Lock+Load

WEAPONS OF THE US MILITARY

Lock+Load

WEAPONS OF THE US MILITARY

Angus Konstam • Jerry Scutts • Hans Halberstadt • Simon Forty • Leo Marriott

SALAMANDER

Produced in 2002 by
PRC Publishing Ltd,
64 Brewery Road, London N7 9NT

A member of **Chrysalis** Books plc

Published by Salamander Books Limited
64 Brewery Road, London, N7 9NT

A member of **Chrysalis** Books plc

ISBN 1 84065 440 6

Printed and bound in China

Acknowledgments by Simon Forty
The US Army and Center of Military History web sites provide an excellent overview of the history and current readiness of the US
Army. The army section of Lock and Load is based primarily on the information provided on these websites, in such material as the
pamphlet *225 Years of Service* by Brigadier General John S. Brown, Chief of Military History at the US Army's Center of Military
History and by material supplied by Hans Halberstadt who is individually credited for his photographs.
Getting photographs in the field is always a team effort, with the photographer simply the front end of a bunch of helpful people
who helped him get in a position to point his lens at the right places. Among the many who helped me I'd like to single out LTC
Ricardo Riera, CPT Pete Fedak, CPT Charles Greene, CPT Reggie Salazar, SSG Lerolland, SFC Tony Bowen, PV2 Lawren
Slockish, PFC William Oliver, SGT Israel Matez, SSG Christopher Dumont, SGT Robert Birchenough, PFC Martens, PFC Garza,
SPC Merrill, SPC Adam, PFC Cira, SPC Richter, SPC Horton.

CONTENTS

ABBREVIATIONS

A

AAA   Anti-aircraft Artillery
AC   Active Component
ACC   Air Combat Command
ADCAP   Advanced Capability
AIC   Action Information Center
ALCM   Air Launched Cruise Missile
ALWT   Advanced Lightweight Torpedo
APC   Armored Personnel Carrier
ARNG   Army Reserve National Guard
ASM   Air-to-surface Missile
ASV   Armored Security Vehicle
ASW   Antisubmarine Warfare
ATACMS   Army Tactical Missile System
AVLB   Armored Vehicle Launched Bridge

B

BFIST   Bradley Fire Support Vehicle
BPDMS   Basic Point Defense Missile System

C

CAP   Combat Air Patrol
CBIRF   Chemical Biological Incident Response Force

CCIP   Common Configuration Implementation Program
CIC   Combat Information Center
CIWS   Close In Weapon System
CMM   Conventional Munitions Module0
CRT   Cathode Ray Tube

D

DPICM   Dual-purpose Improved Conventional Munition
DSMAC   Digital Scene-matching Area Correlator

E

ECM   Electronic Counter Measures
ER   Extended Range
ERGM   Extended Range Guided Munition

F

F&F   Fire and forget
FAST   Fleet Anti-terrorism Security Teams
FCS   Fire Control System
FCS   Fire Control System
FLIR   Forward Looking Infrared
FMTV   Family of Medium Tactical Vehicles

ABBREVIATIONS

G
GPS   Global Positioning System
GWMS   Guided Missile Weapons System

H
HEDP   High Explosive Dual Purpose
HMMWV   High Mobility Multipurpose Wheeled Vehicle
HQDA   Headquarters, Department of the Army

I
IFV/CFV   Infantry/Cavalry fighting vehicles
INS   Inertial Navigation System
IR/UV   infrared/ultraviolet

J
JDAM   Joint Direct Attack Munitions
JSF   Joint Strike Fighter
JVC   Jet Vane Control

L
LBE   Load Bearing Equipment
LO   Low-observable
LOSAT   Line-of-sight Anti-tank

M
MAGTF   Marine Air-Ground Task Forces
MLRS   Multi-launch Rocket System
MMS   Mast-mounted Sight
MOS   Military Occupation Speciality
MPRS   Multipoint Refueling System
MR   Medium Range
MRE   Meal, Ready to Eat

N
NSFS   Naval Surface Fire Support
NSSMS   NATO Sea Sparrow Missile System
NTC   National Training Center

O
OICW   Objective Individual Combat Weapon
OPEVAL   Operational Evaluations
OTH-T   Over-the-horizon-targeting

P
PGM   Precision Guided Munition

R
RAM   Radar Absorbent Material or Rolling Airframe Missile
RC   Reserve Component
RPG   Rocket-propelled Grenade
RPV   Remotely Piloted Vehicle
RSTA   Reconnaissance, Surveillance, and Target Acquisition

S
SAM   Surface-to-air Missile
SAR   Search and Rescue
SAW   Squad Automatic Weapon
SDD   System Development and Demonstration
SLAM   Stand-off Land Attack Missile
STOVL   Short Take-off Vertical Landing

T
TAC   Tactical Air Command
TAINS   TERCOM Assisted Inertial Navigation System
TBMD   Theatre Ballistic Missile Defense
TDD   Target Detection Device
TOW   Tube-launched, Optically-tracked, Wire-guided Missile
TSAAM   Tri-Service Stand Off Attack Missile
TUAV   Tactical Unmanned Aerial Vehicle

U
UBFCS   Underwater Battery Fire Control System
UCAV   Unmanned Combat Air Vehicle
USAR(C)   US Army Reserve (Command)

V
VTO   Vertical Take-off

INTRODUCTION

The production of military weaponry is a necessity in a hostile world. Events such as the attacks of September 11, 2001 on New York and Washington DC, and the recent conflicts in Afghanistan, Iraq, the Balkans, and the Middle East underline the necessity that the United States of America's armed forces stand in readiness for any future conflict, anywhere in the world. At the height of the Cold War, the United State's military was equipped and trained to fight the Warsaw Pact, particularly the armed forces of the Soviet Union. This meant countering the large Soviet nuclear submarine fleet with an antisubmarine capability, spearheaded by the US Navy's nuclear attack submarines. The almost overwhelming numbers of Soviet tanks on the East German border where matched with fewer but better tanks, and with mechanized infantry with a powerful antitank capability. Air-supremacy fighters were developed that were designed to stop the massed ranks of Soviet strike aircraft from reaching their NATO targets. Above all there was a massive commitment to military spending, weapons development and procurement, and in the development of military technology.

All this changed with the end of the Cold War. For the last decade, the United States has been trying to redefine the role of its armed forces, and attempting to decide just what level of military spending is appropriate in an age where the United States of America is the world's only superpower. The change in role from Cold War protagonist to post-Cold War "world policeman" (if indeed that is an appropriate new role) was not an easy process, and indeed, was not the result of a planned strategy. Increasing involvement in peacekeeping forays into the Third World and in former Yugoslavia mandated this new responsibility. Before, America's involvement in Third World affairs had been colored by its role as a Cold War superpower. In the last decade, this changed to one where its armed forces sought to ensure stability, order, and democratic rule if called upon to do so. This meant a change in the way troops, aircraft, ships, and weapons systems were employed, and it also led to a significant change in

RIGHT: A Marine assault amphibious vehicle comes ashore at Port Ploce in Croatia.

old methods of weapons demand and procurement. Put simply, the American military needed to reequip itself and retrain its forces in order to carry out its new role. The commencement of the "War on Terrorism" found the American military largely unprepared for the scale of commitment it was required to undertake. Its fleet had gone through a relatively simple conversion process, with an increasing emphasis on naval airpower and amphibious capabilities rather than attack submarines or antiship capabilities. For the US Air Force, the new demands placed a great strain on a service that was used to operating in certain theaters, and from well-established bases. It now had to devise ways in which its aircraft could operate in new far-flung theaters of war such as Afghanistan, and where its opponent lacked the relatively sophisticated antiaircraft capability of the former Soviet Union. As for the US Army, it was still locked into its commitment to maintain powerful mechanized and armored formations, while its new role demanded the deployment of rapid reaction forces of lightly equipped infantry.

The aim of this book is to outline the arsenal available to the American military in this crucial period in its development, and to explain how effective it is in any current or future conflict. To begin, we must assess the effectiveness of the arms of the American military machine, and examine how its changing role affects its choice and employment of weaponry.

The Changing Role of the Post-Cold War American Military Machine

If an American general was asked what the future held for the US military in 1985, he would be sure of his role, and that of the men who served him. He would know the effectiveness of the weapons at his disposal, and of the way they would be used in combat if the need arose. His enemy was the Warsaw Pact, principally the Soviet Union. Although he might cast condescending remarks at the lower level of technology enjoyed by his Soviet foes, he would retain a certain unease at the numbers of troops, tanks, and aircraft which could be arrayed against his own forces. At the time, the United States was supposed to enjoy a technological advantage in military terms over the Soviet Union. American submarines

were quieter and more deadly, its tanks more powerful, and its fighter aircraft more advanced. Then, a new generation of Soviet weapons systems emerged, such as the MiG-29 fighter-bomber, or the Typhoon Class nuclear ballistic-missile submarine (SSBN). There is a certain truth in the old adage that quality is better than quantity. The Soviets had also proven in the closing days of World War II that quantity has a quality all of its own. These next-generation weapons systems threatened to close the technological gap, while the quantity difference was maintained. This alarming situation continued for another couple of years, until events, which the American military might have thought unthinkable, actually happened. The Cold War ended. Virtually overnight the military stand-off which had existed for four decades was ended, to be replaced by uncertainty, both in terms of world stability and in the future role of the US military.

While the Pentagon was still coming to terms with these dramatic changes, and was facing the prospect of a spectacularly curtailed defense budget, the United States became embroiled in the first conflict fought (in the words of President Bush Sr) on behalf of "the New World Order." The invasion of Kuwait by the forces of President Saddam Hussein of Iraq was seen as an unacceptable act of aggression, and invited the condemnation of the United Nations, followed by a military response. In the Gulf War which followed, American armored divisions, mechanized groups, airborne forces, and Marines fought a conventional war, albeit one preceded by a hitherto unimaginable demonstration of firepower. In a matter of days, the air forces of the United States and its UN allies broke the will of the Iraqi army to fight, decimated its air force and launched strikes against Iraq's command, supply, and transport networks. Warships of the US Navy pounded Iraqi positions using gunfire, and battleships reequipped with cruise

ABOVE, RIGHT: A line of M60A1 tanks and support vehicles at a staging area North of Karlsruhe, Germany.

RIGHT: M60A1 tanks on the inspection line at Rhine Ordnance near Kaiserslautern, Germany. The M60 MBT was the mainstay of US Army armored units for most of the 1970s and 1980s before it was replaced by the M1 Abrams.

missiles launched attacks as far away as Baghdad; a remorseless pounding that demonstrated the firepower available to the US military, and its ability to strike virtually at will wherever it chooses. The ground war which followed was something of an anticlimax, as despite some pockets of heavy resistance, the Iraqi army melted in the face of the allied offensive against it. The war was a clear demonstration that the "New World Order" had teeth, but it also showed that conventional doctrines and political constraints shackled it. President Bush was criticized for not continuing the war, and "finishing off Saddam," but he had no other option, given the political constraints of the UN resolution which had permitted him to assemble his coalition of forces in the first place.

In the ten years following the Gulf War, the US military and successive American governments tried to come to terms with the realities of the post-Cold War world. With no real need to maintain a massive military presence in Europe and in the North Atlantic, the services underwent a process known as "downsizing;" bases were closed, servicemen retired, budgets cut, and new projects shelved. Faced with an incredible uncertainty as to the future role of America's armed forces, strategists in the Pentagon were hard-pressed to decide what shape the future American war machine would take. Even though decisions about the future of research projects, weapons units, and manpower levels were hard to take, given the lack of hard information available as to the future facing America's fighting men and women, the government and the Pentagon had even tougher decisions to make.

At the height of the Cold War, the United States and the Soviet Union both maintained a nuclear arsenal that was capable of destroying all life on Earth several times over. Given that the Cold War was over, and the threat of nuclear war had receded, what was to happen to the nuclear arsenal; the

BELOW: Corporal Carlos Rivera uses a satellite phone to establish communications from the field in the village of Skugrici, Bosnia and Herzegovina, in 1999.

INTRODUCTION

LEFT: A US army M-113 APC prepares to pull an armored Humvee out of the mud in Bosnia and Herzegovina, in 1996, during Operation Joint Endeavor. The spring-time mud presented a challenge to the soldiers and their equipment..

"Weapons of Mass Destruction" (WMD)? Despite wide support for non-proliferation efforts and the gradual dismantling of many Soviet missile silos, the world was not a safer place, and had not escaped the threat of a "nuclear winter." Although states such as the United Kingdom, France, and even China could be expected to abide by existing agreements, the new nuclear nations of India, Pakistan, and to a lesser extent Israel, were more of a problem as all three countries exist in near-continual state of military tension. Other countries such as Iraq or North Korea were also actively trying to gain access to nuclear weapons. The collapse of the Soviet Union also raised the specter that terrorist organizations might be able to gain access to nuclear weapons. Biological weapons were even more prevalent in the Third World, and current diplomatic initiatives had failed to enforce non-proliferation bans. Analysts were even unable to agree under what conditions the United States might use its nuclear or biological weapons in the future. One solution actively sought by successive administrations was some form of protection against rogue nuclear attacks. The "star wars" Strategic Defense Initiative (SDI) has now emerged as a potentially feasible yet extremely expensive option

for the US government. The current American administration has forged ahead with the development of the SDI—despite protests from America's allies, other nuclear powers, and even its own advisors. It is also unable to protect against nuclear weapons triggered from inside US territory by terrorist groups, and is equally unable to prevent a conventional terrorist attack, such as that of September 11, 2001. Today, the recent "anthrax" scare and biological threats have made the specter of these forms of "catastrophic terrorism" more tangible than some vague missile attack from a future nuclear-armed enemy. The fate of America's nuclear arsenal is still in question, but the role of the rest of its military personnel is becoming clearer.

In the decade following the end of the Cold War, war or the threat of conflict is still commonplace around the world. Civil wars, anarchy, and insurrection are still commonplace in Africa, while drug cartels in Venezuela, rebellion in Sri Lanka, and ethnic tension in the Balkans all threaten world stability. Since the Gulf War, America has adopted the role of "world policeman" ceded by Britain in 1945. American troops have been involved in conflicts in Somalia, the Caribbean, Bosnia, Kosovo, and in the

ABOVE: A Hawk surface-to-air missile is launched during the first ever live firing using targeting data supplied by air defense radar at McGregor Range near Fort Bliss, Texas, in 1987.

RIGHT: US Marine Corps Captain Rick Uribe pulls in his parachute at the drop zone in Kuwait.

RIGHT and BELOW: US Army troops have been involved in many of the world's hot spots since the end of World War II. Today technological superiority and skills honed by realistic training – allied to excellent motivation and ésprit de corps – have produced a balanced force that can perform equally effectively in large set-piece operations and smaller mobile engagements. The most important part of this is the quality of the fighting men at the army's disposal.

Middle East. The failure of America's efforts to bring about stability in Somalia in 1993 led to a temporary end to America's involvement in its new role, but the crisis in Bosnia then Kosovo prompted a return to the head of the "New World Order." Supported by Britain and to a lesser extent other European powers, the US fought and won a war in Kosovo using the threat of ground intervention and a well-managed air campaign. This victory was inexpensive in terms of American lives, but it led to a false expectation. After Vietnam, the American public were reluctant to commit American troops to overseas theaters, and were loath to see Americans killed in actions fought far from home. This public posture had to be balanced with the strategic superiority enjoyed by the United States after the collapse of the Soviet Union. There was also its new-found position as the leader of the "New World Order" to consider; this club had also started to encompass the Russian Federation and other former enemies in a supporting role. As the self-styled "leader of the free world," the United States was unable to return to the era of isolationism

ABOVE: A jumpmaster gives a two minute warning to paratroopers as they near the drop zone.

LEFT: A soldier from the 82nd Airborne Division exits out of an Air Force C-141B Starlifter.

ABOVE, RIGHT: M1A1 Abrams main battle tanks from the US Army 1st Armored Division coordinate their fire along with two AH-64A Apache helicopters.

RIGHT: A US Marine Corps M1A1 main battle tank churns the sand as it heads up the beach after off-loading from a US Navy Landing Craft Air Cushion during amphibious training.

during the early 20th century. Like it or not, the United States was a superpower, and had to act the part. For the strategists in the Pentagon, this meant defining a role for the military in the 21st century, and determining how, where, and why troops, weapons, and resources would be deployed. This new role was just emerging when Islamic fundamentalist terrorists struck New York and Washington DC in September 2001. Overnight, the role of the American military machine had changed.

The weaponry described in this book is no longer that of a Cold War protagonist, or the tools of a "world policeman." They represent the arsenal of a nation at war with terrorism, a state locked in a struggle with a largely unseen enemy intent on its destruction.

BELOW: The AIM-9 Sidewinder infrared heat-seeking air-to-air missile is still the most important dogfighting missile available. It has proved its worth in many engagements, including the Falklands War when RAF and RN Harriers cleared the skies of Argentine aircraft.

Weapons Procurement and the American Defense Industry

For nearly 50 years since the end of World War II, the American defense industry was guaranteed orders for new weapons, funding for research, and secure jobs for its workers. The Cold War was good for the sector, and through developing links between the US military, the government, and the leading defense contractors, a continual series of new and ever-more expensive projects ensured that the United States of America maintained its technological edge over its Soviet opponents. Following the end of the Cold War and the collapse of the Soviet Union, this all changed. What followed would be a decade of uncertainty, "downsizing," and job losses as the US military cut back its commitment to military spending, and the size of its armed forces.

Even before the end of the Cold War in 1990, the weapons procurement budget of the United States military was under pressure. In real terms, US

ABOVE: The AIM-7 Sparrow is an excellent standoff weapon but has proved less effective than the Sidewinder in air combat.

RIGHT: The catapult officer gives the final okay signal to the pilot of this EA-6B Prowler to launch from the flight deck of USS *Saratoga* CV-60.

military expenditure on weaponry reached its peak in 1985. After 1990, there was a massive reduction in military effort, which in turn led to a reduction in demand for military equipment. While there is no easy yardstick against which to measure the scale of this reduction in procurement, the employment and sales figures of America's leading warship, plane, and weapon manufacturers help to identify the size of the change. Arms sales and employment levels in the largest arms producing companies fell by an average of 15 percent between 1991 and 1994, and by a further 10 percent in the following six years (1995–2000). At the start of the 21st century, there was a nationwide (if not global) uncertainty as to the nature of the future demand for military hardware. It was an industry without a goal, serving a military without direction. There are certain immovable factors, such as the need of the military to deter any

attack on the national borders and on American interests overseas, and if that fails, to defeat any aggressor. Until September 11, 2001, any further levels of commitment were subject to the vagaries of politicians and their varying levels of commitment to overseas adventures. Even after extensive American military involvement in the global war against terrorism, the requirement for military hardware is there, but the exact nature of the demand is still vague, as strategists try to come to terms with the nature of the new war, and the new enemy.

To figure out what the future holds for the development and procurement of new weaponry from the American military hardware producers, we need to examine the nature of post-Cold War trends in the defense industry. The legacy of the Reagan years was prevalent during the 1980s where many companies, which had previously maintained a significant client base in the civilian marketplace, were lured over to becoming exclusively defense contractors. A prime example is Bath Iron Works, one of two US shipyards who build destroyers for the US Navy. Before the boom in defense spending in the early and mid-1980s, the company was split equally between civilian and military contracts. It switched over to exclusively building warships for the Navy. By the end of the decade, the shipbuilders at Bath and other yards were virtually cut-off from the civilian market, and were so specialized that any return to supplying something other than ships or weapons platforms would entail a complete restructuring of the yard and its work force. These were golden years for these companies; in 1985 alone the US military spent $5.8 billion on warships, which was roughly half its expenditure on military aircraft during the same fiscal year. Missiles and ordnance spending was collectively in excess of $5 billion, while over $1 billion alone was spent on buying new tanks for the army. With post-Cold War hindsight, it seems obvious this level of military expenditure was not going to last forever, but this was not so clear at the time. When weapons procurement was at an all-time high, so too was the level of spending on research into new weapons

LEFT: A Tactical Electronic Warfare Squadron 140 (VAQ-140) EA-6B Prowler aircraft is shown over the nuclear-powered aircraft carrier USS *Dwight D Eisenhower*. Carrier Air Wing 7 is assigned to the *Eisenhower*.

ABOVE: Sailors and aircrew attached to Light Helicopter Antisubmarine Squadron 47 conduct hot-in-flight refueling of a SH-60B Seahawk helicopter from the deck of the USS *Antietam*. Hot-in-flight refueling is necessary when landing to refuel on a smaller US Navy vessel would be too dangerous.

LEFT: A Navy CH-46 Sea Knight helicopter delivers another pallet of bombs to the flight deck of the USS *John F Kennedy*.

ABOVE, RIGHT: A final inspection is made of the firing pins of 500lb bombs mounted underneath an F-14 Tomcat on the flight deck of the USS *Dwight D Eisenhower*.

RIGHT: A Tomcat launches from the the USS *Enterprise* and behind a Hawkeye maneuvers into position.

RIGHT: The frigate USS *Doyle* cruises the Caribbean Sea on its way to Colombia, South America

BELOW: USS *Kitty Hawk* tests the newly-installed Rolling Airframe Missile (RAM). RAM is a lightweight, quick-reaction, high-firepower anti-ship weapon system, designed as an all-weather, low-cost, self-defense system against anti-ship missiles.

systems. Many companies were allocated research and development (R&D) funding direct from the government. In the aerospace industry for example, $20 million, 80 percent of its research funding, came from the government in 1985, which was equivalent to over half of the full government R&D allocation to the private sector. For the military, this was an efficient way to encourage new weapons and technology research; paying private contractors to do the work for them. When the federal government cut the defense budget, not only defense contractors and jobs were hit, but weapons research also suffered.

The end of the Cold War was not the only impetus for change. Increasing concern about the public sector deficit led to calls for a cutback in military expenditure, and in 1987 the defense budget (and more importantly its consequent spending on weaponry) fell in real terms for the first time in a decade. The end of the Cold War four years later meant that the incoming Clinton administration would be able to continue this cutback in government spending on weapons procurement, electing to spend the money on the budget deficit rather than on new (and increasingly redundant) tanks, guns, and aircraft. While the effect of defense cuts on the dependent contractors was clearly understood, the government was largely powerless to help, as

ABOVE: Ground crew at the US Naval Air Station, Patuxent River, MD, load an AGM-65E Maverick onto a wing station of a US Marine Corps AV-8B Harrier 2.

RIGHT: The laser-guided Maverick air-to-ground missile is shown scoring a direct hit on an M53 tracked gun target at Eglin Air Force Base, Florida.

Congress vetoed a restructuring package which would have helped steer many of these defense contractors back into the civilian marketplace.

During the 1990s, there was a retrenchment in US military spending in general, and a reduction in weapons procurement and R&D in particular. The industry had not been hit so hard since the mid-1970s, during the immediate aftermath of the Vietnam War, when a similar number of companies had become dependent on military weapons contracts. Some two to three years after the end of the Cold War defense peak, the cutbacks in spending were reflected in the job market, although overseas exports provided a temporary respite through post-Gulf War arms sales. While cutbacks in America's armed forces resulted in a 25 percent reduction in military personnel between 1991 and 2001, the work

force in the defense industry was cut by a third. The boom of the 1980s, followed by the bust of the 1990s has left the industry in crisis, and has meant that many of America's leading defense contractors have been forced to restructure, and to look elsewhere for contracts. The biggest weapons-producing companies were those in the military aerospace industry, and they responded to the procurement crisis in four different ways. Some, such as General Dynamics and McDonnell Douglas, closed down a few of their less lucrative systems, and concentrated instead on those they did best, or knew would become the mainstays of the US military in the future. Others, such as Honeywell, removed themselves from the market, turning their defense divisions into stand-alone companies. Yet others merged, encouraged (and in some part-funded) by the US government. The Lockheed/ Martin/Loral merger created a defense giant, capable of pooling its resources for weapons research, and ensuring better marketing connections in the Pentagon, and leverage with the US military's procurement offices. The final group (including Boeing and Rockwell) expanded their existing civilian arm, and downsized their weapons divisions. These big companies were able to weather the crisis for the most part because they could adopt the ideal balance between diversification and downsizing. For many

ABOVE: A B-2 Spirit approaches a KC-10A from the McGuire Air Force Base, New Jersey, during a training exercise. The B-2 Spirit is a multi-role bomber capable of delivering both conventional and nuclear munitions.

smaller defense contractors, the options were less appealing. Many of these smaller companies (producing individual weapons systems or electronics) were forced to cut their production and staffing by as much as 50 percent. Others entered new commercial markets, or else expanded their marketing to overseas clients, making up in part for the reduced procurement levels by the US military.

During this crucial decade (1991–2001), the Pentagon was able to offer little in the way of guidance to the US defense contractors who supplied the military with weapons. Wall Street took the lead by encouraging mergers, diversification, and downsizing. Under the Clinton administration an attempt was made to provide some form of guidance for the weapons manufacturers. The Office of Economic Security was charged with researching the future relationship between the military and the defense industries, and to help both parties chart out a policy for the future. Nothing coherent emerged, as the Pentagon took the initiative by canceling several existing weapons research and production contracts,

in order to focus its dwindling resources on other areas. The result was more job losses in some areas, but increased levels of weapons procurement spending in others. For example, in 1999, United Technologies laid off 1,700 workers at its engine-making subsidiary, Pratt & Whitney. At the same time, Boeing, General Dynamics, and Northrop Grumman all benefited from increased investment in projects such the B-2 Stealth Bomber. The primary contractor for the B-2 is the Northrop Grumman Corporation, but Boeing, General Electric, and CTV were all major players in the project, and shared in the boost to their revenue and standing when new aircraft were ordered. In 2000, President Clinton's Defense Secretary William Cohen met with the Chief Executive Officers of the largest weapons corporations. He discussed ways the Pentagon could offer aid to the ailing defense industry. It was at this stage that two watershed policy changes were made. The first was from the Pentagon, which after a decade finally produced a coherent analysis of its future weapons needs for the coming century. This was based on an increased level of commitment to peace-keeping and humanitarian missions, the streamlining of the US military to work more effectively in non-conventional battlegrounds, and a decrease in the weapons of conventional warfare, such as

ABOVE: F-16 "Wild Weasel" aircraft from the 35th Fighter Squadron., Misawa Air Base, fly a training mission over the Japanese coast.

BELOW: A-10s were designed specially for the close air support mission and had the ability to combine large military loads and wide combat radius, which proved to be vital assets to America and its allies during Operation Desert Storm.

ABOVE: A US Air Force E-3 Sentry airborne warning and control system (AWACS) aircraft touches down at 4 Wing Cold Lake, Canada.

LEFT: A member of the USAF 51st Security Forces Squadron talks through his MCU-2P chemical/biological mask as he communicates with other team members via radio while conducting a search.

ABOVE, RIGHT: A paratrooper from the US Army's 2nd Battalion, 1st Special Forces Group, jumps from a C-130 Hercules.

RIGHT: Clouds of dust billow out from behind a USAF C-17 Globemaster III as it lands on the dry lake bed of Bicycle Lake at Fort Irwin, California.

RIGHT and BELOW: During World War II the US Marine Corps proved itself the best amphibious force in the world, and since then it has become the United States' main "Force in Readiness," prepared to respond immediately to international crises. Among its large and potent inventory of arms is the LAV-25 (LAV—light armored vehicle) a wheeled vehicle that comes in a variety of forms including a TOW-armed antitank version (see page 31), a mortar carrier, a command and control vehicle, and as here, armed with a 0.79-in (20-mm) cannon.

ABOVE: The LAV-25 antitank variant is armed with the TOW missile.

antisubmarine destroyers, main battle tanks (MBTs), or state-of-the-art fighter aircraft. The second change was in the field of weapons procurement. As part of the reforms introduced by President Clinton's government, procurement reforms were introduced, aimed at eliminating unnecessary or wasteful military specifications, a tactic which many defense contractors argued was a ploy designed to favor the "chosen" defense companies. It was hoped that by changing the specifications when new systems were tendered, the industries who had diversified away from purely military markets might be able to reap the benefits as well as the main players in the industry. While this opened the marketplace to more competition and lowered procurement costs, it did little to help the industry as a whole, although it made the Pentagon reexamine its procedures.

The whole system of weapons research and procurement was a thorny issue during the late 1990s. Well-publicized examples of sheer incompetence in military procurement, such as the M2 Bradley AFV, clearly cost the American taxpayers billions of dollars through changes in specifications, the use of unsuitable components, and through the suppliers charging what they thought the market could bear for their product. Claims that the US Army spent $1,500 on

a toilet roll holder were often exaggerated, but these "urban myths" also had a basis in fact. Weapons research projects are either allocated to the defense industry, who are tasked with developing proposals, or conducted by the US military. Government research departments such as the US Army Research Laboratory work up their own plans for weapons or weapons systems, then invite appropriate defense contractors to tender for production of the new system. In the past it was considered more efficient to allow the contractors themselves to conduct much of this research, as they were able to adapt the specifications to suit their own weapons manufacturing facilities and production systems. Spiraling costs and intense political scrutiny of research and development methods have led to a cutback in government sponsored weapons research in the private sector, and instead the Pentagon is trying to increase the use of its own in-house weapons development organizations. The Department of Defense is in overall charge of all weapons research programs, and is now instituting a streamlined and fairer method of tendering for production and procurement. Given the long lead

time in weapons research and production, wher*e a weapons system might take a decade or more from initial concept to production, the whole defense industry will still be acclimatizing to these changes for another decade. Military planners consequently have to work in 15-year cycles. It is expected that by 2015, the new kinds of weapons systems, developed and experimented before the start of the war on terrorism, will be in full-scale production; the perfect weapons for an old kind of war. This lag in production and procurement means that the US military has to make do with whatever weapons it has available to fight its new war.

Long-term planning and procurement is by necessity out of date. The Pentagon needs to make a best-possible estimate of the pace of technology, the future role of the US military, and the budget it can expect to receive a decade from now. The current military strategic plan produced during the administration of President Clinton was inherited by President Bush, and although it took into account the expected pace of technological change, it was unable to predict the aftermath of September 11, 2001. Under these existing plans, the annual cost to the Department of Defense to replace its existing arsenal of weapons systems with next-generation weapons or even to replace existing systems in a one-for-one exchange has all been regulated. In 2002–3, $65 billion was set aside for procurement, a sum which was expected to rise to $95 billion in 2015–16. In October 2001, as part of the new commitment to the war on terrorism, an additional $15 billion was made available for new weaponry. In other words, over the next decade, the American defense industry can expect another boom period, just like it enjoyed during the Vietnam War, or during the administration of President Reagan.

One problem with this is that it is far from clear that all of the new next-generation weapon systems called for under the current plan are necessary in this new style of war. The Department of Defense is therefore considering scaling back on new systems, and instead buying larger quantities of current-generation systems (such as F-16Cs or A10As), rather than their high-tech successors. By reducing procurement costs in this way, more money can be channeled to fund changes in the military structures necessary to fight the war on terrorism. This suggestion has met with criticism, as some analysts believe that the budget needed to keep the US military adequately equipped with modern weaponry over the long term is inadequate.

Although research and development teams, military analysts, weapons manufacturers, and politicians all have a say in the commissioning of new weapons systems, recent changes mean that it is difficult to predict future needs. Given the low level of technology expected in the war on terrorism, aging weapons systems such as the venerable B-52 bomber might still have a place in the US Air Force a decade from now. The drawback is that as weapons systems, planes, and warships get older, maintenance costs spiral, and maintenance times get longer. Although next-generation weapons systems may be a preferable option for the future, the large financial commitment needed for their production may not be the best possible use of resources.

The Pentagon is busy trying to work out the ramifications of its first war of the 21st century for its long-term plans. It is highly likely that this fresh look at procurement, planning, and development might force a new approach to planned modernization in the future. In particular, these trends might call into question the current plan for replacing the US military's already large and effective fleet of large surface warships and tanks with costly next-generation systems. Instead, it might make sense to devote greater resources to weapons which are better suited to the new style of warfare. These might include more cruise missile firing warships, converting the SSBN fleet to become Tomahawk platforms, developing "extended-range precision artillery systems" such as the Army Tactical Missile System (ATACMS), or it might even mean concentrating on building more long-range bombers and unmanned combat air vehicles (UCAVs). Until the Pentagon decides what weapons it needs to fulfill its new mission, the soldiers, sailors and airmen of the US military will have to make the best use they can of the weapons they already have.

LEFT: The Hawk surface-to-air missile entered service in the 1960s and since then has been upgraded by the MIM-23B Improved Hawk. It was intended that the Patriot would replace it but the Hawk still continues in service.

Weaponry Developments in the Armed Forces since the Cold War

The US Army

The end of the Cold War caught the army largely unawares. Plans were laid to "downsize," but the army, which had been developed to fight the Soviet Union in Germany, had one last moment of mechanized glory. In the Gulf War (1991), the US Army deployed armored and mechanized infantry formations; M1A1 Abrams tanks, Bradley APCs, plus the full supporting weaponry associated with armored or mechanized warfare. The weaponry deployed by the army during the campaign ensured that the Iraqis were outclassed and outfought. Following an initial overwhelming artillery bombardment that largely broke the will of the enemy front-line formations, the superior weaponry of the American army ensured that victory was swift and complete. The Iraqis were cooperative in that they passively awaited their fate, a bit like a sacrificial lamb to the slaughter. Following

the Gulf War and the shift in emphasis to an interventionist military role, it became clear that not all opponents or battlegrounds would present the army with such a golden opportunity to demonstrate its might. It also provided the military and the American public with a false expectation of what a future conflict might entail. Losses were extremely light, but in a war against a more determined enemy, fighting on ground of his own choosing, then the casualty list would be much higher.

This was amply demonstrated on October 3, 1993 during an operation by Task Force Rangers in Mogadishu, Somalia. An operation to apprehend known Somali warlords in downtown Mogadishu ended in disaster, despite the presence of US Rangers and specially trained operatives from the secret Delta Force. The attack was designed to be a quick insertion, then extraction, and the soldiers were covered by MH-60K Blackhawk gunships, AH-6J Little Bird attack helicopters, and transport versions of both helicopters (MH-60K and MH-6).

RIGHT: The AH-64 Apache is armed with the Hellfire antitank missile whose guidance system is being upgraded with the Longbow targeting system.

INTRODUCTION

LEFT and BELOW: The "Black Hawk Down" episode in Somalia showed that the US Army needed to keep a flexible light – as opposed to mechanized – infantry force such as that provided by the Rangers and the 10th Mountain Division. Armored vehicles and mechanized warfare are essential for operations like "Desert Storm" or to fight the on NATO's Central Front, but the threats of the new millennium require more flexibility.

When two Blackhawk helicopters were shot down, the situation deteriorated, as the troops were required to extend their perimeter to encompass the two crash sites, in the face of growing and heavy Somali opposition. Faced with a city population where almost everyone carried an AK-47, casualties were inevitable. What followed was the virtual siege of the insertion team, and heavy casualties on both sides. The lack of available AC-130H Specter gunships meant that fire support was limited, so the Rangers had to be rescued the hard way, by ground troops. The 2nd Battalion of the 14th Infantry Regiment (nicknamed "The Dragons") was a "light infantry" outfit, part of the 10th Mountain Division. Tasked with the rescue mission, the battalion drove Humvees armed with 1.6in (40mm) Mk. 19 automatic grenade launchers escorting sandbagged trucks. Helicopter gunships and elements of other UN peacekeeping outfits provided support. They fought their way through the Somali city, rescued the Rangers and Delta teams, and managed to extricate themselves without major loss after a bitter running firefight lasting several hours.

The total human cost of the operation for the Rangers was 11 dead, five missing (presumed dead), one captured, and 60 wounded, while two of their

rescuers were killed and 26 wounded. Somali casual-ties have been placed at 1,126, including 312 dead. This bloodbath caused a sensation in America, as the photographs of dead soldiers and aircrew being dragged through the streets by a hostile crowd was not what the American public had come to expect from a supposed relief mission and peacekeeping effort. The operation brought an end to American involvement in the region, and a reevaluation of the role of the US military in future overseas ventures.

If one positive development emerged from the "Black Hawk Down" fiasco, it was the demonstration that well-trained American "light infantry" were a useful part of the Army's reactive force. The Army lists the tasks expected of an infantry battalion, and during the operation in Mogadishu, "The Dragons" performed 23 of the 60 on the list, including "breach of defended obstacles, bypass of enemy forces, fight-ing a meeting engagement, attack of a built-up area, and withdrawal under pressure. During the last decade of the Cold War, American military planners had seriously thought of converting all non-airborne or Ranger infantry formations into mechanized infantry. This was a reaction to the build-up of Soviet mechanized forces in Germany, but following the

ABOVE: The M1 Abrams performed brilliantly in the Gulf War and its armor protection was so efficient that Iraqi T-72 shells simply bounced off.

BELOW: The TOW-armed Bradley also performed with distinction in the Gulf War: the weapon system allowed US forces to keep up the pace of armored thrusts.

LEFT: The M113 has two mortar-carrier versions—the M125 with an 3-in (81-mm) mortar and the M106 with a 4.2 in(107mm).

BELOW, LEFT and RIGHT: Realistic training is essential if troops are to perform their jobs in combat. The "Dragons" in Somalia performed 23 of the 60 tasks expected of an infantry battalion and rescued the Ranger and Delta force operatives in the face of massive numbers of armed but untrained Somalis.

RIGHT: The M47 Dragon antitank missile also proved particularly useful as a bunker-buster in the Gulf War.

BELOW: Many of the Military Occupation Specialities require the ability to use sophisticated technology in a combat environment.

ABOVE: A big advantage for the Army would be having superior night vision and sighting equipment.. This would make target acquisition easier to quantify.

end of the Cold War, these mechanized units were no longer of much use. As one wag put it, the army was perfectly structured for fighting the German Army in 1944–45 by the end of the Cold War. Fortunately it also retained a number of "leg-infantry" units such as the 10th Mountain Division, and these formations were given a disproportionate level of involvement in the decade following the Gulf War, as peacekeepers, interventionists, and humanitarian providers.

The new commitment of the Army to the war on terrorism caught them wrong-footed, as they were still adjusting themselves to a post-Cold War strength, and were in the middle of a reconsideration of their role and mode of operation. During the years following the American withdrawal from Somalia the Army was called upon to operate in the Balkans, and was even readying itself to fight a conventional war in Kosovo. Given the lack of effectiveness of heavy armor and mechanized units, the army necessarily relied on its "light infantry" formations, its Rangers, and its airborne troops. The success of the Kosovo campaign through airpower provided another false

impression; that wars could be won without putting troops on the ground. This myth was dispelled in Afghanistan. As one American colonel put it; "They have yet to make a jet fighter-bomber with a bayonet stud." Further involvement in the war on terrorism also means that both the Army and the public have to be prepared for toe-to-toe fighting with often determined and well-trained opponents, and casualties are inevitable.

Since Korea and Vietnam, the public has become unused to high casualty rates, and consequently the avoidance of casualties has become a cornerstone of "peacetime" American doctrine. This will inevitably change. In an age when other branches of the American military are becoming increasingly reliant on high-tech weaponry, the US Army is finding that the "grunt" on the ground with his rifle is the most important weapon in its arsenal.

The US Navy and US Marine Corps

Warships and the nature of naval warfare have changed radically since the end of World War II, a series of technical developments which was second only to the introduction of the ironclad in its far-reaching effect on seapower. The development of nuclear submarines, new forms of antisubmarine warfare, antiaircraft, and antiship missile systems, along with the revolution in electronic warfare and command and control, evolved during the half century between 1945 and the end of the Cold War. Two new capital ships evolved during this period. The nuclear ballistic missile submarine (SSBN), formed an arm of the Navy which served no function apart from being a covert launching platform for a weapon of mass destruction (WMD); a nuclear missile. As such it was not strictly a naval weapons system, and following the end of the Cold War the SSBN fleet lacked a clear role as the United States was forced to evaluate the effectiveness of its WMD arsenal. The second capital ship of the late 20th century (and the early 21st) is the supercarrier, a weapons platform whose role has changed with relative ease from the Cold War to the post-Cold War world. The aircraft

carrier emerged from World War II as the preeminent warship type of the conflict, and this importance has continued into the 21st century. Another ship type to emerge from the Pacific War was the amphibious assault ship, and its subsequent development has increased the versatility and effectiveness of the US Marine Corps. Today, a combination of naval air-power and marine deployment capability has created a naval force which is well suited to the new demands of the new century, and together they form the backbone of America's rapid reaction capability.

As for warships as weapons platforms, the late 20th century saw a dramatic transformation, from the gun-armed warship to the guided-missile platform. Ships are often referred to as "platforms," as their effectiveness is largely measured by the weapons and control systems with which they are fitted. The old divisions of warships by type (i.e. cruiser, destroyer, frigate etc.) have no longer the same meaning as they did a half-century ago, and their definitions have become blurred. The main elements of this naval revolution have been as much in the fields of electronics and command and control as in weapons. Indeed, all three elements are necessarily combined into a modern naval "weapons system," as a package. Much of these systems are hidden, taking the form of computers, or centralized data-handling systems, such as those found in a US Navy warship's

BELOW: The guided missile destroyer USS *Mitscher* heads out to sea this morning from the channel at Port Everglades, Florida., after a three-day port visit to Fort Lauderdale.

combat information center (CIC) or action information center (AIC). At the height of the Cold War, the US Navy had some of the most efficient weapons control and ship command systems in the world.

Naval warfare has largely become a matter of data management, where special "flagship" vessels were capable of performing complex tasks. A single warship is now capable of analyzing data from its own systems and those of other warships or merchant vessels in its task group. This information could then be redirected to the appropriate weapons system on any of the ships, and the appropriate action taken, whether it be firing an antimissile barrage or computing the data for a shore bombardment. Following the end of the Cold War, the need for these "flagship systems" remains, as was demonstrated during the Gulf War when US task force commanders were able to plan then coordinate strikes by naval guns, cruise missiles, and naval aircraft, all from one CIC. Another important development over the last decade was the degree with which local commanders (or "deployed commanders" as the Navy calls them), can consult with their superiors virtually instantaneously. This means that political decision-makers, task-force commanders, and the Naval staff in the Pentagon can all react to events as they unfold, and dictate the appropriate level of response. This communications revolution means that a phenomenal

ABOVE: At sea with the USS *Essex* Amphibious Readiness Group (ARG) in 2002. The ARG provides a flexible and quick reacting Navy-Marine Corps team.

LEFT: The ARG from the USS *Essex* practice formation steaming during the semi-annual amphibious integration training exercise known as Blue-Green Workups..

RIGHT: During a training exercise, two Navy Special Warfare Rigid-Hull Inflatable Boats (NSW RHIBs) are launched from the amphibious transport dock ship USS *Shreveport* to pick up SEAL team members.

BELOW: USS *John Paul Jones* leads a formation of ships in a series of close ship maneuvers.

BOTTOM: USS *Carl Vinson* launches a "Sea Sparrow" during a missile launch exercise as the ship was sailing toward Hawaii. A "Sea Sparrow" is a surface-to-air anti-missile defense system.

degree of naval firepower and naval airpower can be unleashed against an enemy target within seconds of the order being passed down from the President of the United States to his military advisors.

An example of the effectiveness of this sophisticated command and control system is provided by the employment of Tomahawk antiship missiles during the Gulf War and in Afghanistan. The Tomahawk was a weapon which was largely designed to counter Cold War enemy naval units in the European theater, and was adapted from a missile airframe which was already being developed to attack land-based targets. As a result the new weapon had a dual function, although the US Navy primarily relied on its nuclear attack submarine fleet and its naval aviation units to attack enemy surface task forces.

The missile had an over-the-horizon capability, so the control systems of the launching warship had to coordinate targeting information from satellites, surveillance aircraft, and shore positions to form an over-the-horizon-targeting (OTH-T) solution. This information was passed to a Fleet Command Center, where information was relayed to both the firing ship and the Pentagon. On the ship itself, an OTH-T system took the information, processed it, and readied the missile for launch. Once the Tomahawk was fired, its progress could be monitored, and a second strike

INTRODUCTION

LEFT: The Aegis cruiser USS *Shiloh* fires an RGM-84A Harpoon missile during exercises, while the Spruance-class destroyer USS *Fletcher* awaits her turn to shoot.

BELOW, LEFT: The guided missile cruiser USS *Yorktown* fires her Mark 45, 5-inch, 54-caliber lightweight gun at a target drone during a gunnery exercise.

BOTTOM, LEFT: A standard missile leaves a trail of smoke as it is launched from the starboard side of USS *Vandegrift* and heads on an intercept course with an incoming "hostile" drone.

RIGHT: An F-14 Tomcat catches the wire on the flight deck of USS *Nimitz* during the first day of flight operations after the ship's 36-month refueling.

BELOW, RIGHT: An F/A-18 Hornet, piloted by US Air Force Major Philip Malebranche, from Virginia Beach, Virginia., is launched from the flight deck of USS *George Washington*

BOTTOM, RIGHT: A flight deck director hands off control of a Marine Corps AV-8B Harrier to another director after the aircraft touches down on the deck of the amphibious assault ship USS *Bataan*.

authorized from the highest level within seconds. This was the method used to target Tomahawk strikes during the attack on Al Qaida bases in Afghanistan in 2001–2; the strikes were launched from US Naval units in the Persian Gulf. The result was a weapon which extended the range and accuracy of naval power far beyond the conventional sphere of naval operations.

In a similar fashion, post-Cold War developments have stressed the value of maintaining air and amphibious assets in a constant state of readiness in the Middle East, and off other potential areas of conflict. Tomahawk missiles, for example, can strike targets far inland, and the supercarriers of the US Navy can launch strikes or fight for local air supremacy at considerable distances from their bases. Under this protective umbrella, US Marine Corps personnel can then be deployed virtually anywhere and at short notice, as they lack the cumbersome logistical and mechanical "tail" of most other troop types.

Although in the post-Cold War era the need for nuclear attack submarines or antisubmarine vessels has diminished, the striking power of the US Navy places it at the forefront of America's war on terrorism, as it gives the US government a tool which it can use with very little notice. Of all the three services, the Navy is the best suited to this new war, and to its new role.

ABOVE: A Standard Missile (SM-3) leaves the vertical launch system (VLS) of the cruiser USS *Lake Erie* during a combined Missile Defense Agency and US Navy flight test.

LEFT: Aviation ordnanceman, 2nd class, Alejandro Montalvo of Mocha, Puerto Rico, and aviation ordnanceman, 3rd class, Chris Tucker of Ocala, Florida, prepare a 2000 pound, MK-84 JDAM GPS guided weapon for loading on an F/A-18 Hornet on the flight deck of USS *George Washington*.

ABOVE: The USS *Normandy* fires its 5-in (127mm) guns at the training range on Vieques, Puerto Rico.

RIGHT: The USS *Greeneville* sits atop blocks in Dry Dock at the Pearl Harbor Naval Shipyard, Hawaii. The Los Angeles class attack submarine is dry-docked to assess damage and perform repairs.

FAR LEFT: US and Danish sailors watch as a crane lifts Mark 52 mines to the deck of the HDMS *Falster*.

LEFT: A US Navy diver attaches an inert satchel charge to a training mine.

RIGHT: The US Navy's Deep Submergence Rescue Vehicle Mystic (DSRV 1) is loaded aboard a USAF Reserve C-5A Galaxy aircraft.

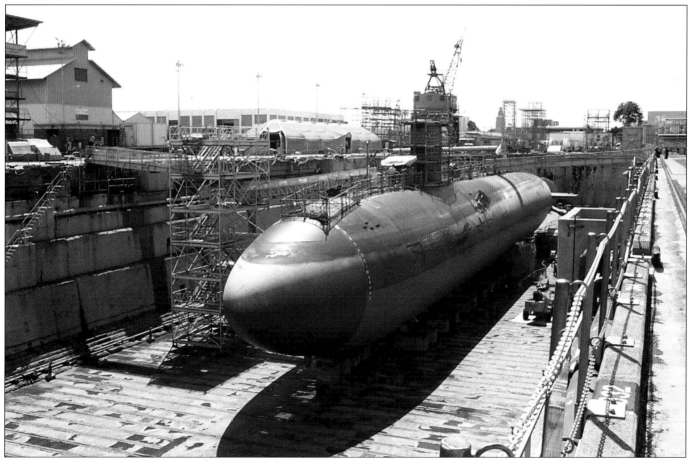

The US Air Force

Like the Navy, the Air Force was designed to fight in a conventional war against the Soviet Union. To this end it developed sophisticated long-range strike aircraft, with complex arrays of electronics equipment, and a supporting fighter wing of the latest air supremacy aircraft. Experience gained during the Vietnam War proved invaluable in determining the best way to equip fighters for air-to-air combat missions, and in protecting strike aircraft with electronics. It also provided an impetus for the development of new types of munitions, particularly specialist antiradar, antirunway, and "bunker-buster" ordnance. These are useful in a conventional war but, together with the latest long-range air-to-air missiles (LRAMs), are less useful in the post-Cold War era.

The new role as a global policeman was one for which the Air Force was ill-prepared. In 1986, F-111s based in Britain bombed targets in Libya, in what might now be seen as an opening round in the war against terrorism. Operation "El-Dorado Canyon" was a relative success, as all five designated targets were hit, but the art of "surgical strikes" still had a long way to go, as civilian targets were also hit in the raid. This prompted further development of precision munition guidance systems. In December 1989, the United States launched "Operation Just Cause" when it invaded Panama, and the Air Force flew over 400 transport sorties with C-130, C-5, and C-141 transport aircraft, placing over 19,000 troops into the combat zone, together with their supplies and equipment. This was made possible by the seizure of Panama's International Airport by airborne forces, and Air Force gunships and helicopters covered the deployment. This operation was unusual in that a high-quality base was available to permit the full deployment of the Air Force's resources. This was not an option in most Third World or Eastern European countries.

RIGHT: Transitioning from trail into diamond formation, the number four slot pilot of the US Air Force Thunderbirds has a very unique perspective.

BELOW: An Air Force weapons loader from the 28th Air Expeditionary Wing prepares a 2000-pound bomb to be loaded into a B-1B Lancer bomber.

RIGHT: HH-60G *Pave Hawk* practices hoist procedures.

FAR RIGHT: An Air Force crew-chief replaces the brakes on a KC-10A Extender in support of Operation Enduring Freedom.

BELOW: The 20th Special Operations Squadron, located at Hurlburt Field, Florida, is one of eight flying squadrons within the 16th Special Operations Wing. Known as the "Green Hornets," the 20th SOS flies the MH-53J Pave Low IIIE, the Air Force's most sophisticated helicopter.

The Gulf War in 1991 came at a time when the Air Force had not yet been forced to implement the post-Cold War cutbacks ordered by the government. Consequently it was able to deploy substantial resources to the Middle East, as part of "Operation Desert Storm." F-15s, F-16s, F-111s, F-4Gs, transport aircraft, electronic warfare aircraft (EWs), and helicopter gunships all had a part to play in the conflict, and for probably the last time they were able to employ the full panoply of Cold War technology. By the time the war ended, Allied air forces had flown over 110,000 sorties, and had devastated the Iraqi army and air force—112 Iraqi aircraft were destroyed, a third in air-to-air combat. The technology employed by the US Air Force proved highly effective, and proved overwhelmingly superior to the weaponry arrayed against it in the form of surface-to-air missiles (SAMs), or aircraft weapons systems. The war also saw the deployment of the old and the new versions of American long-range strike aircraft. B-52 bombers flew 1,624 missions, and dropped 72,000 bombs on enemy targets. This cudgel was

augmented by the latest Lockheed F-117A Stealth fighters, which flew 1,300 sorties, and dropped 2,000 tons of bombs. For the Air Force, the war was personified by the deployment of precision bombing weapons. Infrared, laser-guided bombs launched from aircraft resulted in the virtual destruction of the Iraqi army during its retreat from Kuwait, augmented by even more lethal weapons.

The BLU-82 is a 15,000lb (680kg) free-fall, fuel-air bomb, nicknamed "Big Blue." Also known as "The Mother of all Bombs," the BLU-82 was the largest conventional bomb in the Air Force arsenal, and it was used to great effect during the war. It was found to be effective in clearing enemy minefields, and its use as a platform for "daisy-cutter" munitions and even as a "leaflet bomb" (containing millions of instructions on how Iraqi soldiers could surrender) proved that the Air Force could be innovative in its use of its weaponry. Most air-to-air victories of the US Air Force (35 out of 40) were attributed to F-15C Eagles of the 33d Tactical Fighter Wing, who employed radar-guided AIM-7 Sparrows and even old AIM-9 Sidewinders to shoot down their opponents. Even more Iraqi aircraft were destroyed on the ground than in the air, as precision bombing of

ABOVE: A KC-10A from McGuire Air Force Base, New Jersey, refuels a B-2 Spirit during a training exercise.

airfields helped decimate the Iraqi ability to launch concerted air attacks on Allied forces.

In the ten years between the Gulf War and the commencement of the war on terrorism, the US Air Force became involved in both Africa and the Balkans, first as a supplier of humanitarian aid and as a peacekeeper, then as a combatant. This meant a change of emphasis, and in the Operations "Provide Relief," "Restore Hope," "Provide Promise" or "Provide Comfort," transport aircraft were at the forefront of the Air Force effort. Aircraft such as the C-130E proved capable of delivering food and medical supplies in significant quantities. During this period aircraft designed during the last days of the Cold War entered service, including the B-2A Spirit. Twenty-one of these aircraft have since been built, and while they were designed to carry a varied combination of weaponry – from iron or cluster bombs, nuclear payloads, and near-precision weapons – their most impressive feature is their range. The aircraft incorporates a low-observable (LO) Stealth structure

LEFT: Crew members from the two C-17 Globemaster III airlifters celebrate after returning to Ramstein Air Base, Germany, following a humanitarian airdrop mission over eastern Afghanistan.

BELOW: A B-52H Stratofortress from the 419th Flight Test Squadron from Edwards Air Force Base, California, releases a Joint Direct Attack Munition during a recent test.

LEFT: F-15s from the 114th Fighter Squadron, Kinglsey Field Air National Guard Base, Klamath Falls, Oregon, fly in formation over Craer Lake National Park.

BELOW: Working under nighttime red light, a boom operator shuts down the Pacer Craig navigational system aboard his KC-135.

BOTTOM: Airmen delivered tons of relief supplies, like the daily rations pictured, into poverty-stricken areas of Afghanistan as part of the humanitarian relief effort, Operation Enduring Freedom.

with an incredible aerodynamic design, and employs the latest technology in terms of electronics, navigation, and weapons control. At a time when the US Air Force is hindered by its lack of secure overseas bases close to trouble-spots, the employment of long-range transport aircraft such as the C-141 Starlifter and the C-130J allows it to fulfill its airlift mission from bases on American soil. The deployment of aircraft such as the B-2A takes this one step further, as recent events in Afghanistan have demonstrated. These Stealth bombers flew to Afghanistan from America, dropped their payload with precision, then flew back home. Aircraft have come a long way in the 20th century. The question is whether the US Air Force can maintain this momentum, and design aircraft suited to its new role in the war on terrorism. In order to deploy its full array of Cold War weaponry, it needs a conventional battlefield, or at least conventional targets. The ability of the Air Force to adapt during the Gulf War has still to be demonstrated as it "regears" for the first long-term war in American history. This war is also the first one since 1945 when control of the skies is less important than airborne surveillance, targeting, and the precision bombing of terrorist targets.

ABOVE: A B-1B from the 28th Bomb Wing at Ellsworth Air Force Base, South Dakota, flies over the pyramids in Egypt.

LEFT: MH-53J Pave Low IIIE flies a training mission near Kirtland Air Force Base, New Mexico. The MH-53J's mission is to perform low-level, long-range, undetected penetration into denied areas, day or night, in adverse weather.

ABOVE: The pilot banks his F-15D Eagle as he looks for opposition aircraft while flying a training mission over the Pacific Ocean near Japan.

RIGHT: A 33rd Rescue Squadron HH-60G takes off from the USS *Juneau* during ship landing training in the Pacific. The primary mission of the HH-60G Pave Hawk helicopter is to conduct day or night operations into hostile environments to recover downed aircrew or other isolated personnel during war. Because of its versatility, the HH-60G is also tasked to perform military operations other than war. These tasks include civil search and rescue, emergency aeromedical evacuation (MEDE-VAC), disaster relief, international aid, counterdrug activities, and NASA space shuttle support.

INTRODUCTION

LEFT: A USAF F-16CJ Fighting Falcon soars in the skies over Turkey before being refueled in flight.

BELOW: An A/OA-10 Thunderbolt II is refueled in flight by a KC-135R Stratotanker.

The Future Demands of the US Military

The war on terrorism has been a driving force for change within the US military. Even before the tragic events of September 11, 2001, Secretary of Defense Donald Rumsfeld forced the US Government of President George W Bush to confront the need for drastic changes in the way the US military is equipped, and in its perception of future roles. Since the Gulf War in 1991, several military flash-points have provided signposts to the future of American military involvement; Bosnia, Somalia, and Kosovo being the prime examples. During the decade between the wars in Kuwait and Afghanistan, American political leaders were primarily concerned with the opportunity for "downsizing" their national military machine following the end of the Cold War. This was achieved without reading the signs that the country's armed forces were looking increasingly ill-prepared for the new kind of war which they might be called upon to fight in. The consequence of this lack of direction from above was a growing disenchantment in military circles as servicemen were unable to understand their future role, even though many could see that changes were desperately needed. Secretary Rumsfeld began to address the problem in a series of discussion papers and directives, but the procedure of redirecting the US military to fight a new kind of war had only just started when the airplane hijackers struck on September 11, 2001.

The resulting campaign in Afghanistan came as a real shock to the US military, as it was called upon to launch an air and missile campaign against a distant country. They then had to introduce ground troops, far from the supporting air bases and supply depots which the army required to fulfil its mission, and to resupply or reequip its troops. Of all three services, the US Air Force and the US Army were least prepared to undertake this new role. Given the very nature of the environment in which they operate, the US Navy and the US Marines were better placed to transform themselves into tools to fight terrorist rather than the forces of another global superpower.

It was suddenly discovered that America's military arsenal was virtually obsolete, as it was largely unsuited to its new usage. For a decade the weapons supplied to the US military, as well as the military machine itself, had failed to evolve and it paid the price in its inability to react quickly and efficiently to counter the new threat of global terrorism. The Gulf War was not the war of the future, as many military

BELOW: The aircraft carrier USS *John C. Stennis* executes a sharp turn to starboard.

LEFT: A camouflaged LAV-R tank rolls through the desert, blowing up a cloud of sand behind it.

BELOW: Modern US military doctrine emphasizes speed of reaction and the US Marine Corps plays a significant role in this approach. It is able to land forces by sea or air and support them with its organic air-power. Photo shows a USMC LAV on exercise.

strategists and weapons contractors had imagined. It was probably the last of the great combined tank, infantry, and airpower campaigns fought on a scale reminiscent of World War II, using conventional albeit high-tech weapons. The war was characterized by the massed deployment of heavy M1 Abrams tanks, attack helicopters (such as the Apache), and tank-busting aircraft such as the A-10 Groundhog. Airborne divisions leap-frogged across the battlefield by helicopter, warships provided naval gunfire support, and UN aircraft flew ground-attack sorties which tore up the Iraqi front-line defenses and reserve echelons. The set-piece attack was what the American military had been preparing for since the end of World War II, expect the opponent they had always envisaged was the Soviet Union, and the expected battleground was Central Europe, not the Middle East. This huge military force took time to deploy, and although it was well suited to the relatively open deserts of Kuwait, it was a military cudgel which was as unsubtle as it was obsolete.

The new role of the US military emphasizes speed of reaction and the ability to strike without waiting to build up a huge logistical support base. It means deploying light, well-equipped forces, and supporting

ABOVE: Crew members of the USS *Thomas Gates* stand by at their replenishment station as the ship makes its approach on the USS *Kalamazoo* for underway refueling off the coast of Florida.

LEFT: A Petty Officer uses a sextant to plot the navigational position of the USS *Abraham Lincoln* on route to the Persian Gulf on a routine six-month deployment.

LEFT: An F/A-18 Hornet is directed by a yellow shirt to the forward port catapult on the flight deck of the USS *Enterprise* as the ship conducts flight operations in the Mediterranean Sea.

BELOW: The USS *Kitty Hawk* sits pier side in Apra Harbor, Guam on a routine deployment en route to the Arabian Gulf.

them with airpower and naval gunfire or missile strikes if required. Events in Afghanistan and the Middle East indicate that the US military cannot rely on the use of the airbases and supply infrastructures of other friendly powers, but have to be prepared to fight alone, and far from home. Fortunately the United States of America already has the forces at hand to fulfil this new mission.

The US Navy are the only branch of the US armed services capable of reacting to these new demands, through the deployment of aircraft carrier and amphibious warfare groups. The deployment of US Marines, the use of carrier-based strike aircraft, and the use of naval gunfire support, or ship or submarine-launched cruise missiles are all vital parts of the naval arsenal. Apart from naval gunnery, all of these elements or weapons have been used to great effect in Afghanistan. However, to give them credit,

the US Air Force, as well as naval aviation elements of the US Navy, responded to the attack on the World Trade Center and the Pentagon. They provided Combat Air Patrols (CAPs) along borders of the United States, and around its major cities and military installations.

The sight of F-16s or F-18s patrolling the skies of New York, Washington, and Philadelphia must have provided the inhabitants of these cities some modicum of relief. In addition, both services provide radar and antiaircraft protection from ships and aircraft operating along the Atlantic and Pacific seaboards. In particular, AEGIS-equipped cruisers and destroyers were stationed off Long Island and in the Chesapeake Bay, protecting New York City, Washington DC, and Norfolk, Virginia.

Of all the arms of the military, the Army has the biggest changes to make. Since the end of the Cold War and the Gulf War which followed, the US Army has retained its armored and mechanized formations, which need a large logistical tail, as well as supply bases and time for military preparation. There are

BELOW: Realistic training is essential to prepare US troops for all types of future engagements.

ABOVE and RIGHT: It doesn't matter how heavy the firepower is, it has to be accurate. Training on the ranges and in combat conditions is essential particularly for light infantry forces that rely on their small arms rather than heavy mechanized weaponry.

very few "leg infantry" or light infantry formations available for deployment, and when the decision was made to enter Afghanistan, only the 10th Mountain Division was available for deployment. These light formations rely on infantry firepower, and often highly sophisticated personal or support weapons, but they have the advantage that for all intents, they can be loaded onto a plane, and flown into a trouble-spot. The weakness of these troops, including the Airborne formations (the 101st and 82nd Airborne Divisions) and even the US Rangers is that they need to be flown from established bases.

If friendly powers are reluctant to grant the US military permission to use their bases close to the trouble-spot, or even if they refuse to let them travel through their airspace, then the deployment range of these troops is limited. To transport combat troops in

ABOVE: Two Blackhawks and a Chinook touch down. These new types of helicopter have begun to supercede the older models.

a fleet of transport aircraft such as the Galaxy, the receiving airbase needs to be able to take the huge quantities of planes, stores, and men which are involved in such a deployment. This means that somebody has to secure the base first, and in most cases, to adapt it to take large transport aircraft. While it was envisaged that these troops would be flown into bases in Europe, this was not a major problem. As the US Army now faces the likelihood that it could be called upon to insert troops into Third World countries, or ones lacking substantial airbases, then it needs to reevaluate its method of transportation, and more importantly, the equipping of its troops.

The nature of the new war is something that requires more than military hardware. It needs resolve, and the US commitment to the conflict has demonstrated that at least for the moment, that resolution is shared by both the American public, the government and the military. For the first time in its history, the United States is opposed by an enemy, who if it could detonate a bomb which would kill

every last American would do so with glee. This hatred is not directed at Americans as individuals, but as a nation; a symbol of a corrupt, immoral, and Godless state, preying on the weaknesses of the Third World in general and on Islam in particular. The antagonism of people who hold this viewpoint is exacerbated by the increasing religious fervor encompassing much of the Muslim world, and the involvement of the United States in combating terrorism. In a world filled with weapons of mass destruction, suicide bombers, and religious zealots, the United States is locked into a war involving diplomacy, reason, and intelligence gathering as much as in the deployment of America's formidable arsenal. It is not a clash between civilizations, only one between civilized people and extremists intent on their destruction. These terrorists want to turn it into a war between East and West, Islam and

Christianity, tolerance and barbarism. America is at war, and its leaders, commanders, and above all its public, need to address some difficult issues concerning the waging of this war on terror. In war, you kill your enemies until they stop fighting you. This is particularly true here, as the hard-core terrorists who are waging war against America will not quit while they are alive. In the attack on Afghanistan, innocent civilians were killed.

The fearsome arsenal available to the United States far exceeds that which flattened the cities of Germany in World War II. In that conflict, civilian casualties were inevitable, as they will be in any future campaign in the war on terrorism. The

TOP: M-60 gun. Despite modern advances in weaponry, simple and robust infantry support weapons are still highly effective.

RIGHT: The camouflaged sniper is still frequently used, to deadly effect.

RIGHT: A Petty Officer checks a pump's status on the Auxiliary Engineering Officer of the Watch Central Control Station aboard the Navy's first "Smart Ship," USS *Yorktown*.

FAR RIGHT, TOP: Four A-10A Thunderbolts shimmer in the desert heat waves as they taxi out for a combat patrol.

FAR RIGHT, BOTTOM: A 355th Fighter Squadron A/AO-10 Thunderbolt II moves into position for refueling.

difference is, today the use of less indiscriminate weapons provides military planners with the opportunity to reduce civilian casualties to a minimum. The use of precision guided weapons allow the USA to launch devastating raids at specific targets. This technology will come into its own in the coming decade, but there is still a place in the military toolbox for the sledgehammer as well as the lightsaber.

From the beginning of the conflict in Afghanistan, American service personnel were embroiled in close-combat fighting in caves reminiscent of the struggles on the Pacific atolls during World War II. War is a dehumanizing and horrific experience, and despite all the technological advantages enjoyed by America's servicemen, war can still come down to brutal close-quarters contests; grenades, rifles, knives, and bayonets. As an American Lieutenant said on Pork Chop Hill during the Korean War, "Bayonets … right out of the Stone Age! Where's all this push-button warfare we've been hearing about?" His companion, another Lieutenant, wryly commented in reply, "We're the push-buttons."

This book explores the tools which make up the arsenal of today's US military machine; its aircraft, warships, guns, artillery, missiles, munitions, and rockets. Many of them will stand or fall as weapons systems by their performance in battle. All the B-2

Stealth Bombers, Tomahawk missiles, or AEGIS missile cruisers in the world can't flush out terrorists from a mountain cave complex in Afghanistan. A well-led, well-motivated, and well-trained United States Marine armed with an assault rifle and bayonet is still the best tool for the job, just as he was at Mount Suribachi on Iwo Jima, or the Citadel in Hue City, or the Legation Compound in Peking. Somehow, for all the technology in the world, for all the vast firepower at the beck and call of an American commander in the field or at sea, it often all comes down to a scared young grunt with a rifle.

AIR WEAPONS

A major result of the breakup of the Soviet Union in August 1991 was the so-called "peace dividend" that reduced the need for the Western powers to maintain such a high profile national defense structure. In order not to anticipate too much too soon from a situation that had not prevailed for five decades, the United States relaxed its state of alert around the world at a slow pace. A major restructuring of the US Air Force, implemented on June 1, 1992, resulted in the formation of Air Combat Command and Air Mobility Command. However, the headlines soon shifted from an inert Cold War to smaller, very active, "hot wars." Several conflicts, each on a scale that was minute in comparison to the deadly, nuclear-tipped threat that war with the Eastern bloc had presented, have nevertheless involved US intervention in the two decades since "Glasnost" and "Perestroika" first became familiar words. In the most recent war in Afghanistan, the US made a significant commitment and while Somalia and Bosnia remain quiet, the embers of war are glowing still in the Persian Gulf.

Despite the fact that these were limited conflicts, they have still presented a potential threat if not to world peace then local stability. The US-led coalition that fought in the Gulf reinforced the need to maintain the flexibility inherent in air, sea, and naval forces in the early years after the Cold War and air power still remains at the cutting edge of the Western world's ability to retaliate where military targets are clearly identified.

Restructuring

The closure of bases, mergers in the aerospace industry, and major restructuring were three major results of the end of the Cold War for the US Air Force. In place of the old Tactical and Strategic Air Commands and their clearly defined spheres of responsibility, an integrated Air Combat Command, which to many represents the biggest shake-up that the USAF has ever undergone, brings together the various tactical and strategic strike elements. The AMC directs the passive but vital support of transport, intelligence, and flight refueling units. Despite restructuring and

RIGHT: Modern fighter pilots wear a "bone dome" helmet with an antiglare visor. A current trend is to mount sights on the helmet, thereby reducing workload still further .

downsizing its vast military machine in the last years of the 20th century, the US actually lost little of its combat capability, due mainly to the debut of a number of new weapons and systems. Provided that a battlefield continues to exist, the US can still demonstrate its awesome strike capability.

Although the peace dividend brought about a significant reduction in overall military aircraft numbers compared to the 1970s and 1980s, the USAF inventory of 2002/2003 includes highly sophisticated stealth aircraft such as the F-117 fighter and B-2 bomber. In stark contrast are the old stagers such the AC-130, based on a transport that first flew in 1954. The stealth types have more than made up in capability for the retirement of aircraft perceived to be obsolescent or uneconomical in terms of further technical upgrades.

An overriding factor in the post Cold War atmosphere was a "need for less," which extended to bases and entire military units as well as aircraft numbers. However, this view was certainly not shared by numerous generals and admirals. In budgetary terms, a streamline military force made sense, but the events of September 11, 2001, and the appalling destruction of the World Trade Center, New York, must have convinced many that the US can and should adopt an even higher defense posture. The

ABOVE: US Navy deck handlers prepare an F/A-18 Hornet for launching. The lack of ordnance on the aircraft suggests one of the hundreds of training flights a carrier conducts on every cruise.

RIGHT: Larger visual displays that monitor aircraft state closely are replacing analog instruments in modern combat aircraft cockpits, that of the F/A-18 being very "state of the art."

subsequent pursuit of Osama bin Laden into Afghanistan adds weight to any argument for maintaining strong military forces and the future hardly heralds lasting peace in many areas of the world.

Inventory

In addition to the highly sophisticated aircraft that carry them, current 21st-century, US air-launched munitions have an improved, "all purpose" nature by combining the capability of several different classes of weapon. And to the undoubted satisfaction of the Congressional budget holders, the weapons of today are increasingly developed for use by all US services. This is not exactly a new concept but one that will clearly be expanded upon in the future. The words "joint" and "triple service" appear increasingly in the

identifying acronyms of certain types of hardware, much of it associated with stealth aircraft, which unlike more traditional aircraft cannot be festooned with pods, tanks, bombs, and missiles on external racks. In the coming years, stealth capability will undoubtedly be extended to other aircraft and weapons; cruise missiles such as the AGM-129 have received the treatment and been adapted to boost its low rate of detection during a 1,800-mile target run. Research continues to extend stealth capability to the AGM-137, the shorter range Tri-Service Stand Off Attack Missile (TSAAM).

Historically the single-seat strike aircraft has been the cornerstone of tactical air power and, despite conceding some of this exclusivity to the helicopter, most recent conflicts have incorporated a high proportion of fixed-wing tactical strike aircraft, at least in the early stages. When Iraq invaded the small Gulf state of Kuwait in August 1990, the US led a coalition of 30 nations to restore Kuwait's independence. Operation "Desert Storm" opened with an intensive

ABOVE: Old though it is today, the 2.75-in (70-mm) rocket packed into convenient multiround pods still constitutes an impressive weapon against certain categories of ground target. Here a US Navy F/A-18 unleashes a full salvo from each wing station.

round of "first strike" sorties with the primary aim of destroying or at least significantly reducing the enemy's ability to mount retaliatory air attacks. With loss of radar, and missile and gun defenses in total disarray, Iraq's air force proved to be a paper tiger. The expected large-scale threat from that quarter never materialized, despite the Iraqi air force's potentially strong inventory of modern warplanes built around a core of highly capable Soviet types. Having taken the initiative, the coalition of Western allied countries never lost it and succeeding operations were outstandingly successful.

Blanket aerial surveillance via orbiting AWACs enabled the workhorse F-15 and F-16 to demonstrate that large-scale USAF counter air operations, confined within sensitive national boundaries, present few problems. The F-15 and F-16 had been deployed for many years in a continuing front-line combat role by Israel, but war in the Gulf was the first on such a scale to involve modern fast jets with American personnel. An overwhelming coalition force was ranged against Iraq, supported by extensive and effective ECM and ELINT sorties to disable defense radar. In a conflict where it was impossible to predict the degree of resistance, in the event American fighters and bombers were able to work virtually unmolested.

It would be wrong to underestimate the part played by Allied air forces, particularly the RAF, which undertook many hazardous airfield strikes at minimum altitude; a "high risk" tactic that the USAF all but abandoned after the Vietnam War. The principal reason was that strike aircraft should no longer have to go in at low levels and expose themselves to a hostile defense network if precision-guided munitions could be relied on at a stand-off position. The downside of this argument is the enormous cost of weapons used to destroy low-tech targets such as bunkers. Wars rarely develop in the way that arms manufacturers predict and along with the vagaries of actual combat, variables of weather conditions, enemy defenses, accuracy of target information, and electronics malfunction, these are factors that cannot yet ensure a "one shot, one hit" situation.

A different type of war to that in the Gulf confronted the USAF, Navy, and Marine air units in Bosnia. Deployed initially in a familiar opening phase of intensive strategic air strikes, this NATO-brokered offensive soon peaked, to be replaced by that of peacekeeping in the form of armed reconnaissance patrols to enforce a "no-fly" zone. Fast jet pilots found less and less worthwhile targets in an area that boasted few active missile and gun defenses and could only wait for the painstaking effort on the ground to work through to the opposing sides agreeing truce terms that finally held.

The air action in Bosnia and Kosovo underscored the importance of cooperation by countries friendly to the US in terms of territorial overflight agreements and use of air bases. Operations in the Balkans were particularly aided by the use of Incirlik in Turkey, where the majority of air strikes were mounted from. Bases along the Saudi Arabian coast – Doha, Al Jaber, and All al Salem – together with King

BELOW: S-3A Viking aircraft of Air Antisubmarine Squadron 38 refuels over the Sierra Nevada Mountains. It remain an integral part of any strike force undertaking secondary support roles aboard USN carriers

Khalid and Al Kharj near the capital Riyadh, also enabled US air forces to carry out strikes into Iraq. The US Central Command, which has its headquarters in Florida, has responsibility for operations in the Middle East and South Asia. Nicknamed the "Sandbox," it is controlled from its forward headquarters at Prince Sultan Air Base (also near Riyadh). When "Desert Storm" ended, overflights of Iraq remained necessary to ensure the terms of the ceasefire were adhered to and these bases continued to be very active. The subsequent antiterrorist conflict in Afghanistan, Operations "Enduring Freedom" and "Bright Star," recorded a further increase in the use of foreign bases by US air forces in that region. Thanks to international agreements a limited number of US aircraft have access to bases in Pakistan, Uzbekistan, and Tajikstan.

Afghanistan has some similarities with the Balkans conflict. It has highly difficult terrain in which to pinpoint targets, relatively few effective AA weapons, and a general lack of airborne opposition, meaning that securing a conclusion to the war has not been completely trouble free. Tactical air power has been somewhat overshadowed by the need for strategic battlefield attack by heavy bombers in deference to the well dug-in positions manned by Al Qaida forces. Historically a very difficult country to subdue (as the Red Army found to its cost), Afghanistan's terrain has offered far less hindrance to air strikes than it would to ground armies. The Taliban appear to have met their match as a result of large-scale American bombing of otherwise invulnerable hill positions and underground complexes.

Even though bunker-busting was probably not envisaged as a primary role for the B-2 Spirit, the US has demonstrated its incredible capacity not only to spend billions of dollars on the world's most advanced aircraft, but to deploy them in combat. The B-2 could be seen as a throwback to a Cold War scenario, intended for retaliatory strikes on "hard" targets such as strategic missiles sites, power stations, factories, and petrol, oil, and lubricant (POL) production facilities. However, recent US combat sorties have been mainly against targets with far less resilience, difficult natural terrain aside. In explanation, so lengthy is the gestation period of modern weapons that it is all but inevitable that projections about roles and required numbers will have changed

BELOW: Compact and fitted with a folding fin to enable it to fit into carrier hangers, the S-3A/B Viking ASW aircraft entered USN service in 1974.

by the time they enter service. Bearing that in mind, it remains to be seen whether the USAF will be allowed to order an even more costly replacement of the B-2 when the time comes, but a mission by just two B-2s is reckoned, by one air force general, to be equal to 32 strike aircraft, 16 fighters, 12 air defense suppression aircraft, and 15 tankers. This is the kind of cost saving that the creation of ACC was intended to confirm.

Real veteran aircraft, such as the B-52, remain in air force service as mother ships for cruise missiles, and to prove that some things do not fundamentally change, as carriers of iron bombs. The other heavy punch in the composite wing command structure is the elegant B-1 Lancer, able to operate quite independently of other forces. While the trio of USAF long-range bombers is fully capable of undertaking a nuclear strike, the delivery of conventional ordnance seems to be the requirement they need to fulfill for the foreseeable future.

At the other end of the scale, an A-10 Thunderbolt flying "down in the weeds" is formidable against almost anything that runs on wheels or tracks while dedicated "mud movers," such as the F-15E, can deny large areas of territory to an enemy in a very short time.

With four air services to budget for, the Pentagon has also been obliged to trim the air inventories of the Navy, Marines, and the Army. Here, too, new weapons systems have enabled a greater degree of standardization and the packing of a greater punch into an existing airframe. The Navy has actually broadened its carrier-borne fighter and strike capability by developing the A/F-18 to the point that the strike tasks previously handled by the decommissioned A-6 Intruder and A-7 Corsair II are now largely embraced by the highly capable Hornet. The EA-6B Prowler electronic warfare aircraft remains an integral part of the carrier strike force as does the S-3B Viking in the ASW role, plus helicopter and fixed wing support aircraft.

The carrier task forces and the mighty F-14 Tomcat remain the tip of the naval spear. However, a percentage reduction in the number of first line fighter and strike aircraft, previously vested in several types on a carrier deck, to just two, makes the task of combat missions easier and has some economies in terms of servicing.

BELOW: A US Marine directs a EA-6B Prowler to a spot on the ramp at Aviano Air Base, Italy, as the aircraft returns from a NATO Operation Allied Force mission.

As the only US service to operate the British Aerospace Harrier, the Marines have participated in an ongoing upgrade program for the aircraft. They have taken advantage of the development potential realized by the "big wing" APG-65 radar-equipped Harrier II Plus, which has a 30ft 4in (9.24m) span compared with 25ft 3in (7.7m) of the AV-8B. The larger wing certainly makes the aircraft more combat-capable by increasing stores provision. In late 1998, VMA-214 Black Sheep was selected as the first West Coast unit to receive this variant. Over 200 Harriers remain in the inventory of a force that exists to carry out the primary duty of supporting Marine ground forces. This it does in company with conventional strike aircraft, attack, and transport helicopters which are embarked where necessary, aboard Marine carriers. During more recent events, however, Marine Harriers have been used in combat overseas without a significant Corps ground dimension.

The US Army's helicopter fleet, once larger than many of the world's entire air arms, continues to be streamlined, but again no real lack of attack capability is apparent. Vesting much in broadening the weapons load of its flagship type the AH-64 Apache, the Army has found an able replacement for its original helicopter gunship, the AH-1 Huey Cobra.

At the opposite end of the dimensional scale is the latest development of the fixed wing gunship, the Lockheed/Rockwell AC-130U Spectre. Sired in Vietnam from earlier Hercules adaptations, the AC-130U is but one of a family of modifications of the original aircraft that began in 1965. Special missions variants currently in service with the USAF encompass the roles of tanker, special forces support, and SAR.

Conventional ground forces have been partially sidelined by the increasing adoption of suicide bombings by civilian zealots, which are hard to contain, and air forces too are being sidelined, but in a more positive manner. The development of unmanned Remotely Piloted Vehicles (RPVs) to survey battlefields and convey intelligence information without any risk to human aircrew has been significantly demonstrated in Afghanistan by the General Atomics Predator. Deploying RPVs successfully was but the first step to providing them with their own weapons. Predator carries Hellfire ASMs to attack targets on an "instant update" basis from data supplied by the craft's own computers. Such deployments show a definite swing away from the traditional tactical role of manned aircraft. The attractive "expendability factor" of the RPV has finally proven its worth after decades of testing and theoretical projections of their value in combat. It is certain that increased use will be made of such surveillance systems as the necessary technology expands.

F-117

Dramatically different to any other previous single seat fighter, the Lockheed F-117 Nighthawk or "Black Jet" was the first practical result from years of technological development – much of it clandestine in nature – that enabled the radar signature of an aircraft to be reduced almost to zero. Powered by two non-afterburning General Electric F404 engines which feature "platypus" exhausts to reduce infrared signature, the unique appearance of the F-117 is due entirely to its stealth role. Covered in various radar absorbent material (RAM) coatings and with doors and panels without straight lines to deflect radar energy in all directions, the F-117 is unmistakable. Although quite ungainly on the ground, the aircraft manages to become an angular dart with dramatic purpose once in the air.

First issued to the 37th Fighter Wing, the F-117 represented the most costly development program for a fighter to date. It was so technically advanced that it appeared to guarantee its development costs

would be recouped by proving that stealth design and materials actually work. Coupled with a capability unequaled by any other aircraft in this class, the advent of the Nighthawk was all but inevitable once the technical challenges had been overcome. Entering combat earlier than many generals might have predicted, the first F-117s departed for Saudi Arabia on August 20, 1990 in response to the Iraqi invasion. Flown by crews of the 37th Fighter Wing, the Nighthawk's participation in Operation "Desert Shield/Storm" was highly successful by all accounts.

To support Operation "Allied Force," the NATO bombing campaign over the former Yugoslavia, the 49th FW deployed 25 of its F-117s to Aviano Air Base in Italy. From there the US stealth fighters attacked high priority targets in Serbia and Kosovo.

Combat over the disputed Balkans was not without loss, however, even for the very high tech F-117. Serb SAM missiles were launched in response to Allied air attacks on Belgrade and on the night of March 28/29, 1999, one apparently struck home, bringing down a Nighthawk of the 49th FW. The pilot was rescued.

On the credit side, the F-117A proved highly capable of delivering precision munitions in the face of intense AAA fire over Iraq. The aircraft carries all

BELOW: The F-117A Stealth Fighter is the first operational aircraft conceived to exploit low-observable stealth technology. It is flown by pilots of the Tactical Air Command's 37th Tactical Fighter Wing.

stores in an internal weapons bay and in deference to its stealth role, lacks a built-in gun. The last of 59 production F-117As was completed in August 1982.

F-22 and Joint Strike Fighter

The trend toward integrated weapons systems deployable by a wide range of first line aircraft has led to the concept of a single airframe able to serve in a diversity of roles for different services. The F-22 Raptor, the next generation air dominance fighter, is intended initially to replace the single seat F-15C and later the F-15E and F-117 strike fighters. Fulfillment of the latter plan by the F-22 is years away and could well be overtaken by procurement of the even more advanced X-35 Joint Strike Fighter (JSF). The intention is clear. After the mergers of the US aviation industry that were at least unlikely during the Cold War, one or two strike fighter projects that handle every conceivable combat situation can benefit from the expert input of several companies.

ABOVE: A huge amount of money and faith has gone into the F-22 Raptor. Designed to serve for much of the 21st century, it represents one of the largest military contracts since the end of the Cold War.

As a result the JSF is on course to be the largest military project ever developed by the US.

Lockheed and Northrop were the original contractors for the Advanced Tactical Fighter (ATF), which became the F-22. General Dynamics and Boeing subsequently collaborated to beat the rival F-23 from Northrop McDonnell Douglas. The F-22 flew for the first time on September 29, 1990. The USAF selection of an F-22, powered by two Pratt & Whitney F119-PW-100 afterburning turbojets, followed in April 1991. Two development aircraft were flying by June 1998 and the Air Force currently plans to procure 339 aircraft, with Initial Operating Capability (IOC) testing scheduled.

Despite incorporating a significant degree of stealth technology, such as undetectable and radar

RIGHT: A US Navy version of the Joint Strike Fighter. The JSF is the military's next generation, multirole, strike aircraft designed to complement the Navy F/A-18 and USAF F-22.

absorbent material, construction of the F-22 marks a return to a more conventional design layout compared to the radical F-117. Broadly similar in configuration to the F/A-18, the aircraft's construction has serrated panel and door edges to help deflect radar energy. This is reported to give a radar signature the size of a bee, and enables the Raptor to avoid detection by the most sophisticated air defense systems. The extreme agility the aircraft achieves is built around a power to weight ratio of 1.4 to 1, compared to the 1 to 1 ratio of the F-16.

In terms of combat capability the Raptor has been designed to defeat all current (and projected) fighters in aerial combat under the "first look, first kill" philosophy. Fixed armament is retained in the form of an internal long-barreled GE M61AI Vulcan cannon with up to four AIM-9s in side weapons bays. Ventral bays accommodate four AIM-120A Amraams or six AIM-120Cs. A secondary role is that of precision ground attack with JDAM PGMs

including GBU-32. The future of the F-22, as with any modern combat aircraft, depends on it passing stringent performance, avionics, and weapons integration tests. Overriding everything is the cost. Each F-22 is expected to have a price tag of at least $83 million; adding research and development and support may push the figure per aircraft to $173 million. The USAF, and particularly Congress, will press for an across the board clean bill of health as to the aircraft's capabilities. In short the Raptor's manufacturers have to make it one of the most capable aircraft of all time.

One problem the Air Force faces in its ongoing battles for a military budget elastic enough to absorb inflation projections for aircraft and systems, which are as yet unproven, is the fact that no one aircraft can quite meet all requirements. Air Force chiefs made a case for a future inventory with the emphasis on F-22s and the production of the X-35, wanting to obtain 1,763 of the latter. The US Navy requirement was quoted as 480, the US Marines 609, and a further 150 to equip the British Royal Air Force and Royal Navy.

The JSF, similar in configuration to the F-22, began life as an F-16, F/A-18, and AV-8 replacement. Powered by a single P&W SE611 turbofan, an F-119 derivative, the X-35 is both land and carrier based and adaptable to Short Take-off Vertical Landing (STOVL) via an Allison engine driven lift fan

LEFT: An artist's impression of the US Navy's version of the Joint Strike Fighter. The development program is a joint US–UK effort to affordably replace aging strike assets.

mounted behind the cockpit. This is a system that can be adapted to later more advanced configuration. An internal gun is planned for the USAF version, with AIM-9X, AIM-120, and JDAMs arming the US versions across the board.

Confirmation for the X-35 to enter production came in December 2001, beating the Lockheed Martin design for the unconventional Boeing X-32 that still required further development. One factor that is believed to have helped the case for the X-35 is that the design was virtually fixed and did not require an unspecified sum for further refinement. A figure of 6,000 X-35s was estimated for the world market as the project entered its System Development and Demonstration (SDD) phase of 126 months.

F-15

Big, powerful, hugely expensive, and not without early teething troubles, the mighty Eagle grew to be a potent symbol of the modern USAF. As with most current, highly sophisticated combat aircraft it was closely scrutinized by Congress in its time and was inevitably regarded as too costly. But with "the threat" looming large the Eagle was pushed through. One of its attributes as far as the Air Force was concerned was that the F-15 restored the time-honored single seat fighter concept that had, at least for that service, been somewhat compromised by the two-seat Phantom. Failing to plan its F-4 crew integration as well as the Navy did, the USAF found itself with some serious challenges to morale, particularly in Vietnam. After the war, technical progress in control and monitoring systems enabled the F-15's pilot's workload to be reduced so that it could be flown comfortably by one occupant. Highly successful peacetime integration into tactical air defense and strike wings around the world made the Eagle an Air Force cornerstone, its lengthy service record punctuated by several bouts of combat.

All the computer-simulated, combat scenarios in the world pale into insignificance at the point where an real enemy aircraft is indicated on the head up display. Flown by pilots, who can be very unpredictable in an unreal, undeclared "war skirmish" situation, the F-15's challengers have invariably been Russian MiGs and Sukhois. These challengers have rarely gained the upper hand, but in such situations Eagle drivers have had to engage in one-on-one maneuvering after ensuring that a "Mk. I eyeball" rather than a beyond line of sight missile computer has made positive identification.

All the missile kills in the Gulf War were made by F-15Cs which were ably supported by the crews of the E-3 AWACS who passed range, position, and number coordinates of Iraqi interceptors to the fighter pilots. Of the F-15 missiles expended, 24 kills were made by the Sparrow and 12 by the Sidewinder, with one kill unconfirmed

The Eagle gained a second crew member that of the F-15E, which fortuitously met an early 1980s

LEFT: Modern aircraft gun technology remains with the principle of multiple revolving barrels to aid cooling. The M61A1 79-in (20-mm) cannon in the F-16 has its ammunition coiled in a drum to save space.

requirement for a new multirole fighter under the Advanced Tactical Fighter (ATF) program to supplement the F-111 strike aircraft. The F-15E was selected in February 1984, and its first flight was in December 1986. Disparagingly known as the "mud mover" Eagle to some, the F-15E is highly capable in a ground attack role. Its systems include an APG-70 radar with ground mapping, including seven multifunction CRTs and laser target acquisition, which combine to accurately position the aircraft and achieve the most effective use of its substantial ordnance load of up to 24,500lb (11,113kg).

ABOVE: An AIM-7 Sparrow radar-guided missile, seconds after launching from a 318th FIS F-15A Eagle. Despite a checkered combat career this missile remains an integral part of the US ordnance inventory.

BELOW: Pave Mover's data link and radar components ride in a special pallet-pod, mounted in the bomb bay of an F-111E during evaluation tests at White Sands Missile Range, New Mexico.

ABOVE LEFT: An F-15 Eagle is prepared for launching from Tyndall Air Force Base, Florida.

LEFT: Bombs are loaded onto an F-15 at Aviano Air Base, Italy.

ABOVE: A USAF F-15E takes off from Incirlik Air Base, Turkey.

RIGHT: Preflight checks are performed on precision guided munitions loaded on an F-15E.

F-16

"Electric Jet," "Viper," or even the official Fighting Falcon are names used to describe this outstandingly capable single-seater from General Dynamics. The F-16, in common with most other contemporary combat aircraft, has proven to be highly adaptable to new and improved systems without compromising performance, despite the inevitable weight increase that such changes bring. Evaluation and service has continued since the Viper's first production in 1975 and it is still included in plans for the foreseeable future. The F-16 remains one of the most economical and capable fighters operated by the USAF and the general goal of integrating the type's avionics suite across the different production blocks is currently reflected in the Air Force's Common Configuration Implementation Program (CCIP). Around 700 F-16 Block 40/42s and 50/52s are to be modified, and the latter series of aircraft will also receive PGM targeting pods.

Such upgrades to extend airframe life may mean that the F-16 and other types will be prematurely replaced by the new F-22s of Air Combat Command. That remains to be seen but the USAF maintains numerous slots for upgraded combat aircraft in its Reserve Force and the Air Guard. These are formations that have previously extended the useful life of "nearly new" types in America's highly capable second line forces.

Under Air Combat Command, F-16s have tended to undertake a more diverse role than they had as part of TAC. Nowadays a missile-laden Viper on an

BELOW: Small but highly capable, the F-16 has been a key USAF strike fighter since the mid 1970s. Upgrades will ensure it a place in Air Combat Command inventory for the foreseeable future.

antiradar/SAM suppression mission will usually carry its own ECM and targeting equipment in underwing pods rather than rely on a Wild Weasel (historically an F-4) to set up the target for its AGM-88 or similar antiradiation missiles. Equipment pods have of course long been an integral part of such single-seaters and back up is invariably available if necessary. Here again, economy is the keynote but the revised Air Force policy provides fighter pilots with a greater appreciation of the increasing importance of tactical targets and the flight profiles and weapons required to neutralize them.

B-1 Lancer

A straight spelling-out of the B-1's designation produces the word "Bone," the nickname both air and ground crews have universally adopted to describe the Lancer. With a design that goes back to 1971, the elegant B-1A and its distinctive variable geometry wing faced an uncertain future when the Carter administration suspended production in 1977. Regenerated by Ronald Reagan in 1981, the elegant B-1B appeared to be a highly capable replacement for the USAF's aging B-52. It was, but only in part. Advanced and expensive, the B-1 was in its second manifestation, confirmed for a multi-purpose, high or low level attack role. Budget restrictions keep only 75 of the 95 B-1s in service (100 were ordered) on call at any one time. However, having made its

combat debut over Iraq during Operation "Desert Fox" in 1998, the Bone also went onto action over Kosovo the following year. Operation "Allied Force" showed that, for all their saber-rattling, Serb forces were incapable of adequately defending targets such as the Novi Sad oil refinery. This was heavily bombed by two B-1s that were operating out of RAF Fairford, England on May 1, 1999.

The sophisticated B-1 has proven a little more difficult to integrate into ACC than some other types principally because it is very expensive to operate. Fortunately it is also quite capable of carrying out missions alone, and for that reason Bone crews tend to undertake specific tasks separate to those performed by the rest of their parent Wings and to operate singly at low, medium, or high altitudes depending on the mission.

Whatever the mission of the B-1 the Air Force (in common with other contemporary types) has largely dispensed with the hauling of individual bombs out to the aircraft. Now that its role as a nuclear deterrent role has been shelved, the B-1 utilizes a Conventional Munitions Module (CMM) which is pre-loaded with up to 26 x 500lb (227kg) Mk. 82 general purpose bombs. If necessary the Bone can take three CMMs and further stores, including AGM-86B cruise missiles, on external racks for a maximum load. This may sound impressive but the reality is that scattering sticks or strings of bombs over a target area is a tactic from the days of nuclear strikes, when the allowable margin of error was understandably quite large. That mission profile ran counter to ACC philosophy and for a time Bone crews under-

LEFT: Elegant and able, the B-1 is the mighty "Bone" to its fiercely loyal crews. Designed as a B-52 replacement it has created its own role as an integrated weapons in the current USAF.

RIGHT: An airman rolls a Mk. 82 bomb to the end of the bomb trailer as the munitions crew loads a B-52H Stratofortress.

BELOW RIGHT: A USAF B1-B Lancer bomber from the 28th Bomb Squadron is loaded with Mk. 82 bombs.

took a degree of retraining to reemphasize precision bombing, which the aircraft achieves by utilizing the Global Positioning System (GPS) and Inertial Navigation System (INS) guided versions of the Mk. 80 gravity bomb. By fitting this "dumb bomb" with a guidance system in the tail section, a target accuracy of within 45ft (13.7m) can be achieved. Other modular weapons and a range of JDAMs make the B-1 a very versatile long range bomber, and a single machine is capable of delivering an impressive degree of destruction.

B-2

At the cutting edge of US strategic striking power is the dramatic B-2 Spirit, which has a zigzag "all-wing" stealth design to endow it with virtual immunity from defensive guns and missiles.

With the availability of tankers on a 24-hour basis, the USAF no longer has any problems in deploying aircraft that *per se* have limited range. Types such as the B-2 have to be able to fly sorties to anywhere in the world, as recent conflicts have shown. During Afghan operations in October 2001, a single B-2 of the 509th Bomb Wing took off from Whitemam Air Force Base in western Missouri. Some 44 hours later the aircraft had flown 7,000 miles (11,265 km) and delivered 16 JDAMs on several targets including airstrips, inside Afghanistan. The entire B-2 operation is virtually automatic, and the crew only fly the Spirit off the runway, carry out the designated mission, and land it. The rest of the flight is conducted on autopilot, a flight profile that was deliberately planned according to the crews, to be "monotonous and boringly easy." To offset this on extreme duration

LEFT: Covered in mats to prevent the work force causing any degradation of their sensitive stealth surfaces, B-2 Spirits are seen in the final phase of assembly at Northrop.

BELOW LEFT: A B-2 Spirit has its flying surfaces tested while taxiing out for take-off. To retain stealth integrity external stores cannot be used on this type of aircraft.

missions B-2 crews operate in shifts. As the Air Force dislikes leaving the aircraft on overseas bases because of security considerations and the fact that any maintenance they might require is highly specialized, fresh crews are positioned for the return leg to the States. On the above Afghan sortie the Spirit flew to Diego Garcia in the Indian Ocean, where a relief crew of two took over to fly it back to Missouri.

With 21 Spirits budgeted for (against the original USAF requirement for 133) production was completed in 1997. Even this modest build required a total of US$45 billion, including development costs.

B-52

A weapon popularly associated with serious intent by the US to bring about a result in a difficult tactical situation, the aged B-52 has proven to be a very effective means of persuasion. The Stratofortress has been continually upgraded and is all but decisive in its ability to saturate targets that have proved impervious to small scale ordnance delivered by more conventional means. The current B-52 fleet of 90 plus "short tail" H models represents a milestone of development in that eight 17,000lb (7,711kg), Pratt & Whitney TF-33 turbofans are able to boost the aircraft's range by a third compared to that possible with turbojets.

TOP: A USAF B-2A Spirit bomber approaches the refueling boom of a KC-135R Stratotanker as the two aircraft rendezvous over Alaska for an in-flight refueling procedure.

LEFT: A symbol of American airpower for more than four decades, the B-52's life extension program will see it through several more before final retirement. This B-52G has inboard racks for various loads including cruise missiles.

ABOVE: A pilot of a USAF B-52H Stratofortress scans the horizon for aircraft as he flies in formation with another B-52 on a combat penetration mission toward a target in Kosovo.

LEFT: A B-52H Stratofortress receives fuel through the refueling boom of a KC-10 Extender aerial tanker during in-flight refueling over the Indian Ocean.

RIGHT: Members of the 96th Bomber Maintenance Squadron perform post-mission maintenance on a USAF B-52 Stratofortress bomber at Andersen Air Force Base, Guam.

RIGHT: A USAF airman positions the bomb load truck as members of a weapons load crew prepare to attach a AGM-65 Maverick missile to the wing of an A-10 Thunderbolt II.

FAR RIGHT: The snout of the A-10 Thunderbolt II contains the seven barrel "'business end" of the giant Avenger 1.2-in (30-mm) cannon that is the aircraft's sole fixed armament.

Further engine upgrades are anticipated, possibly using Rolls-Royce RB-211-535s with 43,200lb (19,596kg) thrust, to keep the B-52 in inventory until 2034. If that does indeed prove to be the case, the B-52 will by then have been in service a staggering 79 years (since 1955).

The B-52's maximum load of up to 51 x 750lb (340kg) iron bombs has been enhanced by weapons that are singularly devastating against certain types of structures and terrain. One of these is the AGM-142 Popeye stand-off fire and forget missile, a rare US foreign "buy in," from Rafael of Israel in this case.

The Stratofortress has been successfully integrated into the ACC force structure, as recent combat operations have shown, and the B-52, that shares saturation bombing missions with the B-2, remains an integral part of the USAF's current strategy.

A-10

Historically the dedicated antiarmor aircraft has been a difficult requirement to meet; contenders often lacked the ability to lift enough ordnance or to demonstrate a high enough degree of combat survival. The A-10 Thunderbolt II (otherwise known as Warthog) met the requirement on all these counts and has proved a useful investment for the USAF. Whereas almost any type can be adapted for a specific ground attack role, anticipated high attrition in combat quickly cancels out all but the toughest and most agile of aircraft.

Adopting a low-wing configuration that would provide both an ample number of stores (on 11 hardpoints) while serving to shield the engines mounted on the rear fuselage from ground fire, Fairchild's design also incorporated the largest fixed gun ever fitted to this class of aircraft. This is the 1.2-in (30mm) GAU-8, seven-barrel cannon, which manufacturers General Electric once posed with a VW Beetle to show it was longer than even a family car.

A titanium armor "bathtub" cockpit section offers ample protection to the pilot. The aircraft is designed to lift 16,000lb (7,258kg) of ordnance and demonstrate a loitering time of up to 1 hour 42 minutes. When it entered a combat situation during the Gulf War, the A-10 excelled under harsh conditions, similar to those repeated in Afghanistan.

The 707th example completed the production of the A-10 and although less than half that number currently remain in USAF service, the Warthog has more than proved its usefulness. Its basic attack role has been expanded into that of Forward Air Control, OA-10s carrying smoke marker rockets, and AIM-9 AAMs for self defense.

ABOVE: The humped cockpit identifies this Thunderbolt II as a single conversion intended to meet a night/ all weather attack role in which the second cockpit was filled with electronic equipment.

BELOW: High-vis 'stars and bars' markings confirm this A-10 photo as an early 1970s view of an AIM-4 Falcon missile test. For its attack role the "Warthog" tested all weapons in USAF inventory.

AC-130

The AC-130 gunship, another USAF aircraft of the "old guard" remaining from the vast air inventory of the Vietnam War period, is presently operated by the 16th Special Operations Squadron from the original SOS base, Hurlburt Field in Florida. The gunship unit currently flying the AC-130U Specter/Spooky nicknames this venerable old Hercules variant the "U-boat." Chock full of electronics, guns and ammunition, the AC-130 has been deployed on most of the occasions that the US military has seen action since the Southeast Asian conflict. Able to deluge an area the size of a football pitch with thousands of rounds of automatic weapons fire, the Specter has to be flown "low and slow" and the pilot holds it in a bank over the target area. This inevitably exposes the aircraft to ground defenses and since eight were lost in Southeast Asia, combat over Kuwait and Somalia (in 1994) has claimed a further two.

ABOVE: Large enough to pack in a comprehensive electronics suite as well as a battery of machineguns and cannon, the AC-130 gunship made its combat debut in Vietnam.

LEFT: Ground view of an AC-130E in all black paintwork which emphasized its clandestine ECM/gunship role that remains part of current Air Force inventory.

Support Force

The all important USAF support forces encompassing trainers, transports, and tankers continue to be upgraded. Stretched C-130J-30s have been incorporated at the 143d Airlift Wing of the Rhode Island Air National Guard at Quonset State Airport. Each of the new Hercules features the computer-controlled Enhanced Cargo Handling System, which allows airdrops to be carried out with greater precision than has hitherto been possible with the C-130J. In addition, the new variant meets Army/Air Force requirements for the safe deployment of up to 128 paratroops from both sides of the aircraft.

Tankers

As the ranges over which tactical strike aircraft operate have tended to be extended and the USAF's fleet of venerable KC-135s of Air Mobility Command are still being upgraded, tankers have taken on a steadily increasing importance in recent years. The established reengining program continues and the Flight Refueling Mk. 32B underwing pod is currently being fitted to an initial 35 examples. This Multipoint Refueling System (MPRS) gives the Air Force's first jet tanker the capability to simultaneously transfer fuel to Navy aircraft using the probe and drogue system and USAF machines operating the fixed flying boom. Although the Stratotanker was previously able to fulfill such duel refueling, it was only possible by deploying more than one aircraft. A drogue attached to the boom enabled Navy aircraft to fill up, but a single tanker could not switch to the Air Force system while in flight.

As well as operating the KC-135 and KC-10 Extender, the Air Force is hoping to finalize a ten year, $20bn lease arrangement with the manufacturer covering 100 Boeing 767s. The Boeing 767s will supplement the KC-135s, some 150 of which equip the 22nd, 92nd, and 319th Air Refueling Wings.

The US Navy

In the early stages of impending military action abroad, power projection for the United States is usually vested in elements of her fleet aircraft carriers. The mere presence of one or more of these mighty warships, unrivaled in size and strike capability, is enough to demonstrate that the nation means business. As shown in the Gulf War, once the shooting starts these vessels pack a devastating punch, as befits the world's largest navy. Investing in nine nuclear-powered carriers (with a tenth due to commission) the Pacific Fleet currently has four and the Atlantic Fleet five. Of these the USS *Enterprise* is the oldest ship to enter service and USS *Ronald Reagan* (CVN-76) the most recent. USS *Nimitz, Eisenhower,*

RIGHT: A US Navy A-6E from Attack Squadron 34 lines up its fuel probe with the buddy-store basket deployed by a VA-34 Intruder in preparation for in-flight refueling.

AIR WEAPONS

LEFT: A US Navy F-14A Tomcat releases a GBU-24B/B hard target, penetrator laser-guided bomb, while in a in a 45-degree dive.

BELOW: A Sikorsky SH-3D Sea King creating a typical "ripple" effect on the sea while "dipping" its submarine detection sonar.

ABOVE: An F/A-18E Super Hornet is loaded with two 2,000lb bombs, two AGM-88 High-Speed Antiradiation (HARM) missiles, and two AIM-9 Sidewinder missiles.

RIGHT: The highly versatile SH-60 Seahawk offers shipboard ASW capability to shield task forces from incursions by hostile submarines and carries a range of torpedoes and anti-ship missiles.

BELOW, RIGHT: Navy Seahawks perform multiple roles including ASW, rescue and commando insertion. Further upgrades in armament are currently planned.

Vinson, Roosevelt, Lincoln, Washington, Stennis, and *Harry S Truman* were progressively added throughout the intervening decades.

Each nuclear carrier now carries a complement of some 75 highly capable A/F-18 Hornets and F-14 Tomcats. These are routinely operated from Atlantic or Pacific Fleet stations on an ongoing peacetime training program and launches are carried out around the clock for crews to complete the requisite number of flight hours to maintain efficiency. With their ability to remain on station for months on end due to their highly efficient nuclear reactors, these ships have proven able to impose and maintain an essential blockade of hostile waters without direct assistance from the other US services. Backing the nuclear fleet are several conventional carriers including the USS *Constellation,* USS *John F Kennedy* (the last conventional carrier built for the navy) and USS *Kitty Hawk.*

Four battle groups built around the USS *Enterprise, Vinson, Roosevelt,* and *Kitty Hawk* (converted to a helicopter-equipped depot ship for special forces support with no jet strike capability) were most recently deployed to the Persian Gulf to operate against terrorist forces in Afghanistan.

ABOVE: Engine exhaust shielding gear enables the Sea Hawk to safely patrol "dangerous" waters during antisubmarine patrol exercises.

BELOW: Avenger typically carries four ready-to-fire Stinger missiles on each of its two arms. A forward-looking infrared unit is carried below one pod and a pair of M240 guns beneath the other. Here a Hydra-70 pod containing 19 rockets in mounted on the port arm.

F-14 Tomcat

Tasked with a Combat Air Patrol (CAP) role during the Gulf War, ten squadrons of F-14s totally succeeded in preventing any attack on the US Navy task forces. As such flights took place close to the carriers action was rare, and only a single enemy aircraft fell to Tomcat crews during the Gulf War. However, they were continually airborne and ready, watching every strike package take off.

The F-14 began such duty at the end of the Vietnam War when the VF-1 and VF-2 deployed from the USS *Enterprise*, which patrolled the South China Sea as the 1975 the evacuation known as Operation "Frequent Wind" got underway. No hostile aircraft were encountered but the cruise, which was primarily to evaluate the new fleet fighter under operational conditions, was an outstanding success. During the Vietnam withdrawal enemy ground fire had been aimed at the F-14s but no damage was inflicted.

Six years were to pass before the F-14 came close to combat action again. On August 19, 1981 the Fast Eagle flight of two Tomcats from VF-41 aboard the USS *Nimitz* engaged and shot down two hostile Libyan Su-22s. Monitoring an American naval exercise in the Gulf of Sidra, the Libyan aircraft ran in on the patrolling F-14s and one suddenly launched an Atoll AAM.

Cleared to engage, the F-14s made no mistake. Both Su-22s were dispatched by AIM-9L Sidewinder shots. Tomcats were involved in further action against the Libyan Air Force on January 4, 1989 when F-14s from *John F Kennedy* encountered two MiG-23s. Again the outcome was the same: Americans 2, Libyans 0.

Currently the status of the F-14 in the Navy reflects a broader mission profile since the retirement of the A-6 Intruder. Older F-14As remain in service along with the F-14B and F-14D, which have enhanced air-to-ground capability with digital avionics and radar processing linked to the AWG-9 radar; both the latter variants are also equipped to use the Lantirn designator pod.

The Achilles heel to what is widely regarded as the finest fleet defense fighter extant has been engines.

RIGHT: A sequence of camera frames of an F-14 launching an AIM-54 Phoenix during early compatibility trials. The six missiles carried by the Tomcat are able to deal with multiple threats almost simultaneously.

ABOVE: First of a second generation of nuclear-powered super carriers, the *Nimitz* remains a cornerstone of the US Atlantic Fleet.

RIGHT: A Tomcat comes home to roost. Even the largest carrier looks like a postage stamp until the pilot is committed to the landing and exceptional flying skill is a standard US Navy fighter pilot requirement.

The TF30 turbofan has a history of trouble, including catastrophic blade failures and was considered too underpowered to move the Tomcat's more than 30 tons weight as advertised.

Despite these drawbacks Congress refused to adequately fund the F-14B with improved P&W F401 turbofans, the first example of which made its maiden flight in 1973. The F-14B was subsequently canceled, then effectively reinstated as the F-14A (Plus) in 1984. This variant was an F-14A powered by GE 110-GE-400. It first flew in 1986, and was redesignated as the F-14B. Thirty-eight new build and 32 A model conversions were delivered. The F-14D also suffered from economies as only 37 new build and 18 rebuilds were funded.

BELOW: An artist's impression of an F-14 Tomcat firing an AIM-54 Phoenix missile with a booster attachment.

F/A-18 Hornet

As part of one of the most important aircraft programs for the modern US Navy, the first Hornet development aircraft made its maiden flight on November 18, 1978. Since then it has been built in six single- and two-seater versions and proved to be one of the most versatile aircraft ever to operate from a carrier deck. An outgrowth of the seemingly still-born Northrop YF-17, the Hornet effectively combined the roles of fighter and ground attack, hence the distinctive designation.

Progressive upgrades have resulted in the F/A-18C with improved avionics, including a new central computer, which allowed compatibility with the AIM-120 and AGM-65. The radar fit was from 1994, the APG-73, uprated GE F404-GE-402 engines were fitted two years previously. Current Hornets are able to carry a full range of weapons – up to 15,000lb (6,804kg) – to augment their single

ABOVE: A key feature of the multi-role F/A-18E/F is its payload carrying flexibility. Here the Hornet carries one of many possible strike-fighter loads on its 11 weapon stations. From wingtips inboard are the AIM-9 Sidewinder, the AIM-120 AMRAAM, the AGM-88 HARM, and two 1,000lb (454kg) Mk. 83 bombs.

LEFT: In this sequence of photographs, an AGM-65D imaging infrared Maverick missile smashes a truck target on a test range at Eglin Air Force Base, Florida. The missile, which did not have a warhead, hit the truck parked head-on to the attacking A-10 aircraft.

M61A1 Vulcan cannon. It was F/A-18Cs that scored the Navy's two kills for the type in Operation "Desert Storm," both victories going to aircraft of VA-81 Sunliners.

The first flight of the F/A-18E Super Hornet was in November 1995, which is larger overall than the earlier models it was designed to replace in US Navy service. The original requirement for about 1,000 Super Hornets was however scaled back to 548, the last of which is scheduled to be delivered by 2010. In due course some will undoubtedly pass into Marine hands, as the Corps has been a longtime user of frontline Navy aircraft including the F/A-18.

AV-8 Harrier

The unique vertical take-off (VTO) qualities of the BAe Harrier found a ready acceptance in the Marine Corps, which saw it as an ideal type to offer fire support in amphibious landings. Delivery of 110 license-built AV-8As and two-seat TAV-8As took place in the 1970s. The AV-8A, later upgraded to AV-8C standard, was retired in 1987 because it was seen to have a rather limited capability due to its modest ordnance carrying capacity. Interest was renewed in what had in the meantime become a US rather than British-driven program, and the McDonnell Douglas/ Boeing AV-TAV-8B with an extended wing was delivered to the USMC from 1984. Five years on Marine units began to receive the AV-8B Night Attack version developed specifically for the Corps, equipped with a nose-mounted GEC Marconi forward-looking infrared (FLIR), a head-down display, and color moving map.

A detachment of six Harriers from the VMA-522 Tigers participated in the fighting in Kosovo. The aircraft flew 36 close support and reconnaissance missions and deployed Rockeye LGB and Mk. 82 munitions.

RIGHT: A steeply climbing AV-8B demonstrating the extra ordnance load possible with the extended wing. Triple clusters of Mk. 82 Snakeye bombs can be seen on the midwing pylons.

BELOW: A Night Attack AV-8B Harrier II carries laser-guided Maverick missiles, Mk. 82 500lb (227kg) bombs, and a 1-in (25mm) cannon during a test flight at 29 Palms Marine Base, California.

ABOVE: Seconds after a pair of Snakeye bombs leave the carrier aircraft, retarding fins spring open to slow them down and thus allow the fuzes time to arm and the aircraft to escape the ensuing blast.

BELOW: A Marine Corps AV-8B releases two Mk. 82 Snakeye bombs above the Nevada desert during an exercise at the Naval Air Station at Fallon. The AV-8B is equipped with an angle rate bombing system.

US Army

The deployment to Afghanistan to remove the Taliban from power in 2001–2002 put the major US Army bases, such as Fort Bragg and Fort Campbell, on a Threat Con Delta footing, the highest state of security. The latter base is home to the famed 101st Airborne Division, currently the world's only heliborne air assault division.

In a typical Afghanistan operation USAF A-10s and AC-130s provided close air support for helicopters undertaking troop insertion and rescue missions, such as the UH/EH-60A Blackhawk and MH-47 Chinook. Although the MH-47 Chinook may be armed, its sizeable configuration and relatively slow speed inevitably makes it a prime target for hostile ground forces. In Afghanistan, Al Qaida guerrillas

LEFT: Developed from the original AH-1 HueyCobra, the AH-1N has twin engines and carries a full ordnance load on stub wings.

BELOW: Angular cockpit panels hallmark the Army's AH-1S, one of which is seen here low over the trees during an antitank training sortie.

ABOVE: Despite large fuselage fairings for its twin engines, the AH-1W retains similar nose contours to the original AH-1G. The cannon is an extended barrel M-197, 0.79in (20mm) caliber.

RIGHT: A helicopter crewman getting down to the paperwork. Behind him can be seen a chain gun mounted on an AH-64.

FAR RIGHT, TOP: Awesomely ugly, the AH-64 Apache is an effective battlefield attack helicopter, able to deploy cannon fire and a range of missiles to deal with a variety of targets.

FAR RIGHT, BOTTOM: Heart of the Apache is its chain gun sight which is able to "see" the target via a gimbal-mounted rotating sight linked to the pilot's helmet-mounted sight.

occasionally inflicted damage on Chinooks with the rocket-propelled grenade (RPG), a weapon very widely deployed in the region. For more local air support with greater loiter time over a contested area, the Army can call upon its own gunships in the form of the AH-64 Apache. The amount of destruction that helicopters can achieve is necessarily limited and in the event of a protracted action on the ground with a high risk to friendly forces, USAF, Navy, and Marine fast jets could be called in to neutralize enemy positions. Operating in relays and using flight refueling where necessary, this type of air operation can be maintained for the duration of a threat, as has been proven.

The Army has begun a far-reaching Apache upgrade program under which 530 AH-64As will be converted to AH-64Ds, with improved digital avionics in enlarged cheek fairings. All but 30 will also feature the Longbow mast-mounted millimeter wave radar to guide the radio seeker built into the AGM-114 Hellfire antitank missile. Up to16 Hellfires can be accommodated by the Apache's four stub wing hardpoints which can alternatively carry rocket pods, Stinger or Sidewinders AAMs, or Sidearm ARMs.

Army AH-64D Apache Longbows were deployed to Korea in late 2001, the first such international task

ABOVE: The nose sight on an AH-1 together with podded 2.75-in (70mm) rocket rounds on each fuselage stub wing.

RIGHT: Apache lair is probably Fort Bragg, the US Army's main helicopter training base in North Carolina.

BELOW: An AH-64A Apache attack helicopter is shown armed with Hellfire antitank missiles, rocket pod, and chain gun forward of the undercarriage.

ABOVE: Agile and lethal, the AH-64 is the US Army's main attack helicopter with nearly 500 currently in service.

LEFT: The Apache's "stand off" weapons load includes 2.75-in (70mm) rockets carried in up to four pods and the Hellfire antitank missiles attached to stub wing launchers.

BELOW: A single AGM-114 Hellfire air-to-ground missile round. A practical answer to the perpetual challenge of destroying tanks with helicopters, the Hellfire's semi-active laser homer comes into play during the final phase of flight.

for the type. Initially the Longbows replaced one of three AH-64A units stationed in the country. The Apache's front line success has meant that all examples of the original helicopter gunship, the Bell AH-1, now serve with the Army Reserve and Air National Guard units.

Medium lift transport duties are being mainly handled by versions of the UH-60 Blackhawk, over 1,000 of which are in Army service. As with other US transport helicopters the Blackhawk can be armed and, as the AH-60, it can operate Miniguns or machineguns from pintle mounts in the forward cabin. It is also capable of firing Hellfire missiles or rockets from external hardpoints.

Funding restraints prevented the Army from going through with a planned engine upgrade for its 360-strong fleet of UH-1H/V Iroquois (Huey) utility helicopters, a situation that could change. However, with 838 more transport Hueys in Reserve and ANG service, the bill to upgrade them all would be substantial. It is unlikely that such a program would be carried out, as a more modern type to equip the reserve forces in the future would be preferable.

At least 300 existing airframes of the Army's medium lift Chinooks are being upgraded, however. The first CH-47F upgraded to Improved Cargo Helicopter (ICH) standard was delivered by Boeing in 2002. The Chinook remains first and foremost a transport helicopter, which can be armed if the operational scenario warrants it. Two 0.5-in (1.27mm) M2 machineguns or miniguns can be mounted in the cabin area and there is also provision available for Stinger AAMs to be carried on stub wing hardpoints if necessary.

ABOVE: AN F/A-18C Hornet launches from the waist catapult during flight operations on board the aircraft carrier USS *Nimitz* in the Persian Gulf. It is armed with a AIM-9 Sidewinder, RIM-7M Sea Sparrow, Rockeye cluster bombs, and the AGM-88 HARM.

BELOW: A B-52G bomber with its complement of 12 pylon-mounted AGM-86B Air Launched Cruise Missiles stands ready on the flight line.

Air weapons used by all services

Cruise missiles

Arguably representing the ultimate in conventional weapons is the Air Launched Cruise Missile (ALCM) which can presently be deployed only from the USAF's trio of long range bombers. This is due primarily to weight and prohibitive size, despite the fact that cruise missiles are fitted with folding wings and tailfins. The champion USAF cruise missile platform is currently the B-52, which can accommodate up to six on wing racks in addition to the internal bomb bay load—one triple rack of AGM-129A missiles weighs as much as an F-16.

The AGM-129A has now succeeded the AGM-86 cruise missile—35 of which, fitted with conventional warheads, were launched against Iraqi targets during Operation "Desert Storm." B-52Gs based at Barksdale, Lousiana, carried out the attacks, which involved round trip flight times exceeding 34 hours.

Air-to-air missiles

Although a plethora of air-to-air missiles are available for use by the world's air forces, many are variations or copies of the original, infrared, heat-seeking AIM-9 Sidewinder. The acronym stood for Aerial Intercept Missile and it was developed under a painstaking and often heartbreakingly difficult test program by technicians at the Navy test center at China Lake, California. Under the guiding hand of the irrepressible Dr William McLaren the Sidewinder IR seeker eventually "came good." The resulting series of progressively improvements gave US aircraft one of the most consistently reliable weapons of all time. The Winder program has had its disappointments, but overall its combat kill ratio has been high enough to ensure funding since February 17, 1954, the date of the first live destruction of a QB-17 drone target.

In its early AIM-9B form, the Sidewinder could only home onto the infrared radiation given off by hot metal, preferably from close range and directly behind the target aircraft. One of the greatest challenges was to provide the AIM-9 with the ability to maneuver and shoot down an aerial target even if the parent fighter launched the missile from directly ahead. AIM-9L and M versions were the first of the "all aspects" Sidewinders. The AIM-9X, contracted

ABOVE: Although it has now been phased out the F-4E Phantom was a world class fighter during the Vietnam war armed as here with a 0.79-in (20-mm) gun, AIM-7, and AIM-9 missiles.

BELOW: A ground crew loads an AIM-9 Sidewinder missile onto a F-15 Eagle at Tyndall Air Force Base, Florida.

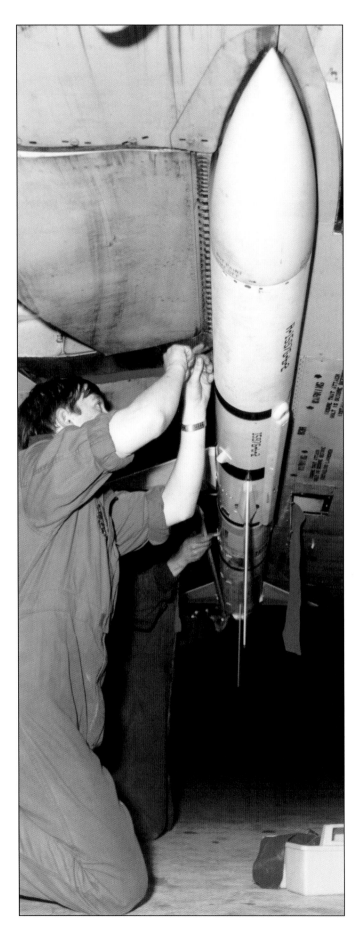

to Hughes/Raytheon, is a missile designed for short range dogfighting (which the US had neglected). It features a constant view IR array with detectors sensitive enough to track a target through all flight aspects; for the first time a Sidewinder is able to maneuver with a very fast target pulling up to $60G$ in the process. Using thrust-vector control, these next generation AAMs are also different in that they are guided by helmet-mounted sights.

The AIM-7 Sparrow went one step further than the Sidewinder in that it incorporated a tiny radar transmitter with which to home onto the returns given off by an airframe. In theory such a missile should have been far more accurate than a less sophisticated heat-seeker but this did not prove to be the case. In Vietnam, the conflict that saw the first large-scale use of AAMs as primary air weapons, pilots found that the kill ratio of Sparrow fell significantly below that of the heat-seeker. The drawback with Sparrow was its rather primitive technology and the fact that it invariably required the parent aircraft to acquire the target on radar to ensure a good missile lock-on. The attendant risk to the fighter in a combat zone was prohibitive and despite improvements, the kill ratio of the AIM-7F/M in Operation "Desert Storm" remained very low.

The AIM-120A is a replacement for the failed AIM-7 Sparrow III, known to pilots as the "Slammer," its suffix standing for Advanced Medium Range Air-to-Air Missile. The AIM-120 had a history of teething troubles and government opposition throughout the 1980s. Despite its early development nearly coming to a halt because it was difficult to perfect (it was technically years ahead of its time), the AIM-120 finally turned out to be one of the most capable weapons available to US air forces. It provides F-15 and F-16 pilots with a missile that has a flexibility and strike capability comparable to that of the F-14's Phoenix.

Navy Phoenix

A missile developed specifically for one type of aircraft is relatively unusual, but the US Navy's F-14

LEFT: Fuselage recesses have enabled the AIM-7 Sparrow and other missiles to be carried by Navy aircraft, thus freeing wing pylons for fuel tanks and ECM pods.

ABOVE: An AIM-54C Phoenix missile undergoes its final visual inspection and cleaning before delivery to the US Navy.

LEFT: Sailors from the ordnance department prepare to load an AIM-54C Phoenix missile onto the wing of an F-14 Tomcat on the flight deck of the USS *Independence*.

Tomcat was designed as are all modern combat air-craft, as an integrated weapons system. Matched with the Hughes AIM-54 Phoenix, the Tomcat was fitted with a large and heavy AAM (nicknamed the "buffa-lo" for that reason) with a potent and effective "fire and forget" punch over a 100-nm (1825-km) range. The Phoenix has an ability to take out multiple tar-gets, but at a million dollars a shot it became a "last resort" weapon for the fleet's primary fighter which can accommodate up to six. Economies adversely effected upgrades of the F-14, and Navy pilots are encouraged to use an AIM-9 or AIM-120 for their opening shots, rather than a Phoenix.

Antiradiation Missiles
The Vietnam War also initiated the development of another highly significant family of missiles, those designed specifically to destroy hostile radars. Turning the radars' own emissions against them by detecting and locking onto the energy beam, the AGM-45 Shrike and the larger AGM-88 HARM were effective enough. However, the enemy radar had to be transmitting in order for the weapon to home onto it. Operators soon worked out that shut-ting down their gun or missile fire control sets, even for short periods, could prevent the destruction of their sites. As a counter to a numerically strong Russian-derived ground defense, the larger and more powerful Standard ARM made its debut in Vietnam.

ABOVE: An AGM-88A HARM high-speed antiradiation missile mounted on a USAF F-4G Wild Weasel aircraft.

RIGHT, TOP: The Standoff Land Attack Missile (SLAM), undergoing a fitting check on an F/A-18 Hornet.

RIGHT, BOTTOM: An F/A -18 Hornet launching a SLAM. The missile shows the tendency of modern air ordnance to get larger but more capable than older weapons.

Currently there is an AGM-88C broadband antiradiation missile, which can duplicate all the functions of an aircraft RWR system, store repro-grammable data in an onboard threat library, and select the specific threat for attack.

Air-to-Surface Missiles
US Naval units, at least in terms of non-carrier surface ships, have been in action in recent wars far less than have aircraft, so the deployment of surface-to-air or surface-to-surface missiles has been modest. The AGM-84A/D Harpoon is a large and versatile air-to-surface missile that can also be deployed by ASW helicopters or land-based aircraft. In its latest form the Harpoon is known as the AGM-84E Stand-off Land Attack Missile (SLAM), and is carried by the F/A-18 Hornet.

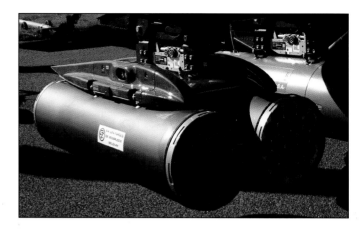

Rocket pods

The very widely used 2.75-in (70mm) folding fin aircraft rocket packed in a convenient pod has been adapted to a range of helicopters and light attack aircraft. American helicopters invariably include a 19-round pod on each fuselage stub wing. Earlier versions were augmented by the Hydra pod, which also contains 2.75-in (70mm) rockets. A larger weapon than other air-to-ground rockets, the 5-in (12.7mm) LAU-97 (Zuni) is packed into a four round tube. Widely adopted by the Navy, the Zuni remains a tri-service weapon.

Antitank missiles

AGM-65 Maverick and AGM-114 Hellfire antitank missiles have proven to be devastatingly effective when used with USAF A-10 Thunderbolt II and Apache helicopters. During the Gulf War, Warthog, or A-10, pilots fired around 5,000 Maverick missiles and claimed a successful hit rate of 80 to 90 percent. The score included 987 of the Iraqi tanks that had appeared so potentially deadly before hostilities commenced.

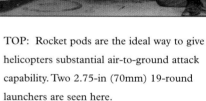

TOP: Rocket pods are the ideal way to give helicopters substantial air-to-ground attack capability. Two 2.75-in (70mm) 19-round launchers are seen here.

ABOVE: A Maverick missile with an infrared seeker, mounted on an F-4 Phantom, receives final checkout prior to being flown to Europe for captive flight tests.

LEFT: Airmen inspect the guidance system assembly on a laser-guided GBU-16 bomb on board the aircraft carrier USS *Nimitz*.

ABOVE, RIGHT: A GBU-24 laser-guided bomb is attached to an F-15 Eagle at Aviano Air Base, Italy.

Bombs

A variety of nuclear bombs in various configurations and different yields were developed for delivery by numerous US combat aircraft, both tactical and strategic, during the Cold War years. Bomb designations include the B-28, B-51, B-61, B-83, and B-93. Today the US air forces rely mainly on an array of free-fall and guided bombs for "force projection" operations. Many of these bombs have now been proven in action. Revising the force structure has led to economies and mission profiles are carefully tailored to minimize costs, if a cheaper weapon is as effective as a prohibitively expensive one, the former is now be the first choice.

A system of steering free-falling aerial bombs onto their target was initiated during the latter stages of the Vietnam War with the Paveway series of "smart" bombs. Utilizing laser technology, GBU-24, -27, and -28 (in various weights) can in a matter of minutes have seeker heads attached to their nose cones and

LEFT: A GBU-15 bomb is prepared before loading onto a Marine F/A-18 Hornet at Aviano Air Base, Italy for a mission over Bosnia Herzegovina.

ABOVE: An F-16 displayed with its total war load. Weapons may be carried in various combinations depending on the mission requirements.

LEFT: Time exposure view of a 2,000lb (907kg) bomb, fitted with a Paveway I guidance unit, about to demolish a truck on a US target range during firing trials.

ABOVE, RIGHT: Laser technology has turned "dumb" bombs into "smart" weapons. Used in conjunction with a designator pod (center), laser-seeker heads give bombs a much greater guarantee of hits than previously.

RIGHT: The "Big Eye" bomb is an aircraft delivered binary chemical bomb. It generates a persistent nerve agent from two non-toxic chemicals, which are shipped and stored separately prior to use.

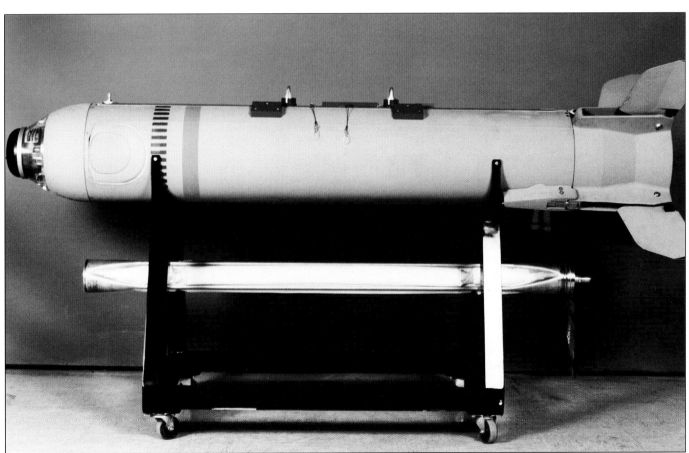

be transformed from humble "dumb" bombs into "smart" munition. Radar and laser guidance has meant a far higher accuracy ratio of launchings to hits than hitherto, although even smart bomb guidance is not totally foolproof. The US is however working toward making precision-guided munitions totally effective.

Cluster Bombs

CBU-59 Rockeye II is the primary US cluster bomb, an air-burst weapon with a streamlined casing designed to split apart just above the ground and spew hundreds of bomblets over a wide area. In the antipersonnel role the effects of such bombs can be devastating. Various other cluster bomb types operating on the same principle, are in the US arsenal. They include the CBU-71 and CBU-71A, which are AP incendiary and antipersonnel types, and have time delay fusing.

RIGHT: Airmen guide a cart of cluster bombs into the staging area for munitions on the flight deck of the USS *Independence* while the ship operates in the Persian Gulf.

BELOW: Rockeye Mk. 20 cluster bombs are designed to split open well clear of the carrier aircraft, which in this case is an A-7 Corsair II, now phased out of USAF inventory.

RIGHT: BLU-109 penetrating bombs, Mk. 84 general purpose bombs, AGM-65 Maverick, AIM-7 Sparrow and AIM-9 Sidewinder missiles are pre-positioned for quick loading onto aircraft.

BELOW, RIGHT: Close-up view of the 1.18in (30-mm) GAU-8A Avenger cannon installed in an A-10 Warthog.

Special Bombs

The CBU-28 Deep Throat bunker-buster is a 4,700lb (2,132kg) penetrator bomb designed specifically to rip apart strongholds buried many feet under ground. It was first used in the closing stages of the Gulf War and in Afghanistan, as the successor to Big Mother, alias the M-121/B-11. Making its debut in Vietnam where it was used to create instant landing pads in deep jungle for helicopters, this 10,000lb (4,536kg) weapon was followed by the 15,000lb (6,804kg) BLU-82 and later the higher tech BLU-109 weighing only 2,000lb (907kg), but with similar characteristics.

The USAF's current inventory includes ample supplies of the 4,700lb (2,132kg) GBU-37B, a bunker-buster that can penetrate three to four layers of 12ft (3.66m) thick reinforced concrete, when released from 45,000ft (13,716m). A sensor in the tail detects how many floors have been penetrated and a signal from the aircraft mission commander then detonates the bomb.

Guns

Slower to adopt cannon as standard aircraft armament than some other countries, the USAF specified 0.79-in (20mm) cannon for the Century series of jet fighters then progressed rapidly to fitting multibarrel weapons to such types as the F-4 and F-105 for Vietnam combat.

Ever larger cannon have been developed for specific aircraft, although the longevity of the 1.2-in (30mm) M61A1 Vulcan, which is also to equip the next generation of fighters (in M61A2 form), marks this weapon out as a standard setter for US aircraft guns designed around the revolver principle. In scaled up form is the 1,350 round General Electric GAU-8 Avenger 1.2-in (30mm) cannon with seven revolving barrels designed for and fitted to the A-10.

The Marines have opted for a weapon using a 25 x 5.4-in (137mm) cartridge (a size suitable for

ABOVE: Longer overall than a small family car, the A-10's Avenger cannon appears to have had the aircraft built around it .

BELOW: GEPOD 30 lightweight 30mm gun pod is shown on body centerline mount on a camouflaged Air Force F4-E Aircraft. The GEPOD 30 fires the family of GAU-8/A ammunition.

ABOVE: A cloud of smoke confirms that an AH-64 pilot has opened fire with his M-230 chain gun during an operational test.

NATO armament compatibility) for the Harrier, known as the GAU-12 Equalizer.

Although the exercise can be expensive, the US has developed several guns for specific aircraft and along with the A-10, the AH-64 Apache has the M-230 chain gun, an externally powered weapon with 625rpg. Using a short 30 x 100lb cartridge, the gun has NATO compatability.

Torpedoes

As the submarine operations of a post-Cold War Soviet Navy represent a much reduced threat to peace, and there is a general lack of surface operations by elements hostile to US forces, the upgrading of torpedoes has a lower priority than it did previously. The Mks. 46 and 50 Barracuda are current developments of the standard ASW aerial torpedoes and these are usually launched by helicopters.

ABOVE: A Mk. 46 torpedo being carried by a Sea King ASW helicopter. With the end of the Cold War the seaborne threat to Allied seaborne forces by conventional navies is much lower than it was.

Joint Service weapons

Among the largest of the US weapons programs is the integration of a range of munitions into "packages" that can be delivered en masse by long range bombers, such as the B-1 and B-2. For these operations the aircraft are fitted with special Combined Effects Munition Rotary Launchers and Advanced Applications Rotary Launchers. Among the advanced weapons they accommodate are the GNM-137 Triple Service Standoff Attack Missile (TSSAM), the Raytheon AGM-154A, GBU-37B Joint Direct Attack Munition (JDAM), and the JSOW—Joint Standoff Weapon.

LEFT: USAF weapons specialists setting a hoist to the correct weight for moving missiles and bombs into position for loading onto a B-1. Until armed, ordnance can be quite delicate and prone to accidental damage.

LAND WEAPONS

The United States Army is, quite simply, the most powerful army on earth. Financed by the world's largest economy, its sophisticated weaponry, trained personnel, and unified vision ensure that it will remain so in the future. It has at its disposal weapons that can eradicate any conceivable enemy, the will and the people to use that weaponry, and the checks and balances of a democratic system of government to ensure that these forces are used properly. Without that proper use of US forces in two world wars and many post-war conflicts, it is doubtful that as much of the world would be free today.

It was all very different on 14 June 1775 – over a year before the Declaration of Independence – when the US Army was born. The fledgling army very quickly had to prove its worth when it was catapulted into the eight-year Revolutionary War against Great Britain. Celebrating its 225th birthday with the new millennium, the US Army has had to struggle against many foes, internal and external, since winning independence for the nation. It has preserved the Union through four years of bitter conflict in the Civil War; it has defended the United States against external threats—from the "second war of independence" with Great Britain in 1812 through the battles against Nazi totalitarianism, Japanese imperialism, and world communism; and it has struck out against world terrorism.

Today the US Army continues to support democracy all over the world: from the home front, attacked in such a cowardly way on September 11, 2001, to Korea where it defends that country against the communists, and with peacekeeping missions in such locations as Haiti, Bosnia, Kosovo, and East Timor. It works closely with the Drug Enforcement Agency, the US Customs Service, and foreign agencies to halt the flow of illicit drugs into the United States. But the US Army does not simply see its role as an armed force. It has aided victims of floods, earthquakes, hurricanes, war, famine, oil spills, forest fires, and other natural and man-made disasters.

RIGHT: Four men comprise a fire team—team leader, rifleman, grenadier, and automatic rifleman. These men are from the 82nd Airborne, a light infantry division designed to go anywhere on short notice. Parachutes are only a way of getting to work—once on the ground, they operate like any infantry unit.

The Army Vision

On October 12, 1999, as the Chief of Staff of the US Army, General Eric K Shinseki unveiled "The Army Vision"—a blueprint showing how the army would transform to meet the requirements of the new millennium. Its basic tenets were that the US Army should "remain the most respected Army in the world and the most feared ground force to those who would threaten the interests of the United States." To do this the US Army would have to undergo a strategic transformation—losing its cold war structure and appearance to prepare for what would come in the 21st century.

The army identified this transformation as being more than just a technological change but a change to a more agile, versatile, and adaptive force—the Objective Force whose mission would be "a combat capable brigade anywhere in the world in 96 hours; a division on the ground in 120 hours; five divisions on the ground in theater in 30 days."

The Army Vision identifies that soldiers – not equipment – are the army's most important asset and that it must inspire its soldiers to have the strength, the confidence, and the will to fight and win anywhere, anytime. It holds that readiness is the key to versatility. "The Army has a non-negotiable contract with the people of America to fight and win our Nation's wars. We must maintain near-term training and readiness to ensure that we are prepared at all times to carry out our obligations." But more than that, readiness means training its forces to ensure that soldiers are not put in harm's way without the knowledge and means to fulfill their mission.

BELOW: A rifle platoon usually has four squads of nine men each, plus machine gunners, an aid man, a platoon sergeant, and leader. This HHC platoon has twice that with the addition of supporting specialists.

The US Army Soldier

Today adaptation to the latest technology is part of life in the army. New threats need new weapons to combat them and a new mindset to use them effectively in the new tactical scenarios that appear on the battlefield. But while the tasks of today's soldier are often very different than hitherto, today's infantryman—the basic component of any army since time immemorial—isn't all that different from his military ancestors. He tends to be rather young, lean, and tough. If he's been in combat for a while, he will be dirty and smelly—and if he's been in particularly bad combat, he may smell really bad. He is profane and can swear as well as any of his forefathers.

Although some of the weapons and equipment would seem very exotic to a soldier of the Civil War or the two world wars, the basics really haven't changed. The modern soldier's rifle will shoot faster, but its effective range is about the same as that of the Civil War infantryman, about 328 yards (300m), no matter what the official specifications say.

The modern infantryman's rucksack is made of nylon and aluminum, but he carries about the same combat load as an infantryman of the Revolution – typically around 60lb (27.2kg) – and sometimes a lot more. The modern infantryman will sometimes ride into the combat zone in a helicopter, armored personnel carrier, or truck, but he is just as adept at walking 30 miles (48.3km) in a day, if he has to, just as the GIs and Yanks and Rebs did long ago.

However, there have been changes, of course. Today's soldier is in extremely good health and

BELOW: A company commander from 3d Battalion, 7th Infantry, 7th Infantry Division (Light) (3/7/7ID) "gets on the horn" to his deployed platoons with a PRC-77. A radio man provides security for the CO.

ABOVE, LEFT: A soldier uses a Humvee to conduct a morning patrol around the perimeter of an Army base camp in the Kuwaiti desert.

LEFT: A pressure washing system is used to decontaminate an M3 Bradley. The decontamination is part of a chemical training exercise conducted by the Army.

ABOVE: These US Army soldiers are attached to the United Nations Command Security Battalion. They are discussing the next maneuver during a regular patrol of the Demilitarized Zone in the Republic of Korea in 1998.

RIGHT: A soldier operates the throttle of his Bridge Erection Boat during a bridge building training exercise on the Imjin River in the Republic of Korea.

condition—far better than soldiers of the past. He is, statistically, stronger, and better educated, than soldiers of even the recent past. He is a professional, too, rather than a conscript; he wears the uniform by choice and commitment. If he fails to perform to an extremely high standard, his punishment is to be kicked out, back into civil society. That is quite a change from the old conscript Army.

But the real combat soldier shares many things with his military ancestors. Once he has finished training and reached his unit his motivation has almost nothing to do with conventional notions of patriotism and flag-waving, but it does have a lot to do with a sense of honor—an infantryman lives and dies as part of his fire team, squad, platoon, and company. More than anything, he will risk his life to play his role in the bloody little drama; he fears missing his cues and forgetting his lines as much as the slings and arrows of the enemy who serve as critics.

Today's soldiers – male or female – are identified not just by rank but by their Military Occupation Speciality (MOS). There are 212 of these falling into nine categories: Administrative Services, Electronic Maintenance, Engineering and Construction, Health Care, Intelligence and Electronic Communications, Mechanical Maintenance, Media, Public and Civil Affairs, Transportation and Supply Services, and Combat Operations. Of these 212 MOSs there are 30 in Combat Operations involving reconnaissance, security, and other aspects of both offensive and defensive combat situations. These can be further broken down (see following page).

BELOW: A fireteam, this time from the 7th ID. All members of the 7th ID have a piece of camouflage netting attached to their Kevlar helmets giving them a shaggy appearance they have nicknamed the "Tina Turner" look.

Air Defense Artillery: Patriot Missile System Enhanced Operator/Maintainer; Early Warning System Operator; Man Portable Air Defense System Crewmember; Bradley Linebacker Crewmember; Patriot Launching Station Enhanced Operator/Maintainer.

Armor: Cavalry Scout; Armor Crewman.

Aviation Operations: Air Traffic Control Operator; Aviation Operations Specialist.

Combat Engineering: Combat Engineer; Bridge Crewmember.

Field Artillery: Cannon Crewmember; Tactical Automated Fire Control Specialist; Field Artillery Automated Tactical Data Systems Specialist; Cannon Fire Direction Specialist; Fire Support Specialist; Multiple Launch Rocket System Crewmember; Multiple Launch Rocket System Automated Tactical Data Systems Specialist; Field Artillery Firefinder Radar Operator; Field Artillery Surveyor; Field Artillery Meteorological Crewman.

Infantry: Infantryman; Indirect Fire Infantryman; Heavy Anti-armor Weapons Infantryman; Mechanized Infantryman.

Special Forces: Special Operations Weapons Sergeant; Special Operations Engineer; Special Operations Medical Sergeant; Special Operations Communications Sergeant.

The equipment used by these MOSs is covered later.

Organisation—Units and Locations

As you might expect, the US Army has a complex structure that runs from the president down to the men on the ground.

It is the Secretary of the Army (Thomas E White was confirmed the 18th Secretary of the Army on May 31, 2001) who has statutory responsibility for all matters relating to army manpower, personnel, reserve affairs, installations, environmental issues, weapons systems and equipment acquisition, communications,

LEFT: Despite all the aircraft, missiles, ships, tanks, and other combat systems used by the US armed forces, the real ultimate weapon remains something called an "Eleven Bravo," the uncommon infantry foot soldier. This soldier is carrying an M16A1 with M203 attached.

and financial management. His department has an annual budget of nearly $82 billion.

The Secretary of the Army is at the top of a team of just over one million divided into: the Active Component (AC), the Reserve Component (RC) – made up of the Army Reserve National Guard (ARNG) and US Army Reserve (USAR) soldiers – and 220,000 civilian employees. The modernization plan in force calls for an AC with an end strength of approximately 480,000 soldiers; a RC with an end strength of approximately 555,000 soldiers (350,000 ARNG and 205,000 USAR), and a civilian work-force of approximately 215,000 personnel.

The Headquarters, Department of the Army (HQDA) is the executive part of the Department of the Army at the seat of Government. HQDA is composed of the Office of the Secretary of the Army, the Office of the Chief of Staff, Army, the Army Staff, and other staff support agencies not just in Washington DC metropolitan area, but in other dispersed locations.

The most senior man is the Chief of Staff, United States Army—General Eric K Shinseki assumed duties as the 34th incumbent on 22 June 1999.

In 2002, the US Army is organized into the following commands:

US Army Europe (USAREUR), Germany.

US Army Forces Command (FORSCOM), GA, United States.

US Army Materiel Command (AMC), VA, United States.

US Army Training and Doctrine Command (TRADOC), VA, United States.

Eighth US Army (EUSA), Korea.

US Army Corps of Engineers (USACE), DC, United States.

US Army Medical Command (MEDCOM), TX, United States.

US Army Pacific Command (USARPAC), HI, United States.

US Army Space and Missile Defense Command (SMDC), VA, United States.

US Army Special Operations Command (USASOC), NC, United States.

Military Traffic Management Command (MTMC) VA, United States.

US Army Military District of Washington DC (MDW), United States.

ABOVE: This soldier carries an M249 SAW.

LEFT: The name, "Eleven Bravo" is derived from the MOS specification, MOS-11B, meaning an Infantryman. His duties are defined as: "[An infantryman] supervises, leads, or serves as a member of an infantry activity that employs individual or crew served weapons in support of offensive and defensive combat operations."

US Army South (USARSO), Puerto Rico.
US Army Intelligence and Security Command
(INSCOM), VA, United States.
US Army Criminal Investigation Command (CID)
VA, United States.
The military forces are divided into four corps
(I Corps, Fort Lewis, Washington; III Corps, Fort
Hood, Texas; V Corps, Heidelberg, Germany; XVIII
Airborne Corps, Fort Bragg, North Carolina), and a
number of smaller units. Of these there are 12 main
AC divisions. The Secretary of the Army is also
responsible for over 15 million acres of land all over
the US.

Weapons and Equipment

History

The Civil War forced warfare into the Industrial Age.
Railways took troops, equipment, and provisions to
the front—railway lines and bridges became significant military assets and required defending and supporting. Communications were improved by both
the railways and by the telegraph. On the battlefield
almost every weapon saw development—the Minie
Ball extended effective rifle range to 600 yards
(549m). This, in turn, rendered mass infantry
advances badly exposed, and Civil War armies started to make more use of trenches, forts, and redoubts.
Artillery – the greatest of all battlefield killers today –
saw major range increases. These technological
advances gained pace as the 19th century continued.
The Spanish-American War saw breech-loading
repeating rifles as standard issue, and an early version of rapid-firing machinegun, the Gatling Gun,
was available as well.

World War I introduced and World War II perfect-
ed mechanized alternatives to trench warfare. This
led to fast-moving wars where land, air, and sea
forces were integrated. There were further improvements to artillery, the arrival and development of the
tank, the first multiple rocket launchers, radio for
communication; fighter, bomber, and transport aircraft; and paratroops. The US armed forces that
entered the Korean War were second to none.

The Korean War saw some improvements in
equipment and the introduction of at least one revolutionary item, the helicopter. By the time that US
servicemen entered the Vietnam War the helicopter

ABOVE: This soldier, with an M16A2 and a round for the Dragon
antitank system on his back, is a Heavy Antiarmor Weapons
Infantryman—a MOS-11H "Eleven Hotel". He "as a member of a
crew-served weapon squad … Assaults and destroys enemy tanks and
armor vehicles, emplacements, weapons, and personnel with heavy antiarmor weapons."

RIGHT and BELOW, RIGHT: An "Eleven Mike"—a mechanized infantryman who "leads, supervises, and serves as a member of a fighting vehicle unit ... Operates both mounted and dismounted to close with and destroy the enemy."

had come into its own—so much so that airmobile units would replace many paratroops. It also contributed materially to improved survival rates of servicemen: medical evacuation (casevac) by helicopter saved thousands of lives.

The successful prosecution of the war with Iraq saw US forces using weapons that would have been classed as science fiction for most of the 20th century—laser-guided ordnance; missile antiaircraft artillery; computer-driven information management, target acquisition, and guidance systems; and low-light capabilities. The Iraqi forces—adequately organized, equipped with Soviet weaponry, and well-versed in the art of war in the desert—were simply blown away. Operations "Desert Shield" and "Desert Storm" saw the forces put in place, the reduction of Iraqi assets by careful, surgical air strikes, and finally a devastatingly brief land campaign.

But the armed forces could not sit back on their heels and congratulate themselves for long. To keep its position as "top dog," the US Army needed to ensure successors to the M1A1 Abrams, Bradley infantry fighting vehicle, Apache attack helicopter, the high-volume, Multiple Launch Rocket System, and Patriot missile. As well as equipment improvements, the army had to ensure the continued high achievement levels by soldiers and their leaders in the demanding world of the high-tech battlefield, thus requiring more skill and initiative than ever from junior officers and NCOs. Now, as always, the success of the soldier is the truest possible measure of the success of the Army. By guaranteeing that soldier the most advanced technology, suitable doctrine, and ample resources available, the United States Army has always sought to accomplish its mission with a minimum loss of life.

Modernization

The goal of the US Army is to remain the top land warfighting force in the world, capable of successfully conducting two nearly simultaneous major theater wars and a wide range of other operations,

such as peace enforcement, disaster relief, or humanitarian assistance.

Paul J Kern, Lieutenant General, GS, Military Deputy to the Assistant Secretary of the Army (Acquisition, Logistics, and Technology) sets out the requirements and goals in the US Army's *Weapon Systems Handbook*:

"At the present time … Army forces are not optimally designed and organized … For the 21st Century, the Army envisions a strategically responsive force that is dominant across the entire spectrum of operations and is responsive, deployable, agile, versatile, lethal, survivable, and sustainable. The requirements for greater lethality, survivability, and deployability across the entire force, resulting in greater versatility and agility for full-spectrum operations, point to the need for fundamental transformation and a new vision."

Much of the information on the weapons outlined in this section is based on the *Weapon Systems Handbook* and shows the army's continued determination to find and use the best possible weapons. The selection of weapons mentioned here is not comprehensive, but provides a flavor of what the US Army uses today and intends to use tomorrow.

M1A1/M1A2 Abrams Main Battle Tank

The US Army's main battle tank, the M1A1, has proved itself in action against the Iraqis. Its 4.73-in main gun, 1,500hp turbine engine, and special armor make it a formidable weapon. Modification and update programs include the M1A1D modification scheduled for 1,535 M1A1s (improved computer and a targeting capabilities) and the M1A2 System Enhancement Program that will see 547 Abrams considerably upgraded. A new engine program—the Abrams Integrated Management Overhaul Program is also underway.

The Abrams' 4.73-in (120mm) gun has the most advanced and lethal tank ammunition in the world. Two types of ammunition can be fired from the can-

RIGHT: The foundation of the infantry, the foot soldier, is a rifleman, grenadier, or machine-gunner with about 20 weeks of initial training plus more training within his unit. He may wear the wings of a paratrooper (as here), a Ranger's tab and black beret, or an Air Assault badge. But he is still fundamentally an infantryman who closes with the enemy and defeats him face-to-face.

non: the M829 family of kinetic energy projectiles that use depleted uranium (DU) hard-rod penetrators, and multipurpose ammunition that uses high explosive, shaped-charge warheads to provide blast, armor penetration, and fragmentation effects. The XM1007 Tank Extended Range Munition-Kinetic Energy (TERM-KE) is planned to be a soft-launch, rocket-boosted, terminally-guided, kinetic-energy munition. The XM1028 Canister Cartridge will provide antipersonnel capability at short ranges.

Wolverine Bridgelayer

Designed to provide the heavy brigade combat team with bridgelayer with a gap-crossing capability of up to 26.25 yards (24m), the Wolverine launcher is

RIGHT: Soldier is shown carrying an M60 machinegun.

BELOW: A M-1A1 main battle tank shown in the field. Its 4.8-in (120mm) main gun, 1,500hp turbine engine, and special armor make it a formidable weapon.

ABOVE: Two M1A1 main battle tanks sit in defensive positions as they prepare to engage targets on Range 2 of the Al Hamra Training Area in the United Arab Emirates.

LEFT: US Army 1st Armored Division M1A1 main battle tanks convoy to the Glamoc Ranges in Bosnia and Herzegovina.

ABOVE, RIGHT: A US Army M1A1 main battle tank is equipped with a mine plow which is designed to push mines out of the tank's path, clearing a lane for other vehicles to follow.

RIGHT: A remote-controlled Panther armored mine clearing vehicle leads a column of armored vehicles down a road near McGovern Base in Bosnia and Herzegovina during Operation "Joint Endeavor." The Panther, based on a modified M60 tank hull, uses metal rollers to set off contact or magnetic mines.

mounted on a M1A2 Abrams and is operated by a two-man crew. The 28.4-yard (26-m) long bridge is launched in five minutes, and retrieved in less than ten minutes. It is a major improvement of the current armored vehicle launched bridge (AVLB) that only minimally supports Abrams.

M88A2 Hercules Armored Recovery Vehicle

Designed to provide a battlefield armored recovery vehicle, the Hercules uses the existing M88A1 chassis but with improvements to its towing, winching, lifting, and braking. The Hercules is the primary recovery support for the Abrams and future heavy systems such as the Grizzly, Wolverine, and heavy self-propelled artillery. It entered into service in 2000 with 1st Cavalry Division.

Armored Security Vehicle

The ASV is a turreted, light-armored, all-wheeled drive vehicle that provides increased ballistic and landmine protection to MPs. It entered service at the end of 2000 and its primary weapons are a 1.58-in (40mm) Mk. 19 grenade machinegun, and an M2 .50cal machinegun. The fully enclosed turret includes a day/night sight for target acquisition. Crew size for the ASV is three, with a jump seat for a fourth soldier. The ASV carries up to 3,360lb (1,524kg) of payload and can be transported by a C-130.

ABOVE, LEFT: The basic form of an infantry platoon is three rifle squads, a weapons squad, plus a small headquarters group. The weapons squad usually has two machinegun, antiarmor missile or mortar teams of two men, a gunner and assistant. Headquarters includes the platoon leader, a platoon sergeant, a radio operator (or RATELO), plus two machinegun teams—a total of one officer and 44 soldiers.

ABOVE: The soldier to the left carries an M16A2 and the man to the right an M249 SAW.

M992 Field Artillery Ammunition Support Vehicle

This fully tracked armored vehicle is designed to accompany artillery weapons—particularly the M109A6 Paladin as an ammunition carrier. It has excellent all-terrain capability and an automated conveyer delivery of ammunition. It has excellent ground mobility for improved battlefield responsiveness and a highly improved survivability that allows extended fire support missions. It carries 90, 6.1-in (155mm) projectiles with 96 propelling charges and 104 fuzes, and three Copperhead projectiles. Its combat loaded weight is 57,500lb (26,082kg).

Bradley M2/M3 Infantry/Cavalry Fighting Vehicles

Modern soldiers don't walk as much as their ancestors, and that means they get to the fight a lot faster and fresher. One very important part of the Army's infantry are the "mechanized" units. They have their own "organic" fighting vehicles – traditionally called "battle taxis" – and their own specialized missions. Traditional infantry is now called "light" infantry, and they have another set of missions and skills.

The current battlefield taxi of choice is the M2 Bradley, a fast, agile, well-armed and armored combination of fighting vehicle and personnel carrier that delivers infantry to critical areas of the battlefield while engaging enemy targets with chain gun, coax, and TOW (Tube-launched, Optically-tracked, Wire-guided) missiles.

The specifications and "school solution" will tell you that seven combat-equipped soldiers will fit in one, but the people who came up with that figure don't seem to have tried it. For most of the troops, the Bradley is pretty comfortable. But there is one seat, right behind the driver, that requires its assigned

ABOVE and LEFT: M2 Bradleys weigh about 25 tons and have a 600hp diesel engine. The primary armament on the M2 is a 1-in (25mm) chain gun. TOW missiles launched from the M2 can out-range an enemy tank by engaging it at 9842ft (3,000m).

passenger to squeeze through a very small and cluttered tunnel on the right side of the turret. It is quite possible for a soldier to get into this seat—but nobody can do it while wearing their LBE and expect to get back out again. The Bradley crews and the infantry who ride in them refer to this seat as the "hell hole." Sometimes a soldier will actually sit in there, but he leaves his LBE and weapon in the main passenger compartment and tries to get it on as he dashes down the ramp, far behind the rest of the men in his squad. Normally, the seat is empty and the squads either fight short-handed or split up the men into multiple Bradleys.

The Bradley was initially designed to help the M1 Abrams MBT fend off potential attacks during a possible world war. It is almost as fast as the Abrams in open terrain and faster when the going gets really rough. Bradleys are often confused with tanks, but they are quite vulnerable to the cannon of even old and obsolete MBTs such as the T-55s and T-72s used by threat nations all over the world. The 4.14-in (105mm) and 4.43-in (120mm) projectiles from these tanks would slice through a Bradley without slowing down—if they ever get a shot at one.

ABOVE and RIGHT: The current "battlefield taxi" of choice is the M2 Bradley. Seven combat-equipped soldiers are meant to fit in one, but this is only possible at a tight squeeze and if one soldier sits in the "hell hole" behind the driver's seat. Usually this seat is left empty and the squads fight short-handed or men are carried in several Bradleys.

BELOW and LEFT: Bradleys mount a M240C co-axial 0.3-in (7.62mm) machinegun with 800 rounds in the ready boxes and another 1,400 stowed.

Bradleys have thin armor only intended to protect against small arms and machinegun fire and the shrapnel from nearby artillery impacts.

Bradleys weigh about 25 tons, less than half the weight of a MBT, thanks to the lighter armor and smaller size. They are propelled by a 600hp diesel engine that will move the M2 along at 45mph (72kmph) or better (although the Army says top speed is only 38mph – 61kmph). With a full tank of 175 USgallons (145 UKgallons) of fuel aboard, a Bradley can travel about 175 miles (281km) under ideal road conditions although that tank will need refilling much sooner when the vehicle operates in tactical conditions.

Primary armament on the M2 is a 1-in (25mm) chain gun optimized for engaging enemy lightly-armored vehicles and "thin-skinned" trucks, but can also engage area targets such as troops in the open, helicopters, and fortified positions. The infantry version of the Bradley, the M2A2 and A3, carry 600

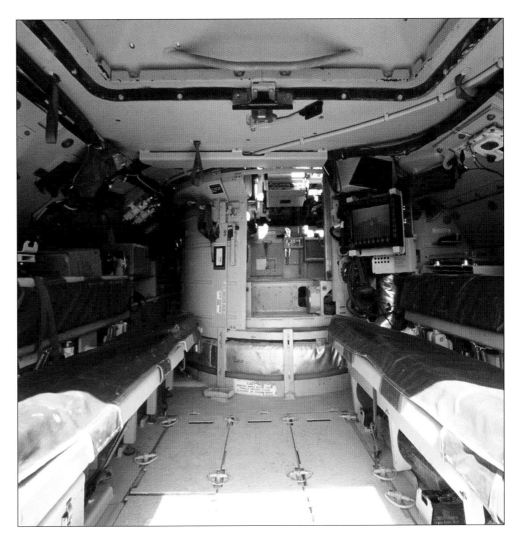

rounds for the chain gun, in two types—high explosive (HE) for trucks, troops, and aircraft, and armor-piercing (AP) for enemy APCs.

Bradleys may not be able to take a hit from a MBT but they can certainly inflict one with TOW missiles. The TOW missile can out-range an enemy tank by engaging it at 3,281 yards (3.000m), beyond the target's weapon's effective range. Although it takes 14 seconds for the missile to get to the target at that range, it is extremely accurate and lethal; the most recent variants of the missile will defeat any modern tank, with or without reactive armor.

For those situations when enemy infantry swarm around your position, Bradleys mount a M240C co-axial 0.3-in (7.62mm) machinegun with 800 rounds in the ready boxes and another 1,400 stowed.

Bradley Fire Support Vehicle (BFIST)

One of the M2/M3 Bradley derivatives, the FSV is designed to provide an integrated Bradley based fire-support platform so that officers can plan, coordinate, execute, and direct timely, accurate, indirect fires. It is planned to upgrade the BFIST to both Bradley M2A2 Operation "Desert Storm"-based improvements (M7 BFIST) and M2A3 variants (A3 BFIST).

M6 Bradley Linebacker Air Defense Vehicle

The Linebacker is the air-defense variant of the Bradley modified by replacing the TOW missile launcher with a four-missile Stinger standard vehicle-mounted launcher.

M707 Striker Fire Support Team Vehicle

The Striker replaces the M981 Fire Support Team Vehicles used by Combat Observation Lasing Teams (COLTs). It operates as an integral part of the brigade reconnaissance team, providing COLT and fire support mission planning and execution. The crew on board Striker locates and designates targets for laser-guided ordnance. It is built on a HMMWV chassis.

BELOW: A Hummer shown here with a TOW antitank missile system mounting.

M998 High Mobility Multipurpose Wheeled Vehicle

One of the Army's big success stories of recent years is the sturdy little vehicle called the High Mobility Multipurpose Wheeled Vehicle, known affectionately as the "Hummer." It has been in the infantry motor pool since 1983 and was a hit from the beginning. Fifteen versions of the basic design have been built, and over 70,000 have been put in service.

The basic Hummer is much bigger than the traditional jeep of old: the basic model weighs about three tons (5,900lb/2,676kg), has a 2,500lb (1,134kg) payload, and has a kind of odd, low, wide stature. It has full time four-wheel drive, independent suspension, and a very reliable 6.5-liter V-8 engine. You can take one up a 60 percent slope or ford a stream five feet deep. The HMMWV's long wheelbase and wide track make it remarkably agile and reasonably comfortable when rattling around the wadis and deserts of the Valley of Death or the Goat Trail at the National Training Center (NTC).

The main body material, is aluminum, one of the factors that make the Hummer so easily air-deployable. They are dropped by parachute or delivered to austere forward airstrips from C-130s. CH-47 heli-

LEFT: The M998 High Mobility Multipurpose Wheeled Vehicle is otherwise known as the Hummer.

BELOW: TOW missile being fired from a Hummer.

copters easily carry two of them as sling loads to inaccessible locations, and a UH-60 can carry one.

It can be configured to become a troop carrier, armament carrier, S250 shelter carrier, ambulance, TOW missile carrier, and a Scout vehicle. The heavy variant, with a payload of 4,400lb (1,996kg), was developed as the prime mover for the light howitzer, towed Vulcan system, and heavier shelter carriers. It is a tri-service program that also provides vehicles to satisfy Marine Corps and Air Force requirements. Company commanders and platoon leaders all have Hummers of their own, complete with driver and stuffed with SINCGARS radios, and with a case of MREs, a water cooler, and field gear during tactical operations. Most infantry soldiers will spend at least some time riding around in one of the versions, and all agree that the ride is better than walking.

M113 Armored Personnel Carrier

Although too slow and vulnerable to play much of a role on the modern battlefield, the old M113 is still part of the inventory and still performing essential missions for the modern infantryman. Bradleys have taken over the battlefield taxi business, but the basic M113 (in a modified version called the M577) provide the foundation for a mechanized infantry

battalion's tactical operations center. You will generally find a large coffee pot in one of the M577s clustered together at the TOC, and the others will be home to the fire support officer, the S3 Operations crew, and all the other staff that keep the battalion in business. The M113s that remain in service provide a highly mobile, survivable, and reliable tracked-vehicle platform designed to keep pace with Abrams and Bradley-equipped units. The current list of models include:

M58 Mechanized Smoke Obscurant System
M548A1/A3 Cargo Carrier,
M577A2/A3 Command Post Carrier
M901A1 Improved TOW Vehicle
M981 Fire Support Team Vehicle
M1059/A3 Smoke Generator Carrier
M1064/A3 Mortar Carrier
M1068/A3 Standard Integrated Command
    Post System Carrier, and OPFOR Surrogate
    Vehicle (OSV).

BELOW: Although it no longer plays much of a role on the modern battlefield, the M901A1 Improved TOW vehicle still forms part of the Army's inventory.

ABOVE: The M901A1 Improved TOW Vehicle (ITV) consists of a standard M113A1 APC with an M27 cupola mounted on the roof.

BELOW: When traveling, the launcher head is retracted level onto the hull top so making the ITV difficult to distinguish from the standard M113A1 series APC.

TOP: The M901A1 Improved TOW provides a highly mobile, survivable, and reliable tracked-vehicle platform.

ABOVE: The M901A1 is designed to keep pace with Abrams and Bradley-equipped units.

RIGHT: Soldiers assigned to C Troop of the 4th Squadron, 7th Cavalry Regiment drive an M113A1 Armored Personnel Carrier to the live fire range at the Korea Training Center, Republic of Korea. Armored units use the range to meet annual, live gunnery training requirements.

M16A1/A2 Rifle and M4 Carbine

The most common weapon in the whole Army is certainly the M16 rifle and its several variants. The design is almost 50 years old at this point, and has been in US service for 35 years. Dozens of nations around the world also use it, a testament to its excellent design and manufacture.

Most soldiers today love the weapon; it is light, strong, accurate, reliable, and it puts a killing round downrange. But American soldiers haven't always been so fond of it. During the late 1960s, shortly after it was introduced, the propellant used in the ammunition for the weapon was changed and soldiers reported numerous problems with failure to feed and jamming. Those problems have long been solved and today's soldiers seldom have any stoppages with the weapon.

The current basic variants found in infantry units are the M16A2 rifle and M4 carbine. The M16A2 weighs 8.7lb (4kg), is 39in (1m) long, and has a maximum range of 3,937 yards (3,600m). Its maximum effective range is rated at 634 yards (580m)—an extremely optimistic official figure for real-world combat engagements against individual soldiers.

The old A1 version offered a choice of single shots or fully automatic. The predictable result was that in combat during the Vietnam War inexperienced soldiers switched to auto, forgot all their training about fire discipline, and aimed fire, executing an engagement technique known as "spray and pray." Their first rounds might possibly have been in the general vicinity of an enemy soldier but the rest of the 20 or 30 in the magazine almost certainly pruned the trees over the opposing team. These soldiers rapidly found themselves running low on ammunition without having done any damage at all to the Viet Cong or NVA.

When it came time to take another look at the M16, and the A2 went onto the drawing board, the full auto feature was deducted in favor of a three-shot

LEFT: A soldier patrols near a US observation post in Mijak, Kosovo, Serbia. US troops in Mijak regularly patrolled the area in an attempt to prevent shipments of arms from crossing the border into Macedonia.

RIGHT: M16A1 with M203 attached. The A1 uses a special upper hand-guard with the M203. A ramp sight attached to the hand-guard helps put the 1.6-in (40mm) rounds on target but, because of the projectile's steep trajectory, precision fire is difficult to achieve.

ABOVE: Soldier with M16A1 with M203 attached. The A1 version offered a choice of single shots or a fully automatic feature. This automatic feature was changed in favor of a three-shot burst on the A2.

burst. This feature still lets the inexperienced soldier waste a lot of ammunition, but forces him to engage targets with a weapon that is more controllable.

The round fired by the rifle was a radical shift from infantry tradition when it was introduced, too. It is a tiny little bullet, dwarfed by the projectile used with the old and beloved M1 Garand of World War II and Korea and even the 0.3-in (7.62mm) NATO round fired by the M14. But its light weight and small diameter has a couple of virtues that have gradually won over the troops. For one, the soldier can carry a lot more rounds for a given weight—210 are a typical combat load. For another, the bullet comes zipping out of the muzzle at 2,800ft/sec (853m/sec); it is a very flat-shooting round within its normal engagement ranges, and inflicts devastating wounds before the velocity falls off around 219 or 328 yards (200 or 300m) out.

The weapon is capable of firing 800rpm but 12 to 15 is a realistic maximum sustained rate of fire. If a soldier really gets into some deep trouble and has to use that three-shot-burst capability, 90rpm is possible. Thirty-round magazines are standard with the weapon but 20-round versions are sometimes used, and even Rambo has to change them once in a while.

According to the Army, the M16A2 can be used to engage "point" targets out to 634 yards (580m). That's a third of a mile, and at that range an enemy soldier has very little to fear from about 95 percent of riflemen—for the first shot, at least. It takes a very good marksman to hit a man at that range, even if he is just standing still and in the open like an idiot.

The Army says the weapon is useful to 1094 yards (1000m) for "area" targets—that is a gaggle of troops in the open, for example; you may annoy them with your three-shot bursts, and if you are very lucky (and he is not) you might even hit one at that distance, if you fire enough rounds. But killing engagements are typically at 218 yards (200m) and closer – generally a lot closer – and the M16 in its long history and several variants has been in a lot of them.

A lot of soldiers are surrendering their rifles for the lightweight M4 carbine. It is almost the same weapon but has a collapsible stock and shorter barrel making it even lighter than the original. The shorter

sight radius makes it a little less accurate at long range, but that is seldom a problem. It is much easier to carry when hopping in and out of helicopters, trucks, Bradleys, trench-lines, and enemy bunkers.

M203 Grenade Launcher

Direct fire weapons such as the M16 rifle are excellent for certain kinds of targets but utterly useless for

ABOVE: An M16A2 uses a small bullet that seems dwarfed in comparison to the old projectile used with the memorable M1 Garand of World War II.

BELOW: M16A1 and M203 with 1.6-in (40mm) rounds in bandolier. The 203 fires high-explosive, illumination, smoke, flechette, dual-purpose, training, and "beanbag rounds." The training round is only filled with red powder but works well for marking the point of impact.

LEFT: A soldier of Bravo Company, 1st Battalion, 8th Marines, engages the enemy with his M16A2 rifle.

BELOW, LEFT: A soldier uses a M16A2 rifle to maintain his marksmanship qualifications at a range near Handalici, Bosnia, and Herzegovina, during Operation Joint Endeavor.

BELOW: A Mark 19 automatic grenade launcher is fired at the Marine Corps Base in Virginia. This grenade launcher is capable of a maximum range of well over a mile and a maximum effective range of 1750 yards (1600m). It can fire 350rpm but 60rpm is usually the case.

others. During the war in Vietnam and Southeast Asia, infantry soldiers were issued the M79 grenade launcher, a stubby little single shot weapon that fired a 1.58-in (40mm) low velocity round. The M79's high-explosive, smoke, and "bean-bag" rounds proved to be extremely effective against VC and NVA in all sorts of situations. The HE round could be fired into bunkers or at enemy soldiers behind the crest of a hill; the smoke round could provide a bit of screening for an attack or withdrawal; the "bean-bag" round was very effective at temporarily incapacitating an enemy soldier, like a massive punch to the torso, without doing (much) permanent damage—a great way to collect a prisoner for questioning.

Today's grenadier uses a similar weapon, the M203, but his launcher is attached to the same M16A2 used by the riflemen in the squad, and his

ABOVE: A 1st Platoon, Lima Company Marine uses his ski poles to steady his M16A2 rifle equipped with a M203 grenade launcher during part of his training in cold weather survival and arctic warfare.

weapon has a tremendous variety of ammunition available. Among these are HE, dual purpose, several varieties of smoke rounds, several star-cluster signaling rounds, non-lethal projectiles, a "buckshot" projectile, and the really nasty flechette round. This latter sprays several dozen small, heavy, extremely sharp steel darts downrange, any one of which will likely make even Rambo drop his weapon and quit.

The launcher adds 3lb (1.36kg) to the weight of the M16 making the assembly almost 12lb (5.44kg) with a full mag in the rifle. The grenades can be used to engage point targets such as a bunker aperture, a window, fighting position, or vehicle out to 164 yards (150m). For area targets, such as troops in the open, it is used to 383 yards (350) or so. Maximum range is 437 yards(400m).

M240B Medium Machinegun

The M240B is a ground-mounted, gas-operated, crew-served machinegun. This reliable 0.3-in (7.62mm) machinegun delivers a bigger punch than the smaller caliber M249 SAW. It will be issued to infantry, armor, combat engineer, and special force units that require medium support and will replace the M60 series machineguns currently in use.

RIGHT: The M60 machinegun is capable of firing 200rpm and 100rpm of sustained fire, just the kind of weapon needed to initiate an ambush on an enemy platoon.

M60 Machinegun and M249 Squad Automatic Weapon

The M60 sucks up 0.3-in (7.62mm) NATO rounds at a rapid rate—550 rounds cyclic rate, 200 rpm when the bad guys are coming through the wire, and 100rpm sustained. Even 100 rounds of M60 ammunition is a heavy load, and somebody has to carry it. That somebody is every guy in the squad, each of whom gets a box or belt to stuff in his backpack.

But that firepower is just what you need when it comes time to break contact, or when the assault elements are rushing the enemy bunker. It is also just the job when you initiate an ambush on an enemy platoon—you either cut down those 45 NVAor they are going to put you in (so to speak) a "world of hurt."

The M60 has been largely replaced by the M249 Squad Automatic Weapon, known as the SAW. This machinegun is a Belgian design from Fabrique Nationale Manufacturing and has become quite popular—especially with soldiers who used to have to "hump" the "pig" over hill and dale. Complete with bipod and tools, the weapon weighs just over 15lb (6.8kg) empty; a 200-round plastic "battle pack" box magazine adds another 7lb (3.17kg), but that is still far less than an M60 and 200 rounds.

SAWs fire the same 0.22-in (5.56mm) cartridge used by the M16 and can even accept the standard 30-round magazines carried by every rifleman. This allows the SAW gunner to beg, steal, or borrow more ammunition when he runs out, not an option for the M60 gunner. He starts out with 600 rounds for his basic load, though, and it will take him a while to get through it all.

M249s have a cyclic rate of fire of 600rpm but the gunner will have the squad leader screaming at him if he keeps that up for long. Sustained fire is 85rpm or less. The SAW is good for area targets out to 875 to 1,094 yards (800m to1,000m) or against point targets to 656 yards (600m).

ABOVE, RIGHT: Soldiers call the big M60 machinegun the "pig," and if you had to carry one and a basic load of ammunition for a mile or two, you would understand why. Weighing 23lb (10.4kg) when empty, it is a hefty load.

RIGHT: Even 100 rounds of M60 ammunition is a heavy load and each soldier gets a belt or box to stuff in his backpack.

Although it doesn't have a three-shot burst control, the gunner should be able to manage that on his own. With practice, a gunner can squirt three, four, or six rounds downrange, under control and with reasonable accuracy. Long bursts are for the movies—in the real world, the barrel starts to glow cherry red very quickly and the ammunition starts to "cook off" as soon as it chambers, and then the gun is out of control.

During sustained engagements the gunner is very careful to manage his rate of fire, and will swap out barrels quite frequently, allowing one to cool while he heats the other one up with those well-disciplined bursts of carefully aimed fire.

Mk. 19 1.58-in(40mm) Grenade Launcher

An industrial-strength grenade launcher is the Mk. 19, a kind of machinegun for 1.58-in (40mm) projectiles. Although it fires ammunition that appears similar to that used with the M203, the Mk. 19 throws its rounds out much farther with a maximum range of well over a mile and a maximum effective range of 1750yards (1,600m). It is a heavy weapon, weighing 137lb (62kg) in total, so it isn't carried by the foot soldiers. Instead, it is mounted on humvees and trucks, or carried in them and dismounted for use in defensive positions. The Mk. 19's cyclic rate of fire is about 350rpm but 60rpm is tops for the real world and 40rpm the maximum rate of fire for sustained engagements.

One of the rounds fired by this weapon, the M430 HEDP (High Explosive Dual Purpose), will punch through two inches of armor. Fragments from this round and the HE version will kill enemy soldiers within 5.47yards (5m) of impact and probably wound anybody within 16.4 yards (15m).

ABOVE, RIGHT: The Barrett .50cal sniper rifle is testimony to the renewed interest in the Army and Marine Corps in extreme long-range precision shooting. They call it "target interdiction," and with one of these weapons a trained shooter can make first-shot kills at ranges exceeding 1094 yards (1000m). The Barrett weighs 28.5lb (13kg), fires as a semi-automatic, and its magazine holds ten rounds.

RIGHT: M18 smoke grenades are frequently used to signal a position and to obscure.

ABOVE and RIGHT: M18 smoke grenades such as the ones illustrated here come in several colors—red, yellow, white, green, and violet.

BELOW: The M67 hand grenade weighs about a pound and is a potent little package. Up to six may be carried by combat infantrymen during operations. Once the pin is removed from the M67 (and NOT with your teeth!) and the "spoon" is released, the soldier has between four and five seconds to take cover before the weapon detonates. This hand grenade once detonated will kill anybody within 16.4ft (5m) and wound most within a range of 50ft (15m).

M2 .50cal Machinegun

Soldiers call this fine old weapon "Ma Duce," and it is an affectionate nickname. The M2 heavy machinegun design goes all the way back to 1923 and is still in the inventory because of its tremendous effectiveness, reliability, and range. Fired single shot, it is so accurate that M2s were used as sniper weapons in Vietnam, making single-shot kills on NVA soldiers at distances up to a mile. But the Ma Duce is normally employed against enemy soldiers in the open, sometimes at great distances, against trucks, light armor, and slow-flying aircraft.

Several types of ammunition are issued: M33 ball and M17 tracer are the most common, mixed at a five-to-one ratio in belts of 100 rounds. Armor-piercing, armor-piercing-incendiary, and even discarding-sabot armor-piercing rounds are also issued, all highly effective against thin-skinned enemy vehicles. Sustained rate of fire is just 40rpm—and that requires regular barrel changes.

A new round, the Mk. 211, combines an delayed explosive charge with an armor-piercing projectile.

BELOW: At 128lb (58kg), the M2 and its tripod are carried by vehicles. They are frequently found on mounts attached to M113s (as here), 5-ton trucks, and HWWMVs. An M2 can reach 5905ft (1.8km), or take out a point target 3937ft (1.2km).

Instead of exploding on impact, the Mk. 211 projectile is designed to penetrate light armor first, then detonates once inside creating more damage than earlier projectiles.

2.36in (60mm) Mortar and 3.19in (81mm) Mortar

So what do you do when the bad guys are on the far side of a building, berm, hill, in a trench, or hiding behind something solid? Call up the mortars! The three-man mortar squad and their M224 Lightweight 2.36-in Mortar can drop rounds on the opposing team in their holes where no direct-fire weapons can reach them.

The 2.36-in (60mm) mortar is light enough to travel with the infantry wherever they go. Its crew—squad leader, gunner, and ammunition bearer—split its 46.5lb (21kg) up into two loads, the tube and mount forming one and the base-plate the other. The ammo bearer has enough to carry already so the squad leader and gunner will hump the weapon. Once they get the call for fire, the mortar squad can pump out high-explosive, white phosphorus, and illumination rounds, helping the infantry unit with immediate, organic indirect fire support. They can hammer any target from just 76.6 yards (70m) to almost 3828 yards (3,500m).

The HE round is certainly the most common and is used to kill enemy soldiers and to damage vehicles, structures, and similar unarmored objects. The HE and other rounds have one of two kinds of fuzes installed, one, the M935, that explodes on impact, and the very useful M734 Multioption fuze. The latter version allows the mortar team to set the round to explode about 10ft (3m) above the surface, just above the surface, on impact, or a half-second after impact. The first two options work well against troops in the open or in hasty defensive positions, the delay setting will help defeat troops in prepared positions with over head cover.

Besides the normal high-angle fire typical of mortars, the M224 has the capability of low-angle direct fire. The weapon can be fired with a manual trigger and when the base of the tube is supported by a substantial tree trunk or similar suitable object, the mortar becomes a kind of small howitzer or huge shotgun. Employed in this way, targets as close as 76.6 yards (70m) can be engaged.

In an emergency, 30rpm can be fired for a total of four minutes—but that takes a lot of ammunition, much more than is likely to be available to a squad mortar section in normal combat. During sustained operations, 20rpm is more likely to be the practical maximum that can be obtained.

Although quite heavy at almost 90lb (40kg), the M252 3.19-in (81mm) mortar system is still an essential part of the infantry's bag of tricks. For real

ABOVE: The 2.4-in (60mm) mortar is light enough to be taken with the infantry wherever they go. Its 46.5lb (22kg) weight is split into two loads, the tube and mount forming one and the base-plate the other.

hardcore units, the weapon can be broken down into its components—the 35lb (15.8kg) tube, the 25.5lb (11.6kg) baseplate, 26lb (11.8kg) bipod, and 2.5lb (1.1kg) sight—and man-packed off into the weeds where it will provide industrial-strength fire support.

It is accurate to 6,234 yards (5,700m) firing HE, illumination, and smoke rounds at the rate of 15rpm. One illumination round will light up the night with 600,000 candlepower for a minute, revealing any enemy sappers trying to sneak through the wire.

4.73-in(120mm) Mortar

The 4.73-in (120mm) mortar system is a conventional smoothbore, muzzle-loaded mortar system that is a great improvement on the World War II-vintage 4.2-in (107mm) heavy mortar system it replaced. It is employed in towed (M120) and carrier versions (M121) and fires enhanced ammunition.

The Mortar Fire Control System (MFCS) will provide Paladin-like fire control capability that greatly improves mortar lethality, responsiveness, and crew survivability. New infrared illumination ammunition, the first of its kind in the world, provides enhanced nightfighting capability. Other improved munitions include the XM395 Precision Guided Mortar Munition (PGMM) – extended-range precision-guided munition with a strap-down laser detector seeker – and the XM984 Dual Purpose Improved Conventional Munition (DPICM)— extended-range munition that incorporates composites to maximize the number of dual-purpose grenades that can be carried.

Javelin Antitank Missile System

The Javelin is a portable, antiarmor system in service with the US Army and US Marine Corps. Javelin was designed to replace the Dragon. It is highly lethal against tanks with both conventional and reactive armor. The Javelin system weighs 48lb (21.7kg) and has a maximum range in excess of 2,734 yards

BELOW: The M47 Dragon's complete system consists of the launcher, the tracker, and the missile, which is installed in the launcher during final assembly and received by the army in a ready to fire condition.

(2,500m). The key feature of Javelin is the use of fire-and-forget (F&F) technology that enables the gunner to fire and immediately take cover.

TOW Antitank Missile System

TOW is designed to defeat tanks and armored vehicles equipped with advanced armors at close ranges with minimal exposure time. A fire-and-forget (F&F) missile system, the intention is to ensure it is given increased range, lethality, and platform survivability shelf life extension efforts.

M47 Dragon multipurpose weapon

A medium-range complement to TOW, this antitank or assault weapon has a range from 65.6 to 1,094 yards (60–1,000m), and a 5.4lb (2.45kg) warhead. In service since 1971, it has been replaced by the more effective Javelin.

TOP: The M47 Dragon is a medium-range, wire-guided, line-of-sight antitank missile weapon capable of defeating armored vehicles, fortified bunkers, concrete gun emplacements, and other hard targets.

ABOVE: The M47 is too heavy to be carried permanently on a soldier's shoulder. In order to use it, a soldier needs to deploy, changing the M16A2 for self defense to an M47 Dragon.

LEFT and BELOW, LEFT: The Swedish-designed AT4, weighing is a multipurpose weapon used in the antitank and bunker-buster roles, firing shaped-charge ammunition.

RIGHT: The M72A3 LAW is a lightweight, self-contained, antiarmor weapon consisting of a rocket packed in a launcher. It is is man portable and may be fired from either shoulder.

AT4 Lightweight Multipurpose Assault Weapon

This single-shot throwaway 3.31-in (84mm) antitank rocket was produced to replace the LAW. It entered service in 1989. It has a range of over 328 yards (300m), firing fin-stabilized HE-shaped charge ammunition.

M72 Light Antitank Weapon

Now obsolescent, this is a throwaway antitank system that gave the infantry a useful antiarmor capability.

ABOVE: The launcher on the M72A3, which consists of two tubes, one inside the other, serves as a watertight packing container for the rocket and houses a percussion type firing mechanism that activates the rocket.

Stinger Antiaircraft Missile System

A short-range air defense missile, Stinger is a fire-and-forget infrared/ultraviolet (IR/UV) missile system and is mounted on a variety of platforms including Avenger, Kiowa Warrior, Special Operation Black Hawks (MH-60), Bradley Linebacker, and the US Marine Corps' Light Amphibious Vehicle—Air Defense. This missile homes in on the heat emitted by aircraft and other targets. Stinger uses an eject motor to propel the missile a safe distance away from the gunner; a flight motor then ignites and propels it to the target.

Avenger Antiaircraft Missile/Gun System

The Avenger system is a lightweight, highly mobile, and transportable surface-to-air missile/gun weapon system mounted on an M998 HMMWV. It has a two-man crew and can operate during the day or night and in clear or adverse weather conditions. The system incorporates a rotating turret and standard vehicle-mounted launchers which support and launch multiple Stinger missiles. Avenger can be operated remotely up to 54.7 yards (50m) from the fire unit and can shoot on the move.

ABOVE: Marines launch a Stinger antiaircraft missile at a target aircraft during a live fire exercise. This missile homes in on the heat emitted by aircraft and other targets.

BELOW: An Avenger Gunner from the 2nd Low Altitude Air Defense Squadron, keeps a lookout for hostile aircraft. The Avenger has a two-man crew and can operate during the day or night.

M270 Multiple Launch Rocket System

With its origins back in the 19th century – Congreve's rockets – and more recently in the form of the World War II Katyusha, the MLRS is an artillery weapon system that supplements cannon artillery fires by delivering large volumes of firepower. It delivers freeflight basic and Extended Range (ER-MLRS) rockets and Army Tactical Missile System (ATACMS) Block I missiles. Growth programs are underway to extend the range and accuracy of the rockets and to upgrade the launcher to fire precision guided rockets and missiles to include Guided MLRS (GMLRS) and ATACMS/Brilliant Antiarmor Submunition (BAT)

Block II weapons

M109A6 Paladin Howitzer

The Paladin is the most technologically-advanced self-propelled cannon system in the US Army. The "A6" designation identifies several changes to the standard model—a fully automated FCS, a computer-controlled gun drive, improved ballistic and nuclear, biological and chemical protection and is capable of firing within 45 seconds from a complete stop. Its ammunition has 18.6 miles (30km) range with HE RAP and M203 propellant.

Patriot Antimissile Missile System

The Patriot is designed to provide defense against aircraft, cruise missiles, and tactical ballistic missiles. Each of eight launching stations contains four ready-to-fire missiles sealed in canisters that serve the dual purposes of shipping containers and launch tubes. Patriot's fast-reaction capability, high firepower, ability to track numerous targets simultaneously, and ability to operate in a severe electronic countermeasure environment are significant improvements over previous air defense systems. Currently underway is the Patriot Advanced Capability-3 (PAC-3) upgrade program that will incorporate significant upgrades to

BELOW: Soldiers from the 31st Air Defense Artillery Brigade load a Patriot missile onto a transfer vehicle at McGregor Test Range, NM, during Exercise "Roving Sands."

the RS and ECS, and will add the new PAC-3 missile, which utilizes hit-to-kill technology for greater lethality against TBMs armed with weapons of mass destruction. Additionally, it will be possible to have up to 16 PAC-3 missiles per launcher, increasing firepower and missile defense capabilities.

AH-64 Apache Longbow attack helicopter

The McDonnell Douglas AH-64 Apache helicopter is the US Army's main attack helicopter utilizing the Hellfire antitank missile, 2.75-in (70mm) rockets, and 1.2-in (30mm) chain gun. The AH-64D Apache Longbow has an upgrade of the Hellfire targeting system making it capable of full fire-and-forget all-weather, use. Longbow integrates a mast-mounted millimeter-wave fire control radar, a radar frequency interferometer, and a radar frequency fire-and-forget Hellfire II missile on the Apache. The modernized

LEFT: A Hughes AH-64 Apache advanced attack helicopter firing 2.75-in (70mm) rockets at a ground target.

BELOW: The UH-60 Blackhawk, the US Army's battlefield utility helicopter, gained notoriety known after its use in Somalia and the film "Blackhawk Down".

Apache heavy attack team will now be able to provide a truly coordinated rapid-fire capability (servicing 16 separate targets within a minute).

UH-60 Blackhawk Helicopter

The Sikorsky Blackhawk provides air assault, general support, aeromedical evacuation, command and control, electronic warfare, and special operations uses. The UH-60 utility tactical transport helicopter has enhanced the overall mobility of the Army, due to improvements in troop capacity and cargo lift capability, compared to the UH-1 Huey it replaces. An entire 11-person, fully equipped infantry squad can be lifted in a single Blackhawk; it can reposition a 4.14-in (105mm) howitzer, its crew of six, and up to 30 rounds of ammunition in a single lift.

Tactical Unmanned Aerial Vehicle (TUAV)

A TUAV is designed to provide reconnaissance, surveillance, and target acquisition (RSTA) at an initial range of 31 miles (50km), day or night, in limited adverse weather conditions with a future, objective range extending to 124 miles (200km). A TUAV system consists of two ground control stations, a minimum of three air vehicles (AVs), modular mission payloads, and launch and recovery equipment. The

ABOVE: US Army Blackhawk helicopters lift off at Cairo West Air Base, Egypt, during Exercise Bright Star.

RIGHT: US Army UH-60L Blackhawk helicopters load soldiers at Allen Army Air Field.

BELOW: An Army National Guard soldier conducts maintenance on the tail rotor of a UH-60Q Blackhawk medevac helicopter in Romania.

complete TUAV system can be transported by two C-130 aircraft. Mission capability will be enhanced as advanced mission payloads become available, maximizing battlefield digitization to increase the effectiveness of other weapon systems.

CH-47 Chinook/Improved Cargo Helicopter

Designed by Boeing Vertol in the 1950s, the Chinook first flew in 1961. A medium transport, the army uses it for the transport of ground forces, supplies, and ammunition. The CH-47 is the Army's only heavy-lift cargo helicopter capable of cargo movement of payloads greater than 9,000lb (4,082kg). It is due for an upgrade—the CH-47F Improved Cargo Helicopter program will remanufacture 300 of the current fleet of 431 CH-47Ds, install a new digital cockpit, and make modifications to the airframe to reduce vibration. Other airframe modifications reduce the time by about 60 percent required for aircraft tear down and build-up after deployment on a C-5 or C-17.

RAH-66 Comanche Helicopter

The RAH-66 Comanche is a next-generation helicopter, designed to perform armed reconnaissance and light-attack reconnaissance missions. The Comanche will significantly expand the Army's capability to conduct reconnaissance operations in all battlefield environments, day or night, and during adverse weather. The Comanche will replace three types of helicopters (AH-1, OH-58, and OH-6) that currently perform the armed reconnaissance mission. Currently Comanche is in the last phase of development, with two prototype aircraft in active flight test status.

Kiowa Warrior

The Kiowa Warrior is a rapidly deployable, lightly armed reconnaissance helicopter. The Kiowa Warrior

BELOW: Two US Army CH-47 Chinook helicopters sling load Humvees at Allen Army Airfield, Fort Greeley, Alaska.

includes advanced visionics, navigation, communication, weapons, and cockpit integration systems. The mast-mounted sight (MMS) houses a thermal imaging system, low-light television, and a laser rangefinder/designator. These systems allow target acquisition and engagement at stand-off ranges and in adverse weather conditions. The Kiowa Warrior is rapidly deployable by air and can be fully operational within minutes of arrival. The armament systems combine to provide antiarmor, antipersonnel, and antiaircraft capabilities at standoff ranges. Although Kiowa Warrior fielding is complete, the Army is currently installing a series of safety and performance modifications to keep the aircraft safe and mission effective until it is retired.

Family of Medium Tactical Vehicles (FMTV)

The Family of Medium Tactical Vehicles (FMTV) consists of a common truck chassis that is used for several vehicle configurations in two payload classes and two tactical trailers with complementary payloads. The Light Medium Tactical Vehicle (LMTV) is available in van and cargo variants and has a 2.5-ton payload capacity. The Medium Tactical Vehicle (MTV) has a 5-ton payload capacity and consists of the following models: standard- and long-wheel base cargo (with and without matériel-handling equipment), tractor, wrecker, and dump truck. The FMTV is replacing the over-aged and maintenance-intensive trucks currently in the medium tactical vehicle fleet.

The Army has awarded a new four-year contract to Stewart & Stevenson Services and they have begun full production of the FMTV A1 series. The FMTV A1 includes a 1999 Environmental Protection Agency-certified engine, with an upgraded transmission, electronic data bus, an anti-lock brake system and interactive electronic technical

BELOW: The Family of Medium Tactical Vehicles will replace standard trucks in US Army use.

ABOVE: The Family of Medium Tactical Vehicles (FMTV) consists of a common truck chassis used for several vehicle configurations.

manuals. Also under contract are the new FMTV 2.5-ton and 5-ton tactical trailers that have the same cube and payload capacity as their prime mover.

The Future

Although the US Army infantryman still carries a weapon that is almost unchanged from the one his father carried in Vietnam, there are some major changes happening to the soldier's gear. The M16 is likely to remain the soldier's primary weapon for many years to come, but there are some very interesting new systems currently being fielded to make it and its user more efficient and effective.

Actually, the whole process of using advanced technology for the common foot soldier goes back almost as far as the M16, to the war in Vietnam. Back in the late 1960s the Army started introducing the first generation of night vision systems, particularly the early "starlight" scopes used on some weapons. At the time, there were lots of problems with this

technology and lots of critics who said it would never work. Well, the scopes worked well enough to start picking off the VC and NVA in the middle of the night, and that changed the nature of battle in a significant way.

Night vision technology has been developed to such a high state of perfection that soldiers now depend on it and battle doctrine is written around its use. The same is true of GPS that lets a squad leader know exactly where he is, in the middle of the night, far behind the lines. These and other technologies have confounded the critics—they are dependable, durable, and give the American foot soldier another little edge when the poop hits the propeller.

There is currently another program developing another kind of technology. As with NVG and GPS, it is having its teething problems and it has its critics. This technology is based on digital communications and an integrated system of devices that combine different kinds of information from different places into one big, highly detailed, almost-real-time resource. At the soldier-level, it is a package called "Land Warrior." At the battalion and brigade command level, it is a related package called FBCB2" (see page 184).

Land Warrior

The Land Warrior system makes a soldier look like something out of a Robo-Cop movie. His helmet has a small monocular display linked to a compact computer stowed in his pack. The display can show the soldier a map of the area, complete with symbology for enemy and friendly units, target sensor display (day or night), and navigational information. A Global Positioning System transmitter/receiver provides constant real-time information about the soldier's location—to both the soldier and to his parent command.

There are five basic parts to the Land Warrior system: First is a modified M4 carbine with laser-aiming pointer and a sight that includes video capture, a digital compass, thermal sensor, and close-combat optics. If it all works as advertised, that will let a soldier shoot around corners, exposing only the weapon and his hands, while aiming the carbine with the video display.

Part of the kit includes a new helmet that is quite a bit lighter than the current kevlar but with improved ballistic protection. And, it reduces somewhat the problems some soldiers had with limited visibility and restricted hearing when using the standard-issue kevlar.

The whole package weighs 16lb, including body armor. That sounds like a hefty addition to the soldier's load but he actually will be lighter by a half-pound because the new body armor is so much lighter than the old.

The virtues of the system are in its ability to improve everybody's situational awareness—the soldier on the ground will have a better idea of where the bad guys are, and where the good guys are, too. The soldier's commanders will also know where the squads and fire-teams are, when they are moving and when they are taking a break.

The possibilities for mischief and mayhem with Land Warrior technology are endless. If a squad leader can transmit video from his weapon sight back to the TOC, there is always the possibility that it will be intercepted by the opposing team or (worse yet) by CNN.

And with the squad leader or platoon leader on an electronic leash, there will always be the temptation for those on high to micromanage tactical operations. Digital, real-time, secure communications will allow

ABOVE: Modern training aids do much to enhance tactical awareness in combat—much as the USAF's Top Gun programs achieved for aircrew.

squad leaders – under fire and in close contact with the enemy – to get messages that sound something like: "HATCHET ONE SIX, THIS IS GUN-FIGHTER CONTROL; THE SECRETARY OF DEFENSE THINKS YOU SHOULD SHIFT YOUR POSITION ONE HUNDRED METERS TO THE WEST ... DO YOU COPY?"

To which the squad leader is likely to do what his Vietnam era forebearers did ... he'll reply "GUN-FIGHTER CONTROL, HATCHET ONE SIX— DID NOT COPY YOUR LAST; TRANSMISSION WEAK AND BROKEN. HATCHET ONE SIX, OUT." Then he will turn off the radio and drive on with the mission.

FBCB2 and the Tactical Internet

One of the great developments in modern military technology, and another product of the whole Force XXI program, is a pair of linked developments nobody will want to shut down. One is called FBCB2, and that stands for *Force XXI Battle Command, Brigade and Below*. FBCB2 is primarily a software program that allows lots of players on the battlefield talk to each other in a controlled, focused way. Each of these players has a computer and GPS receiver/transmitter, all linked together by secure radios in what is called a Tactical Internet. The name is complicated but the basic idea behind it is simple—put everybody on the same sheet of music, all the time, from the squad leader and his fire-teams to the brigade commander in his TOC.

In essence, FBCB2 connects all the players in an operation on a wireless, secure, real-time internet. All the Bradleys, most of the HWWMVs, and all the combat leaders are equipped with a compact, rugged, computer. This computer is tied to a GPS system that provides continuous position updates and is linked to a very high resolution display, a keyboard, and a stylus. The display uses "touch screen" technology and standard menus similar to those found on any PC or Apple computer. But unlike your home computer, FBCB2 will show you exactly where you are, in near real-time, exactly where all the other "friendlies" are, where the enemy is reported to be, all superimposed on a very detailed map that scrolls and zooms as required.

If one of your scout Bradleys spots an enemy tank, they will laze it. That laze will provide both a precision bearing and a precision distance from an accurately known position, and the enemy tank can be automatically displayed on everybody's display. The combination of very accurate information with near real-time display and the ability to share this information with everybody who needs to know is going to revolutionize the conduct of some kinds of infantry operations.

The system allows the transmission of ACE (ammunition, casualty, equipment) and spot reports, orders, and communications of all kinds—complete with address books just like most of us use for office email. But unlike most office computers, the screen is touch sensitive—you work your way through menu items by pressing icons on the screen, as well as making keyboard entries.

Line-of-Sight Antitank (LOSAT) weapon system

LOSAT is designed to provide highly lethal, accurate missile fire, effective against heavy armor systems and field fortifications at ranges exceeding tank main gun range, reducing the light infantry force lethality shortfall against heavy armor. The Line-of-Sight Antitank (LOSAT) weapon system consists of four hypervelocity Kinetic-Energy Missiles (KEM), and a Second Generation Forward-Looking Infrared (FLIR)/TV acquisition sensor, mounted on an air-mobile HMMWV chassis.

Objective Individual Combat Weapon (OICW)

The OICW will replace selected M16 rifles and M4 carbines. The modular, dual-barrel OICW will combine the lethality of 0.8-in (20mm) air-bursting munitions, 0.22-in (5.56mm) NATO ammunition, with a full-solution fire control to affect decisively violent and suppressive target effects and to greatly improve small arms performance. This fire control will incorporate a laser rangefinder, ballistic computer, direct view optics, video sight, electronic compass, thermal capability, and a target tracker.

The OICW's high explosive air bursting munitions will be capable of defeating not only exposed targets, but those in defilade (targets that have taken cover behind structures, terrain features and/or vehicles), a capability lacking in current rifles and carbines. The OICW will provide an overmatch in

ABOVE: Laser training aids and other modern systems increase the realism – and therefore the usefulness – of modern training .

system effectiveness while increasing the versatility and survivability of the soldier by:
- doubling the infantryman's stand-off range to 1,094 yards (1,000m);
- providing effective day/night operation; and
- providing significant improvements in lethality and target effects.

XM777 Joint Lightweight 6.1-in (155mm) Howitzer (LW155)

The XM777 Joint Lightweight 6.1-in (155mm) Howitzer (LW155) is a joint Marine Corps/Army program, in which the Marine Corps funds the howitzer research, development, test, and evaluation (RDT&E) and the Army funds the RDT&E for Towed Artillery Digitization (TAD) and other automation enhancements. It will replace the M198 howitzer as a general support system for Army light forces. The Marine Corps will use it in direct support, replacing existing cannon systems. The XM777 incorporates innovative designs to achieve lighter weight, without sacrificing the range, stability, accuracy, or durability of the current system. The lighter weight is achieved through lower trunnion height and the use of high-strength titanium, a primary component of the lower carriage and cradle assembly.

Chow

If there is one great Army tradition, it is that soldiers bitch about their chow. If the mess hall recruited Sergeant Wolfgang Puck and Corporal Julia Child to prepare Châteaubriand, a proper Caesar salad, good French bread, excellent wine, with some Stilton cheese and 100-year-old port to follow, you can bet that ten soldiers out of a hundred will be complaining about the meal.

But you don't hear quite as much whining about the chow these days as back in the legendary "old"

army. Millions of soldiers survived in the field on C-rations (or "C-rats" to an entire generation) and before that the dreary K-rations of our World War II forefathers. C-rats weren't too bad, if you like canned lima beans and ham, but almost nobody did. The little boxes often contained a chocolate bar that seemed to be manufactured from petrified chocolate—it wouldn't melt in the heat or in your mouth. The author of this section survived for much of a year in Vietnam on canned pound cake and fruit cocktail, for which he diligently searched through cases of rations, leaving lima beans for others less fortunate.

MREs

Despite what the troops call MREs – "Meal, Rejected by Ethiopians," or "Meal, Ready to Excrete" – the initials actually stand for Meal, Ready to Eat, and they are amazingly good. Instead of cans, the MRE uses pouches to keep the food fresh. There are about 12 entrées, including a couple of vegetarian options—chicken with rice, spaghetti and meat sauce, red beans and rice, beef stew, chili con carne, chicken stew, and others.

ABOVE: Force morale is essential for efficient operations and the old maxim "an army marches on its stomach" is as true today as it was in the 19th century.

Each MRE is packed in a pouch that provides some protection against the inevitable rough handling for anything that goes to the field. The packet fits neatly in a BDU pant pocket or in the outside pockets of a backpack.

Inside the pouch is the entrée, a packet containing two large, thick, extremely dry crackers, a tube of peanut butter or jam, sometimes a pretty good little fudge bar, and a packet of either cocoa or kool-aid-type drink (called invariably "bug juice"). Current pouches contain a wonderful addition, a little chemical heater that is activated with a small amount of water—it will heat your entrée (and, if it is chilly, yourself) for about 15 minutes. There is also an accessory packet with an impossibly small quantity of toilet paper, a book of water-resistant matches (although the old five-pack of extremely stale cigarettes found in C-rats are gone), a little moist

ABOVE: A US Marine and a British Royal Marine chat while heating up English rolled oats as they break for chow.

towellette, some hard candy or gum, and—an inspired addition—a very tiny bottle of hot sauce. This latter component is big enough for just one serving for most soldiers, and adds horsepower and spice to anything.

Tray Rats

MREs are generally issued individually and used by soldiers when they are out in the weeds, away from the unit, but once every day in the field or so the platoon sergeant will try to get hot chow for the men. In the old days, that meant that the company cooks set up a field kitchen, did their best to fabricate soggy pancakes, scrambled eggs, and half-cooked bacon. The soldiers had mess kits to receive this issue, all of which was slopped together in a somewhat disgusting mélange. After the meal, the mess kit was cleaned in a garbage can filled with lukewarm water, soap, and the dregs of previous cleaning efforts. The result was that the mess kits didn't get very clean and the soldiers often got sick. But no more.

The company cooks still provide hot chow, and sometimes they prepare it from scratch (when it is

officially called "A rations") in the field, but it is often trucked out in insulated marmite containers. But even more often they show up with Tray Rations, or "t-rats," and a big stack of paper plates.

T-rats can be quite good, and some people love them. Not everybody loves every entrée but most are extremely good—particularly, in the experience of the author, the canned omelet and the crumb cake. Others include sliced turkey, chicken, pork, hamburgers, sausage links, and the ancient and honorable SOS (as it has been called since World War II—"shit on a shingle," or creamed beef on toast).

These are flat aluminum "cans" about 14in by 20in. They can be heated in hot water, on top of a truck or tank engine, or even over a few bits of burning C-4. One tin will feed about 18 men, depending on their appetite and the generosity of the cooks. The problem with "T-rats" is that they start out warm and

RIGHT: Stacked boxes become tables as US Marines from the 26th Marine Expeditionary Unit eat at a field mess at Camp Monteith, near Cernica, Kosovo.

BELOW: Soldiers from the 5th Long Range Reconnaissance Patrol Company, Royal Thai Army, (right) share their traditional field chow with a member of the US Army's 6th Infantry Division (left).

BELOW, RIGHT: British Royal Marines (right) from 42 Commando offer hot water for making coffee and tea to US Marines from Kilo Company as they break for chow at Camp Lejeune, N.C.

the first half dozen men in line get hot chow. The next three or four get warm food, and the rest get theirs cold.

The US Army Reserve

The US Army Reserve is made up of ready-to-go combat support and combat service support forces that can move on short notice to give the active army the resources it needs to deploy overseas and to sustain combat troops during wartime, contingencies, or other operations. It is the Army's main source of transportation, medical, logistical, and other units, and it is the Army's only source of trained individual soldiers to augment headquarters staffs and fill vacancies in units.

The United States has always relied on a very small Regular Army augmented in time of crisis by militia or civilian volunteers. The training and preparedness of these troops was always suspect at best and non-existent at worst—something that cannot be tolerated today.

Today's US Army Reserve consists of more than a million men split into three categories—the Selected Reserve, the Individual Ready Reserve, and the Retired Reserve, totaling more than 1,000,000 reservists, upon whom the government can call when needed.

The invasion of Kuwait by Iraq in 1990 led to the largest call-up of Reserve Component personnel since the Korean War. More than 84,000 Army Reservists provided combat support and combat service support to the Total Force in Southwest Asia and site support elsewhere.

A key step in the continued development of the Army Reserve took place in 1991 with establishment of the US Army Reserve Command (USARC) in Atlanta. The USARC has responsibility for command and control of Troop Program Units nationwide and the 65th Army Reserve Command in Puerto Rico. The Chief, Army Reserve commands

LEFT: The US Army's small number of regular soldiers is supplemented when required by more than a million reservists.

the USARC, and also serves as Deputy Commanding General for Reserve Affairs, US Army Forces Command (FORSCOM).

In December 1995, the president authorized the call-up of Reserve Component forces as part of America's support to the NATO peacekeeping forces in the Bosnia-Herzegovina area. Within a short period of time the Army Reserve provided civil affairs, postal, medical, engineer, transportation, psychological operations and firefighting units, the first arriving in Bosnia in mid-January 1996. The initial manpower ceiling from the Reserve Component was 3,888, with soldiers activated for up to 270 days. In May 1996, the ceiling increased to 7,000 to allow overlap of deploying and redeploying units and individual soldiers. The majority of Army Reservists ordered to active duty served as backfill for active Army soldiers in Germany, but substantial numbers pulled duty in Bosnia and Hungary.

Today, the Army Reserve has almost 40 percent of the Army's combat support (CS) and combat service support (CSS) units. With over 92 percent of those units assigned a role under Army regional operational plans, the USAR is positioned to support almost any type of mission worldwide.

The Army Reserve is in the final stages of its strength drawdown and unit reorganization plan. The fiscal year 1998 programmed end strength of 208,000 will mean a reduction of 35 percent since 1989, when America began reducing its armed forces (the USAR will take the largest cut of any Reserve Component). Future unit activations and inactivations, tied to the off-site agreement with the Army National Guard, will reinforce the Army Reserve's core competency of combat service support.

The Army Reserve of the 21st century, with its core competency firmly planted in combat service support, will be a more relevant and better trained cornerstone of our nation's defense. While managed change is still in the Army Reserve's future, the basic values of its citizen-soldiers—duty and selfless service—will remain steadfast.

TOP RIGHT and RIGHT: Battlefield communication systems are likely to see major improvements as new technology comes in. FBCB2 and the Tactical Internet will be the first stage of this.

NAVAL WEAPONS

Since the end of World War II the US Navy has deployed a wide spectrum of weapon systems designed to enable its ships to fight and survive at sea. The main strike power was vested in the aircraft of the various Carrier Air Groups and considerable effort was put in to systems designed to defend task forces from all forms of aerial, surface, and undersea threats. In particular, given the size and power of the Russian submarine fleet, antisubmarine warfare (ASW) was given a very high priority. Amphibious warfare, involving landing forces against opposition, also needed support weapon systems, but these were generally limited to covering the immediate beachhead area.

In the last decade of the 20th century the end of the Cold War considerably lessened the likelihood of a major conflict between superpowers, but in its place US forces have been involved in an almost continuous series of small wars and peacekeeping actions including the Gulf War in 1991, subsequent strikes against Iraq in 1994, the various Balkan conflicts which followed the break up of the former Yugoslavia, and action in Afghanistan. The latter resulted from the September 11, 2001 terrorist attack against America and will almost certainly be followed by further action against states deemed to pose a threat to the US and other nations.

As these wars and actions have occurred, it has become apparent that the US Navy has had to reconsider its prime role and reevaluate the weapons needed to support this type of warfare. Instead of blue water oceanic deployments, US ships are now engaged in so called Littoral Warfare in which the target and objectives are land, rather than sea based. This poses a whole host of problem scenarios, which have to be faced and overcome.

In order to successfully engage land targets, ships must operate much closer to hostile shores where they can come under attack from land-based aircraft and missiles, and where ASW operations are much more complex in relatively shallow, littoral waters. From an offensive viewpoint, naval weapon systems must be capable of striking deep inland. Tactical cruise missiles now form a vital part of the US naval armory and even conventional guns have been

RIGHT: USS *McFaul*, an Arleigh Burke class AEGIS destroyer commissioned in 1998. This view clearly shows the phased arrays of SPY-1D radar set into the sides of the bridge superstructure. Also of note is the single SPG-62 target illuminating radar atop the bridge.

ABOVE: The nuclear-powered USS *Virginia* was one of a class of four built in the mid-1970s. Heavily armed for their time, they lacked AEGIS air defense systems and were retired in 1998.

BELOW: Built during World War II, the Iowa class battelships played an active part in the Gulf War. With limited modernization their land attack capability was improved by Tomahawk TLAM missiles.

RIGHT: USS *Spruance* (DD 693), lead ship of a class of 31 ships. On the foredeck is a Mk. 45 5-in (127mm) gun and immediately in front of the bridge are the silos of the 64 cell Mk. 41 Vertical Launch System (VLS). Atop the bridge is a single Mk. 15 Phalanx Close In Weapon System (CIWS).

BELOW: For self protection all US carriers are fitted with the Mk. 15 Phalanx and the RAM short range missile system. These can be seen either side of the forward flight deck in this view of the USS *Harry S Truman* (CVAN 75).

improved to offer accurate fire support far inland from coasts and beachheads.

In this section all major US naval weapon systems are described and it is noticeable how many are now focused to support the new appreciation of the Navy's role in the post-Cold War era.

Missiles—Strategic and Land Attack

Trident

The most powerful weapon in the US Navy's arsenal, and probably one of the most destructive weapon systems ever devised, is the Trident submarine launched ballistic missile (SLBM). In its most developed D5 form, this has a range of 6,500nm (12,000km) and can carry up to 12 Multiple Independent Reentry Vehicles (MIRV) each with a 100 or 475 kiloton (maximum) nuclear warhead. The destructive power embodied in a single Trident II999 missile can barely be imagined, and the awesome potential of a full 24 missile complement carried by one Ohio class nuclear powered strategic missile submarine (SSBN) does not bear contemplation.

The original Trident I became operational in 1977 aboard the USS *Francis Key Scott,* but the US Navy first deployed strategic missiles at sea in 1960 when the 1,200nm (2,222km) range Polaris A-1 was test fired from the newly commissioned USS *George Washington.* Further development led to the Polaris A-3 with a range of 2,500nm (4,630km) and this remained in service until 1977. In the meantime it had been supplanted by the Poseidon SLBM, which entered service in 1970, and offered an increase in

ABOVE: USS *Wisconsin*, last of the great battelships which once rule the seas with 16-on (406mm) guns in the Norfolk Naval shipyard.

LEFT: The US Navy amphibious assault ship USS *Wasp* comes to the aid of the merchant cargo vessel *Sea Land Mariner* in the Mediterranean.

RIGHT, ABOVE: The USS *Theodore Roosevelt* conducts a Vertical Replenishment weapons on-load with the ammunition ship USS *Santa Barbara* as they steam in the waters off the Virginia coast.

RIGHT, BELOW: The USS *Vincennes* steams in front of three other classes of USN ships as they operate in the Pacific Ocean.

range to a maximum of 3,200nm (5,926km), although the more significant improvement was in the payload which could consist of up to 14 warheads compared to a maximum of six carried by Polaris. Poseidon remained operational until 1991, when as result of international treaty agreements, it was decided to decommission the ten Benjamin Franklin class SSBNs which still carried this missile.

Successor to both Polaris and Poseidon was the Lockheed Martin Trident I (C-4) whose development could be traced back to a study of US strategic forces in 1966. A requirement for a range of 6,000 miles (9,600km) was identified but a missile capable of this would be too large to be accommodated in the launch tubes of the Lafayette and Franklin class SSBNs then in service or building. Consequently the Trident I had a range of only 4,350nm (8,056km), although this represented a considerable increase over the older missiles and gave the US strategic submarine fleet a substantial increase in flexibility. Trident I was a three stage missile powered by solid fuel rocket motors. Overall length was 34ft (10.4m) and it weighed 31.75 tons at launch. (Polaris and Poseidon were single and two stage missiles respectively). The first Trident test firing took place in January 1977 and it became operational in 1979. Twelve Lafayette/ Franklin class SSBNs were converted to carry Trident I between 1978 and 1982, but these were all decommissioned in the early 1990s as the later Ohio class entered service.

The Ohio class SSBN were designed to carry the longer ranged Trident II (D-5) which has an overall length of 46ft (14m) and weighs 57.15 tons at launch. In fact the first eight Ohio's were armed with the older Trident I but this version has now been almost entirely superseded as a modernization program has updated the boats to carry the Trident II. Unlike earlier SLBMs, the Trident is capable of pinpoint accuracy thanks to a precision stellar-inertial guidance system augmented by GPS for terminal guidance. Consequently it can be used to accurately deliver non-nuclear warheads although the development of various cruise missile systems makes this an expensive way of delivering conventional ordnance.

LEFT: A Trident missile D4 is launched from the USS *John C Calhoun* during 1980s test firing. The Lafayette class were not large enough to carry the Trident D5, and were decommissioned in1994.

ABOVE: The US Navy provisions its strategic missile submarines at coastal bases in the states of Washington, South Carolina, and Georgia. The Ohio class submarines are designed to carry the 44ft (1.5m) long, 83in (2.1m) diameter Trident II missile.

LEFT: A torpedo room aboard the nuclear-powered ballistic missile submarine Ohio (SSBX-726).

Tomahawk Sea Launched Cruise Missile

The 1991 Gulf War saw the first operational use of a powerful new naval weapon system—the Sea Launched Cruise Missile (SLCM). Fired from installations mounted on the battleships *Wisconsin* and *Missouri*, and later from submarines positioned in the Red Sea, Tomahawk SLCMs were among the very first ordnance to hit strategic targets within Iraq. Although this was Tomahawk's baptism of fire, the missile system had been under development since 1974 and was initially deployed by the USN in 1983. General Dynamics were awarded the original development contract under the designation BGM-109 and the first Tomahawk test firing took place in 1976.

Tomahawk was originally envisaged as a submarine launched weapon and this immediately fixed the maximum dimensions as it was to be fired from a capsule loaded in a standard 21-in (0.5-m) torpedo tube. As developed, this version is ejected from the tube by the hydraulic torpedo firing gear and the 7,040lb (3,200kg) thrust Atlantic Research rocket booster is fired by a lanyard when the capsule is approximately 30ft (10m) ahead of the submarine. At this point the missile leaves the launch capsule and, angled up at 50°, accelerates to over 50mph (80kmph) before breaking the surface at which point an external protective shroud is cast off and the aerodynamic surfaces are extended. The 598lb (272kg) thrust Williams F107 jet engine is spun up by means of a starter cartridge ready to take over as the expended booster is detached. Nosing over into level flight the missile begins cruising toward the target.

Following closely on initial development of the submarine launched version, a number of other variants were proposed which included the short ranged antiship BGM-109B and the closely related land attack BGM-109C. Both of these carried conventional warheads as opposed to the nuclear armed BGM-109A fired from submarines, while the later

LEFT: The USS *Ohio* (SSBN-726) was the lead ship of a class of 18 SSBM commissioned 1981–97. They were specifically designed to deploy the Trident D5 strategic missile.

RIGHT: A Tomahawk is fired from a Vertical Launch System aboard the US Navy trials ship USS *Norton Sound*.

RIGHT: A completed Tomahawk undergoing final factory checks. The two engineers help convey its size.

BELOW: Tomahawk TLAM in flight. Note the aerodynamic surfaces and the scoop intake for the jet engine just under the rear of the missile body.

BOTTOM: Several warships were equipped to fire Tomahawk TLAM from a deck-mounted, armored four round launcher. These included the four Iowa class battleships and Virginia class cruisers. These are now decommissioned and all current surface warships utilize the Mk. 41 VLS.

D variant was similar to the C except that it carried a specialized submunitions warhead.

Although the antiship variant used relatively conventional guidance methods (inertial platform and active radar terminal homing) the others used a completely new system which relied heavily on digital computer techniques. This was known as TERCOM which stands for Terrain Comparison and is a technique of comparing a real time radar derived picture of the ground below the missile's flight path with a series of digitally stored spot heights for various sections of the route. Information derived from comparison of the two sets of data is used to establish position and update the missile's inertial navigation system. For the nuclear tipped missiles, this system offered a highly satisfactory degree of accuracy, although it was dependant on the provision of adequate amounts of mapping data, usually derived from satellite surveys. The Tomahawk's computer is capable of storing over 20 TERCOM maps which enable complex routings to be achieved, avoiding and decoying enemy defenses. The whole system is designated TERCOM assisted inertial navigation system (TAINS).

After launch, the Tomahawk is guided initially by its inertial navigation platform which is programmed with the required route. Between each TERCOM check the missile steers to preprogrammed waypoints in straight lines at predetermined speeds and altitudes. This ensures not only that it will reach the target but also that the precise time of impact can be

ABOVE: USS *Los Angeles* was the first of 51 similar nuclear-powered attack submarines commissioned between 1976 and 1996.

BELOW: USS *John Young* is a modern, multimission warship whose primary mission areas are offensive strike warfare and undersea warfare. *John Young* uses gas turbine power.

arranged to suit a specific tactical objective (e.g. to coincide with a conventional airstrike). Once in the vicinity of the target, guidance passes to a system known as the digital scene-matching area correlator (DSMAC). This uses a nose mounted TV camera from which images are compared with digitally stored images of the target or surrounding area. By steering the missile to give optimum correlation, the DSMAC guidance can achieve accuracies of around 30ft (10m), which is absolutely amazing after a flight of up to 700 miles.

The BGM-109B antiship variant (now known as TASM) was the first to enter service, and was carried aboard Los Angeles and Sturgeon class SSNs from 1983 and aboard surface vessels from 1984. Currently Tomahawk arms versions of the Spruance class, while the current DDG-51 Burke class are equipped to fire Tomahawks from the Mk. 41 vertical launcher which can also fire Harpoon, Vertical ASROC and Standard missiles. In 1985, a new launch system for submarines, consisting of 12 vertical launch tubes between the pressure and outer hulls, was introduced aboard the USS *Pittsburgh* (SSN 720), although in most submarines the missile is launched from conventional torpedo tubes.

The Tomahawk variant which saw service in the Gulf War was the BGM-109C, also called the Tactical Land Attack Missile (TLAM-C). It entered service in 1986 and carries a 1,000lb (455kg) HE warhead. At the start of the war it was reported that the US Navy had some 900 TLAM-Cs in service, of which around 500 were deployed in the region. In the first two weeks of hostilities no less than 300 missiles were launched, including at least one on January 19, from a submarine, although the majority came from two battleships. Since the Gulf War, Tomahawks have been fired operationally in the September 1995 Bosnia strike (Deliberate Force), strikes against Iraq in 1996 (Desert Strike), and more recently against Al Qaida targets in Afghanistan. Many of these were fired from submarines, including British Trafalgar class SSNs which are now armed with Tomahawk following successful firing trials by an RN SSBN in 1998. Since 1994, the latest Block III TLAM-C, deployed by both the USN and RN, has a range increased to 914nm (1,693km) and has a GPS back-up to the TAINS.

The nuclear armed TLAM-N (originally BGM-109A) is now capable of ranges up to 1,400nm (2,593km) at a cruising speed of Mach.0.7 and can

carry a 200 kiloton nuclear warhead. The adaptability and relative low cost of this weapon, combined with the restrictions of the START treaty mean that no more Trident armed SSBNs are likely to be built and their successor is the new Virginia class SSNs due to enter service from 2004 onward. These will be armed with TLAM-N and TASM, as are the three Seawolf SSN and there are also plans to convert some Ohio class SSBN to carry up to 154 Tomahawk missiles in 22 vertical launch silos.

The Tomahawk missile has proved to be most effective weapon system and enables warships to strike accurately at precise targets hundreds of miles inland. Before the demonstration of its capabilities under wartime conditions, its true potential had not been understood by many strategists but the Sea Launched Cruise Missile is now established as one of the prime assets of American seapower. To date some 950 TLAMs have been fired in action with an 85 percent on-target success rate.

SLAM—Stand-off Land Attack Missile

The successful development of cruise missiles led in the 1980s to a Navy requirement for a shorter ranged missile employing similar technology for use by tactical aircraft such as the carrier based F-18 Hornet. In this case the object was to provide the aircraft with the means to launch precision strikes from a distance in excess of 50 miles (80km), outside the range of the target's air defense systems.

In an effort to reduce costs and lead times it was decided to base the new weapon, known as the Stand-off Land Attack Missile (SLAM), on the existing air launched McDonnell Douglas AGM-84 Harpoon antiship missile. Following the award of the development contract, trials began in 1987 and McDonnell Douglas delivered the first SLAM to the US Navy from its production facility at St Charles, Missouri, in November 1988.

Although SLAM used the airframe, warhead, propulsion, and control systems of the basic Harpoon, there were significant changes in the guidance system to reflect the change of role. For navigation a Global Positioning System (GPS) was incorporated to update the missile's inertial navigation system and allow a suitable flight profile to be followed. In the final stages of the attack an infrared seeker is activated and this sends a video image to the pilot or the bombardier/navigator, who then selects the specific aiming point by means of crosshairs on

LEFT: Artist's concept of the SSN-21 Seawolf class nuclear-powered attack submarine.

RIGHT: Sea SLAM is a ship launched version of the air launched SLAM. Principal difference is the addition of booster motor for initial acceleration at launch.

LEFT: A Stand-Off Land Attack Missile (SLAM) is launched from an F/A18. SLAM was first operationally in the 1991 Gulf War against an Iraqi hydro-electric plant.

BELOW: A standard AGM-84 SLAM under the wing of a F/A18 Hornet. Note the hemispherical dome covering the IR seeker in the nose.

BOTTOM: SLAM-ER (Expanded Response) is currently in production for the USN. Designated AGM-84H, it offers increased range and upgraded guidance systems. External differences from the standard SLAM are the folding wings and revised nose geometry for the IR seeker

their cockpit display. Once the target is designated in this way, the seeker locks on to it and the missile completes the attack autonomously and with great accuracy. The use of an infrared seeker allows attacks to be carried out at night or in periods of poor visibility and, following a policy of using existing components wherever possible, this unit is identical to that used by the Maverick air-to-ground missile and the associated data link is taken from the Walleye guided bomb. The data link is extremely flexible, to the extent that the aircraft controlling the final attack may not be the one which launched the missile. This allows for considerable variation of tactics to further confuse defense systems and increase the chance of a successful attack.

Although still undergoing operational evaluation testing in 1991 when Operation "Desert Storm" commenced, the US Navy took the opportunity to try SLAM in action and it was successfully launched against an Iraqi hydro-electric plant. Since then the missile has passed into front line operational service and is currently available to all F/A-18 squadrons. SLAM has been the subject of improvements under a contract awarded to McDonnell Douglas in August 1994 for an Expanded Response program (SLAM ER). This retrofit program offers improved range and maneuverability through the use of redesigned wings, an improved and more lethal warhead, and new software to ease the task of the missile controller.

A ship launched version of SLAM, appropriately designated Sea SLAM, has been developed and this is entirely compatible with existing shipboard Harpoon command and launch infrastructure. There are some software modifications and a standard Harpoon missile booster kit is all that is required to convert the air launched SLAM into a Sea SLAM which can be fired from the standard Harpoon container launchers although some form of airborne control is still required for the final attack phase. Typically this could be carried out by the ship's helicopter. As well as the conventional high explosive warhead, Sea SLAM can also carry a variety of sub-munitions to attack soft targets or concentrations of

armored vehicles. At present this version is not deployed by the US Navy.

Antiship Missiles

RGM-84D/AGM-84/UGM-84 Harpoon

Harpoon is one of the most flexible naval weapon systems ever developed and is widely deployed throughout the navies of the United States and its allies. It was originally conceived as an air launched antiship weapon to be carried by P-3 Orion maritime patrol aircraft and the development program began around 1970 leading to the original AGM-84 Block 1 entering service in 1978. A requirement for long range led to the adoption of 600lb (1,320kg) thrust J402-CA-400 turbojet as the main propulsion and consequently the missile is subsonic with a cruising speed in the region of Mach 0.85. It is guided to

BELOW: Harpoon antiship missile being launched from a fixed deck mounted canister. Note the rear mounted booster motor which will fall away on completion of the launch phase.

ABOVE: An RGM-84 Harpoon antiship missile speeds toward its target at Mach 0.85.

RIGHT: A Harpoon missile blasts off from a deck mounted canister. Most destroyers can be fitted with two quadruple canister launchers.

its target by an onboard inertial navigation system with an active, frequency agile, J-band radar being switched on at a predetermined point for the terminal homing phase. The initial Block 1A variant flew directly to the target but subsequent Block 1B and 1C versions were capable of complex maneuvers in order to evade defenses and countermeasures. In parallel with the air launched AGM-84, a ship launched RGM-84 was developed and this could be fired from fixed deck mounted canisters or from various launcher systems, now including the Mk. 41 VLS. This latter version differed from the AGM-84 in that it incorporated a solid fuel booster rocket for initial acceleration from the launcher. This subsequently fell away as the missile continued toward the target using its jet sustainer motor. The surface launched RGM-84 has a range of approximately 80nm, while the AGM-84 can manage up to 120nm (222km). A 488lb (227 kg) high explosive warhead is capable of causing significant damage to any surface vessel. The RGM-84 has an overall length (including booster) of 15ft (4.6m) and a body diameter of 1.13ft

(0.343m). Wingspan over the fixed aerodynamic surfaces is 3ft (0.914m). Launch weight is 1,496lb (680kg). The air launched AGM-84 does not require a booster rocket and overall length is consequently shorter at 12.4ft (3.8m)

Britain's Royal Navy became a Harpoon customer in the wake of the Falklands War and their requirement for a sea-skimming capability resulted in the Block 1C variant which is the standard production version today. A Block 1D variant which featured a larger fuel tank and the ability to make a second attack if the first pass resulted in a miss was successfully tested in 1991, but production was shelved due to changing priorities with the end of the Cold War.

The US Navy's first operational use of Harpoon was in 1986 when AGM-84 missiles launched from A-6E Intruders sank two Libyan ships and further

ABOVE: This torpedo-shaped capsule is the container for a UGM-84 Sub Harpoon. The guide vanes at the rear ensure that the capsule reaches the surface at a suitable angle to discharge the missile.

LEFT: A standard quadruple container launcher for the Harpoon missile. Once installed aboard the ship, the missile requires no servicing and is permanently ready for activation and firing at short notice.

engagements against Iranian vessels in the Persian Gulf occurred in 1988. Harpoon was also used in the 1991 Gulf War.

Harpoon was also produced in the UGM-84 submarine launched version. The actual missile is enclosed in a torpedo sized capsule (ENCAP) which has positive buoyancy so that it floats to the surface after discharge from conventional torpedo tubes. Fins on the ENCAP ensure that it reaches the surface at a suitable angle for missile launch. At this point the capsule nose is blown off and the missile booster motor fired. One problem with the UGM-84 is that accurate long target information is not always available to the parent submarine and this may have to be provided by an external source such as an aircraft or surface ship. At shorter ranges, sonar derived information can provide accurate enough data for an

attack. The UGM-84 arms all current US Navy attack submarines.

Harpoon was developed by the McDonnell Douglas company, now part of Boeing, and the missile family was originally envisaged to remain in service until 2015. However, constant improvements and upgrades have maintained Harpoon as a creditable weapons system and no replacement is currently scheduled. To date well over 6,000 missiles have been produced and it is in service with navies and air forces around the world.

AGM-119 Penguin

In US Navy service the Penguin antiship missile arms SH-60 Seahawk helicopters deployed aboard cruisers, destroyers, and the FFG-7 class frigates. Originally developed by Norway as a surface-to-surface missile to arm Fast Attack Craft, it proved to be most adaptable and can now be launched from ships, helicopters and aircraft.

ABOVE: The Norwegian designed Penguin antiship missile arms SH-60 and SH-2G Seasprite helicopters carried aboard destroyers and frigates. Note the folding fins which are deployed after launch.

BELOW: Artist's impression of a Penguin antiship missile being launched from a SH-60B helicopter whose search radar will have been used to provide target data prior to launch.

Its history goes back to the 1950s when the Norwegian Navy conducted a searching review of its role in the light of the massive growth of the Soviet Navy and a decision was made to concentrate on a force of small, fast, well-armed patrol boats and, in particular, the future importance of the surface-to-surface missile was recognized (even though no operational examples existed at the time). As a result, in 1962, development of a suitable missile was initiated under a contract awarded to Kongsberg, who at that time were heading up a European consortium that was about to commence production of the US designed air launched Bullpup missile for various NATO air forces. It was natural, therefore ,that several Bullpup components, including the warhead, should find their way into the new Penguin. The other significant feature was the guidance system, which relied on passive infrared for final target acquisition, as opposed to the more conventional radar seeker used by almost every subsequent antiship

TOP: An AGM-114B Hellfire missile roars off the rails of a US Navy SH-60 Seahawk helicopter toward a laser designated surface target during training off the coast of California.

ABOVE: An SH-60 Seahawk helicopter assigned to Helicopter Antisubmarine Squadron Seven hovers off the bow of the aircraft carrier USS *Enterprise*.

missile. This was partly for practical reasons, since at that time radar seekers were relatively bulky, but also because in the likely area of operations around Norway's rocky coast and steep sided fjords there would be considerable radar clutter to be overcome.

Although developed and produced in Norway, there was actually considerable US involvement in the program including financial assistance and the provision of test facilities. A total of 60 development and evaluation rounds were produced between 1964 and service entry in 1971, when it armed Storm class missile boats of the Royal Norwegian Navy. The original Mk. 1 Penguin weighed 750lbs (340kg) at launch and was powered by a Raufoss dual thrust solid fuel rocket motor. Housed in a fiberglass container bolted to the deck, the missile was launched by a two second firing of the boost stage after which the sustainer stage continued to accelerate the missile to its cruise speed of Mach 0.8 out to a maximum range of 12.4 miles (20km). Prior to launch the missile's inertial guidance system was provided with basic target data (e.g. bearing, range, rate of crossing, etc.) to enable it to close to within 3 miles (5km) at which point the infrared seeker was activated. During the cruise, the missile maintained a height of approximately 328ft (100m) using information derived from a pulsed laser altimeter (heady stuff for the early 1960s!). The 250lb (113kg) Mk. 19 Bulldog warhead was sufficient to cause significant damage, even to large ships. A missile could be activated and launched in two minutes, but this reaction time was cut to seconds if the seeker head cooling was already functioning. Time of flight was around 85 seconds to maximum range. A modified Mk. 2 with longer range was subsequently adopted and test firings of a Mk. 3 variant developed for launching from airborne platforms was test fired in 1984.

When the Norwegian Air Force developed the Mk. 3 for use aboard fast jets, the US Navy investigated the possibility of arming the standard SH-60B Seahawk helicopter with the missile in order to provide an effective antiship capability. The version selected for trials was designated Mk. 2 Mod. 7 and the first contract, for 64 missiles, was signed in 1989. In the meantime, a test program culminated in the first successful launch from an SH-60 in December 1989 and further firings in 1990. In US service the Penguin is designated AGM-119B and is in fact a hybrid, combining features of both the Mk. 2 and 3. Although air launched, the two stage motor of the Mk. 2 is incorporated to provide acceleration to cruise speed as the launch helicopter has a relatively low airspeed. However the guidance system is substantially the same as that of the Mk. 3 and incorporates a radar altimeter instead of the pulsed laser type used in the shipboard variants.

An obvious external difference between the two air launched versions is that the Mod. 7 has folding wing surfaces to facilitate storage aboard ship and carriage on the UH-60 weapon pylon. The use of the Raufoss two-stage, solid fuel, rocket motor reduces range to around 21 miles (34km) compared to 34 miles (55km) for the Mk. 3. Overall dimensions: length 9.8ft (3m), span 4.5ft (1.4m), 1.8ft/0.56m with wings folded and body diameter 0.9ft (0.28m).

The UH-60 is equipped with a Texas Instruments AN/APS-124 search radar which is used for target location and designation. Coordinates are fed to the missile's inertial guidance system and after launch, a preprogrammed route is flown to the point at which the IR seeker is activated. Alternatively, targets can be designated from visual sightings. For launch, the helicopter must have some forward airspeed to prevent an initial pitch up of the missile which free falls for less than half a second to allow the wings to extend before the booster motor phase ignites. Although the Mod. 7 does not have a sea-skimming capability, its small radar cross section, agility, and passive infrared homing system makes it difficult to detect and consequently gives it a good chance of defeating modern countermeasures including fast reaction CIWS.

AAW (Antiaircraft Warfare Missiles)

AEGIS/Standard

The Standard Missile is the US Navy's primary surface-to-air fleet defense weapon and its development goes back to the 1960s when it evolved as a replacement for the earlier Terrier and Tartar from which it utilized many components. The original SM-1 missile was produced in MR (medium range) and ER (extended range) versions, the former having an overall length of 14.4ft (4.4m) and was powered by a single-stage, dual thrust rocket motor, while the lat-

RIGHT: The Standard missile was developed from the Tartar and Terrier surface-to-air missiles, which armed destroyers, frigates and cruisers in the 1960s and 1970s. Photo shows a Tartar test firing aboard the trails ship *Norton Sound*.

BELOW RIGHT: An SM-1MR Standard missile on a single arm Mk. 13 launcher aboard a FFG-7 class frigate.

BOTTOM RIGHT: The Mk. 13 launcher is raised to the vertical position to allow missile loading from the magazine below.

ter featured two-stage booster and sustainer motors and consequently length was increased to 26ft (8m). Maximum ranges were approximately 25nm (40km) and 100nm (160km) respectively. The SM-1 employed a conventional command guidance system, with semi-active homing for the terminal phase, which required a target illuminating radar on the parent ship. SM-1R is now only deployed aboard Oliver Hazard Perry class frigates which utilize the SPG-60 fire control radar.

The larger Tioconderoga (CG-47) class cruisers and Arleigh Burke destroyers are armed with the developed SM-2MR/ER which is similar in to the SM-1 in terms of size and propulsion system but achieves greater flexibility and range through the introduction of a more sophisticated guidance system based on an onboard inertial platform—the first to be fitted to any tactical missile system. Terminal guidance is still by semi-active homing using an illuminating radar. Aboard the early CG-47 ships the SM-2MR was fired from a Mk. 26 twin launcher on the foredeck but later vessels incorporated the Mk. 41 VLS, as do all of the Arleigh Burke class destroyers which deploy the SM-2ER. The SM-2MR weighs 1,380lbs (621kg) at launch while the figure for the larger SM-2ER is 2,980lbs (1,341kg). Both attain speeds of Mach 2 and carry a high explosive fragmentation warhead triggered by a proximity fuze.

The current Standard SM-2 is an integral part of the AEGIS weapons system (named after the shield of Zeus in Greek mythology) based on the distinctive SPY-1 phased array radar which utilizes electronic scanning instead of the traditional rotating antenna associated with conventional radar. This enables simultaneous search and tracking functions, and allows AEGIS to meet its intended purpose of dealing simultaneously with multiple aerial targets. In the

ABOVE: A close up of the midships section of the USS *Winston S Churchill* (DDG-81) showing two more SPG-62 radars aft of the funnels.

face of such an attack, an AEGIS equipped ship can launch numerous Standard missiles in rapid succession and each is tracked toward its designated target by the SPY-1 radar. In the closing stages of the engagement, AEGIS directs an SPG-62 target illuminator briefly at the target while the SM-2 completes the interception using semi-active homing. The SPG-62 is then directed at the next priority target, which is already being closed by another SM-2. This method of engagement is significantly different from that used by the SM-1 and some non-AEGIS equipped ships deployed the SM-2, where the illuminating radar was required to track the target throughout the whole engagement, from missile launch to interception. In order to permit rapid multiple missile launches from the Mk. 41 VLS, a special version of the SM-2MR/ER, was produced in which the booster uses thrust vectoring instead of movable tail surfaces for directional control immediately after the launch.

Further development of the SM-2 was initiated to meet the Navy's requirement for a Theater Ballistic Missile Defense system (TBMD). The resulting Block IVA version was test fired in 1997 and successfully intercepted a ballistic missile target. However, the problems associated with producing a fully operational and effective TBMD capability have proved more difficult than anticipated and the program has currently been shelved.

RIM-7 Sea Sparrow

By the early 1960s, the US Navy began to realize that a considerable gap was opening up between the performance of a long-range system, such as Talos and Terrier, and the outdated short-range gun systems then in service. In order to save on costs and development time, the US Navy decided to adapt the highly successful AIM-7 Sparrow air-to-air missile for shipboard use as part of what was termed the Basic Point Defense Missile System (BPDMS).

AEGIS WEAPON SYSTEM MARK 7

ABOVE: USS *Arleigh Burke* (DDG51) was launched in 1989 as the lead ship of a class of AEGIS destroyer and is named after an able and distinguished destroyer captain (later admiral) who fought several successful actions in the Pacific during World War II.

LEFT: This schematic of the AEGIS weapon system gives some idea of the major components which together form a complex, but effective defense against multiple simultaneous air attacks. Core of the system is the SPY-1 phased array radar together with the SM-2 standard surface-to-air missile.

ABOVE: A standard eight-cell Mk. 29 launcher system for the Sea Sparrow. short range surface-to-air missile. This type of launcher arms the Spruance class destroyers and also a number of NATo warships.

BELOW: A Sea Sparrow missile leaps from the aft Mk. 29 launcher aboard a Spruance class destroyer. Maximum engagement range is in the order of 8 miles (12.8km), covered in less than 15 seconds at Mach 2.5.

The Sparrow missile itself was an early generation air-to-air missile, which had begun development in 1946 and eventually entered full-scale service in 1956. It has subsequently been updated several times and is still in widespread service today. The initial version selected for shipboard use was the AIM-7E which utilized semi-active radar homing whereby the missile homes onto reflected radar signals from a target illumination radar mounted on the launch vehicle (aircraft or ship).

BPDMS was a relatively crude system and suffered from a number of limitations, particularly against low flying targets. However, its relative simplicity and low cost led to its adoption by NATO as the basis for a standard short range antiaircraft missile system under the designation NATO Sea Sparrow Missile System (NSSMS). Development of this improved version followed from a Memorandum of Understanding signed by the US, Belgium, Denmark, Italy, and Norway in 1968 (subsequently The Netherlands and Germany joined the program) and Raytheon, the manufacturers, were awarded an initial contract for three systems. The first of these was fitted to the Knox class frigate USS *Downes*, which began test firings in 1972. NATO Sea Sparrow

differed from BPDMS in several key areas. The missile itself was the RIM-7H, which featured folding fins to fit a much smaller, purpose designed, lightweight, eight-cell launcher (Mk. 29). New digital electronics and components for the FCS were developed by companies from Italy, Denmark, and Norway while a new power driven Mk. 91 director incorporated an I/J band continuous wave radar for target tracking and illumination and also a TV camera for visual monitoring of the engagement. A complete NSSMS shipboard outfit weighed 28,648lbs 12.994kg), including the eight missiles in the launcher. Following successful trials, full production of NATO Sea Sparrow began in 1975.

Meanwhile in the United States development of the basic Sparrow missile continued and in 1980 tests began on a new version, the AIM-7M, which featured a monopulse radar seeker in the nose together with an on-board autopilot and other electronic improvements. These changes meant that target illumination was not required continuously, but only for mid-course corrections and terminal guidance. This, in turn meant that the launch vehicle could fire several missiles at different targets in rapid sequence. The new Sea Sparrow variant was designated RIM-7M and was capable of being fired by all existing systems. However, following successful tests,

ABOVE: A sequence of photos showing a VLS Sea Sparrow arching over onto the target bearing immediately after launch.

BELOW: The Mk. 91 fire control radar associated with the Sea Sparrow Missile System. There are separate transmit and receive aerials and this example also incorporates a boresighted electro-optical tracker between the antenna.

which began in 1981, a new vertical launch system became available for Sea Sparrow and the RIM-7M could be adapted for this mode of firing. Sea Sparrow missiles modified for VLS incorporate a jettisonable jet vane control unit (JVC). Bolted to the missile's tail section, the JVC has its own built-in processor and a hydraulic system that moves vanes within the rocket motor's exhaust to turn the missile on course to the target after the launch. As with all VL systems, this arrangement does away with complex launchers and offers a 360° coverage from a single installation.

Sea Sparrow is today in service aboard over 100 ships operated by ten navies and continued improvement has resulted in the current production version, the RIM-7P. The naval version of this multipurpose missile features folding wings and clipped fins to allow compatibility with all launch systems and can be fitted with a JVC for vertical launch. A new missile borne digital computer includes Erasable Programmable ROM chips, which allow quick and easy reprogramming of the guidance software to counter new threats. It also has an improved Low Altitude Guidance Mode, which enhances the discrimination of very low targets against a background that is heavily cluttered.

Other electronic improvements include a data link for mid-course guidance and built-in test circuitry to enhance maintainability and confirm readiness on the launcher. A further version is the RIM-7R, which incorporates an infrared guidance and homing system to complement the standard semi-active radar seeker. In addition, it has a more powerful rocket motor with a new autopilot to allow rapid response and high energy maneuvers against the late detection of high speed agile threats. The RIM-7R is compatible with existing launcher systems including the NATO standard Mk. 29 and the Mk. 41 and Mk. 48 VL systems.

BELOW: All US Navy carriers are armed with NATO Sea Sparrow for point defense, each ship carrying three Mk. 29 launchers. This example is being fired from the USS *John F Kennedy* (CV67).

ABOVE: A RIM-7 Sea Sparrow missile launches from the destroyer USS *Cushing* (DD985), a Spruance class destroyer completed in 1979. these ships carry a single Mk. 29 launcher abaft of the helicopter flight deck.

RIM-162 Evolved Sea Sparrow Missile (ESSM)

As its name implies, this is a development of the RIM-7P Sea Sparrow. A larger diameter after body contains a new rocket motor incorporating thrust vectoring for directional control and eliminating the need for winged control surfaces. The onboard guidance system is improved and a variety of operating modes are available. The ESSM has been designed to be fired from the standard Mk. 41 VLS with a quad pack of four missiles in each silo. It is also compatible with the Mk. 48 VLS and Mk. 29 multicell trainable launchers. An initial production order was placed in late 2001.

RIM-116 RAM (Rolling Airframe Missile)

The initial impetus for a new short range air defense system came from the German Navy in the mid 1970s, backed by a similar requirement from the Danish Navy, while the US Navy saw the new system as a candidate to arm the Tarawa class LHAs and the Iwo Jima class LPHs. Accordingly a joint US, German, and Danish program was launched and development began in 1976. Although loosely based on the Sidewinder, the new missile adopted a new and entirely novel method of aerodynamic control which was intended to increase maneuverability and safe weight by reducing the number of active control surfaces. In flight, the missile would slowly but continuously rotate under the effect of the four fixed tail fins, while directional control would be exerted by two canard surfaces on the forebody, these being sequentially deflected to provide the required change of course. A conventional missile, such as the original Sidewinder, would normally have required four canard control surfaces, each with its own actuator, so there was an immediate weight advantage to be gained by adopting the more unusual approach. This unique control system led to the name Rolling Airframe Missile (RAM), which was applied to the new weapon that was otherwise designated as the RIM-116A.

The final configuration meant that the only Sidewinder components incorporated in the RAM were the rocket motor, warhead, and fuze. The original infrared seeker was replaced by a more compact

IR unit from the shoulder launched Stinger missile, but an additional target seeker in the form of RF (Radio/radar frequency) seeker was also incorporated. It was intended that the IR unit would home onto the forward aspect glint of a missile or aircraft or, alternatively, the RF seeker would home onto any radar emissions from the target (typically a radar-guided antishipping missile). A bonus of the rolling airframe concept was that only two RF aerials were required to obtain a three-dimensional tracking capability rather than the four needed in a conventional missile.

In action the missile would be fired in response to active radar, passive electronic, or optical warning and would be launched on a selected bearing and elevation. RF mid-course guidance is available, but RAM normally shifts to IR guidance for the final homing, although RF guidance can continue if weather conditions are unsuitable for IR functioning. This method of operation means that RAM is effectively a "fire and forget" system, a characteristic, which coupled with the relatively small size of the shipboard installation, opens up the possibility of

ABOVE: A Marine AV-8A Harrier light attack jet aircraft lifts off the flight deck of the 820ft (250m) multipurpose amphibious assault ship USS *Tarawa*.

providing small ships with the capability of dealing effectively with multiple targets. It is this capability which sets RAM apart from other similar short range defense systems.

It was hoped that the use of proven components in the missile and launcher systems would reduce the development period of the missile system, but in fact the reverse was true and when RAM finally entered service in the mid 1990s, it was some 12 years behind schedule. Most of the delays were due to practical problems related to the unique control and guidance system, but political and cost difficulties also contributed to the ever lengthening timescale.

The main US Contractor is the Hughes Corporation, and missile production is centered in Germany where it is carried out by the RAM System GmbH Consortium consisting of MBB, AEG-Telefunken and RTG. In US service the Mk. 31 RAM Guided Missile Weapons System (GWMS)

ABOVE: The Tarawa class amphibious assault ships were among the first to be armed with RAM for close-in self defense. Two Mk. 49 launchers are carried; above the bridge and starboard side, right aft.

includes a Mk. 49 Guided Weapon Launching System and a Mk. 44 Guided Missile Round Pack. The weapon system is extensively fitted throughout the amphibious warfare fleet including Tarawa class LHAs and Wasp class LHDs. Following various test firings and operational evaluations (OPEVAL), the first fleet firing of RAM was carried out from USS *Peleliu* (LHA-5) in October 1995.

Weighing 33lb (15kg), Ram carries a 6.6lb (3kg) proximity fused fragmentation warhead out to a range of 6 miles (10km) at speeds up to Mach 2. The initial production RIM-116A (Block 0) used a combination of RF/IR homing but the current RIM-116B (Block 1) missile has upgraded IR seeker which allows engagement of non-RF-radiating targets. Block 1 development trials were successfully completed in 1999; RAM was demonstrated against a variety of antiship missiles such as Harpoon and Exocet. Further software changes will enable other targets, such as helicopters, fixed wing aircraft, and small surface craft, to be engaged. RAM is also being tested in a new hybrid system known as SEA RAM which is described in the gun section of this chapter.

USW (Undersea Warfare) Weapons

RUR-5 ASROC

ASROC (the acronym for Antisubmarine Rocket) development began in 1955 to meet a USN requirement for an automated weapon system capable of deploying a Mk. 44 homing torpedo at ranges initially in excess of 10,000 yards (9,144m), which coincided with the ranges then being attained by contemporary shipboard sonars. The actual missile, designated RUR-5A, was simple enough and comprised an NPP (Naval Propellant Plant) boost solid fuel rocket with a thrust of 11,000lbs (4,990kg) in tandem with the Mk. 44 torpedo. Cruciform aerodynamic surfaces were attached to the rocket motor body and a parachute assembly was employed to lower the payload into the water after the booster separated on command from the fire control system.

LEFT: An eight-cell Mk. 112 ASROC launcher was standard when the anti submarine missile was introduced in 1960. It has now been almost entirely superseded by the Mk. 41 VLS although a few CG-47 class cruisers still retain the Mk. 26 twin Launcher.

RIGHT: An ASROC (RUR-5A) antisubmarine missile is launched from USS *Brooke* during fire power demonstrations.

BELOW, RIGHT: A huge underwater explosion following the launch of an ASROC antisubmarine missile during exercises from the destroyer USS *Agerholm*.

The missile had an overall length of 15ft (4m) (including the torpedo 8.75ft/2.67m long), body diameter of 12.75in (0.33m) and a wingspan of 2.8ft (0.85m). Launch weight was 957lbs (435kg).

In order to make effective use of the missile, a new sophisticated fire control system known as the MK. 114 Underwater Battery Fire Control System (UBFCS) was developed by the Singer Company under contract from Honeywell who were awarded the prime weapon system contact in 1956. In a typical engagement the target submarine is located by sonar and range and bearing data are passed to the Mk. 114 FCS, which then continuously computes the projected future target position while, at the same time, setting the separation point for the booster motor and launcher onto the correct bearing for firing. As soon as a solution is reached, the firing circuit is activated and the missile is launched. After separation the torpedo drops into the water close to the target, the parachute is released, it homes onto the submarine. ASROC was also designed to carry a W-44 nuclear depth charge instead of a torpedo and the accuracy of the system was enough to ensure target destruction in this mode of attack.

Although ASROC was designed to use a variety of launchers, the most common was the distinctive Mk. 112 eight-cell box which could rotate through 360°, while each vertical pair of boxes could be elevated to 45° for firing. Later ships could fire ASROC from the simplified Mk. 26 twin arm launchers, which could also fire Standard MR surface-to-air missiles. In this configuration each launcher is fed from one of three rotary drum magazines below decks, which respectively hold torpedo armed ASROC, depth charge ASROC or Standard MR SAMs, and loading of the appropriate weapon is controlled from the ship's operations room.

ASROC entered service with the US Navy in 1961 and the system was upgraded in 1965 when it was adapted to carry the Otto fuelled Mk. 46 lightweight torpedo (cf). The eight-cell Mk. 112 launcher became a familiar fitting on almost all new major US warships, although the first installations were aboard modernized wartime Gearing class destroyers which were converted to specialized ASW vessels under the FRAM 1 program begun in 1959.

When the Terrier SAM missile evolved into the current Standard surface-to-air missile, the dual purpose Mk. 26 launcher capable of handling ASROC was introduced and subsequently fitted to many ships completed from around 1976 onward. This included: the four Virginia class CGN, the Ticonderoga class AEGIS cruisers, and Kidd class DDGs. An exception to this were the 31 Spruance class DDGs, which continued to use the eight box launcher, although a new loading system was incorporated whereby the missiles where stowed vertically below the launcher that was in turn elevated to the vertical for reloading.

ASROC is widely deployed as the standard medium range ASW system in the US Navy and consequently it is unsurprising that the system has been widely adopted by foreign navies. Customers include Brazil, Canada, Greece, Italy, Japan, Pakistan, South Korea, Spain, Taiwan, Turkey, and Germany.

RIGHT: A Vertical Launch ASROC (VLA) emerges dramatically from its silo in a Mk. 41 launcher system.

RUM-139 Vertical Launch ASROC (VLA)

ASROC has proved adaptable to a wide range of launcher systems and the Arleigh Burke class DDGs introduced a new vertical launch variant of ASROC fired from the ship's Mk. 41 VLS launchers. This incorporates a total of 90 silos, which can carry either ASROC or Standard MR missiles. VLS ASROC (VLA), which entered service in 1987, has an increased range (9nm/16.7km) and is slightly longer than the standard version as it incorporates an additional booster for the launch and initial turn over maneuver. It carries a Mk. 46 Mod. 5 homing torpedo. The VLS system has also been fitted to later units of the Ticonderoga class AEGIS cruisers.

Prior to launch, the missile can be programmed through the Mk. 116 Underwater Fire Control System (UFCS) with tactical data from a wide variety of sources including hull mounted AN/SQS-53B sonar, NTDS data links with other ships and aircraft, AN/SQR-19 towed array sonar, and helicopter laid sonobuoys. The missile is housed in a canister, which is inserted directly into the launcher silo and no shipboard maintenance is then required prior to firing.

At one stage ASROC/VLA was scheduled to be replaced by the XMGM-52B Sea Lance intended to carry a Mk. 50 Advanced Light Weight Torpedo or an optional nuclear warhead. However, this was cancelled and VLA remains in service. A submarine launched version of ASROC (Subroc) carrying a W55 nuclear warhead was also deployed from 1962 onward, but this was withdrawn in the early 1990s.

Mk. 46 ASW Torpedo

The Mk. 46 is the standard NATO antisubmarine weapon and is deployed by a wide variety of ships, helicopters, and fixed wing aircraft. It became operational in 1967 and subsequently replaced the earlier Mk. 44 torpedo. Capable of speeds in excess of 45 knots and carrying a 98lb (44kg) PBXN-103 high explosive warhead, it has a maximum range of 12,000 yards (11km) although a more typical running distance is 8000 yards. The current version is the Mk. 46 Mod. 5 Neartip which has a length of 8.5ft (2.6m) and a diameter of 12.75in (0.33m). Its

ABOVE: An air drop version of the Mk. 46 torpedo shown on its handling trolley.

RIGHT: The Mk. 46 is designed to seek out and destroy high-speed submarines. These extremely effective weapons can be launched by more than 20 different launch platforms from antisubmarine warfare surface ships as well as aircraft.

total weight is 517lb (235kg) and propulsion is supplied by an Otto fuelled (monopropellent) two-speed reciprocating engine. With a running time of 6–8 minutes, the Mk. 46 commences a circular search on reaching the target area and uses Active or Active/Passive homing in during the terminal phase. Aboard surface ships, the Mk. 46 is fired from the NATO standard deck mounted Mk. 32 triple torpedo tubes.

The Mk. 46 also forms an integral part of other weapon systems, notably the ASROC long-range ASW system described above. All current ASROC systems carry the Mod. 5 Neartip versions as the payload. The Mk. 46 Mod. 4 is a version specifically produced for incorporation in the CAPTOR mine system described later.

Mk. 48 Torpedo

The modern torpedo is a complex weapon system of possibly greater sophistication than airborne guided missiles and their design and development consequently spans decades rather than years. The Mk. 48 is no exception and initial work began in 1960, although it did not become operational with the US Navy until 1972. In its original form it could reach speeds of 55 knots and, at a slower speed of 40 knots, was capable of ranges up to 24nm (45km).

Propulsion was by means of a 500hp Otto cycle swashplate motor and total weight was 3,434lb (1545kg). The engine drives twin contra rotating propellers enclosed in a ducted shroud. Overall length was 19ft (5.8m) and the Mk. 48 was designed to be discharged from standard 21in (0.5m) torpedo tubes aboard surface vessels and submarines, although today there are no surface ships equipped in this way.

After firing, the Mk. 48 can follow programmed target search, acquisition, and attack procedures using active and/or passive homing for the final stages. Alternatively it can be wire-guided from the parent submarine throughout part or all of the engagement. If it misses the target at the first pass, it can then conduct multiple attacks until successful.

In 1978, development of a new heavyweight torpedo began, although this utilized many components of the basic Mk. 48. The resulting Mk. 48 ADCAP (Advanced Capability) became operational in 1988 and has now completely replaced the earlier version aboard all US submarines. The main difference related to the guidance and control system, which utilized modern digital technology, and the warhead fusing system was also upgraded. Engine performance was enhanced and additional fuel carried to allow an increase in range. The torpedo body shell was strengthened to allow greater diving depths, reputedly down to 3,000ft (900m), in order to counter deep diving Russian submarines such as the Alpha class. A speed in excess of 60knots has been quoted for the Mk. 48 ADCAP and range at 40knots is believed to be almost 30nm (55km). Both versions carry a 650lb (293kg) high explosive warhead but the ADCAP improvements resulted in an overall weight increase to 3,695lb (1,663kg).

Development of the Mk. 48 ADCAP continues with the emphasis on improved performance in shallow littoral waters against conventional diesel powered submarines and also to reduce its vulnerability to countermeasures.

ABOVE, LEFT: A Mk. 48 torpedo undergoes fuel tank stress measurement tests at the Naval Torpedo Station, Keyport, Washington.

LEFT: At 1.5 tons the Mk. 48 torpedo needs careful handling, as shown by this example being loaded aboard the USS *Pargo* a Sturgeon class SSN, at Cape Kennedy, Florida.

Mk. 50 Torpedo

Otherwise known as the Advanced Lightweight Torpedo (ALWT), the Mk. 50 is intended as the successor to the ubiquitous Mk 46. Development began in 1974 and OPEVAL started in 1990, although the latter highlighted some serious shortcomings, mainly software related and redesign and testing continued throughout the 1990s. Many problems were identified as being related to operator competency and familiarization and efforts have been made to improve matters in this respect, although at a cost of $70,000 for each exercise firing, training has been restricted. The current Mk. 50 Block 1 Upgrade torpedo can be air dropped from P-3 maritime patrol aircraft and a variety of helicopters including SH-2, SH-3, and SH-60. The Mk. 50 is also deployed in limited numbers aboard surface ships that also still carry substantial numbers of the earlier Mk. 46. Both can be fired from the standard Mk. 32 triple tubes.

The Mk. 50 torpedo is 111in (0.29m) long, has a diameter of 12.75in (0.3m), and weighs 775lbs (352kg). An active/passive sonar is mounted in the nose and torpedo operation is software controlled to define search and attack profiles. The warhead consists of a 100lb (45kg) shaped charge. Basically a fire and forget weapon, the Mk. 50 is faster (45kts) and deeper diving (to 2,000ft/600m) than the Mk. 46. Propulsion is by means of a closed cycle chemical reaction system utilizing a lithium-based fuel.

Mines

The US Navy no longer deploys specialist minelaying surface ships and all current mines in the US inventory are capable of being laid by aircraft or submarines. Today mines are a very sophisticated weapons systems and bear little resemblance to the traditional World War II contact mine. The most common air dropped mine is the Mk. 55, which contains a 1,275lb (577kg) HBX-1 high explosive charge and is produced in a variety of versions including Mod. 2 (magnetic influence), Mod. 3 (pressure/magnetic influence), Mod. 5 (acoustic/magnetic influence), Mod. 6 (pressure/acoustic/magnetic), and Mod. 7 (dual channel magnetic).

This combination of influences, which can be set to detonate the mine and enable minefields to be set up, will only be activated by very specific targets. Total drop weight is in the region of 2,200lb (997kg).

The other common air dropped weapon is the Mk. 56, which is of similar size and weight, but is a moored magnetic influence mine.

Submarines are equipped to lay the Mk. 60 CAPTOR mine, which is a moored capsule containing a sensing element to detect and track targets, and a standard Mk. 46 homing torpedo. Intended primarily as an antisubmarine weapon, the Mk. 60 is capable of being moored in depths up to 1,000ft (300m), and its acoustic processor can track and classify targets. On acquiring a suitable target, the Mk. 46 is released vertically and then completes a standard engagement. The submarine version can be launched from standard 21-in (0.5-m) torpedo tubes and weighs just over 2,000lbs (907kg). There is also an air dropped version which is slightly heavier.

Submarines also carry the Mk. 67 SLMM (Submarine Launched Mobile Mine). This is basically an obsolete Mk. 37, conventional 21-in (0.5-m) torpedo modified to act as a mine. It is fired from the submarine and, at the end of its run, settles in a precalculated position enabling the submarine to remain clear of the area to be mined. The 326lb (148kg) HE warhead can be detonated by either pressure, magnetic, or acoustic target detection devices (TDD). The new Virginia class SSNs, due to be commissioned from 2004 onward, will be equipped with a mobile mine version of the Mk 48 torpedo.

The US Navy can also call upon large quantities of aircraft dropped Quickstrike mines. These are in effect standard Mk. 82/83/84 streamlined bombs, which are modified by the attachment of an exploder triggered by a TDD to act as a bottom mine in relatively shallow waters. These can be quickly produced and laid, obviating the need to hold stocks of more conventional moored mines.

Guns

The gun is the traditional naval weapon, although it has been eclipsed by the guided missile since World War II. However, it is making something of a comeback as modern technology is applied to the weapon itself, advance ammunition, and fire control systems. Although the US Navy has long since standardized on the 5-in (127-mm) gun, the recent emphasis on littoral warfare has led to the requirement for heavier weaponry, and the new DD(X) class destroyers will almost certainly carry a 6in (155mm) Advanced Gun System. This will fire a guided munition weighing approximately 120lb (54kg), substantially heavier than the 70lb (32kg) shell fired by the current Mk .45 5in (127mm)/54cal. although maximum range will be similar to that achieved by the later 5in (127mm)/62cal. Rate of fire will be about 12rpm.

The development of guided munitions, equipped with folding aerodynamic surfaces and boosted by rocket motors, opens the possibility of an entirely new type of gun with a fixed vertical barrel mounted within the ship. After firing, the projectile can be turned onto the desired trajectory by its guidance system in a manner similar to vertically launched missiles. Such a weapon would do away with complex turrets and mountings, and ammunition supply could be much simplified, leading in turn to increased rates of fire.

Technology of this nature is beginning to blur the distinction between guns and missiles. In the meantime, most ships carry relatively conventional gun systems, which are described next.

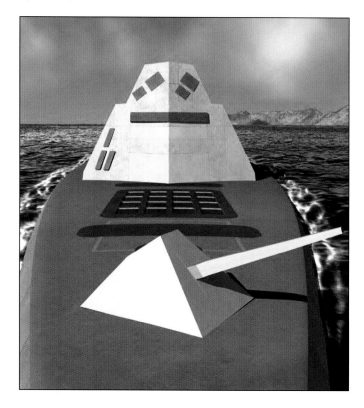

RIGHT: An impression of the 6.1-in (155mm) Advanced Gun System (AGS) aboard the DD21/DD(X) project.

Mk. 45 5-in (127-mm) Gun

The United States Navy has used the 5-in (127mm) gun as its standard medium caliber gun since it was introduced in 1907 as the secondary armament of contemporary battleships.

In World War II the ubiquitous dual purpose 5in (127mm)/38cal. weapon was used to arm everything from destroyer escorts up to battleships and aircraft carriers and, as a legacy, it has been widely adopted by many of the world's navies. In the postwar era, the USN developed automatic mountings that used the longer barreled 5in (127mm)/54cal. gun introduced at the end of the war. The first of these to see service was the Mk. 42 system, now replaced by the current lightweight Mk. 45 mounting.

The Mk. 45 gun system consists of two component groups, an upper and a lower structure. The former is defined as everything above deck level and includes all components necessary to load the ammunition, aim the gun, fire the ammunition, and eject the empty cartridge cases. To save weight, the gun and mounting is protected by a reinforced aluminum enclosure. The lower structure, below deck, is designed to deliver an uninterrupted ammunition supply to the gun and includes the gun system controls, loader drum, fuze setter, and the lower accumulator system to provide hydraulic power. An

ABOVE: A Mk. 45 5-in(127mm)/54 caliber gun aboard a US destroyer. The gun is enclosed in a lightweight gunhouse which is unmanned when firing.

BELOW: To provide greater support for amphibious operations, the Mk.45 5-in(127mm)/62 caliber gun is now entering service. The longer barrel and rocket assisted munitions give ranges in excess of 63nm (117km). Note the faceted "stealth" shape of the gunhouse.

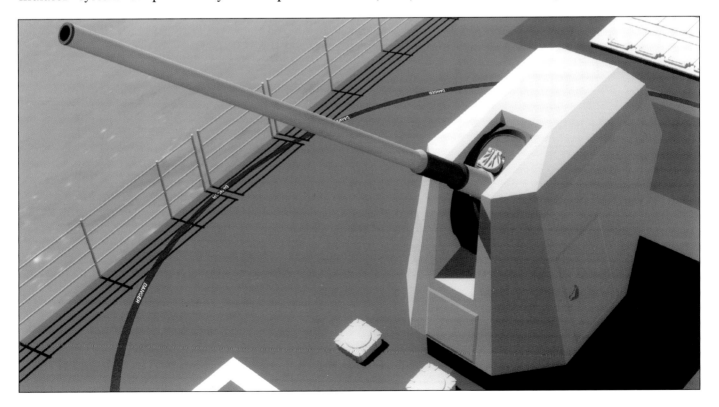

RIGHT: A dramatic view of a Mk. 45 5-in(127mm)/54 caliber at the moment of firing. The 70lb (32kg) shell can be clearly seen in flight.

optional Mk. 6 lower ammunition hoist provides an ammunition load station and transfer mechanism for ships, such as cruisers and assault ships, whose magazines are located below the loader drum deck level. The whole system (excluding the optional hoist) weighs in at 49,000lb (22,226kg) which compares very favorably with the 149,930lb (68,150kg) of the previous Mk. 42 and is why the Mk. 45 is referred to as a "lightweight" system. The normal gun crew, none of whom are actually in the gunhouse, consist of six operators—a mount captain, a control panel operator, and four ammunition handlers. When action requirements are limited to ammunition already preloaded onto the loader drum, one crew member can activate and operate the entire system.

The system loader drum in the lower structure can hold 20 conventional 5-in (127-mm) rounds, or ten extended length projectiles with separate cartridge cases, or a mixture of both. It is replenished through its own manual load station or via the Mk. 6 hoist if fitted. The Mk. 45 is designed to utilize all current US Navy 5-in (127-mm)/54cal. ammunition, which includes a wide variety of specialized projectiles, fuze types, and cartridge case loads.

The firing cycle is relatively simple in operation and normal rate of fire is 20rpm. The Mk. 45 can also handle extended length ammunition, which can include guided and precision rounds, and these generally feature separate propellant cartridges. In this case the firing cycle is modified to include a double hoist and ram cycle before firing.

The operation of the gun and its loading cycle is controlled from the operators station control panel, which includes all switches and indicators required to select operational modes and monitor the functioning of the gun. In addition the operator can monitor the distribution of ammunition types in the lower hoist, loader drum, and upper hoist. The mounting utilizes the ship's 440 volt electrical supply via a power control panel, and a battery system is incorporated to allow completion of a firing sequence in the event of a power failure.

In US Navy service the Mk. 45 is normally paired with the Lockheed Mk. 46 Fire Control System (FCS), which incorporates an SPQ-9 track-while-scan radar, an SPG-60 target tracking and illuminating radar, and an electro-optical sensor system.

The Mk. 45 has been produced in several versions, the initial variant being the Mod. 0 as installed aboard the early Spruance class ships. This was replaced by the Mod. 1, first tested in the early 1980s aboard the USS *Briscoe* (the 15th Spruance class), which introduced automatic handling of different ammunition types and electronic fuze setting. The current production version is the Mod. 2, which introduces new microprocessor control circuitry and a number of other modifications designed to enhance its reliability.

Despite being over 20 years old, the basic design is currently being modernized and upgraded to fulfil a requirement for a near term improvement in Naval Surface Fire Support (NSFS) capabilities. This program relates mainly to the gun itself, which is modified to allow the use of advanced solid propellants together with conventional or improved ballistic projectiles to produce a staggering improvement in

maximum range. Structural modifications, including a lengthening of the barrel to 62 caliber, increased recoil length, and strengthening of major components, allow the Mk. 45 to operate at higher chamber pressures and to cope with greater recoil forces. The new 5-in (127mm)/62 caliber mounting is now being introduced aboard destroyers and frigates and is capable of ranges up to 63nm (117km) using the EX 171 Extended Range Guided Munition (ERGM). Using GPS guidance and a solid fuel rocket motor, the ERGM is capable of pinpoint accuracy even at maximum range and is intended to support ground forces up to 62 miles (100km) inland from a beachhead.

LEFT: A close up of the 5in (127mm)/54 cal. gun barrel of the light-weight Mk. 45 mounting. Its main function is Naval Surface Fire Support of forces ashore, as well as antiship and antiaircraft capability.

BELOW: This Mk.45 has obviously just carried out a sustained fired detail as evidenced by the cartridges cases on the deck and scorch marks on the barrel. It can fire at 20rpm.

Mk. 75 3in/62 Gun

This 3in (76mm) automatic gun was originally designed and manufactured in Italy by OTO Melera and has achieved considerable success in the export market. Following a successful evaluation in 1975, it was ordered for the US Navy and initially manufactured under license by the Naval Systems Division of the FMC Corporation. Subsequently orders were shared between OTO Melera and FMC. First deliveries were made in 1978 for installation in the first of the new Oliver Hazard Perry class frigates of which 51 were eventually completed for US service. The gun also armed some hydrofoils and US Coastguard Hamilton and Famous class cutters.

The fully automatic Mk. 75 3in (76mm)/62 caliber gun has a rate of fire of 85rpm and fires a 13lb (6kg) shell to a maximum range of 8.7nm (16km) against surface targets although it has a full dual purpose capability and is effective against aircraft and missiles. The gun is water cooled to dissipate the heat created by the high rate of fire and a tank type muzzle brake reduces recoil forces. The turret is unmanned; ammunition is stored immediately below

the mounting in ready use drums containing 40, 80 or 115 rounds. Only three crew are required to operate sustained fire, one at the mounting remote control station in the ship's operations center, and two others replenish the ammunition drums. However, fire can be opened almost instantaneously against unexpected targets using the preloaded ammunition. Overall mounting weight is 16,500lbs (7,484kg).

Aboard the FFG-7 frigates, the Mk. 75 is teamed with the Mk. 92 fire control system (FCS), which is a license produced version of the Dutch Signaal M28 FCS. The twin X-band radar antenna for this system are installed in a distinctive egg-shaped housing prominently mounted atop the frigates bridge.

These ships also carry a SPG-60 STIR (Separate Tracking and Illuminating Radar) that can also be integrated with the FCS to illuminate targets for

BELOW: The Mk. 75 3-in (76mm) gun is unusually mounted high up amidships in the FFG-7 class frigates. Also visible in this view of the USS *Estocin* (FFG-15) are the Mk. 13 single rail missile launcher forward and a Mk. 15 Phalanx aft atop the hangar.

NAVAL WEAPONS

RIGHT: A model of the 3-in (76mm)/62 gun showing the below deck arrangement of the ready use magazine.

BELOW: This egg-shaped housing contains the two antenna of the Mk. 92 fire control radar associated with the Mk. 75 3in (76mm) gun.

BOTTOM: An SPG-60 STIR (Target indicating radar) aboard an FFG-7 class frigate.

both the gun and the ship's Standard missiles. Unusually, the gun itself is mounted amidships atop the superstructure so its arcs of fire against low-level targets are restricted fore and aft by the ships funnel and masts.

Mk. 38 1-in (25mm) Automatic Cannon (Bushmaster)

This the US Navy's standard lightweight gun system, installed for self defense purposes aboard many support and amphibious warfare vessels, is effectively a replacement for the 0.79in (20mm) Oerlikon cannon of World War II vintage. The gun is an electrically driven M242 autocannon, or chain gun, which takes its name from the roller chain that operates the firing mechanism and transports the ammunition rounds. Rate of fire is variable; it can be set at 100 or 200rpm in addition to a single shot capability. Maximum effective range is in the region of 8,202ft (2,500m). The gun is carried on a Mk. 88 heavy machinegun mounting and is manually elevated and trained.

Development of the M242 for Army use began in 1971 and it was adopted for naval use in 1986. As early as 1988 it was deployed aboard ships operating in the Persian Gulf and was fitted to the frigates *Fahrion* (FFG-22) and *Mahlon S Tinsdale* (FFG-27) during the Gulf War in 1991. The weight of the complete mounting is 1,250lb (567kg), including the attached magazine holding 150 rounds.

20mm Phalanx Mk. 15 Close In Weapon System (CIWS)

Despite the increasing sophistication of missile and medium-caliber gun systems, experience has shown that low flying aircraft and missiles can sometimes evade them and a need was identified for some form of last ditch point defense system. In the 1970s, the US Navy developed the Phalanx system to provide a short-range, self defense capability and operational tests of the prototype were conducted aboard the destroyer USS *Bigelow* in 1977. These were completely successful: full-scale production began in 1978, since when it has been widely deployed by the US and allied navies.

Phalanx is a completely self contained weapon system based around a standard M61A1 Vulcan 0.79in (20mm) multibarreled cannon firing up to 4,500rpm in continuous fire or bursts of 60 or 100 rounds. That actual ammunition is made of heavy tungsten or depleted uranium for greater kinetic energy. Co-mounted with the gun is a dual purpose search and track radar and an associated fire control system. When the search radar detects a target, it is tracked and evaluated. If its profile indicates that it is a threat then it will be engaged once within range. As well as tracking the target, the radar can also track the path of the cannon shells and this information is utilized by the FCS to correct aiming errors until the target is destroyed. Although maximum gun range is in the order of 6,000 yards (5,486m), effective range is 1,500–2,000 yards (1,371–1,829m).

The original Mk. 15 Block 0 was designed to counter low flying antiship missiles but the Block 1 introduced from 1986 incorporated a new search antenna to detect high altitude targets. The firing rate was increased from 3,000 to 4,500 rpm and ammunition capacity was increased while tungsten rounds were introduced. Block 1A offered substantial improvements to the FCS computer. Block 1B offers various enhancements including a Forward Looking

ABOVE, LEFT: A close of the rear of the Phalanx mounting showing the ammunition feed to the M61A 0.79in (20mm) cannon.

LEFT: The muzzle of the Phalanx M61A multibarreled cannon literally spits fire in this dramatic night shot.

LEFT: The USS *Ticonderoga* has the AEGIS class guided missile cruiser and Phalanx, a radar-controlled gun system. It is designed to protect ships against low altitude missiles or hostile aircraft that penetrate the fleet's lower defenses.

Infra Red (FLIR) and a thermal imaging video tracking system to enable day and night capability against small surface targets and helicopters. The need for this was demonstrated during operations in the Persian Gulf from 1988 onward when US ships came under attack from Fast Inshore Attack Craft whose high speed and small size made them difficult to counter. In the latest versions the M61A1 gun has been upgraded with longer and heavier barrels and additional bracing to reduce wear and tear, and to reduce projectile dispersion.

Despite weighing over 5 tons, the Mk. 15 Phalanx can easily be installed on any suitable area of clear deck, and can just as easily be removed and installed on another ship. Thus systems are recycled as ships,

are decommissioned for refits, or placed in reserve. Over 800 Phalanx systems have been delivered and these are in service with 22 navies.

Phalanx is currently providing the basis for a new Inner Layer Defense system known as SEA RAM in which the 0.79in (20mm) Vulcan cannon is replaced by an eleven cell RAM (RIM-116B) missile launcher. The full range of radar, infrared, and optical sensors developed for the Block 1B Phalanx is incorporated in SEA RAM, which is currently undergoing development and evaluation trials with both the US Navy and British Royal Navy. The SEA RAM system is completely interchangeable with a standard Phalanx mounting and weighs some 900lb (400kg) less than the gun version.

US Marine Corps

Today the USMC is the nation's main "Force in Readiness" and is prepared to be catapulted into a war zone at any time. With major inventories of aircraft, armor, and infantry equipment, the USMC is a significant weapon and major part of the United States' armed forces.

With a remarkable record of achievement in World War II and beyond, the USMC showed itself to be the world's premier amphibious force. In the western theater it was involved in the major amphibious operations landing forces on the coast of West Africa, Sicily, Italy, Southern, and Northern France. In the Pacific it was the Marine Corps that spearheaded the drive to push the Japanese back to their homeland and reclaim the Pacific territories Japan had conquered. Operations such as Iwo Jima, Okinawa, Pelelieu, and Tarawa were bloody battles that honed the corps into the best combined-arms fighting unit in the world. Postwar it showed its strength in the Korean War at Inchon and fought with distinction in the Vietnam War.

Today, its current strategic role is set out in *Marine Corps Strategy 21* as "the continuous forward presence and sustainable maritime power projection of Naval expeditionary forces ... scalable, interoperable, combined-arms Marine Air-Ground Task Forces (MAGTFs) to shape the international environment, respond quickly to the complex spectrum of crises and conflicts, and gain access or prosecute forcible entry operations." *Marine Corps Strategy 21* also identifies a number of USMC specialist forces – such as Fleet Anti-Terrorism Security Teams (FASTs) and the Chemical Biological Incident Response Force (CBIRF) – which show that the USMC has a wider responsibility than amphibious assault.

To be able to achieve their missions Marines need to be able to move quickly to trouble spots around the globe, arrive there and organize themselves quickly and efficiently, and then fight as air-ground task forces—integrated organizations of air, ground, and logistic forces under a single commander. The equipment they need to do this incorporates, therefore, much of what the US Army and US Air Force need – tanks, artillery, infantry weapons; fixed-wing aircraft and helicopters – as well as specialized equipment for amphibious operations.

BELOW: A "herd" of CH-53D Sea Stallion helicopters prepare to make a landing during D-Day operations.

ABOVE: Two Marine CH-53E Super Stallion helicopters are led by an KC-130 aircraft.

LEFT: The black and red AH-IW Supercobra touches down to ground.

LEFT: The AH-IW Supercobra in camouflage colors.

FAR LEFT: A US Marine Corps AH-1W SuperCobra equipped with Bell Helicopter Textron's Advanced 680 Rotor System makes its first flight at Bell's Flight Research Center, Arlington, Texas, in 1989.

BELOW: A US Marine Corps AH-1W SuperCobra fires a missle across the desert.

ABOVE: CH-46 Sea Knight helicopters stir up a cloud of dust as they launch behind a CH-53 Sea Stallion near Yuma, AZ. during Exercise Desert Punch. This was a simulated helicopter assault mission involving over 60 helicopters from nine squadrons of Marine Aircraft Group 16.

LEFT: A US Marine Corps reconnaissance team braces against the blast of rotor wash from a CH-53E Sea Stallion as the helicopter lifts off from the Marine Corps Air Ground Combat Center, 29 Palms, Calif. The Sea Stallion inserted the recon team from 1st Battalion, 8th Marines, as part of the Combined Arms Exercise 3-98.

ABOVE: Two US Marine AH-1W
Super Cobra helicopters from the
26th Marine Expeditionary Unit fly
over the live fire range at Glamoc,
Bosnia and Herzegovina. Assigned to
the Strategic Reserve Force of the
Stabilization Force, the Marines were
taking part in Exercise Dynamic
Response 98, a training exercise
designed to familiarize the reserve
forces with the territory and their
operational capabilities within this
region.

RIGHT: US Marine Corps
parachutists free fall from an MV-22
Osprey at 10,000ft above the
drop zone.

LEFT: A Bell Boeing MV-22 Osprey comes in for a landing at the Pentagon to demonstrate its capabilities before an audience. The Osprey utilizes tiltrotor technology. Taking-off like a helicopter, its engines then rotate forward 90 degrees to create a conventional aircraft configuration permitting high-speed, high-altitude, fuel-efficient flight. For landing, the engines rotate to the vertical allowing it to land in helicopter fashion. The Marine version can transport 24 combat-equipped personnel or a 15,000-lb (6,804kg) external load.

ABOVE: A soldier cleans his M203 1.6 in (40mm) grenade launcher before a battalion live fire exercise.

LEFT: Navy Chief WO uses a GPS receiver to calculate coordinates for a amphibious landing at a beach near Makuto, Venezuela. US service personnel gave humanitarian assistance to flood victims in January 2000.

ABOVE, RIGHT: US Marine Corps Assault Amphibian Vehicle Recovery Model 7A1 arrives to take part in exercise Tandem Thrust 1997, a combined military training exercise to train US and Australian staffs in crisis action planning and contingency response operations.

RIGHT: Marines perform a live fire exercise with an M-198 6.1in (155mm) howitzer during Exercise Tandem Thrust.

ABOVE: US Marines from the 10th Marine Regiment prepare their M-198 6.1in (155 mm) howitzer for firing while taking part in Combined Arms Exercise 4-98.

RIGHT: Two Marine cannoneers hustle a 6.1in (155mm) white phosphorus round to the breech of a M-198 howitzer during live-fire exercise. The Marine Air Ground Task Force exercise allowed these Marines of Golf Battery, 2nd Battalion, 10th Marines, to practice their desert warfare.

ABOVE: US Marines from the 8th Marine Regiment train for close quarters combat on the flight deck of the USS *Ponce* (LPD 15) during its transit to Liberia.

LEFT: Marines from Communications Company, Headquarters Battalion provide command and control via radio at Range 400 of the Marine Corps Air Ground Combat Center.

ABOVE: US Marines from Kilo Company, 3d Battalion, 8th Marine Regiment, 2d Marine Division, form a perimeter after unloading from Amphibious Assault Vehicles.

RIGHT: Marines from Bravo Company, 1st Battalion, 6th Marine Regiment, rush toward the target at Range 400 of the Marine Corps Air Ground Combat Center.

BELOW: Marines from Charlie Company protect the Advanced Surgical Suite for Trauma Casualties medical tent at the Military Operations in Urban Terrain facility during Urban Warrior.

ABOVE: US Marines on snow shoes patrol across a meadow at the Mountain Warfare Training Center, California.

LEFT: Two Marines try to collapse a billowing cargo parachute dropped from a helicopter.

RIGHT: Marines from 2nd Marine Regiment head back down to base camp at the Mountain Warfare Training Center, California as near white-out conditions set in. Marines are there to train in cold weather survival and arctic warfare.

ABOVE: Charlie Company Marines use a M-9 Armored Combat Earthmover for cover as they patrol the medical area during role playing at Camp Lejeune, North Carolina.

LEFT: US Marines from 3d Battalion, 8th Marine Regiment patrol the streets of Gnjilane, Kosovo. Elements of the 26th Marine Expeditionary Unit were deployed from ships of the USS *Kearsarge* Amphibious Ready Group.

ABOVE, RIGHT: A US Marine Corps Light Armored Vehicle patrols in the village of Zegra, Kosovo.

RIGHT: US Marines from Charlie Company patrol the Military Operations in Urban Terrain facility in a Helo Transportable Tactical Vehicle (HTTV) at Camp Lejeune, North Carolina.

INDEX

INDEX

ACKNOWLEDGMENTS

The publisher wishes to thank the following photographers and photo-libraries, who kindly supplied the images for this book:

Front cover photograph, and pages 131, 132, 133, 136, 137, 138, 139, 140, 141 (top and bottom), 142, 143 (top), 146 (left and right), 147 (top and bottom), 148 (top and bottom), 149 (top and bottom), 150 (top and bottom), 151 (top and bottom), 152, 153 (top and bottom), 154, 155 (top and bottom), 156 (top and bottom), 159, 160, 161 (top and bottom), 164 (right), 165 (top and bottom), 166 (top and bottom), 167 (top left, top right, bottom left and bottom right), 168, 169, 170, 171 (top and bottom), 172 (top and bottom), 173 (top and bottom), 181, 182, 183, 185, 186, 190 and 191 (top) and back cover photograph (main), courtesy of Hans Halberstadt;
Pages 2, 11 (top and bottom), 14 (top), 18, 19 (top and bottom), 20-21, 25 (top, middle and bottom), 30 (top and bottom), 31, 32, 69, 70, 71, 72, 73, 74, 77, 78, 80, 81 (top and bottom), 84, 86, 88 (top and bottom), 89 (bottom), 93, 94 (top and bottom), 99 (top), 100 (all), 101 (top and bottom), 102, 103 (upper middle, lower middle and bottom), 105, 107 (top and bottom), 108 (top and bottom), 109 (top and bottom), 115 (top), 116, 117 (top), 118, 120 (middle), 126 (bottom), 128-129, 143 (top and bottom), 194 (top and bottom), 198, 199 (top and bottom), 200, 201, 203 (top and bottom), 204, 207, 210 (bottom), 215 (top and bottom), 218, 220, 221, 236, 237 (top and bottom) and 238-239 (main, bottom left and bottom right), and back cover (inset, top and bottom), courtesy of Chrysalis Images;
Pages 9 (Chief Petty Officer Steve Briggs), 22 (top) (Petty Officer 2nd Class Ty Swartz), 22 (bottom) (Petty Officer 3rd Class Natalie Nolen), 23 (top) (Airman Justin K. Thomas), 24 (top) (Photographer's Mate First Class Martin E. Maddock), 24 (bottom) (Photographer's Mate 3rd Class John E. Woods), 40 (Ms. Grace Kelly), 41 (top and bottom) (Photographer's Mate Airman Apprentice Stephanie M. Bergman), 42 (top) (Photographer's Mate 2nd Class David C. Mercil), 42 (middle) (Photographer's Mate Airman Joshua J. Pina), 42 (bottom) (Photographer's Mate 3rd Class Martin S. Fuentes), 43 (top) (Photographer's Mate 1st Class Chris Desmond), 43 (middle) (Photographer's Mate First Class Martin E. Maddock), 43 (bottom) (Intelligence Specialist 1st Class Matthew C. Ruble), 44 (top) (Photographer's Mate 2nd Class Shawn Eklund), 44 (middle) (Photographer's Mate 3rd Class J. Scott Campbell), 44 (bottom) (Photographer's Mate 3rd Class John Taucher), 45 (top), 45 (bottom) (Photographer's Mate 3rd Class J. Scott Campbell), 46 (top left) (Petty Officer 2nd Class Richard Rosser), 46 (top right) (Petty Officer 2nd Class Andrew McKaskle), 46 (bottom) (Petty Officer 2nd Class Shane McCoy), 47 (top) (Petty Officer 1st Class Jason Everett Miller), 58 (Photographer's Mate Airman Tina Lamb), 59 (top), 60 (top) (Petty Officer 2nd Class Richard Rosser), 60 (bottom) (Airman Apprentice Mason Cavazos), 61 (top) (Petty Officer 2nd Class Michael W. Prendergrass), 56 (bottom), 66 (Petty Officer 1st Class Jim Hampshire), 96 (Lt. John McVay), 114 (top) (Petty Officer 3rd Class Christopher Mobley), 117 (bottom) (Petty Officer 2nd Class Charles Neff), 120 (bottom) (Petty Officer 3rd Class Heather Humphreys), 124 (top) (Petty Officer 2nd Class Felix Garza), 134 (top) (Petty Officer 2nd Class Jeff Viano), 188 (bottom left) (Petty Officer 2nd Class Gloria J. Barry), 196 (top) (Petty Officer 3rd Class R. David Valdez), 196 (bottom) (Airman Angus D. Stokes), 197 (top) (Petty Officer 2nd Class Michael Tuemler), 197 (bottom) (Petty Officer 1st Class Wade McKinnon), 211 (top) (Petty Officer 1st Class Spike Call), 230 (Petty Officer 2nd Class Felix Garza), 240 (top) (Petty Officer 2nd Class Jeff Viano), 241 (top) (Chief Petty Officer Steve Briggs), 241 (bottom) (Vernon pugh), 244 (bottom) (Petty Officer 2nd Class Russell Carter), 245 (top) (Lt. John Protz), 245 (bottom) (Petty Officer 3rd Class Jennifer A. Smith), courtesy of the Department of Defense/US Navy;
Pages 12 (Staff Sgt. James V. Downen Jr.), 13 (Staff St. Jon Long), 15 (top and bottom), 17 (top) (Pfc. R. Alan Mitchell), 34, 35 (top and bottom), 36 (top and bottom), 37 (top, bottom left and bottom right), 38 (top and bottom), 39, 59 (bottom), 144 (bottom) (Pfc. R. Alan Mitchell), 62, 63 (top and bottom), 64, 65 (top and bottom), 145 (bottom) (Staff St. Jon Long), 162 (inset left) (Pfc. Luis A Deya), 177, 180 (Spc. Cory Montgomery), and 191 (bottom), courtesy of the Department of Defense/US Army;
Pages 14 (bottom) (Cpl. Mike Wentzel), 17 (bottom) (Sgt. Thomas W. Farrar Jr.), 144 (top) (Cpl. Branden P. O'Brien), 162-163 (main) (Lance Cpl. Donald R. Storms), 163 (inset right) (Pfc. Andrew Revelos), 164 (top left) (Lance. Cpl. E.J. Young), 174 (top) (Cpl. Manuel Valdez), 187 and 189 (bot-

tom right) (Cpl. A. Olguin), 188-189 (main) (Sgt. Craig J. Shell), 240 (bottom), (Sgt. T. M. Dale Jr.), 246 (bottom) (Pfc. J.L. Shelhart), 246 (top), 247 (bottom) and 248-249 (main) (Lance Cpl. S.A. Harwood), 247 (top) and 248 (top left) (Cpl. A. Olguin), 248 (bottom left) (Sgt. Jason J. Bortz), 250 and 251 (top and bottom) (Lance. Cpl. E.J. Young), 252 (top) and 253 (bottom) (Staff Sgt. David J. Ferrier), 252 (bottom) and 253 (top) (Sgt. Craig J. Shell), courtesy of the Department of Defense/US Marine Corps;
Pages 16 (top) (Staff Sgt. Jerry Morrison), 16 (bottom) (Kenn Mann), 26 and 52 (Gary Ell), 27 (top) (Master Sgt. Ray Conway), 27 (bottom), 28 (top) (Senior Airman Diane S. Robinson), 28 (bottom) (Tech. Sgt. Lance Cheung), 29 (top) (Staff Sgt. Cary Humphries), 29 (bottom) (Staff Sgt. John E. Lasky), 48 (Staff Sgt. Shane Cuomo), 49 (Tech. Staff Sgt. Justin Pyle), 50 (top), 50 (bottom) (Staff Sgt. Andy Dunaway), 51 (Staff Sgt. Larry A. Simmons), 53 (top) (Master Sgt. John Snow), 53 (bottom), 54 (top) (Staff Sgt. Jeffrey Allen), 54 (middle and bottom), 55 (top), 55 (bottom) (Master Sgt. Dave Nolan), 56 (top) (Master Sgt. Marvin Krause), 57 (top) (1st Lt. Dave Westover), 57 (bottom) and 67 (bottom) (Tech. Sgt. David W. Richards), 67 (top) (Senior Airman Greg L. Davis), 75 (Senior Airman Stan Parker), 82 (top) (Staff Sgt. Kevin J. Gruenwald), 82 (bottom) (Tech. Sgt. James D. Green), 83 (top and bottom) (Staff Sgt. Vince Parker), 87 (top), (Staff Sgt. Randy Mallard), 87 (bottom) (Staff Sgt. Krista M. Foeller), 89 (top) (Master Sgt. Kevin L. Bishop), 90 (Senior Airman Eric D. Beaman), 91 (top) (Senior Airman Greg L. Davis), 91 (bottom) (Staff Sgt. Efrain Gonzalez), 92 (Senior Airman Stan Parker), 115 (bottom) (Staff Sgt. Kevin J. Gruenwald), 121 (top) (Senior Airman Jeffrey Allen), 121 (bottom) (Tech. Sgt. Russ Pollanen), 125 (top) (Senior Airman Greg L. Davis), 134 (bottom) and 135 (top) (Senior Airman Jeffrey Allen), 135 (bottom) (Tech. Sgt. James Mossman), 157 (Tech. Sgt. James Mossman), 174 (bottom) (Airman Benjamin Andera), 175 (Staff Sgt. Jerry Morrison), 178-179 (main) (Staff Sgt. Bill Morris), 178 (top left) (Staff Sgt. Jim Varhegyi), 178 (bottom left) (Tech. Sgt. David W. Richards), courtesy of the Department of Defense/US Air Force;
Pages 23 (bottom) (Photographer's Mate 3rd Class Jason D. Malcom), 47 (bottom), 61 (bottom) (Photographer's Mate 1st class Mark Foughty), 79 (top and bottom), 85 (top), 97 (top) (Vernon Pugh), 145 (top), 158 (R. D. Ward), 211 (bottom) (Petty Officer 3rd Class Timothy Smith), 219 (Petty Officer 1st Class John Guzman), 228, 242-243 (R. D. Ward) and 244 (top) (Sgt. Bob O'Donahoo), courtesy of Department of Defense.
Page 76, 97 (bottom), 98 (middle and bottom), 99 (bottom), 103 (top), 104, 106 (top), 111, 112, 119 (bottom), 120 (top), 122 (top), 123 (top and bottom), 124 (bottom), 125 (bottom), 126 (top), 127 (top and bottom), 225 (bottom), courtesy of Military Archive and Research Services, Lincs.;
Page 85 (middle), 95 (top and bottom), 122 (bottom), courtesy of Military Archive and Research Services, Lincs. (U.S. Air Force photo, Department of Defense);
Page 85 (bottom) courtesy of U.S. Air Force, Department of Defense, photo by Paul Reynolds; print from Military Archive and Research Services, Lincs.
Page 98 (top) photo by Kevin Flynn, courtesy of McDonnell Douglas.
Page 106 (bottom), 110 (bottom), 113 (top), 176, courtesy of McDonnell Douglas; print from Military Archive and Research Services, Lincs.
Page 110 (top) courtesy of Military Archive and Research Services, Lincs./D. Moore.
Page 113 (bottom) courtesy of Rockwell International/Military Archive and Research Services, Lincs.
Page 114 (bottom) courtesy of Boeing Aerospace; print from Military Archive and Research Services, Lincs.
Pages 119 (top), 202 (top, middle and bottom), 205, 206 (top, middle and bottom), 208 (left and right) and 209 (right) courtesy of Boeing, and back cover (inset, middle), via Leo Marriott.
Page 193 courtesy of Ingalls Shipbuilding, via Leo Marriott.
Pages 195 (top and bottom), 232, courtesy of U.S. Navy/Leo Marriott.
Pages 209 (left), 210 (top), 213 (middle and bottom), 214, 216 (top), 217 (bottom), 222, 225 (top), 233 (top, middle and bottom), 234 (top), courtesy of Leo Marriott.
Page 213 (top) and 234 (bottom) via Leo Marriott.
Page 216 (bottom), 217 (top three), Raytheon, via Leo Marriott.
Page 223 (top and bottom), 226 (top and bottom), 231 (top and bottom), courtesy of U.S. Navy/Military Archive and Research Services, Lincs.
Page 224 Lockheed Martin, via Leo Marriott.
Page 229 (top and bottom) United Defense, via Leo Marriott.
Page 235 courtesy of Geneva Dynamics; print from Military Archive and Research Services, Lincs.

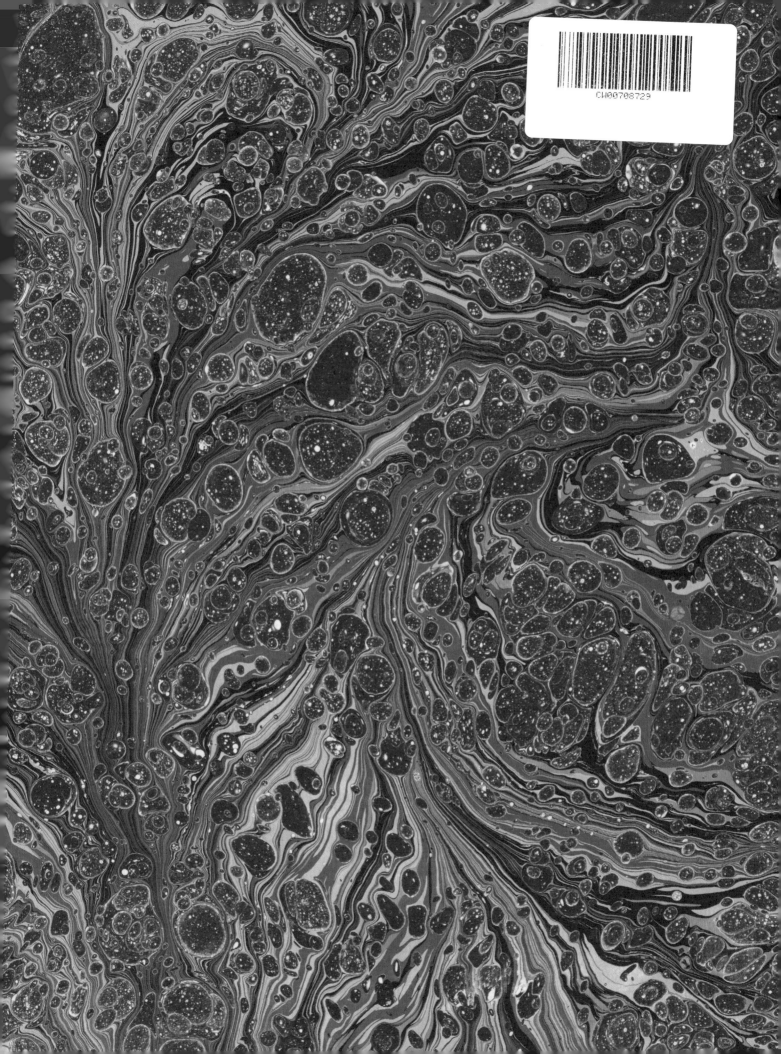

GERMAN GLIDERS IN WORLD WAR II

GERMAN GLIDERS IN WORLD WAR II

Luftwaffe Gliders and Their Powered Variants
**DFS 230 – Go 242 – Go 244 – Go 345 –
Ka 430 – Me 321 – Ju 322 – Me 323**

Heinz Mankau and Peter Petrick

Schiffer Military History
Atglen, PA

Book Design by Stephanie Daugherty
Translated by David Johnston.
Copyright © 2010 by Schiffer Publishing, Ltd.
Library of Congress Control Number: 2009939140

Printed in China.
ISBN: 978-0-7643-3519-8

This book was originally published in German under the title
Deutsche Lastensegler by Motorbuch Verlag.

We are interested in hearing from authors with book ideas on related topics.

Published by Schiffer Publishing Ltd.
4880 Lower Valley Road
Atglen, PA 19310
Phone: (610) 593-1777
FAX: (610) 593-2002
E-mail: Info@schifferbooks.com.
Visit our web site at: www.schifferbooks.com
Please write for a free catalog.
This book may be purchased from the publisher.
Please include $5.00 postage.
Try your bookstore first.

In Europe, Schiffer books are distributed by:
Bushwood Books
6 Marksbury Avenue
Kew Gardens
Surrey TW9 4JF, England
Phone: 44 (0) 20 8392-8585
FAX: 44 (0) 20 8392-9876
E-mail: Info@bushwoodbooks.co.uk.
Visit our website at: www.bushwoodbooks.co.uk
Try your bookstore first.

CONTENTS

FOREWORD

Nowadays air forces keep their aircraft in service for years, sometimes decades. The *Luftwaffe*'s transport gliders, on the other hand, were conceived with a short service life in mind, sometimes just a single mission, and consequently they were simple designs constructed using cheap materials. The operational profile originally conceived made it appear that a fixed undercarriage could be dispensed with. Despite their simplicity, I found it interesting to learn about and construct models of these aircraft. In the process I became interested in the various subtypes. In order to build accurate models of the different variants, it was necessary to delve into the literature and original documents, and the results may be seen in the following pages.

The first usable books came from Pawlas and Kössler, but the description of the variants was insufficiently detailed for my purposes. Pawlas provided some contradictory information. To clear up these contradictions I turned to the German Technical Museum in Berlin (Historical Archive) and there examined the sources on which Pawlas based his work. I found that the contradictions were not inventions on Pawlas' part, rather they were present in the original documents. He did, however, draw some erroneous conclusions, wrongly identified photographs, and made errors in the sequence of events.

Apart from the German Museum in Munich, my main sources were the German Technical Museum in Berlin and the Federal Archives in Freiburg and Coblenz. The staff there were generous in their support, for which I am grateful. The DFS wrote reports on its work, and I found some of these in technical school libraries. The cited handbooks, pilots' notes, replacement parts lists, etc came from the Hafner Aviation Archive.

My partner, Peter Petrick, contributed most of the photographs. I am grateful to Manfred Griehl, Karl Kössler, Manfred Krieg, Rainer Nidrée, Christoph Regel, Georg Schlaug, and Marton Szigeti, who also contributed photos and information. Hans-Peter Dabrowski was of great help to me in searching for sources on the Me 321/323.

In my opinion, placing the documents in the proper chronological order was important in describing the course of German transport glider development. I therefore decided to present the information in the form of a sort of diary, with accompanying comments. This gives the reader the opportunity to assess the information for himself and possibly draw different conclusions.

Rothemühle, March 2008
Heinz Mankau

OVERVIEW

The first flight by an aircraft-towed glider took place in Kassel in the spring of 1927. The idea gained wide acceptance, and it became particularly popular in sport aviation for towing single-seat gliders into the air. The RRG, or Rhön-Rositten Association, played a particularly important role in perfecting the procedure. The idea of larger gliders towed by commercial aircraft was conceived in the period 1930 to 1934. The concept envisaged gliders landing at airfields too small to justify the landing of a large passenger aircraft. The RRG also built a larger glider for research purposes. In 1933, as part of the National-Socialist government's aviation and rearmament activities, the RRG was reformed, eventually becoming the German Aviation Research Institute for Gliding Flight (DFS) in 1936. The State Ministry of Aviation (RLM) assigned a number of projects to the DFS, including one for the development of a glider capable of delivering a squad of soldiers to the battlefield. Development looked so promising that the Luftwaffe began training glider pilots in 1937. Construction of the first batch of the new DFS 230 A-0 transport glider also began in 1937, and in November trials at Stendal showed that troops landed by glider became combat ready more quickly than parachute troops. An order was subsequently placed for more DFS 230s, and training of glider-borne troops began in 1938. Also in 1938, work on developed versions of the DFS 230 began and quantity production was transferred to an experienced aircraft manufacturer, Gothaer Waggonfabrik. It developed the DFS 230 A-1, which was designed for mass production and conceived as a combat glider. Training of pilots and troops for the planned attack on Belgium and France followed in 1939. At the same time the idea crystallized of using the DFS 230 to transport guns and equipment as well as troops, resulting in the DFS 230 A-2 with an additional loading hatch. On 10/5/1940 42 Ju 52/DFS 230 glider-tug combinations transported Assault Battalion Koch to Belgium, where it captured the fortress of Eben-Emael and several bridges over the Albert Canal. This was the first success by the DFS 230 glider. The DFS 230 was subsequently used more and more for transport duties,

with second-line types like the He 45 and He 46 serving as tugs. As the war progressed, the Hs 126, Avia 534, Ju 87 R, Do 17 E, and He 111 were also used as glider tugs.

The success at Eben Emael was so convincing that the RLM increased its order for DFS 230s to 2,500 and issued a contract for development of a larger transport glider. The maximum size of the new glider was determined by the available tugs, the Ju 52 and He 111. The DFS and GWF each developed a new glider: the DFS 331 and Go 242. Prototypes of both were completed in autumn 1940 and were flight tested in the winter of 1940-41. As no suitable production company could be found for the DFS 331, the RLM decided in favor of the Go 242. So much greater did its operational potential appear, that the RLM reduced the production contract for the DFS 230 to about 1,500, intending to use production capacity for the Go 242. The Go 242 lived up to expectations, and for a long time the RLM and General Staff planned to build it throughout the war. Not until August 1944, when the worsening military situation forced Germany to concentrate on the production of fighter aircraft, was production of the Go 242 halted after about 1,500 had been built.

In October 1940 the Junkers and Messerschmitt companies were issued contracts to build a large glider capable of delivering tanks, other heavy equipment, and entire contingents of troops behind enemy lines. The Ju 322 developed by Junkers proved to be unflyable. Messerschmitt's Me 321 could be flown, but the use of three glider tugs was dangerous. The Me 321 was never used in its intended role of combat glider, transporting equipment and troops behind enemy lines. Instead, it served as a transport glider carrying fuel and other cargoes. In this role it proved to be an expensive and dangerous failure. 200 examples were built, but few saw action. The last were scrapped in France in autumn 1943.

At the beginning of 1941, the GWF began work on the Go 244, an interim transport aircraft based on the Go 242. The RLM viewed these activities so optimistically that, for a time, thought was given to building only the

Go 244. The GWF received a contract for 450 Go 244s in 1942, and for capacity reasons these were to be built at the expense of the Go 242. Production began in 1942, but experiences in Russia in the summer of 1942 were so bad (inadequate payload and range) that production was halted in the fall. Completed Go 244s were subsequently converted back into Go 242s and full production of the Go 242 was resumed. Gotha Waggonfabrik tried to develop a better interim transport, culminating in the Go P-39 project, but at an early stage the RLM decided on the Ju 352 for this role.

At about the same time that the Go 244 was being developed from the Go 242, the powered Me 323 was derived from the Me 321. Whereas the RLM initially viewed the Go 244 as highly promising and then had to accept its failure, exactly the opposite was true of the Me 323. The Air Armaments Minister was highly skeptical at first, but the aircraft proved reliable and usable. The numbers desired by the RLM soon ran into problems because of shortages of the French engines that powered the Me 323. The situation eased somewhat at the end of 1943, but by then the RLM had to restrict production of the Me 323 in favor of fighter aircraft and then halt it altogether at the beginning of 1944.

While the Ju 52 was initially the main glider tug for the Go 242, as time went on the He 111 increasingly took over this role. RLM planning in 1942 foresaw the end of He 111 production in 1944, however. The only other suitable tug was the Ju 188/388, but it was incapable of towing the Go 242 and DFS 230. In 1943 this situation resulted in a contract for the development of a new glider. In terms of size it was to fall between the Go 242 and DFS 230, but was to be capable of higher towing speeds. The DFS and GWF developed the DFS 230 V7 and worked on several other projects, and the Erla Repair Works developed the Ka 430. The latter was chosen for development; however, the deteriorating military situation meant that it never entered production.

In summer 1943 the RLM saw a reason to develop transport gliders capable of water landings. The manufacturers therefore developed projects with suitable new aircraft (Go P-52 and Ka 430 on floats) or placed existing gliders on floats (DFS 230). A corresponding version of the Go 242 was also developed (Go 242 C-1). None of these types entered production.

CHRONICLE

1904 to 1921

According to the magazine Luftwissen of March 1943, the Frenchman Voisin began experimenting with towed gliders on wheels in 1904. In 1912 Anthony Fokker was granted a patent titled "Towing a Lilienthal Glider by Means of a Powered Aircraft" (see section Spring 1927). No further progress was made because of the low power of existing aero-engines. In 1917 Fokker (again according to Luftwissen) came up with the idea of a D-VII fighter towing a D-VIII from which the engine had been removed. This concept also failed to reach fruition, however, and in 1918 Fokker built a special high-wing glider with floats. Because of the war this was not tested until 1919/20, when it was towed aloft by a motorboat from the Ymuiden-Amsterdam Canal in Holland. The flight lasted six minutes at a height of 2.5 meters. The experiments were subsequently abandoned. At the Paris Salon in 1921 Fokker displayed another glider for towing trials, but it is not known if it was ever tested.

1924 [6]

At the recommendation of *Ministerialdirektor* Brandenburg, head of the Aviation Department in the State Ministry of Transport, the Rhön-Rositten Society Research Institute (RRG) is founded with the objective of promoting the development of gliders in Germany. The RRG concerns itself with the training of the next generation of pilots, the development of gliders, and the exploitation of new atmospheric gliding possibilities.

Kassel, Spring 1927

According to Gerhard Fieseler [G. Fieseler: *Meine Bahn am Himmel*, Bertelsmann Verlag 1979], he conceives the idea of a powered aircraft towing a glider as an attraction for an air day planned for Easter 1927 in Kassel-Waldau. He invites the glider pilot Gottlob Espenlaub to bring his machine. According to Fieseler, the first towed flights by an old LVG BIII with Fieseler at the controls and Espenlaub in his glider took place on 12/3/1927. A total of three towing tests are

No matter who came up with the idea, it is indisputable that the first towing experiments were carried out with a LVG BIII. (Nowarra)

Gottlob Espenlaub in his E7 glider, 1927. (Espenlaub)

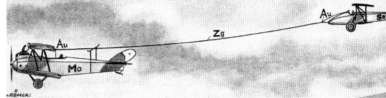

Above: Raab-Katzenstein RK 7 (Schmetterling). The towed vehicle was 8.5 m wide, 6.15 m long, and weighed 125 kg. (Nowarra)

Above right: the RaKa Kranich with the RaKa Schmetterling (Fieseler)

Right: This drawing shows the arrangement of the tow cable, for which Raab-Katzenstein applied for a patent. (von Römer)

Der fliegende „D=Zug" von Raab=Katzenstein

said to have been carried out, but in each case Espenlaub allegedly releases the tow cable just before takeoff because he himself plans to apply for a patent for an aircraft-towed glider. According to Fieseler's account these experiments serve to test the concept, but Espenlaub informs the press. At this time Fieseler is an employee and shareholder of the Raab-Katzenstein Aircraft Works in Kassel. He goes on to write that the shareholders Raab and Katzensteiner subsequently oust him, and he thus has no further part in the development of towed flight.

According to Fieseler's account, on 20/3/1927 Antonius Raab and Espenlaub conduct what they claim to be the first flight by a glider towed by a powered aircraft for the benefit of the press. Espenlaub's glider loses its fin and rudder during the flight; nevertheless, he is hailed by the press as the inventor of the aircraft-towed glider. Because of the poor results achieved with the Espenlaub glider Raab-Katzenstein-Flugzeugwerke hastily designs a new glider, the *Schmetterling* (Butterfly). The new machine completes a circuit at the air day that year, with Raab and Katzenstein as pilots.

But Antonius Raab [A. Raab: *Raab fliegt*, Konkret Literatur Verlag 1984] also lays claim to having reinvented the concept of an aircraft-towed glider. He maintains that the whole thing was based on an idea of Anthony Fokker's from the year 1912, which he, Raab, brought to fruition in 1927. Raab writes that Fieseler was at the controls of a Raab-Katzenstein *Kranich* (Crane) when the Espenlaub glider it was towing lost its tail. The Raab-Katzenstein Aircraft Works subsequently built the *Schmetterling* glider in three weeks. Raab claims that he carried out the first successful

towed flight on 15/3/1927 with Katzenstein at the controls of the RaKa *Kranich*. The RaKa *Kranich* was essentially an unpowered copy of the LVG BIII.

After the first experiments on 12/3 Espenlaub had portrayed himself to the press as the inventor of the towed flight, and Fieseler as merely the pilot of the powered aircraft. Even after the flight on 20 March the press still considered him the inventor of the procedure (statement by Gerhard Fieseler).

Luftwissen writes that in 1926 Fieseler proposed to the Kurhessisch Aviation Society that demonstrations of aircraft-towed gliders be used to increase the drawing power of air displays. The first flight with Espenlaub in the glider allegedly took place at Kassel-Waldau on 13/3/1927, and the first public demonstration on 20/3/1927. The Aviation Society subsequently grounded Espenlaub's glider as non-airworthy. The Raab-Katzenstein Aircraft Works subsequently constructed the RK 7 *Schmetterling*, which from 13/4/1927 appeared at other air displays all over Germany.

Fieseler and Raab obviously had a falling out in 1927. Their written accounts contradict each other and are marked by mutual antipathy. But as both admit that Espenlaub also claimed to have been the inventor of the aircraft-towed glider, we must now live with the fact that there are three supposed initiators. I do not have the documents required to prove one version of events as the correct one. Luftwissen is mentioned here for the sake of completeness, but it is unreliable because of the censorship of the day (Raab and Katzenstein were silenced for political reasons).

Parked in front of the Raab-Katzenstein Flugzeugwerke hangar in 1928 are an RK 6 "Kranich" (third aircraft from left) and two RK 7 "Schmetterling." Four RaKa RK 7 (also designated RK 7) may be found in the German Aviation Registry, registered between April and June 1928: D-1351 (Werk.Nr. 301), D-1352 (Werk.Nr. 305), D-1379 (Werk.Nr. 302), and D-1392 (Werk.Nr. 303). (Lange)

Gottlob Espenlaub also continued working on the aircraft-towed glider. At Rositten in 1927 Espe demonstrated the E 11, a powered aircraft with a 35 hp Anzani motor, and the E 7 glider. (Nowarra)

The Espenlaub EA 1 towed vehicle was registered in May 1928 (D-1396). Another EA 1 followed in May 1929 (D-1637). The vehicle was also called the E 12 in the contemporary press.

In 1928, Ing. Botho von Römer was convinced that, based on the success of experiments, the commercial use of glider trains was only a matter of time. (von Römer)

3. Luft-D-Züge der Zukunft

The DFS used the OBS as a flying observatory. (DFS)

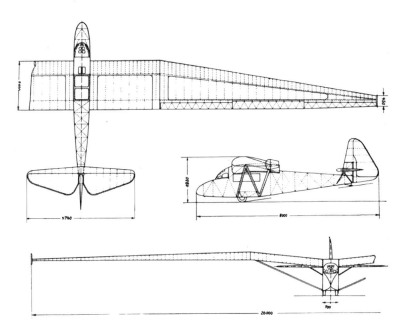

The OBS was a large aircraft for the conditions of its day. (Schlaug)

1927 to 1930

Raab writes that soon after the maiden flight of the *Schmetterling*, the Raab-Katzenstein Company made flights with two towed gliders, and sold combinations of a tug and two gliders to Italy and the USA. Katzenstein also writes an article that appears in America in which he describes the "air train of the future." Thus, by 1927 there is already speculation about larger gliders.

In Germany, the aircraft-towed glider is mainly a feature of air displays, but some overland flights are carried out (for example Karlsruhe to Frankfurt/Main to Kassel). In 1928 Lola Schrödter organizes towed flights through all of Germany and Frank Hawks makes a towed flight from San Diego to New York in eight days.

1930 [6]

The RRG's research institute develops towed glider flight in cooperation with the Darmstadt Academic Aviation Group. Together with the discoveries concerning thermal gliding flight from the year 1928, towed glider flight leads to the universal expansion of unpowered flight.

1931

According to *Flugwissen 3/43*, a Soviet towed glider crossed all of Russia.

1932 [6]

The RRG builds the OBS, a three-seat glider with an enclosed cockpit.

22/7/1934

The Röhn-Rossitten Society becomes the *Deutsche Forschungsinstitut für Segelflug* (German Research Institute for Gliding Flight).

Berlin, 22/7/1934

In the magazine *Deutsche Luftwacht*, World Edition, Volume 1, No. 14, p. 271, it is reported that Aeroflot is instituting scheduled service by commercial aircraft towing gliders on the Moscow to Bataisk run. The gliders are capable of carrying loads of 1.5 to 3 tons. The tug is said to be a P-5 and the glider a two-seat SCH-5 (designer Sheremetyev) or single-seat G-9 on the 1600-kilometer route.

1936 [6]

While the RRG had 20 to 35 workers until 1932, by 1936 the figure climbs to 220 (and by 1940 to 680). The *Deutsche Forschungsinstitut für Segelflug der RRG* is renamed the *Deutsche Forschungsinstitut für Segelflug (DFS)*.

The design and construction of the first cargo-carrying glider (LS aircraft) is begun and completed in 1936. Flight testing of this aircraft begins at the end of 1936.

This information came from Professor Georgii (head of the DFS), but not until 1941. The information is probably not correct.

1/10/1936 Aircraft Development Program LC II [8]

An order is placed for three examples of the DFS LS1 cargo carrier (V1 – V3). The project was taken over by LC I. Mockups are completed in September 1936. The anticipated first flight date is March 1937. Testing by the *E-Stelle* (proving center) is supposed to follow in the months May to July 1937. No pre-production series (0-series) has yet been ordered.

The abbreviation "LS" originally meant "cargo carrier." LC I was the research department in the RLM (State Aviation Ministry) under *Ministerialrat* Baeumker. The DFS, headed by Prof. Georgii, was subordinate to this department. Working under Georgii was Chief

Fallschirmjäger werden aus Transportflugzeugen abgesetzt . . .

Parachute troops landed widely dispersed and had to assemble before going into action. (Buch der Luftwaffe)

Designer Jakobs, who designed the DFS 230. LC II was the designation for the RLM's development department, which was responsible for ordering and supervising the development of aircraft.

20/1/1937 [8, RL6/215] LC II Development Conference No. 120/37

At a meeting of the LC II department head with *Fl.-Oberstabsing.* Lucht, *Major* Junck, and others, a discussion is held concerning current and future projects assigned to the aircraft companies. Among the decisions made: "Aircraft types designated SV are to be categorized as study devices, for which drawings will now be required which meet RLM guidelines. The drawings must only be of a standard required to construct the anticipated number of prototypes."

It is also decided that, in the future, a number of aircraft types, such as the Do 19, Ju 89, He 119, and Bf 163, are to be treated as SV types, if this had not already happened.

This decision spelled the end for a number of aircraft development programs. The prototypes already ordered would be completed, however, the pre-production aircraft were cancelled. The RLM clearly wanted to reduce the number of development projects. The reason for this was the shortage of development engineers required to work on all the active projects. As well, from a production point of view it made more sense to concentrate on a few types with significantly higher production rates. The change in the development programs became clear, with the designation V 1 becoming SV 1 and so on. The Fi 157 V 1 thus became Fi 157 SV 1.

3/1937 Darmstadt-Griesheim [13], [37]

A glider trials unit is formed in Darmstadt under *Leutnant* Kies and the first transport glider course is held.

I have no original documents to support this claim and must rely on the cited sources. As there were as yet no transport gliders, the training must have been carried out using normal gliders. The timing is not entirely in keeping with the RLM's hesitant approach to transport gliders described in the following text.

1/4/1937 Aircraft Development Program [8]

The three transport gliders are now designated DFS LS SV 1 – SV 3. The first ready-to-fly date was in January 1937. Testing at the *E-Stelle* and procurement authorization are not anticipated and no pre-production series is planned.

The designations SV 1 to SV 3, absence of a plan to test, and no anticipated pre-production series lead to the conclusion that the RLM saw no useful role for transport gliders at the beginning of 1937 and had no interest in a production program. This attitude lasts only a few months, as subsequent developments show.

10/5/1937 LC II Department Head Conference No. 770/37 [8]

The department head (Udet) decides that 40 DFS 230 towed gliders should be manufactured as intended by GERNER (Frankfurt/Main) and HARTWIG (Sonneberg). If test results are favorable, a follow-up series is to be built, not by GERNER, but by small companies in areas where unemployment is high.

1/10/1937 Aircraft Development Program [8]

The three transport gliders are still called SV 1 – SV 3, but procurement authorization is given in March 1937. Type testing is completed and trials begin at the DFS and in Stendal. Work begins on a batch of 30 aircraft.

According to the table dated 17/2/1941, HARTWIG built 18 DFS 230 A-0. GERNER must therefore have constructed twelve examples. The parachute battalion's first parachute school was established at Stendal in the period February to April 1936.

16/11/1937 Stendal, [5]

A comparative exercise between transport gliders and parachute troops is held at the training grounds opposite the Stendal airfield. A reinforced platoon of paratroopers, which jumps from Ju 52s at a height of about 350 meters, takes about 15 minutes to achieve combat readiness after touching down, as the weapons containers have to be inspected and emptied before the paratroopers arm themselves and assemble. By comparison, the 70 infantrymen landed by 10 DFS 230 gliders are combat ready in less than three minutes.

Based on this, at least seven more machines must have been built in addition to the three prototypes. However, a quartermaster general's list prepared later (see 4/12/1944) reveals that the Luftwaffe did not take the first 28 transport gliders on strength until 1939. From 1937 to 1939 the gliders were probably the property of the RLM.

25/1/1938, DFS Darmstadt [8]
Further development of the DFS 230 is discussed at a meeting between DFS and the General Staff Dept. 1.

1938, DFS Darmstadt [9]
The DFS begins systematic towing experiments using short cables, with the objective of making the glider-tug combinations capable of instrument flight.

At the conclusion of the experiments, the DFS 230 aircraft is towed behind the Ju 52 on cables 1 to 1.5 meters long. The method's suitability for instrument flying is demonstrated in a number of day and night instrument flights over the triangular course Darmstadt—Hamburg—Munich—Darmstadt. Of course, the procedure demands a high level of concentration on the part of the aircrews, and for this reason it is rejected as an operational procedure.

9/3/1938, RLM [5]
The *Reichminister* orders the formation of a "Transport Glider Training Detachment," the first transport glider unit.

1/4/1938 [13]
The Transport Glider Training Detachment is established.

7/1938 RLM, [5]
The training detachment is disbanded and its personnel transferred back to their parent units.

Senior air force officials were still obviously uncertain as to the practicality of the transport glider. It is unlikely that additional gliders were ordered in this situation, and production was initially limited to the 30 pre-production aircraft already ordered. In the end, though, they came to the decision that they wanted it [the transport glider].

22/11/1938 Gothaer Waggonfabrik [8, RL 3/180]
The Gothaer Waggonfabrik receives from the RLM a preliminary order (LC 6 Az. 89 al. 12.35 LC 6 IIa Contract No. 73/381b) for the "Production redesign, construction of the 1st prototype V5, design and production of jigs and tools" for the DFS 230.

Developed and built by the DFS (a research institute), the DFS 230 was too expensive for mass production. An experienced aircraft company was therefore given the task of simplifying the DFS 230 and readying it for quantity production. The GWF was to supervise and develop the DFS 230 until the end of the war. The DFS 230 V1 to V3 were mentioned previously, here the V5. I have no knowledge of the V4.

Short-tow tests (here with a towline length of about 1.5 m) began in 1938 using a small glider. (DFS)

Short-tow trials by a Ju 52 and DFS 230 A-0 with a towline length of approx. 3 m. (DFS)

Training was initially conducted using pre-production aircraft. (Mathiesen)

Illustration of the DFS 230 from the aircraft handbook. (Handbook)

DFS' original rigid-tow configuration. (DFS)

Gothaer Waggonfabrik, 31/3/1939 [8, RL 3/180]

The GWF produces a summary of the existing development contracts. Concerning the DFS 230, it is noted that the DFS 230 V5 is to be ferried to Rechlin in approximately eight days.

1939 [13]

Formation of 17./K.Gr.z.b.V. 5, which is to be used in the attack on Belgium.

1939 DFS Darmstadt, [9]

The DFS proposes a rigid tow bar which places the glider approximately 1 meter behind the tug, in order to reduce the stress on crews towing close-coupled gliders. Later that year the DFS builds and flight tests such a rigid tow bar.

3/9/1939 Air Armaments Minister No. 4351/39

The GL (Air Armaments Minister) issues service manual L.Dv. 559 (Draft) DFS 230 A and B Aircraft Handbook. The foreword reads: "This handbook deals with the DFS 230 A and B. (L.S. = *Lastensegler*, or transport glider). The A model has single controls, the B model dual controls for training. The handbook is applicable in particular to the A-1 series. The specifics of the DFS 230 B-2 dual-control machine are described in greater detail in Part 8 (L.Dv. 559) Appendix."

The A-2 and B-1 series were obviously not planned. All of the illustrations in the handbook depict pre-production machines, which are painted silver and wear codes (here D-5-2xx) prescribed for gliders. Some of the drawings depict pre-production series aircraft, while others show the DFS 230-A1, which had by then entered production.

2/11/1939 Hildesheim [1]

Under conditions of extreme secrecy, "Assault Battalion Koch" is formed for the attack on the Belgian fort of Eben Emael.

1/1940 Brunswick [9]

The DFS demonstrates the rigid-tow unit to *Generaloberst* Udet, the Air Armaments Minister, and *General* Student, the commanding general of XI Air Corps. Factors that weigh against its introduction into service are the rigid tow bar's weight (approx. 200 kg) and the loss of performance compared to the long-towline method.

18/1/1940 *E-Stelle* [8, RL 36/75]

DFS 230 type testing: following the demonstration in Brunswick on 11/1, work immediately begins on the introduction of the rigid-coupled towing procedure. The 7th Air Division submits documents needed by the *E-Stelle* for the loading of various guns.

24/1/1940 Robert Hartwig, Sonneberg [8, RL 3/556]

The Robert Hartwig Company delivers the last of 30 DFS 230 A-1s to the *Luftwaffe* and begins deliveries of the DFS 230 A-2 gun aircraft.

As the DFS 230 had not yet seen action, the introduction of a new variant could only have resulted from experience gained in exercises or the addition of new roles.

8/2/1940 *E-Stelle* [8, RL 36/75]

Tests with the semi-rigid coupling reveal a significant improvement compared to cable-tow.

29/2/1940 *E-Stelle* [8, RL 36/75]

DFS 230 type testing: special modification for 7th Air Division completed; flight distance tables completed; braking spur installation under development by GWF.

I do not know what the special modification involved. It may possibly refer to the new hatch on the right side of the fuselage, which in combination with the removable rear row of seats enabled the transport of guns. This modification led to the switch in production from the A-1 to the A-2.

11 and 18/4/1940 *E-Stelle* [8, RL 36/75]

DFS 230 type testing: flight performances and ranges with one and two towed gliders are measured and range tables completed.

9/5/1940 German Research Institute for Gliding Flight, Ainring

In Studies and Reports No. 624 the DFS describes <u>Short Towline and Rigid-Tow Flights by Ju 52s and DFS 230 Transport Gliders</u>. The DFS conducted towed flights with towlines less than 10 m long to determine the operational potential of transport gliders. Advantages were the small amount of space required during takeoff and direct view of the tug from the glider even in heavy cloud. Towlines as short as 1½ meters were used in the trials. From them arises

Ju 52 / DFS 230 combinations in flight. (Schlaug)

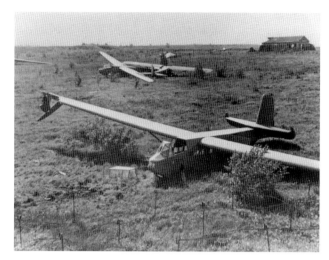

Most of the crew climbed out through the cockpit. (Schlaug)

A DFS 230 A-1 after landing. The machine wears neither an aircraft code nor national insignia. (Schlaug)

the idea of coupling the glider directly to the end of the Ju 52's fuselage, to relieve the strain on the glider pilot (rigid-tow). The report also details a first step in this direction. (See DFS: Research Aircraft)

10/5/1940 Fort Eben Emael / Albert Canal Bridges [1]
After taking off from Cologne in 42 Ju 52/DFS 230 glider-tug combinations, Assault Battalion Koch captures the Belgian fort of Eben Emael and several bridges over the Albert Canal. This is the first use of the DFS 230 in combat. As only 30 DFS 230 A-1s were built, the DFS 230 A-2 must also have been used by the unit.

17/05/1940 Conference GL1/Genst. 6. Abt. [7]
(GL means Generalluftzeugminister or Air Armaments Minister, Genst. 6. Abt. means General Staff Dept. 6)

Genstab. 6. Abt. requests a report on delays in delivery of the transport glider (DFS 230) and subsequent project planning.

The He 45 (top) and He 46 were used as tow planes. (Schlaug / Stiepdonk)

The Genstab. 6. Abt. requests that a number of types be examined for suitability as tow planes: He 45, He 46, Hs 126, Ju 87, and He 111. Previous results: He 45 and He 46 suitable, He 111 unsuitable.

Genstab. 6. Abt. previously ordered the conversion of 50 He 46. An additional He 45 and He 46 aircraft cannot be made available, so both the Hs 126 and Ju 87 must be tested for suitability as glider tugs.

The success in Belgium surely strengthened the general staff's desire for more transport gliders, but the decision to expand the transport glider fleet must have predated this. The DFS 230 was, after all, capable of transporting cargo—after the removal of the bench seat—as well as armed troops. Long-obsolescent aircraft could be used as tugs, creating relatively inexpensive transport capacity. As not even the "old kites" were available in sufficient numbers, the general staff intended to also equip active frontline aircraft (Hs 126, Ju 87, and especially the Ju 52) with tow couplings to enable them to be pressed into service if the need arose.

24/05/1940 Conference GL1/Genst. 6. Abt. [7]
LC 2 informs LE 2 of a DFS 230 production schedule. General Staff passes comment on the delivery plan.

The request for examination of aircraft types for suitability as glider tugs is expanded to include the He 50. LE stated the number of aircraft available for conversion (probably 50 He 50).

General staff asks for information on construction plans for "enlarged transport gliders," especially the pre-production series production schedule.

A He 46 tow plane in flight. (Mathiesen)

The multiple glider tow employing two to three DFS 230s behind a Ju 52 was tested at Hildesheim, but was never used operationally. (Seifert)

This is the first mention of the enlarged transport glider, which resulted in the Go 242, that I am aware of. The success at Eben Emael likely spurred interest in this aircraft.

31/5/1940 Conference GL1/Genst. 6. Abt. [7]

In the event that the He 50 proves a suitable glider tug, LC 2 is asked to preplan 50 aircraft for conversion. A request was made for the probable timetable.

General Staff advises that *Major* Trettner of the 7th Division is still of the opinion that deliveries of the enlarged transport glider will begin in June/July. LC 2 is asked for information on construction plans—especially the production schedule for the pre-production aircraft.

7/6/1940 Conference GL1/Genst. 6. Abt. [7]

General Staff requests a "Transport Glider Program." A request is also made to deliver an undercarriage with each glider for use at intermediate landing fields. The first prototype (enlarged transport glider) will probably fly in August. Delivery schedule in the new program.

14/6/1940 Conference GL1/Genst. 6. Abt. [7]

25 He 46 are already in Hildesheim, as are towing kits. Installation to be carried out by the units themselves.

25/6/1940 Conference GL1/Genst. 6. Abt. [7]

General Staff states a requirement for 1,000 transport gliders (DFS 230) by the end of the year for the formation of units. General Staff is advised that 2,500 transport gliders have already been ordered.

The first enlarged transport glider will come at the end of August, and a further four by the end of the year (pre-production series). Quantity production is to be expected by the middle of the following year.

It is declared that 600 aircraft of the Ju 52 type must have towing equipment installed at all times. The necessary towing equipment is to be procured. Installation of towing equipment on new-production Ju 52s is to be initiated as quickly as possible. Information on timing is requested. Conversion of existing Ju 52s is to begin immediately. For the time being, only aircraft under repair, in the manufacturers' hands, or with LE are available. LE provided LC 2 with a list of Ju 52s available for conversion.

1/7/1940 C-Amt Program [8]

Deliveries of the DFS 230 total 109 with another 1,963 on order.

Five prototypes of an enlarged transport glider are being built by Gothaer Waffonfabrik. The first is to be completed in September 1940, the others to follow in October. The designation is DFS 230/? or Go 230.

As with the DFS 230, while the DFS was able to conduct preliminary development, it was up to the manufacturers to make the preparations necessary for production. Under the existing conditions it seemed logical that GWF would again serve as partner and even build the prototypes. As subsequent developments would show, the five prototypes were of two different designs. The misleading designations are probably attributable to an error on the part of the stenographer.

12/7/1940 Conference GL1/Genst. 6. Abt. [7]

LC 2 offers for inspection a report on the situation of Ju 52 aircraft under repair. This shows that a total of 95 aircraft are in the hands of the aircraft industry. General Staff requests that, as per the plan (Appendix 1), the program to convert Ju 52s for use as transports and glider tugs be initiated at once. The report appears to have overlooked the Dutch repair industry, as the figure of 95 Ju 52 aircraft under repair seemed improbably low. A request is made to check the report and provide the General Staff with a delivery plan and a list of serial numbers (*Werknummer*).

After it was replaced as a frontline aircraft by the Ju 87 D in 1942, the Ju 87 R was used as a tug for the DFS 230 glider. (Bundesarchiv Koblenz 10 11-567-1519-30)

As not enough of the obsolete He 45 and He 46 aircraft were available, the Hs 126 initially became, along with the Ju 52, the standard glider tug. (Bundesarchiv Koblenz 10 11-565-1425-11A)

Arado was the main supplier of undercarriages for the DFS 230. (Schlaug)

General Staff requests opinions on the question of glider tugs for transport gliders: He 45, He 50, Hs 126, and Ju 87.

18/7/1940 Gotha [15]

Representatives of the RLM inspect a mockup of the large transport glider (Go 242) at the Gothaer Waggonfabrik.

19/7/1940 Conference GL1/Genst. 6. Abt. [7]

General Staff requests opinions on the question of glider tugs for transport gliders: He 45, He 50, Hs 126, and Ju 87. Based on a position taken by the 7th Division, it had already been decided to equip 200 Hs 126s with towing equipment, 80 of these as a high-priority project. LC 2 is asked for a timetable. 30 aircraft are already ready in Kölleda. There is a possibility that additional aircraft could be flown there, so that a more capable working headquarters can be established. The ferrying of aircraft there is only possible, however, if a preliminary timetable is known, so that the aircraft are not taken away from the units for too long. In terms of priority, equipping 200 Hs 126s with towing equipment is secondary to the equipping of Ju 52s with towing equipment.

23/7/1940 RLM LC 2/IA [8, RL 3/556]

An order is placed with the Arado Company for the production of 1,975 undercarriages for the DFS 230, to be built between August 1940 and June 1941. Of these, 1,350 are allocated to series production (415 for Hartwig, 190 for Bücker, 272 for Erla, 227 for Gothaer Waggonfabrik, and 246 for C.K.D.). The rest are to go to operational units and spares depots.

26/7/1940 Conference GL1/Genst. 6. Abt. [7]

The revised report on the Ju 52s undergoing repair is promised for the coming weeks. Effective immediately, towing equipment is to be installed in every transport aircraft coming out of repair. Towing equipment is to be installed in transport aircraft only. Deliveries of aircraft to Wittstock have not achieved the specified rate—20 per day—consequently deliveries are late.

On the question of glider tugs, the General Staff requests opinions about the He 50 only. This type is only being used for training and will be available if it proves a suitable glider tug. As well, it is requested that the He 111 be evaluated as a tug for large transport gliders.

According to information from the 7th Division—*Major* Koch—the Hs 126 glider tug is unsuited to night operations. Progress of the conversion program in Jena-Rödiger is as follows: 70 examples by 31/7, ten by 4/8. The 120 parts still to be delivered are being stored temporarily by LE. LE is seeing to the procurement of the necessary towlines, about 400 in total.

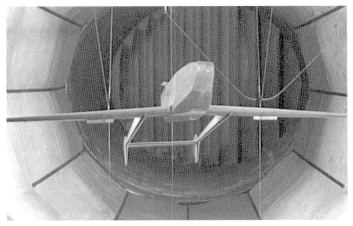

9/8/1940 Conference GL1/Genst. 6. Abt. [7]

The revised report (Ju 52 with towing equipment) is tabled. The General Staff and LE are to be advised in writing of the serial numbers of the Ju 52s in Holland. 72 Ju 52 aircraft, which were to have been equipped with PVC in Paderborn, Ütersen, by Blohm & Voss, and in Dessau, are also to be retrofitted with towing gear. This will be accomplished by restarting a line in Wittstock. 95 aircraft have been converted in Wittstock. Another 105 sets of towing equipment are in storage there. Arrangements are presently being made to convert three Ju 52s which were not available when the work was carried out on the others.

The He 50 has been found suitable for glider tug work. The final test results are to be revealed later. The He 111 is currently under test for suitability as a tug for large gliders, with results to follow.

General Staff is presented a report on the question of night towing by the Hs 126. Night towing by that time presented no problems.

10/8/1940 Gothaer Waggonfabrik [9]

The GWF tasks the Hermann German Aviation Research Institute in Brunswick with carrying out wind tunnel tests on a model of the Go 242. After construction of the models tests begin in October.

1/9/1940 C-Amt Program [8]

Three prototypes of the DFS 331 are under construction at the Gothaer Waggonfabrik. Delivery is planned for

As was typical of a 1940s wind tunnel, the model was suspended upside down, as the scale was located above the instrumented chamber. The instrumented chamber had a diameter of 2.5 m. (Aviation Research Institute)

Once replaced as a reconnaissance aircraft by the Fw 189, the Hs 126 was widely used as a glider tug for the DFS 230. (Schlaug)

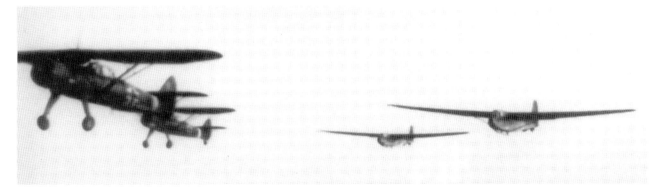

Vordruck 10 — Nr. 18, Blatt 12a von 12, Ausgabe 2, Nr. 80, g.Kdos.-Nr. 984/40

C-Amts-Programm
Lastensegler

Lieferplan — Ausfertigung

Muster	Motor	Fa.	Ges.	bis 30.6.	vom 1.7.	1940-7	8	9	10	11	12	1941-1	2	3	4	5	6	7	8	9	10	11	12	1942-1	2	3
DFS 230	A 3	Go	40	-	40		5	5	10	10	10															
		Erla	40	-	40			10	10	10	10															
		CKD	34	-	34			1	6	12	15															
			114	-	114			6	21	32	35	20														
								27			114															
	A 2	Har	809	109	800	30	40	40	40	40	40	40	40	40	40	40	40	40	40	40	40	40	40	40	30	20
		Bü	360	-	360			1	3	6	10	15	20	25	25	25	25	25	25	25	25	25	25	25	20	10
		Go	332	-	332					1	3	8	15	25	25	25	25	25	25	25	25	25	25	25	20	10
		Erla	477	-	477					1	3	8	15	20	25	35	40	40	40	40	40	40	40	40	30	20
		CKD	377	-	377					1	3	8	15	25	25	30	30	30	30	30	30	30	30	30	20	10
			2455	109	2346	30	40	41	43	49	59	79	105	135	140	155	160	160	160	160	160	160	160	160	120	70
								220			371			690			1145			1625			2105			2455

Delivery plan of 1/10/1940 with the planned numbers for the DFS 230.

The DFS 331 V1, still without an aircraft code. (Petrick)

the months of September, October, and November 1940. Construction of two prototypes of a parallel design is also supposed to be complete in October and November. The designation is: Go/DFS 242.

13/9/1940 Conference GL1/Genst. 6. Abt. [7]

It is revealed that the report on towing tests involving He 111 with large transport glider cannot be submitted until the large transport glider became available.

27/9/1940 Conference GL1/Genst. 6. Abt. [7]

The large transport tglider can only be towed by the He 111 F, H, or P, or the Ju 52. The General Staff inquires whether the large transport glider with the 3000 landing skid can be towed, as this is a vital factor in selecting a design.

30/9/1940 *Luftwaffe* Airfield in Gotha (Blendermann Logbook) [24]

Pilot Karl-Heinz Blendermann pilots a Ju 52 (H4+BH) towing the DFS 331 V1 on its first flight. Hanna Reitsch pilots the glider. More than 100 towed flights are subsequently carried out.

1/10/1940 C-Amts Program/ Transport Glider [8]

(The C-Amt Program contained fixed dates with information on aircraft that had actually been built by then. As a rule, plans concerning aircraft to be constructed after those fixed dates were not adhered to. Therefore, the programs are only of limited value when making statements about total production figures.)

This C-Amts Program includes the DFS 230 A-3, 114 examples of which were supposed to be built in parallel to the DFS 230 A-2. I cannot state with certainty what it [the A-3] was. The period for construction of this variant was, however, precisely during the phase when the Luftwaffe was converting aircraft for use in the tropics, in the campaign in Africa. To me, the most logical explanation is that the DFS 230 A-3 was a tropical version.

1/10/1940 Gotha/Erfurt see 2/12/1940

Albert Kalkert moves from the Gothaer Waggonfabrik to the Erfurt Repair Works. At this time he is also the Air Armaments Minister's deputy for the DFS 230 industry program.

After this move Kalkert surely had no further responsibilities with the Gothaer Waggonfabrik, and could not have been responsible for many developments attributed to him in the literature.

Autumn 1940 Operation Large Glider (Me 321, Ju 322)

Publications dealing with Willy Messerschmitt credit him with the idea of the large glider; however, I consider it entirely possible that the concept came from somewhere else and was passed on to him for development. In any case, the Junkers firm received a contract for a large glider concept study at the same time. While Messerschmitt was permitted to design the load-bearing sections of the fuselage and wing using steel tube, Junkers was allegedly instructed to use wood even for these critical components. The Ju 322 was a total failure. Junkers consequently destroyed all documents related to the project and no official photographs or drawings survived. What knowledge we have comes largely from an article by Heumann in Flugrevue 12/64 and

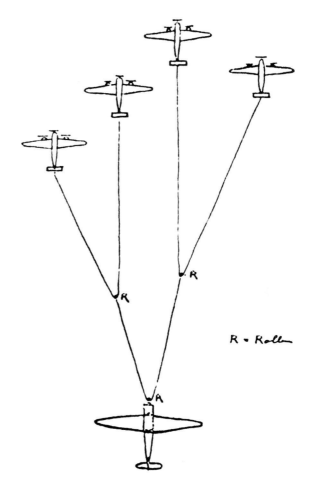

Messerschmitt sketch dated 4/10/1940.

subsequent letters from readers, and is based on personal recollections.

In the literature the development contract for the Me 321 is usually linked to "Operation Sea Lion," Hitler's planned invasion of England. This version of events seems doubtful to me. Hitler gave the order for "Operation Sea Lion" on 16/7/1940. On 22/7 Hitler declared that England had to be subdued by September so that he could turn to Russia. Not even the Go 242 or DFS 331, which existed only as prototypes, could have been built with sufficient speed. Even the time gained when the Luftwaffe failed to achieve air superiority over England in August and September 1940, and Sea Lion was postponed on 12/10/1940, was not such as to have allowed the development and construction of the desired 400 large gliders.

In my opinion the large glider was considered exclusively for future attacks, like the one on Russia.

4/10/1940 Messerschmitt [18]

Willy Messerschmitt proposes to the RLM that large gliders with minimal equipment and aerodynamic shapes be designed within a few weeks. These would be capable of transporting large, bulky loads behind the enemy lines. The gliders would be able to transport heavy guns and similar items within the fuselage; however, it would also be possible to suspend tanks beneath the wings and use just the rear fuselage as a tail unit bearer, attached to the tanks with bolted-on fittings. He believes it possible to construct a large number of gliders, essentially made of pine and thick plywood with metal fittings, within a few months. He envisages the glider being towed by four Ju 52s. He had discussed this towing arrangement with the Research Institute for Gliding Flight, then in Ainring. There were no reservations, and test flights with small glider tugs could begin immediately.

8/10/1940 Messerschmitt [18]

A small team (about 15 to 20 designers) under the direction of Josef Fröhlich begins initial development of the Me 261, a predecessor of the Me 321. Design work starts on 15/10. The first known drawing of the Me 261 W is dated 1/11/1940.

9/10/1940 Conference GL1/Genst. 6. Abt. [7]

Ju 52 glider tugs for the large transport glider are to be taken from the production line on such dates as to match the large transport glider.

19/10/1940 Ainring / Grand Venice Glacier [1]

Using the DFS 230 V1 (D-5-289), the German Research Institute for Gliding Flight (DFS) carries out a landing and takeoff from the glacier. Takeoff is achieved with the assistance of a catapult consisting of six elastic ropes. The purpose of the exercise is to demonstrate the feasibility of transport glider flights in the high mountains. After taking off from a makeshift airfield at Matrei, the DFS 230 (pilot Lettmayer) is towed over

the glacier by a Ju 52 (pilot Zitter, radio operator Roschlau). Released at an altitude of 4250 meters, it lands on the glacier at an elevation of 3500 m. The experiment proves the feasibility of the procedure, however, the manpower required to get the DFS 230 airborne again is high, and tensioning the elastic ropes takes a long time. For this reason further development of the procedure involves rocket-assisted takeoffs.

October 1940 Junkers [28]

The Junkers design bureau, headed by H. Gropler, has to release an aerodynamicist and a design engineer for the top secret pre-development work on the Ju 322. As there is no consultation with experienced experts in flight characteristics (such as dynamic and static longitudinal stability), the fuselage is subsequently designed too short and the vertical tail surfaces too small.

1/11/1940 RLM

Deadline for submission to the RLM of design plans and initial estimates for the large glider. Junkers and Messerschmitt each subsequently receive an order for 100 gliders.

26/10/1940 Conference GL1/Genst. 6. Abt. [7]

The General Staff agrees to reduce deliveries of the DFS 230 (for 20 examples of the 331 by spring 1941).

1/11/1940 C-Amts Program [8]

The DFS 331 V1 with the *Werknummer* 331 0000001 is in general testing. The DFS 331 V2 and V3 and the Go/DFS 242 V1 and V2 (*Werknummer* 242 0000001 and 2) are to be completed in November. All aircraft are located in Gotha.

20 pre-production examples of the Go 242 are to be constructed in Gotha from January to May 1941. 20 DFS 331 pre-production aircraft are to be built in Erfurt during the same period.

2/11/1940 Gotha, Registered Letter from GWF to the RLM [8, RL3/1860]

Referring to a meeting in the RLM on 24/10/1940, GWF offers to construct an initial batch of ten prototypes using extremely primitive means. After construction of the main jigs, a second batch of ten prototypes is to begin even as the first series is being built. Following completion of the jigs, a production batch can begin with an output of ten machines per month. All of this will depend on cancellation of the DFS 230 and the cessation of Fw 58 production and Bf 110 repair work.

6/11/1940 Messerschmitt [4], [18]

Willy Messerschmitt telegraphs Fröhlich from Berlin (after an audience with Hitler the previous day) and informs him that the Warsaw-South program is to begin immediately, but with double the quantity. Fröhlich views this date as the start of design work. 200 aircraft are to be completed by spring 1941. Because of the tight schedule the aircraft are envisaged as gliders.

The DFS 230 V I approached the glacier, landed there, and was manually hauled into takeoff position. (DFS)

There the DFS 230 was positioned for takeoff and anchored to the ground with a steel cable. 25 men then tensioned the catapult's elastic cable. (DFS)

After taking off, the DFS 230 flew to the improvised landing site at Matrei.
Waiting for it there was a He 46, which towed it back to Ainring. (DFS)

The fuselage sides of the DFS 331 V1 were painted RLM 70. (German Museum)

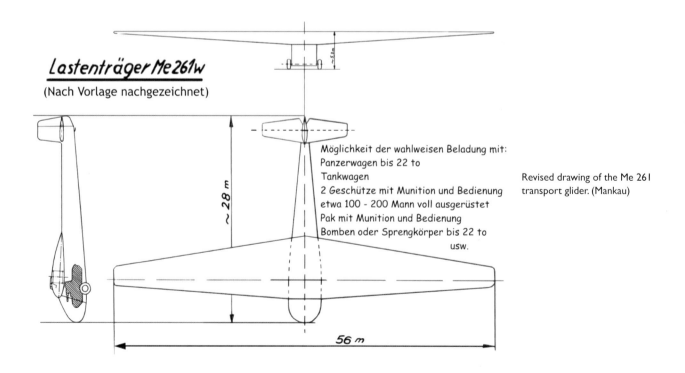

Lastenträger Me 261w

(Nach Vorlage nachgezeichnet)

Möglichkeit der wahlweisen Beladung mit:
Panzerwagen bis 22 to
Tankwagen
2 Geschütze mit Munition und Bedienung
etwa 100 - 200 Mann voll ausgerüstet
Pak mit Munition und Bedienung
Bomben oder Sprengkörper bis 22 to
usw.

Revised drawing of the Me 261 transport glider. (Mankau)

~28 m

56 m

There are no confirmed photos of the Go 242 VI, but it must have been similar to this pre-production aircraft. (Nowarra)

Four He 72s (D-EFHU, D-EYRI, BB+XE, and D-EPQE) tow the DFS 230. (DFS)

6/11/1940 Junkers [19]
Junkers also receives a development contract for its Warsaw-North glider.

9/11/1940 Gothaer Waggonfabrik Factory Airfield Gotha (Blendermann Logbook) [24]
Blendermann pilots the glider tug as the Go 242 V1 made its first flight. Two further towed flights take place on 10/11.

11/11/1940 Gotha [15]
Representatives of the RLM inspect the Go 242 V1 in the Gothaer Waggonfabrik.

21/11/1940 Conference GL1/Genst. 6. Abt. [7]
The Air Armaments Minister presents the large glider project, code name "Warsaw," to the General Staff. The General Staff promises to state its position on the resulting

questions (training, provision of aircraft for conversion to glider tugs, parking areas).

For some time the large glider was referred to only by the code name Warsaw. The Me 321 was Warsaw-South and the Ju 322 Warsaw-North.

26/11/1940 DFS Ainring [9]
In the report "Towing of Coupled Aircraft by Multiple Powered Aircraft" Stamer and Georgii write about the experiences of experiments with 2 to 5 tow aircraft. It remains to be determined whether a glider of large dimensions *(meaning the Me 321 and Ju 322)*, which cannot be towed by a single powered aircraft, can be carried into the air and towed by several powered aircraft. In order to create conditions as close as possible to those that will arise as the project progresses, a DFS 230 is towed by two He 72s. It is immediately decided to use one towline per tow plane, so that the formation will not

be impacted by the loss of one of the powered aircraft. The testing carried out in November 1940 (16 flights) reveals the need for unrestricted visibility between the tow planes. This eliminates from consideration the echelon left formation with one aircraft in front and the others staggered behind and 10 meters to the side. It is found that positioning the first tow plane 80 m in front of the glider on the outer left is a more favorable arrangement. The second [aircraft] flies 90 meters in front of it on the outer right. The other tow planes each fly 10 m farther forward and to the inside, so that the middle of the five tugs is 120 m in front of the glider. The flights are made with empty and loaded DFS 230s. They demonstrate the feasibility of the procedure and suggest that no major difficulties are to be expected.

2/12/1940 Erfurt/RLM LC 2/IA [8, RL 3/556]

The Air Armaments Minister's deputy for Industry Program 230, Dir. Albert Kalkert, Erfurt Repair Works GmbH, writes to the RLM LC 2/IA that he has not received various letters in his above-named capacity because the RLM sent them to GWF. He points out that he has not been with GWF since 1/10/1940, but on the other hand is responsible for Industry Program 230. As a result, he has only now learned that the entire stock of wings has been given to the Fokker Company. His planned capacity allocation to the Fokker Company and the shape of the entire program have thus been overturned, and he has to develop a new program with Fokker. Furthermore, it is not clear whether Fokker is now supposed to build 350 or 450 sets of wings. He asks the RLM to decide once and for all how many wings Fokker is to build.

18/12/1940 Conference GL1/Genst. 6. Abt. [7]

The LE 2 brings to the attention of those present that the increased production of the transport glider (DFS 230) has resulted in considerable difficulties in the storage of these aircraft. General Staff is asked to check with the air force to determine if the affected units might be able to make available the required dispersal space.

10/1/1941 Conference GL1/Genst. 6. Abt. [7]

General Staff asks for confirmation that all DFS 230s produced from February on will have dual controls.

11/1/1941 Erfurt Repair Works [8, RL 3/556]

Kalkert (Air Armaments Minister's deputy for Industry Program 230) informs the GWF by letter that he and the RLM (*Obersting.* Reidenbach) have reached two decisions in principle concerning the DFS 230:

1. In the event that a Go 242 follow-up contract is not forthcoming, GWF is to deliver 8 DFS 230s in January 1941, in February 15, in March 25, in May 22, in June 19, in July 15, and finally in August ten.

2. In the event that test-flying of the Go 242, which is to begin on 21/1, proves successful, and a follow-up contract is issued, then, after delivery of the pre-production series, GWF is to produce ten Go 242s per month as a bridge contract until other license companies can begin production of the type. In this case production of the DFS 230 will run down at the end of March with the following numbers: January eight examples, February 15, and March 25. To make good the resulting shortfall in fuselages, a contract will probably be given to the Bohemian-Moravian Machine Factory AG Prague (previously CKD) to cover the period until the factory in Konstanz is up and running.

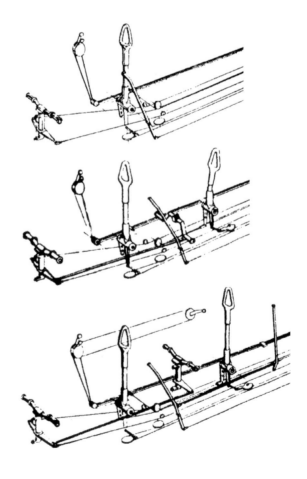

The top drawing, from the 1939 handbook, illustrates the simple controls of the DFS 230 A-1, the center those of the A-2 with auxiliary stick and the bottom the dual controls of the B-2. The last two drawings are from the 1942 issue of the pilot's notes for the DFS 230 A-1, A-2, and B-2. On the left side of the fuselage was the lever for operating the spoilers located on the wings. According to former DFS 230 pilots, the A-2 did not have the auxiliary control stick. (Handbook)

19/1/1941 Gotha [24]

Flugkapitän Franke from Rechlin takes the DFS 331 up on a test flight and is enthusiastic about its flight characteristics.

21/1/1941 Gotha [15]

According to Regel, the Go 242 was also test-flown by the *E-Stelle* in January 1941.

Regel offers no results of these acceptance tests, but the fact that preparations for production of the Go 242 begins just one month later suggests that the test flights were a success.

22/1/1941 Conference GL1/Genst. 6. Abt. [7]

LC 2 informs those present that both the Bf 110 C/D and the He 111 H-3/H-5 are suitable tow planes for Warsaw. The General Staff's decision as to how many of each type will be used is urgent.

LC 2 confirms that as of February all DFS 230s had been built with dual controls.

30/1/1941 Conference GL1/Genst. 6. Abt. [7]

LC 2 to immediately supply General Staff with delivery dates for aircraft to be modified (to tow Warsaw). Once it has received the schedule, the General Staff will determine the numbers of Bf 110s and He 111s intended for this role. The next six Bf 110 Es off the production line are to be assigned to XI Corps for tests and are to be equipped for their special role. Air Armaments Minister suggests that for secrecy reasons a remote airfield (for example Fassberg) be used for the testing. Required are two large hangars and associated ground personnel, as well as a takeoff support team.

Beginning of 1941 Junkers [28]

According to Gropler, the design bureau first learns about the Ju 322 and the task of assuring acceptable flight characteristics at this time. Recalculations reveal aerodynamic instability, specifically a tendency to yaw, with loose control surfaces. As the center of gravity is already far to the rear, it is not possible to extend the tail or increase the size of the rudder. It was only possible to solve the problem of excessively high control forces. As it is not out of the question that the pilot might be able to compensate for the yawing motion manually with the aid of powered controls, the Ju 322 is to be tested with the required caution.

1/2/1941 C-Amts Program [8]

By direction of the DFS, in February the DFS 331 V1 is sent to Darmstadt for general testing. The V2 is in the Erla Repair Works and is supposed to be completed in March. The V3 has not yet been built and its future is uncertain. The Go 242 V1 is under test in Gotha and is supposed to be converted into a motorized test-bed. The V2 is destined for general testing at Rechlin and is complete. The V3 is supposed to be completed in February and begin general testing by the air force. The pre-production plan is the same as that of 1/11/1940. The large transport glider is not mentioned in the program.

I have no information as to what type of engine was planned for the Go 242 V1 at this time. However, as this plan was not realized, and the first prototypes of the Go 244 later had to be converted from other aircraft, I suspect that what was under consideration was a version with a central auxiliary motor (As 10 C). As estimates showed that this version offered no advantages, it was decided not to construct a prototype and the Go 242 V1 was used for other tests.

6/2/1941 Ernst Heinkel Flugzeugwerke Rostock/Marienehe

According to an internal company memo (Heinkel Archive), the firm has received a contract to equip 200 He 111 H-3 to H-5 aircraft with a 10-ton tow coupling; a rearview mirror is to be installed at the same time. The installation is carried out as a high-priority project.

6/2/1941 Gothaer Waggonfabrik [8, RL 3/556]

The Gothaer Waggonfabrik writes to the Air Armaments Minister's deputy for Industry Program 230 that production of the DFS 230 is to run down in April and that production of the Go 242 will continue after the pre-production series is completed. The following DFS 230 production is planned for 1941: from January to March eight per month, and four in April. The jigs are functioning normally and will be free at the end of February. If the jigs are to be inspected, converted to dual controls and overhauled, this cannot take place before the end of April, as GWF will be 100% engaged with the jigs for the Me 210 until then.

6/2/1941 Conference GL1/Genst. 6. Abt. [7]

In addition to the six Bf 110s for XI Corps, six new-production He 111 H-5 aircraft are to be assigned to the Warsaw project immediately. The Chief of the General Staff cannot make a decision as to which units are to be equipped or the type to be chosen until XI Corps submits its report on the results of trials.

10/2/1941 Gothaer Waggonfabrik [8, RL 3/556]

The GWF advises Dir. Kalkert, the Air Armaments Minister's deputy for Industry Program 230, of the following allocation of serial numbers:

The "7" in the Werknummer identifies this DFS 230 as having been built by C.K.D. or BMM. (Mankau)

The Werknummer 22077 does not fit the list below, however, the 22 could be interpreted as a reference to Hartwig. (Aders)

Gotha	230.01.20 137	bis	230.01.20 176
	230.01.21.397	bis	230.01.20 405
	230.02.20.406	bis	230.02.20.723
Sonneberg	230.01.2.2.803	bis	230.01.2.2.922
	230.01.2.2.667	bis	230.01.2.2.694
Erla	230.01.2.5.112	bis	230.01.2.5.151
	230.01.2.5.347	bis	230.01.2.5.358
	230.02.2.5.359	bis	230.02.2.5.833
C.K.D.	230.01.2.7.017	bis	230.01.2.7.050
	230.01.2.7.194	bis	230.01.2.7.575
Bücker	230.01.2.1.016	bis	230.01.2.1.040
	230.02.2.1.041	bis	230.02.2.1.065
	230.02.2.1.216	bis	230.02.2.1.545

The serial numbers issued by the companies Hartwig, Sonneberg, and Bohemian-Moravian Machine Factory AG Prague differ from those of Gotha because the DFS 230 aircraft delivered by these companies have dual controls.

The list is reproduced as it appears in the document. One can presume that the Gotha Company's serial numbers were actually supposed to have followed the same format as those of the others. If so, additional periods should have been added and the fourth to last number should have been a "0". The manufacturers would then have been identified by these numbers (0 = Gotha, 1 = Bücker, 2 = Hartwig, 5 = Erla, and 7 = C.K.D.). It was common practice for only the last three digits to be painted on the aircraft, making it impossible to determine from this the company or variant.

12/2/1941 PRAGA Company, Prague [8, RL 3/556]

A meeting is held at the Praga Company. The minutes reveal that Praga has delivered 34 DFS 230 A-3s and 29 DFS 230 A-2s, and also has a contract for 503 DFS 230 B-2s. Among these 503 B-2s are 105 complete fuselages, for which MIAG is to deliver wings. Praga is to acquire

the materials for the 105 fuselages from Gotha. It has yet to hear from the RLM as to whether Miag can also supply Praga with the wings.

17/2/1941 Erfurt Repair Works [8, RL 3/556]

Kalkert writes to the RLM LC 2 IA that the Bohemian-Moravian Machine Factory AG Aircraft Construction Division in Prague is only capable of taking GWF's place in the delivery of 105 fuselages, as the wings have to be built by the Miag Company until production by Schwarzwald-Flugzeugbau in Donaueschingen is up and running. He requests clarification of the question of whether all aircraft to be built in the future should have dual controls. Kalkert offers the following figures for planned total deliveries of the DFS 230:

Type	Total	Total by 31/10/40
1) Gothaer Waggonfabrik, Gotha		
A-3 immediate program	40 by 12. 40	23
A-2 series	9 by 1.41	0
B-2 series	23 by 4.41	0
2) Erla Maschinenwerk GmbH, Leipzig		
A-3 immediate program		20
A-2 series	12	
B-2 series	195	
3) Bücker-Flugzeugbau GmbH, Rangsdorf		
A-2 series	25	9
B-2 series	397	0
4) Bohemian-Moravian Machine Factory AG Prague		
A-3 immediate program	34	
A-2 series	29	
B-2 series	503	
5) Robert Hartwig, Sonneberg		
A-0 series	18 by 30/9/38	18
A-1 series	30 by 24/10/40	30
A-2 series	357 by 15/3/41	
B-2 series	566 from 16/3/41	

DFS test pilot Anderle in a Prague-built DFS 230. (Petrick)

Takeoff with rocket power. (DFS film)

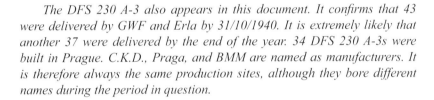

The DFS 230 A-3 also appears in this document. It confirms that 43 were delivered by GWF and Erla by 31/10/1940. It is extremely likely that another 37 were delivered by the end of the year. 34 DFS 230 A-3s were built in Prague. C.K.D., Praga, and BMM are named as manufacturers. It is therefore always the same production sites, although they bore different names during the period in question.

18/2/1941 Erfurt Repair Works [8, RL 3/556]

Kalkert writes to the Gothaer Waggonfabrik that the Bohemian-Moravian Machine Factory AG Prague (BMM) will build the aircraft lost in the transfer [of production], specifically 105 complete DFS 230 fuselages for the GWF. The Miag Company will continue to supply the necessary wings and the Eka-Werk Company of Friedrichsroda the tail sections. As Gotha is subsequently going to transfer the program to the Schwarzwald-Flugzeugbau Wilhelm Jehle Company of Donaueschingen, which, according to department LC 2 IA, however, is to build complete aircraft, a cancellation of further contracts to the Miag and Eka-Werk Companies has to be anticipated. GWF is to deliver materials stored by it to BMM for the 105 fuselages and other materials to the Schwarzwald-Flugzeugbau Company.

25/2/1941 Messerschmitt [4]

The Me 321 flies for the first time, towed by a Ju 90. It has an empty weight of 11,290 kg and is loaded with 3,590 kg of ballast.

In subsequent flights the Me 321 carries 3,910 kg and more of ballast. It cannot fly empty as it is then much too tail-heavy. This can be seen in photos of empty large gliders resting on their tail skids.

27/2/1941 Ainring / Seethaleralpe [9]

To demonstrate that gliders can be used to supply troops in the high mountains, a tug and DFS 230 glider take off from the Schmelz training camp, after which the DFS lands on a 250 x 80 m area of the Seethaleralpe. As soon as it has landed the machine is turned around, and it then takes off with the aid of two Rheinmetall rockets.

This still from a Messerschmitt film probably depicts the prototype with small crosses and no aircraft code. (Pawlas)

The experiment is repeated on 28/2. DFS assesses the procedure as suitable for regular use and declares that a landing area of 40 x 60 meters is sufficient. Three to five ground personnel are needed for the rocket-assisted takeoff, in particular to position the glider. One DFS 230 glider can make six flights in one day, delivering enough supplies for a 500-man battalion for two-and-a-half days (see chapter DFS 230: Experimental Aircraft).

1/3/1941 C-Amts Program [8]
The Go 242 V1 and V3 are undergoing trials with *Luftlandegeschwader Hildesheim*; the V2 is at the Rechlin proving center.

8/3/1941 Messerschmitt [4]
The first flight by the Me 321 V1, towed by three Bf 110s with [DB 601] N motors, takes place on this day.

7/3/1941 Erfurt [8, RL 3/556]
Dr. Kalkert writes to the RLM LC 2 concerning the DFS 230 and Go 242 production programs referring to meetings, first with *Generalstabsing* Alpers, and second between the RLM and the Gotha, Messerschmitt, and Junkers companies.

It emerged from the meeting with Alpers that the Go 242 is to replace the DFS 230, production of which is to be reduced to 1,000 examples. It is to be determined how much capacity for the Go 242 will be created as a result. If possible, the Schwarzwald-Flugzeugbau Company is not to begin production of the DFS 230. The Bohemian-Moravian Machine Factory AG is not being considered for production of the Go 242 and is to continue building the DFS 230. Alpers has further decided that Erla will cease production of the DFS 230 in October. The Bücker, Hartwig, and Gotha companies are also to completely halt production of the DFS 230, as is the Miag Company, which builds wings for Gotha.

According to GWF, the RLM has contracted the entire Go 242 program with Gotha. The sizes of the contracts for Warsaw-North (Ju 322) and Warsaw-South (Me 321) are based on the construction methods used (wood and steel). The Warsaw-North and Warsaw-South organizations are to complete 100 aircraft per month. In addition, Gotha and Hartwig are each to start construction of a small batch of Go 242s as a backup. To this end the full capacities of Hartwig and Eckhardt Sonneberg will be required from about July 1941. Gotha believes that from July 1941 it will also have to request Bücker's capacity for production of the fuselage nose and components of the control system. No value is placed on Erla's capacity, and also not on Schwarzwald-Flugzeugbau, as they are involved in work on the wood-construction Warsaw-North.

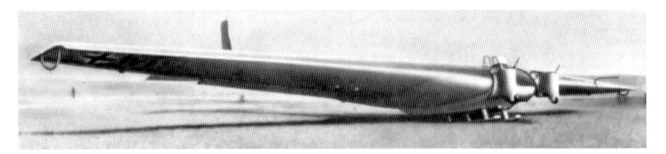

Fritz Buchwald, member of an anti-aircraft searchlight unit in Blösien, near Merseburg, photographed the Ju 322 immediately after its forced landing. This is the retouched version first published by Heumann. The gondolas forward of the wing contained the 4 tons of ballast. There were no gun positions. (Flugrevue)

In a few cases the Me 321 was towed by the Ju 90 V5 equipped with BMW 132 engines. (Kössler)

Kalkert observes that the rundown of DFS 230 production by Hartwig should be carefully coordinated with Gotha's capabilities, in order to avoid a complete shutdown of production. Kalkert doubts that, after DFS 230 metal work stops, Bücker will be fully engaged by producing fittings for the Go 242. Altogether, Kalkert feels that the rundown of DFS 230 production will be of very little benefit to the Go 242, as neither production capacity nor raw materials savings will result in a significant gain for the Go 242. Of the materials in storage for the DFS 230, only a few sections of steel tube can be used in the Go 242, and there is plenty of wood available. To Kalkert's knowledge, the Go 242 is supposed to take over the entire production capacity of Warsaw-North and –South <u>and</u> the DFS 230. This has to be verified, for according to previous estimates the Go 242 only requires one-third of the plywood currently being produced and one-third of the steel tube capacity available for Warsaw-South.

The Luftwaffe initiated development of the Me 321 and Ju 322 large transport gliders for effective attacks behind enemy lines, and development had been under way for a long time under the codenames Warsaw-South (Me 321) and Warsaw-North (Ju 322). The Ju 322 was to have been built largely of wood. As the Ju 322 displayed unacceptable flight characteristics, the wood capacity of Warsaw-North (various woodworking companies) became available for the Go 242. On 23/5/1941 the Air Armaments Minister planned a total of 250 examples of the Me 321 and its motorized derivative (110 gliders, 100 4-engine, 40 6-engine). It appeared that Warsaw-South's capacity would also be available for the Go 242 after this contract was filled.

10/3/1941 Erfurt [8, RL 3/556]
At the Erfurt Repair Works in Erfurt, Dir. Kalkert receives a telegram from RLM LC 2/IA with the prospective definitive program for the DFS 230.

Company	April 41	May 41	June 41	July 41	Aug. 41	Sept. 41	Oct. 41	Nov. 41	Dec. 41	Jan. 42	Feb. 42
Gotha	Running down as per Plan 19										
Hartwig	40	25	10								
Bücker	25	25	25	25	25	25	25	20	15		
Erla	25	25	25	25	20	10	5				
BMM	30	30	30	30	30	30	30	30	30	20	10

This sequence of photos shows the Go 242 breaking up during maximum speed trials. The breakup was caused by oscillations about the normal axis. (E-Stelle Rechlin)

12/3/1941 Junkers [28], [19]

The Ju 322 takes off from Merseburg on its maiden flight, flown by *Flugkapitän* Hesselbach and Alfred Funke. A Ju 90 (KB+LA) serves as tug. The combination just manages to get airborne at the airfield perimeter. The Ju 322 fails to separate cleanly from the 8-ton takeoff trolley, which bounces and strikes the glider, inflicting severe damage. Because of its small rudder, while under tow the glider yaws uncontrollably, and it also appears to be loaded tail-heavy. Although it failed to leave the ground properly, it is reported that, after takeoff, it climbed so sharply that it pulled up the tail of the Ju 90 and the towline had to be released to avoid an accident. The yaw was controllable in the glide and the Ju 322 landed in a field without sustaining further damage. 14 days later, two tanks towed it back to the airfield after about 4 tons of ballast had been removed. Gropler, head of the design bureau, characterized further attempts to make the Ju 322 flyable as a waste of time.

13/3/1941 Meeting at the RLM [18]

The RLM assigns the type number Me 323 to the motorized version of the Me 321, and the company received a preliminary contract for development of the machine.

14/3/1941 Conference GL1/Genst. 6. Abt. [7]

The General Staff receives from XI Corps the news that the Messerschmitt Company has declared that the Hansa model of the Ju 90 (BMW 132) is capable of towing Warsaw. The General Staff requests comments immediately.

20/3/1941 Conference GL1/Genst. 6. Abt. [7]

As *Lufthansa* is to continue operations, the RLM drops its request for Ju 90s to tow Warsaw.

18/3/1941 Lärz [15]

During a test flight by an early Go 242 to determine the type's maximum speed (part of testing by the *E-Stelle* Rechlin) the horizontal tail breaks off, followed by the tail booms and one wing. Pilot Harmens of GWF is able to parachute to safety, however, flight mechanic Thomas is killed.

The aircraft involved was probably the Go 242 V2, which, according to the C-Amts Program of 1/3/1941, was at Rechlin. Regel [15] reported another incident during testing at Rechlin, in which the tail booms of a prototype broke off during landing.

24/3/1941 Erfurt Repair Works [8, RL 3/556]

The RLM/LC 2/IA sends a telex to Dir. Kalkert, head of the repair works, with the following news: "All work on the DFS 331 is to be stopped. The necessary notifications to the individual production participants, including DFS-Darmstadt, are to be undertaken from there."

27/3/1941 Conference GL1/Genst. 6. Abt. [7]

The General Staff inquires whether the Go 242 has to be flown with the tow frame when attached to the Ju 52 or if the Type 3000 tailwheel suffices. The question is considered urgent on account of preparation of the aircraft.

3/4/1941 Conference GL1/Genst. 6. Abt. [7]

The LC 2 is currently investigating whether the Type 6000 tailwheel can be installed in Ju 52s with the Type 3000. This would make it possible to quickly equip the Ju 52 to tow the Go 242.

10 and 17/4/1941 Conference GL1/Genst. 6. Abt. [7]

A Ju 52 experimental aircraft has been fitted with a Type 6000 tailwheel. A report will be submitted after testing.

14/4/1941 Messerschmitt [4]

The Messerschmitt Company presents an offer sheet for the four- and six-engine Me 323. The Me 323 is a development of the Me 321 large transport glider and differs from it in having engines and associated equipment and a fixed undercarriage with brakes instead of skids. The Me 321 can be retrofitted with engines and also with a wheeled undercarriage.

The aircraft is designed to carry a 22-ton tank or other loads weighing up to 22 tons.

While the offer sheet also mentions the six-engine version, it concerns itself primarily with the four-engine version. In the period that followed, the RLM also clearly requested more four-engine Me 323s. The payload estimates would prove to be highly optimistic, however, and with four power plants takeoff performance was poor, even with a reduced load.

17/4/1941 DFS Ainring [8, RL 3/556]

In a letter to the RLM, the DFS responds to the accusation that it contributed to DFS 230 A-0 production difficulties by not delivering production documents (drawings) on time. The DFS had delivered the drawings to the REWE Company

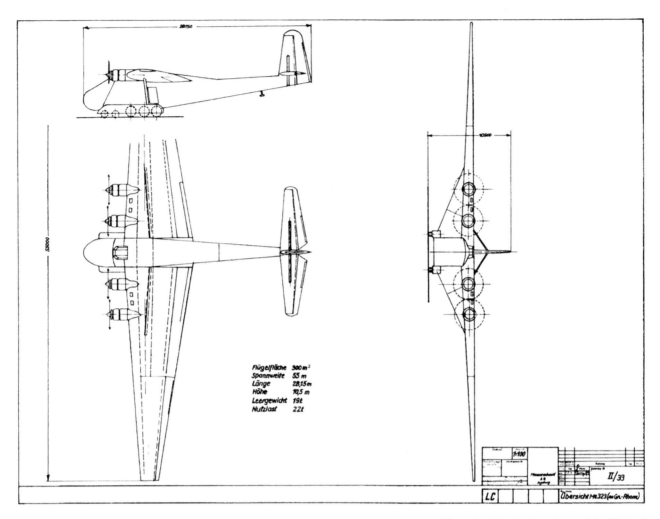

Flügelfläche   300 m²
Spannweite   55 m
Länge   28,15 m
Höhe   10,5 m
Leergewicht   19 t
Nutzlast   22 t

Three-view drawing from the portfolio. (Mankau)

(Erfurt Repair Works) on time, but REWE did not build the pre-production series itself as DFS expected, instead dispersing it among six to eight subcontractors, most of whom had no experience in building aircraft. Furthermore, REWE had failed to send the first set of drawings received from the DFS to the subcontractors, and so the DFS had to deliver the drawings to the subcontractors itself, resulting in a delay of about six weeks. As well, after inspecting the DFS 331 V1 on 21/1/1941, the *E-Stelle* Rechlin demanded various changes that resulted in further delays; for example, two sets of rudder pedals, cockpit armor, a revised canopy, etc. Finally, the RLM sent ten engineers loaned to Fieseler by the DFS to the GWF in Gotha for more urgent work.

The DFS believes that the production difficulties that have arisen may be traced to the following causes:

1. Steadily increasing difficulty in procuring materials since the contract was issued.

2. Unnecessary spreading of the work for the current contract among many individual companies.

3. Difficulty in assigning the work to suitable companies as a result of the current overloading of all companies.

The RLM thus abandoned the DFS 331 not because the Go 242 was better, but because production of the DFS 331 A-0 did not begin. As GWF was itself the manufacturer of the Go 242 it had a much better grip on the production process than the DFS, which had to deal with an incapable or unwilling main contractor and numerous, some of them inexperienced, subcontractors.

Piquantly, the father of the Go 242, Albert Kalkert, was head of the REWE at precisely this time, meaning since 1/10/1940. He was presented with the unique opportunity to help the Go 242 succeed simply by forgetting the drawings of the DFS 331. Kalkert is generally considered to be the designer responsible for the Go 242. He was also head of the responsible design department, although the actual designer was a Herr Laiber.

As the Go 242 met the expectations of the RLM and production was assured, the decision against the DFS 331 was understandable.

21/4/1941 Leipheim

According to Baur's logbook, on this day he carried out the maiden flight of the four-engine Me 323, a V1. The aircraft still had no code, and it continued to appear in the logbook without a code until 20/6/1941. The Me 323's maiden flight took place barely two months after that of the 321. By then the Me 321 V1 had made seven flights, the last of which, on 14/3, resulted in an accident. The Me 321 V2 had made two flights, and the V3 to V5 one each. Test flying of production aircraft had not yet taken place. The prototype's undercarriage was an interim design, for in April 1941 Messerschmitt submitted an offer sheet for the Me 323 in which the undercarriage looked completely different. The two-seat cockpit

These stills from a film show the Me 321 a V1 among various Me 321s and in front of a Me 321 as it takes off. (Messerschmitt film)

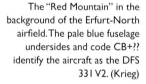

The "Red Mountain" in the background of the Erfurt-North airfield. The pale blue fuselage undersides and code CB+?? identify the aircraft as the DFS 331 V2. (Krieg)

This machine is often identified in the literature as the Go 244 V1 with BMW 132 engines. It is the Go 244 V1 (Werk.Nr. 2420000018, VC+OR), but with Gnôme et Rhône 14 M engines whose cowlings have been removed. (German Museum)

This aircraft combination was used to test the DFS 230 with rigid tow. The towing fixture on the Ju 52 was still a very heavy piece of equipment. (DFS)

Testing a braking parachute. The production version was different in appearance. (DFS)

was also a prototype at this point, for quantity production had not yet begun.

24/4/1941 Conference GL1/Genst. 6. Abt. [7]

The General Staff requests an investigation into the procurement situation (Ju 52 with the Type 6000 tailwheel for the Go 242), the installation time, and whether the installation might be carried out at the unit level. Comments requested.

The General Staff requests that 400 sets of conversion parts for Bf 110s (including radiators) be prepared. Schedule requested. LE 2 reports that major difficulties have arisen in the installation of towing equipment. LE 2 is unable to carry out the conversion.

25/4/1941 MIAG Brunswick [8, RL 3/556]

MIAG issues a memo, according to which MIAG was originally supposed to construct 337 sets of wings for the DFS 230 B on behalf of the Gotha Company. Of these, 125 were cancelled before 27/3/1941. On 23/4/1941 MIAG received a telegram from Kalkert, which stated that delivery

of more than a total of 110 sets of wings was not possible. By that time 110 sets had been delivered, seven completed, and material was in various stages of construction up to set 212.

26/4/1941 Corinth

During the fighting in Greece transport gliders land at the Corinth canal bridge.

End of April 1941 Junkers [19]

After repairs, installation of a new tail section, and strengthening of the takeoff trolley, the Ju 322 makes its second test flight, this time towed by three Bf 110s. The Ju 322 yaws again, resulting in a collision between two of the Bf 110s, and the test flight ends with a crash landing by the Ju 322 and one Bf 110. The RLM subsequently halts work on this unfortunate design. The wood amassed for its construction and associated resources are assigned to other projects.

1/5/1941 Conference GL1/Genst. 6. Abt. [7]

The General Staff again requests 400 sets of conversion parts for the Bf 110 as tow plane for Warsaw. The conversion will

During trials in the high mountains, a DFS 230 takes off from the Seethaleralpe with the aid of two powder rockets. A takeoff from a snow-covered field is depicted in [37]. (DFS)

now be carried out by Hansen & Co. of Schneidemühl. In order to convert 80 Bf 110s by 1/6, beginning immediately 40 aircraft must be delivered per week for conversion.

1/5/1941 C-Amts Program [8, RL 3/556]

The DFS 331 is at the DFS in Darmstadt for general testing. The V2 was 80% completed in Gotha and is now in Erfurt.

Go 242 *Werknummer* 24200000018 was tested in Gotha with two Gnôme et Rhône power plants.

In the records of the E-Stelle Rechlin, 00019 with Gnôme et Rhône motors is designated Go 244 V2, thus 00018 was probably the V1.

6/5/1941 Erfurt Repair Works [8, RL 3/556]

Kalkert advises the RLM LC 2 IA that MIAG is to finish construction of 128 sets of complete wings which were intended for use by Gotha in production of the DFS 230, of which Gotha has already used 47. The rest are to be sent to Bücker and Erla. The Fokker Company is to take over production of spare wings. The Eka-Werk Friedrichsroda built tail sections for Gotha; 23 of these are surplus to requirements and are to be sent to the Bücker Company.

14/5/1941 [6]

The German Academy for Aviation Research publishes a history of German aviation science and technology. In it Prof. Walter Georgii describes the German Research Institute for Gliding Flight and the work carried out there. He mentions the DFS 331 transport glider, capable of carrying a 2.5-ton payload, which was flight tested in November 1940.

Also mentioned is the development of a blind flying method for towed aircraft, the rigid tow, in which the glider was attached to the powered aircraft by a rotating Cardan shaft. A combination of rigid and long-towline tow is also described. The installation of a cable winch in the tow plane

allowed the crew to select the more suitable method based on the type of mission or weather conditions.

The DFS and the Stuttgart Aviation Technical Institute jointly developed a braking parachute to allow gliders to operate in the high mountains. This enabled a fully-loaded glider to approach the landing site at a speed of 150 kph and a dive angle of 45°. When combined with the use of spoilers, a dive angle of 70° was possible at a speed of 190 to 200 kph. This made it possible for the glider to make an approach to very small landing surfaces.

To enable the aircraft to get airborne again from a short field, it was fitted with two takeoff aids (powder rockets each producing 500 kg of thrust) on each side of the fuselage. These made it possible for the glider to make a short takeoff and even climb over obstacles after becoming airborne. Georgii referred to the considerably enhanced operational potential of gliders equipped with these landing and takeoff aids.

These powder takeoff rockets are not to be confused with the Argus-Schmidt pulse jets, which were also tested on the DFS 230 and installed in a similar location. They were not intended as takeoff aids and were only to be tested in flight.

Georgii mentioned new towing methods in which one Ju 52 could tow up to three DFS 230s or, conversely, several tow planes could tow a single glider. Working closely with XI Air Corps, the DFS had taken part in simulated operational testing of a combination of three Messerschmitt 110s and one heavy transport glider (*meaning the Me 321*).

14/5/1941 Messerschmitt [4]

The company advises the RLM LC2 of the following delivery schedule for 200 321 gliders.

	1-seat cockpit		2-seat cockpit	
	Leipheim	Obertraubling	Leipheim	Obertraubling
April	8	4		
May	16	15		
June	26	31	8	2
July			36	36
Aug.			6	12

14/5/1941 RLM LC2 No. 6121/41 [4]

The RLM writes to Professor Messerschmitt that the numbers contained in the production plan for the Me 321 with single- and two-seat cockpits are far lower than what had been promised. He is directed to have the schedule rechecked so that the air force, as per a telephone conversation between him and *Generaloberst* Udet, will receive the dual-control version as soon as possible. At the same time, Me 323 conversions are also to be included in the Me 321 plan.

15/5/1941 Conference GL1/Genst. 6. Abt. [7]

The General Staff is asked for a decision as to whether the engines in the approximately 20 Bloch 175s in use by

A Ju 52 tows three DFS 230s. (DFS)

Five He 72s tow a DFS 230. (DFS)

The second man in the two-man cockpit was only there to assist in controlling the aircraft and had no instruments of his own. (Nowarra)

the Chef AW (Commander of Training Units) are to be immediately made available (for the Me 323).

At present, 24 of the 80 Bf 110s have been converted for use as Warsaw tow planes. Additional parts will be available for each of the 400 requested sets of conversion parts so that they will be on hand for a possible further conversion.

Information on installation time and the procurement situation for the Type 6000 tailwheel (in Ju 52) will be submitted later.

As a result of favorable test results, it is anticipated that an initial batch of 50 powder takeoff rockets will be procured for the DFS 230 for broad-based testing. Delivery schedule as yet undetermined.

15/5/1941 Erfurt Repair Works [8, RL 3/556]
Kalkert sends to Miag the ultimate decision that it is to deliver 128 sets of DFS 230 wings. 47 of these have been delivered to Gotha. 35 are to be sent to the Bücker Company and 46 to Erla. Other prepared materials are to be sent to Fokker.

16/51941 Messerschmitt [4]
A testing report describes the initial flights by the Me 321 V1 to V5 during the period 25/2 to 10/4/1941. The V1 made seven flights, six with a Ju 90 tow plane and only the seventh behind three Bf 110s. The seventh flight, the first by an air force crew, ended in a forced landing after a tow coupling broke. The glider overturned on landing, but the crew escaped injury.

The V2 completed five flights, all towed by Bf 110s. Three takeoffs were made using takeoff-assist rockets, two of these while carrying 21,890 kg of ballast. The V3 to V5 each made one flight, likewise towed by Bf 110s. The V2 and V3 were subsequently brought up to production standard, making one flight each in this condition on 7/5 and 10/5.

According to the test report, after ten test flights the Me 321 was so trouble free that it could easily be flown by glider pilots with transport glider experience. It was even claimed that takeoffs with a full load using eight takeoff-assist rockets were scarcely more difficult than in an empty machine.

Aborted takeoffs were common during the early stages of testing. The report claimed that these were caused by the left tow plane being struck by propwash from the lead aircraft, causing it to veer slightly. To alleviate this problem, an outrigger is installed on the tail of the left-

The outrigger is visible beneath the tail of this Bf 110. Also note the larger radiator fairings and rearview mirror. (Schlaug)

hand tow plane in such a way as to cause the towline to pass almost through its center of gravity. This eliminates the moment on the rear fuselage that tries to force the aircraft to the outside, and the danger of a swing on takeoff is significantly reduced.

20/5/1941 Messerschmitt [4]

To the RLM's letter of 14 May, Messerschmitt replies that production of the Me 321 cannot be accelerated on account of testing results and additional equipment requested by the air force. Manufacture of the two-seat armored cockpit by the subcontractor has just begun, consequently, a switch to this cannot be made any sooner. However, 200 two-seat cockpits have been ordered; consequently, single-seat aircraft can be converted later. In any case, beginning with the first machine a second control column for elevator control has been installed, and even in the single-seat cockpit a second man can use this to adequately reduce elevator control forces.

Concerning the Me 323, the extraordinary difficulties in the procurement of materials have not yet been overcome, and there are still unanswered questions as to the availability of engines and their type and model. It is therefore not yet possible to complete planning.

20/5/1941 Crete

69 DFS 230s of LLG1 take part in "Operation Mercury," the airborne invasion of Crete.

23/5/1941 Conference GL1/Genst. 6. Abt. [7]

The engines are being removed from all of the Chef AW's Bloch 175s for use in the Warsaw program. Those aircraft that are flyable will be moved to an airfield to be determined by the Chef AW. LC 2 will send a vehicle column there to remove the engines. Chef AWS is to provide the locations of the remaining aircraft. Removal of engines will then take place at the locations of the unserviceable aircraft.

The current plans for production of Warsaw are 250 Warsaw-South aircraft, 100 of them motorized, with four

Many DFS 230s were wrecked landing in the rocky terrain of Crete. (Schlaug)

engines, and 40 aircraft motorized, with six engines, type Gnôme et Rhône 48/49.

The General Staff requests the order of an initial series of 50 improved motorized aircraft follow the series earmarked for XI Corps. A request is made to determine if this series can be completed in the interim.

The RLM was thus expecting just 110 gliders at that time, and not, as Messerschmitt said a few days earlier, 200. However, 100 four-engine and 40 six-engine Me 323s with Gnôme et Rhône engines were planned, to be fitted initially with power plants from captured Bloch 175s. 400 Bf 110s were to be converted as tugs for 110 gliders.

The latest test results show that the He 111 H-3 to H-6 can also be used as tow planes in addition to the Bf 110. Performance is better than with the Bf 110. The General Staff is asked to clarify whether operational planning should include the He 111 instead of the Bf 110. As a precaution, the Air Armaments Minister orders 200 sets of towing components.

The Bf 110 was ill-suited for the low speed of the glider-tug combination. The towing speed of about 230 kph was only slightly higher than the twin-engine fighter's landing speed, and larger radiators were installed just to provide adequate cooling for the Bf 110s flying at high power settings. Cables also had to be run from the tail, where the coupling was located, to the force application point on the wing spar. On account of its larger wings, the He 111 was much better suited to the low towing speed, had retractable radiators and therefore no need for modification, and was capable of accommodating the tow coupling completely in the tail.

There is no need to make good the arrears in the DFS 230 production program. End of DFS 230 production as proposed by LC 2 General Staff requests accelerated production of the Go 242.

30/5/1941 Conference GL1/Genst. 6. Abt. [7]
The meeting is advised that, at present, a total of just 250 Warsaw-South aircraft can be delivered. Of these, 100 will be equipped with four engines and 40 with six engines. Production start date depends on the delivery of power plants. It is planned to deliver the last 50 Warsaw-South as gliders. 20 gliders will be delivered by 1 June. The General Staff requests with all urgency the maximum possible number of gliders and motorized aircraft for June.

The General Staff also requests information as to how the Bf 110 and He 111 are to be equipped to ensure trouble-free takeoffs with the necessary range (information about the equipment to be removed and the remaining fuel quantities). General Staff requests that preparation of tow planes with available means at the unit level be carried out in the shortest possible time.

12/6/1941 Conference GL1/Genst. 6. Abt. [7]
The company (Messerschmitt) is presently reinforcing the horizontal stabilizer; thus, the 28 aircraft reported delivered on 1 June are unserviceable again. The V1 to V4 have already been delivered. 45 Warsaw-South to be delivered in June, 65 in July, 70 in August, and 19 in September. The 45 aircraft for June include the 28 unserviceable ones from the May delivery. Airframes for motorized Warsaw are being removed from these numbers as power plants are delivered. Only very small quantities can be anticipated by 1 September. In these months Warsaw-West is to deliver 13, 40, 170, and 92 aircraft.

Here approx. 200 Me 321/323 (Warsaw-South) are initially planned by September 1941. There was still no plan for the remaining 50. The 315 Warsaw-West (this is how it appears in the document) aircraft are unclear to me. Perhaps this refers to the Ju 322 (otherwise designated Warsaw-North).

After industry-level conversion of the Bf 110 and He 111 tow planes (Bf 110 approx. eight days, He 111 about half a day), the units can themselves equip the aircraft for use as glider tugs or combat aircraft as required. Removed for towing: armor plate, PVC, auxiliary fuel tanks, and in some cases weapons. At present range is 450 km, penetration depth approx. 280 km (return flight at economical cruise). Attempts are being made to increase range to 450 km.

There is a typing error in the minutes, for stating the range as 450 km twice makes no sense. Actually the range was less than 450 km.

The General Staff agrees to the sending of an aircraft (DFS 230) to Japan.

27/6/1941 Conference GL1/Genst. 6. Abt. [7]
Only 20 Warsaw-South are coming in June, as the air force is using the Ju 90 glider tugs for other purposes. Increasing range to 450 km is to be further investigated. 40 Type 6000 tailwheels (Ju 52) will be available for installation by 10/7.

1/7/1941 C-Amts Program [8]
The DFS 331 is at the DFS in Darmstadt for general testing. Two Go 242s (*Werknummer* 24200000018/19), each with two Gnôme et Rhône 14 M power plants, are being tested in Gotha.

6/7/1941 C-Amts Program [8]
Delivery Proposal A-1 anticipates a reduction in DFS 230 production from the current 55 per month to 10, with the subsequent maintenance of this production rate from April 1942. There is no mention of the Go 242, and as to the Go 244 with Gnôme et Rhône 14 N power plants, the current production rate of 20 per month is to continue until March 1944.

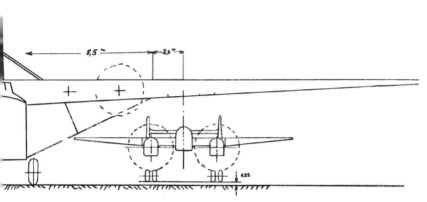

Chr. Tilenius thought of using, for example, two twin-engined Ar 240s to power the Me 321 into the air. (Tilenius)

The Go 242 was not yet available when the Russian campaign began, but later proved a success in that theater. (Nidree)

The rigid-tow equipment envisaged at this time was already 60 kg lighter than the original design. (DFS)

15/7/1941 Heinkel [9]

The stress tables for the He 111 Z are set down in a meeting with RLM officials. The He 111 Z is a twin aircraft consisting of two He 111 H-6 joined by a new wing center-section. Airspeed will be 395 kph at low level and 480 kph at 6,000 (maximum boost altitude). Its intended role is glider tug, with the towed aircraft weighing a maximum of 35 tons.

This is the first mention of the He 111 Z I have found in the Heinkel archives. As stress tables were already being prepared, the He 111 Z must have been conceived at an earlier date. By this point in time only about 20 Me 321s had been delivered. Thus, the concept of the He 111 Z had its origins during the Me 321 testing period. According to Koos [17], development of the He 111 Z went back to a proposal by Flugbaumeister Tilenius of the RLM in the spring of 1941.

17/7/1941 Paper by Tilenius R. and *Luftwaffe* CIC LC2 [9]

Tilenius proposes using Warsaw-South as a takeoff aid for single- and twin-engine fighters and Stukas. Four Me 109s, or two Me 110s, or two Ar 240s or two Ju 87s are to be suspended beneath the wings of a Me 321 with two engines and carried into the air by it. As the fighters use no fuel for takeoff their range is extended significantly.

On 1/8/1941 Tilenius proposed another use for the Me 323 as a tanker for the He 177, He 111 Z, or BV 222 immediately after takeoff. In this way the He 177 reconnaissance aircraft could carry an additional 9,000 liters of fuel, which would extend its endurance to 25 hours.

17/7/1941 Conference GL1/Genst. 6. Abt. [7]

The General Staff's request for snow skis is drawn up in two procurement periods for winter 1941/42 and winter 1942/43, with identical quantities and types in both periods. Being prepared for the Warsaw Program are:

30 sets each for the Go 242 and Go 244 and 10 sets each for the Me 321 and Me 323.

This is the first time that the designation Me 321 appears in [the minutes of] the Air Armaments Minister's meetings instead of the codename Warsaw.

Rigid tow is being introduced by XI Corps, initially with DFS 230s. General Staff requests immediate rigid tow tests with the Go 242. The Ju 52 equipped for rigid towing (currently at Hildesheim) is being made available to the DFS for this purpose. If rigid tow proves unsuitable, <u>long rigid tow</u> is to

The first six-engined Me 323 was initially designated Me 323 BVI. (Radinger)

be investigated. Tests with various towline lengths are currently taking place in Ainring. General Staff requests rigid towing equipment [be made available] as an equipment set (*Rüstsatz*) if possible.

22/7/1941 Russia

Hitler launches the Russian campaign, during which transport gliders will be used almost exclusively on supply missions.

24/7/1941 Conference GL1/Genst. 6. Abt. [7]

As installation of rigid tow equipment in the Ju 52 results in a considerable weight increase (at least 200 kg), LC 2 will contact XI Corps to determine how many aircraft it will require with rigid-tow equipment for special missions.

31/7/1941 Conference GL1/Genst. 6. Abt. [7]

The weight increase associated with conversion to rigid-tow results is 205 kg. Installation as an equipment set requires the installation of 64 kg of permanent parts. It is agreed with XI Corps that, in the interim, only eight aircraft will be converted for rigid-tow.

8/1941 Gothaer Waggonfabrik [8, RL 3/556]

In August 1941 the *Luftwaffe* accepts the first Go 242 A-1s built by AGO and GWF.

2/8/1941 RLM/LC 2 [4]

Based on the materials and personnel situation, concerning the Me 321 and Me 323 the Air Armaments Minister has decided that the following quantities of each type should be built in Series 1: 200 Me 321, five Me 323 six-engine, and ten Me 323 four-engine. Anticipated in Series 2 are: 300 Me 323, 100 with four N 48 engines, and 40 with six N 48 engines. The rest are to be equipped with captured Russian engines, as many as possible with six engines.

The RLM has again decided that it wants 200 Me 321 gliders. The failure of the Ju 322 and delays in the start of Me 323 production were probably factors. The 15 Me 323s in the first production batch were most likely the planned prototypes (see 1/11/1942).

4/8/1941 German Research Institute for Gliding Flight, Ainring [9]

Prof. Georgii issues Report No. 638: "Landing and Takeoff by Transport Glider Aircraft in the High Mountains." The report describes tests which demonstrated that transport gliders could be advantageously used to supply troops in the high mountains and to transport a variety of materials in mountainous regions. The report first describes the tests made with the DFS 230 V1 on 19/10/1940 on the Grand Venice Glacier at an elevation of 3500 m. It then describes the tests of 27 and 28/2/1941 on the Seethaleralpe, which involved rocket-assisted takeoffs (see chapter DFS 230: Rocket-Assisted Takeoff).

6/8/1941 Messerschmitt Leipheim

According to Baur's logbook, on this day he carried out the first test flight of a six-engine Me 323 (W9+SA).

7/8/1941 Conference GL1/Genst. 6. Abt. [7]

As before, just eight are to be converted for DFS 230 rigid-tow. XI Corps is to provide the aircraft. Tests to determine the feasibility of GO 242 rigid-tow are currently under way.

14/8/1941 Conference GL1/Genst. 6. Abt. [7]

On account of the unfavorable procurement and capacity situation, only three aircraft can be converted for DFS 230

The Go 242 flew supplies to Africa from Sicily and Crete. (Petrick)

The snow skid resembled the standard skid, but was wider. (JET & PROP)

The He 111 succeeded the Ju 52 as the principle glider tug. (ECPA)

rigid-tow. The aircraft are being supplied by XI Corps. Unit trials requested.

A Go 242 is required for Go 242 rigid-tow feasibility trials, as flight and performance tests are necessary.

The DFS 230 can be made capable of taking off from snow by fitting a broader skid (snow skid) on the three attachment points of the standard landing skid. General Staff is asked for its opinion as to the likely scale of production of such snow skids.

General Staff is asked to advise how many braking parachutes are to be procured for the DFS 230.

21/8/1941 Conference GL1/Genst. 6. Abt. [7]

General Staff announces its request for snow skids (DFS 230).

General Staff requests an initial batch of 500 braking parachutes (DFS 230) for XI Corps. Contract is in preparation. Message asks whether braking parachutes are to be attached to the tail or at the center of gravity.

Autumn 1941 Mediterranean Theater

The first Go 242 glider/tug trains of the *Go-Kdo/X. Fliegerkorps* (Gotha Detachment/X Air Corps) are transferred to the Mediterranean Theater and fly supply missions to Africa.

25/9/1941 Conference GL1/Genst. 6. Abt. [7]

The 200 sets of DFS 230 snow skids will be delivered in the months December to February. Monthly delivery figures to follow.

16/10/1941 Conference GL1/Genst. 6. Abt. [7]

The bulk of the DFS 230 snow skids ordered are to be delivered in February.

28/11/1941 Messerschmitt Leipheim

Pilot Fries conducts undercarriage tests with the Me 323 B V1, taxiing the aircraft over obstacles.

12/12/1941 Meeting of Department Heads at the Headquarters of the Air Armaments Minister [7]

The operations staff requests a review to determine the feasibility of advancing the date in the previous planning for the interim transports to May 1942. Moving up the date for the Go 244 is probably possible, however, for the Me 323 there is no chance. A proposal is made for use of the He 111 H-6 as a tug for the Go 242. The Technical Office will investigate the possibilities and report the results to Headquarters, Air Armaments Minister.

12/1941 GL/C C-Amt Monthly Report 4105/41 – 4111/41 [4]

Me 321 Delivery Numbers	
May 1941	4
June 1941	21
July 1941	4
August 1941	50
September 1941	34
October 1941	36
November 1941	17
Total	166

7/1/1942 *E-Stelle* Rechlin [15], [9]

The Go 242 V2, Werk.Nr. 00019, is ferried from Gotha to Rechlin as part of the type approval process. After

The Me 321 production line. In the foreground are ballast boxes, which were part of every glider. (Messerschmitt)

acceptance checks, flight testing begins on 10/1/1942.

17/1/1942 Messerschmitt AG Obertraubling [4]

A report entitled "Description of the Me 323 with Flettner Powered Controls" states that the initially high forces exerted on the control column can be considerably reduced

In the background, on final approach, is the Me 321 a V1 (W1+SZ), while the aircraft in the center is W1+SY. The tail section in the foreground has an unpowered, narrow Flettner tab on the rudder.

The control surfaces of the Ju 52 were designed in such a way that little force was required to operate them. (Mankau)

through the use of the tabs, which in turn deflect the control surface.

The control surfaces of the Me 321/Me 323 were not cleverly designed. Instead of putting mounting rods through the axis of rotation, as on the old Ju 52, Messerschmitt tried to employ control surfaces with leading edge hinges similar to those used on the Bf 109. It was this, and not the size of the control surfaces, that resulted in excessively high control forces. The adoption of dual controls was only a stopgap. The power-operated Flettner surfaces were also only the second-best solution. The ultimate solution, with internally-balanced control surfaces in the style of the Ju 52, did not enter production until the Me 321 F of 1943.

17/1/1942 Messerschmitt AG Augsburg [22]

The Messerschmitt AG proposes the following delivery program for the Me 323:

Type	Number	Production Site	Delivery Period
1 Me 323 GR 14 N 48/49	24	Leipheim	July 42- Oct. 42
	30	Obertraubling	July 42 - Nov. 42
2 Me 323 GR 14 N 48/49	64	Obertraubling	Oct. 42 - March 43
3 Me 323 Jumo 211	70	Leipheim	Oct. 42 - June 43
	105	Obertraubling	Jan. 43 - Aug. 43
4 Me 323 Alfa Romeo	24	Leipheim	April 43 - Sept. 43
5 Me 323 Jumo 211	116	Leipheim	July 43 - March 44
	20	Obertraubling	Aug. 43 - Nov. 43
Total	453		July 42 - March 44

20/1/1942 Meeting of Department Heads at the Headquarters of the Air Armaments Minister [7]

The *LC-Chef* is given the powers necessary for the operation of the intended committee and for carrying out the cannibalization of the Me 322 in favor of the motorized LS (transport glider).

Me 322 is surely a typing error in the minutes and stands for the Me 321. The experience gained in the first six months of operations with the Me 321 appears to have been so negative that cannibalization is being considered.

He 111 glider tug as seen by the pilot of a Go 242. (Nidree)

20/1/1942 Messerschmitt AG Obertraubling [4]

Maiden flight of the first four-engine Me 323 from Obertraubling.

Probably the Me 323 V4 with LeO power plants.

27/1/1942 *E-Stelle* Rechlin [15], [9]

The *E-Stelle* Rechlin compiles the first test results with the Go 242 V2 and comes to the conclusion that the Go 244 is an aircraft which is easy to handle on the ground and in the air. Takeoff and landing are very simple and, apart from a few minor failings, handling characteristics are good. The aircraft is more comfortable to fly than the Ju 52. In terms of performance and handling, however, single-engine flight with a load of 1.2 tons is just manageable for experienced pilots. On one hand engine performance has reached a limit. At the same time, because of excessively high pedal forces, the rudders are fully engaged. Rudder trim is insufficient for single-engine flight. Single-engine flight is not possible at gross weights of more than 6.8 tons (which means also with the maximum allowable payload of 2.5 tons).

28/1/1942 *E-Stelle* Rechlin [15], [9]

The *E-Stelle* reports on the state of testing of the Go 242 V2 after 45 flying hours. No serious complaints arose with a payload of 1.3 tons, however, the nosewheel mount failed during a normal landing. The attachment point has already been redesigned by GWF.

1/2/1942 C-Amts Program [8]

The DFS 331 and Go 242 are no longer mentioned. Aircraft 24200000018 is now called Go 244 and is being tested with wooden propellers in Gotha.

7/2/1942 *E-Stelle* Rechlin [4]

A testing report by the Rechlin Proving center states that the two-blade Heine fixed-pitch propellers of the Me 323 were found to be unbalanced, which caused serious vibration. Consequently the propeller cannot be used in production. Use may be possible if the motor mounts are changed.

10/2/1942 *E-Stelle* Rechlin [15]

The first 100-hour endurance test of the Go 244 is completed without significant complaints about the engines or airframe. The only area which receives significant criticism is handling while taxiing, however, Gotha is already making modifications to address this. The aircraft is operational up to a gross weight of 6.8 tons.

10/2/1942 GL/-B2 Aircraft Program [8]

Draft 1009 envisages the average production of 15 Go 244 A-1 aircraft with two Gnôme et Rhône 14N power plants per month until May 1943. The Go 244 A-2 variant with two M 25 power plants is to be built in parallel, resulting in the production of approximately 35 aircraft per month. As of June only 20 Go 244 A-2 are to be built per month, with the power plant situation uncertain as of 12/1943. Concerning the Me 323, the power plant situation is uncertain at present. After an initial delivery of approximately 100 aircraft in October-November 1942, production is to continue at a rate of ten per month.

There were other plans at this time, but the anticipated production quantities were similar. The delivery situation for the Russian M 25 motor turned out to be so uncertain, however, that this variant was dropped. I am not aware of any document that confirms the published claim that the M 25 was experimentally installed in a Go 244.

27/2/1942 Messerschmitt AG Augsburg

A status report notes that the Me 323 V1 and V11 were completed in 1941. Since then an additional five four-engine aircraft and three six-engine machines have become flyable. The remaining three six-engine examples are to be ready to fly by April. The Me 323 with Ju 88 power plants will not be ready to fly until April because of delays in the delivery of engines, and work on the prototypes with Alfa-Romeo engines has been halted because of considerable delays in delivery and the questionable availability of production power plants.

The question of power plants for production aircraft has only been clarified for 54 machines with Bloch

This early drawing shows the closely-cowled LeO 451 power units. These provided an inadequate flow of cooling air, resulting in overheating problems. (Messerschmitt)

This may have been one of the mock-ups mentioned in the text. (Messerschmitt)

The Go 244 B-1's axle undercarriage only permitted a payload of 1.2 tons (German Museum)

power units. There is uncertainty as to which propeller should be used for the additional 65 with LeO power units and whether adequate cooling can be achieved. A LeO power unit has been installed in the V11 for flight testing. [Translator's Note: The term power unit, sometimes "power egg," refers to a combination of the engine, engine accessories, engine cowling and engine mounts as a single component.]

11/3/1942 Messerschmitt AG Obertraubling [4]

According to a Messerschmitt AG memo, the *E-Stelle* Rechlin carried out vibration tests using the Me 323 V4 fitted with Bloch power units and Heine fixed-pitch propellers.

16/3/1942 Messerschmitt AG Augsburg

Messerschmitt reports that deliveries of the Me 321 are six aircraft in arrears. The aircraft are ready to fly. Another six-engine Me 323 prototype was completed on about 27/2, and the remaining two are to be ready to fly by the beginning of April. The prototypes with Alfa-Romeo and Ju 88 power plants have been delayed by late deliveries of power plants and are expected to be ready to fly in April. The 65 Me 323s which are to be equipped with LeO power plants are still experiencing cooling difficulties.

21/3/1942 Conference Memo No. 58/42 secret command matter, Rominten [8]

Feldmarschall Milch: "Messerschmitt's 321 glider (Gigant) is a swindle. *Feldmarschall* Milch has initiated a thorough investigation by *Oberstleutnant* Dinort. 36 people have already been killed in test flights. The aircraft is poorly constructed, trimming is impossible, control forces too high. Messerschmitt even made a film for the *Führer's*

birthday using mockups. Director Tank of Focke-Wulf has a contract to develop a glider capable of carrying the new 32-ton tank."

> *Reichsmarschall* Göring: "What have the transport gliders achieved in action so far?"

> *Generaloberst* Jeschonnek: "Four missions, two by fleet four and two at Ösel. The cost, as *Feldmarschall* Milch describes it, is, however, out of all proportion to the result. Towing by three aircraft is very difficult, 50-80% of all takeoffs go wrong."

> *Reichsmarschall* Göring: "Decision?"

> *Feldmarschall* Milch: "Wait for *Oberstleutnant* Dinort's investigation, then decide."

14/4/1942 Meeting of Department Heads at the Headquarters of the Air Armaments Minister [7]

The Me 321 is cancelled, with the authorization of the *Reichsmarschall*. Two or three aircraft are to be retained and equipped for towing trials with the He 111 Z.

15/4/1942 *E-Stelle* Rechlin [15], [9]

Go 244 type testing is complete, except for the radio equipment. Flight testing is also 80% complete. Takeoff and range measurements and diving tests have been completed. The results conform completely to the company data. Still to be rectified, in addition to minor complaints, are single-engine flight characteristics and the [fuel] tank selection system. The new system shall also allow fuel to be transferred from containers mounted in the fuselage while in the air. The undercarriage has only been authorized to a gross weight of 6.8 tons. Problems immediately arise at higher gross weights. These include the appearance of significant cracks at the nosewheel axle

The Go 244's handling characteristics were only acceptable as long as both engines were operating. (German Museum)

bosses on almost all aircraft. The date at which the new tricycle undercarriage can be introduced into production has yet to be determined because of the very late delivery dates of the accessory companies. The *E-Stelle* requests that the new undercarriage be capable of being retrofitted onto all aircraft delivered prior to the start of production [of the new undercarriage].

Unit familiarization (K.G.z.b.V. 106) on the Go 244 by the *E-Stelle* Rechlin is currently under way at Hagenow.

K.G.z.b.V. means "Kampfgruppe zur besonderen Verwendung" (the designation for a transport unit, which translated literally is "battle group for special use"). Other forms of the abbreviation sometimes encountered are KG.z.b.V. and KGzbV.

The poor single-engine flight characteristics led to modification of the rudders. It was impossible to achieve sufficient trimming effect with the old rounded rudders with small trim tabs (see 12/1/1944). GWF therefore developed internally-balanced rudders with significantly larger trim tabs. They came too late for the Go 244, but were planned for the Go 242 B-5 variant. The undercarriage complaints resulted from the undercarriage with one-piece axle extending to the outrigger mainwheel legs, although this was only a feature of the Go 242 B-1.

15/4/1942 Hagenow [27]
K.G.z.b.V. 106 receives orders to return to Hagenow, turn in its Ju 52s, and train on the Go 244.

21/4/1942 Meeting of Department Heads at the Headquarters of the Air Armaments Minister [7]
In connection with the cancellation of the Me 210, it is decided that the labor forces released as a result are to be assigned to the Bf 110 and Go 244.

Stabsing. Volpert reports on production of the Go 244. GL/C-B is tasked with seeing to it that the production program is carried through. The excuses offered by the company cannot be accepted. Production is to continue for the next two years at a rate of 60 aircraft per month. Operations Staff I T is asked to determine whether, in the future, the Go 242 can be dropped completely in favor of the Go 244. As of 1 June 1942 the Ju 87 and Go 244 are to lose their special priority status.

5/5/1942 Meeting of Department Heads at the Headquarters of the Air Armaments Minister [7]
Oberst Vorwald proposes that the Gotha Company (Director Berthold) be relieved of responsibility for the Go 244 so that the company can concentrate exclusively on production of the Bf 110. Responsibility for the Go 244 is to be transferred to Director Tiedemann. The *Generalfeldmarschall* (Milch) approves the proposal for the Ju 52 and Go 244 to be equipped with interior heating. The technical costs must be acceptable.

15/5/1942 *E-Stelle* Rechlin [15], [9]
The proving center compiles the test results to date for single-engine flight in the Go 242. Single-engine flight characteristics are not acceptable because of high rudder pedal forces. The spring-assisted rudders tested on *Werknummer* 39 were completely ineffective. GWF is

Aircraft TE+DU was used for testing at Dorpat by the E-Stelle Rechlin. (E-Stelle Rechlin)

continuing its efforts to address the problem of excessive control forces in single-engine flight by modifying the aerodynamic balancing of the rudders. In addition, level flight at a gross weight higher than approx. 6.3 tons is not authorized, even at 30-minute power (650 hp combat power for a maximum of 30 minutes). To avoid trim ballast, the proving center also approves flight with the cg at its most forward position (empty weight, two-man crew, tanks emptied).

19/5/1942 Meeting of Department Heads at the Headquarters of the Air Armaments Minister [7]

Under the condition that Gotha's operations manager is relieved of responsibility for production of the Go 244, the factory general manager offers a monthly output of 75 Bf 110 aircraft. Director Tiedemann is unable to assume responsibility for the Go 244 on account of overwork.

GL/C-B is ordered to determine how many Go 242s can be delivered on account of the reduction of the Go 244 and report the results to Genst. Gen Qu 6 (General Staff Quartermaster General).

The Me 323 program put forward by Director Croneiß foresees the delivery of the first five aircraft in July 1942, with production increasing to 30 aircraft per month in February 1943. The planned July startup is contingent on a positive outcome of the 100-hour trials currently under way. It is stressed that any increase beyond the offered program is not possible.

Generaling Hertel reports on the possibilities of increased Ju 87 production by the Weser Company. This appears to be possible under certain circumstances. In any case the Ju 87 must receive priority in 1943 at the cost of power plants for the Me 323.

This refers to the Me 323 D-3 and D-5 with Jumo 211 J engines.

20/5/1942 *Erprobungsstelle* Rechlin

In testing report No. 1787, the Rechlin Proving center describes trials with a Go 242 glider fitted with snow skids. The tests took place in the winter of 1941-42 in Dorpat with a He 111 H-6 (also on skis) as tug. The Go 242's maximum load was 2,500 kg. The *E-Stelle* has no reservations about operation of the Go 242 with skis.

21/5/1942 Messerschmitt AG Obertraubling [4]

It is mentioned in the minutes of a meeting that series production of the Me 323 will begin in July with five aircraft.

26/5/1942 Meeting of Department Heads at the Headquarters of the Air Armaments Minister [7]

Obersting Platz assumes overall responsibility for production of the Go 244.

29/5/1942 Heinkel [9]

A field report states that the He 111 Z V1 was at Leipheim and Obertraubling for towing trials from the middle of May until the 27th. With the Me 321 carrying a load of 16 to 17 tons, the train's rate of climb was still 1 m/sec, with a 20-ton load just 0.8 m/sec. It is extremely urgent that several minor improvements be made before the He 111 Z V1 and V2 are released to the air force, as both aircraft must be ready for operational use in a very short time.

1/6/1942 Conference GL/Genst. [7]

The export request (Rumania) for the Go 242 can be responded to in August at the earliest; DFS 230s can possibly be delivered in the interim.

Opinion concerning the Go 242 braking parachute urgently needed.

FuG X P is envisaged as the radio equipment for installation in the Go 244 and Me 323. As the aircraft will have only limited blind flying capabilities, the request appears too far-reaching.

Sufficient MG 15s are available as armament for the Go 244 and Me 323; installation investigation under way.

1/6/1942 GL/A-Rü [8, RL 3/66]

The RLM prepares a summary of all aircraft deployed in Germany and abroad for the Air Armaments Minister. Among the types listed:

DFS 230 A-2	Transport glider, crew 1 + 6, gun or ammunition aircraft
Go 242	Transport glider, crew 3, payload 3.3 t or 33 men
Me 321	Transport glider, crew 2, payload 22 t or max. 175 men
Go 244	Crew 2, 2 x Gnôme Rhône 14 M, payload 1 t or 26 men
Me 323 D-1/D-2	Crew 5; 6 x Gnôme Rhône 14 N, payload 12 t or max. 175 men
Me 323	6 x Jumo 211 J, payload 19.5 t (*designation missing, was Me 323 D-3*)
Me 323	6 x Alfa-Romeo, payload 20 t (*designation missing, probably D-4*)
Me 323 D-5	Glider tug (along with He 111 H-5/H-6 and He 111 Z) for Me 321

Despite its inadequate payload, the Go 244 B-1 was placed in quantity production. (German Museum)

A Go 242 A-1 ready for takeoff. This type was designed as a successor to the DFS 230. (Obermaier)

The Walter Company's R I 202 b rocket was reliable; nevertheless, its acceptance was not recommended by the experimental station. While the rockets shortened takeoff distance, they restricted the glider-tug combination's climb rate until it reached rocket jettison height. (E-Stelle Rechlin)

Four Rheinmetall R I 502 rockets mounted on a framework on the rear fuselage of a Go 242 prior to static tests. This arrangement was preferred by the experimental station, provided there was a significant improvement in operating reliability. (E-Stelle Rechlin)

The designation Me 323 D-6 had obviously not yet been issued at that time. The type designations are reproduced as they appear in the original.

The DFS 230 A-2 is designated as a gun aircraft for a pilot and six-man crew plus one gun weighing 646 kg. Delivery numbers for 1942 are given as 25 to 30 per month. No further production is envisaged in 1943. Production of the Go 242 in 1942 is to be 90 to 100 per month, and likewise no production is envisaged in 1943. Production of the Go 244 begins in January 1942 with 18, reaching 35 per month by June and remaining at that level for the rest of 1942. Production is planned to drop to 20 per month by mid-1943.

3/6/1942 Messerschmitt AG Obertraubling [4]
The operational potential of the Me 321 is restricted because of the serious difficulties associated with the use of three tow planes and the limited availability of other glider tugs (He 111 Zwilling or Ju 90). Messerschmitt AG therefore proposes equipping the Me 321 with pulse jets. Twelve Argus pulse jets each producing 300 kg of thrust, or 24 each producing 150 kg, are to be mounted beneath the wing center-section on the lattice mast. The use of takeoff-assist rockets or tow planes will be necessary to achieve a reasonable takeoff distance. Anticipated range is 300 km with a 14-ton payload.

4/6/1942 Heinkel [9]
Heinkel official Beu reports to E. Heinkel that the He 111 Z V1 is presently in Leipheim and will be tested after modifications to the towing equipment. After returning from Leipheim a change is to be made to the instrument panel, after which the machine is to become operational. The He 111 Z V2 will also be completed in a few days.

9/6/1942 Meeting of Department Heads at the Headquarters of the Air Armaments Minister [7]
Go 244 heating is causing insulation-related problems, as the fuselage is fabric-covered. Even if it is possible, the insertion of a second wall is to be avoided for cost reasons. Tests are being made with the same heating equipment (similar to a hot air blower) envisaged for the Ju 52.

A new program was under consideration for the Go 244. The *Generalfeldmarschall* demands that the company not be released from Program 21 ü and required to produce a catch-up program. The decision for Klemm to halt production of the Kl 35 in favor of the Go 244 has been reversed with the approval of the General Staff.

12/6/1942 Meeting of Department Heads at the Headquarters of the Air Armaments Minister [7]
250 braking parachutes for the Go 244 are requested. Development is in the hands of Prof. Madelung and is not yet complete. Supply has provided the materials.

12/6/1942 Peenemünde-West Experimental Station [9]
The experimental station issues Report 1770/42 concerning function testing of the two takeoff aids installed in Go 242 Werk. Nr. 24: the R I 202 b Walter rocket and the Rheinmetall R I 502 powder rocket (also see Go 242: Short Takeoff Rockets).

19/6/1942 Meeting of Department Heads at the Headquarters of the Air Armaments Minister [7]
The General Staff requests 20 examples of the Go 242 for XI Corps. The *Generalfeldmarschall* doubts that construction of the Go 242 will continue until 1945.

In June 1942 the Go 244 B-1 was approved for use by the Luftwaffe.
(German Museum)

Oberstleutnant Petersen reports that testing has revealed that the rigid-tow developed by Prof. Georgii is better than the cable-tow used previously. It is proposed that units operating the DFS 230 and Go 242 convert to rigid-tow.

The Go 244 has been a success in trials and is cleared for operational use. Strengthening of the undercarriage and enlargement of the radiators are necessary. One shortcoming is a range of just 400 km.

Oberstleutnant Petersen reports that Me 323 aileron and elevator control is still unsatisfactory. The Messerschmitt Company is not dedicating enough effort to eliminate the problems identified during testing. *Oberst* Vorwald states that Croneiß (director at Messerschmitt) has asked that the Me 323 be given to someone else. In response to a suggestion by Petersen, and with the agreement of Vorwald, *Generalfeldmarschall* (Milch) will examine and discuss with the affected companies

The Go 244 B-1's low-level cruising speed was on the order of 200 kph.
(German Museum)

Go 244 B-1 of K.G.z.b.V. 106 in Russia. The antenna mast reveals that radio equipment was installed in this machine. (Petrick)

With the He 111 Z as tow plane, the Me 321 was capable of carrying even large loads with relative reliability. Here a Panzer IV is being loaded into W7+SC, possibly as part of a loading exercise. (German Museum)

Failures of the Go 244's nosewheel were common when the aircraft was overloaded. (Petrick)

A DFS 230 B-2 fitted with two Argus pulse-jets beneath the wings. Metal shields were placed between the tubes and the wings to protect the wing surface. This DFS 230 was used several times by DFS as an experimental aircraft. (Aders)

the question of transferring the Me 323, together with the airfield and installations at Leipheim and all the workers from the Messerschmitt Company, to the Blohm & Voss Company. Stabsing Friebel reports that the Me 321 made a half-hour flight carrying an army assault gun. It was towed by a He 111 Z.

Very high costs have so far been incurred in the development and production of the Me 321 and Me 323. To date the aircraft have not yet seen any proper action. The *Generalfeldmarschall* asks for a reckoning of the costs, taking into account all the redesigns, scrapping, and personnel casualties. As well, the commitment of an extraordinarily high share of steel consumption means that a decision on the viability of the Me 321 must be made soon.

22/6/1942 Hagenow [27]

K.G.z.b.V. 106 receives orders to move to Kirovograd with its Go 244s. It accepted the first 13 aircraft in April, and at the end of June has 37 aircraft on strength. In the months that follow strength will vary between 32 and 37 aircraft.

23/6/1942 *E-Stelle* Rechlin [15]

During testing of the Go 242 braking parachute in Lärz, a crash-landing results in the death of a soldier.

23/6/1942 Heinkel [9]

Meschkat, the representative of Heinkel's Berlin office, asks on behalf of the RLM/LC 2 when the additional ten He 111 Z ordered will be delivered. There is great interest in these machines following the successful towing trials at Leipheim with the 321 carrying a 20-ton payload. There are still 100 examples of the Me 321 in existence, and the first ten He 111 Z are badly needed for these. Heinkel

replies that one should be delivered in each of August and September, two in October, and three each in November and December 1942.

24/6/1942 *E-Stelle* Rechlin [9]

The *E-Stelle* comments on four reports by K.G.z.b.V. 106 concerning its experiences with the Go 244 (from 15/4 to 20/6/1942).

Among the information contained in the reports:

- The Go 244 is to be armed with 4 x MG 15 or 4 x MG 34 machine-guns.

- The first Go 244s delivered are being modified by KG 106 so that fuel can be pumped by hand into the wing tanks from containers in the fuselage. Gotha will be installing the interim system in new aircraft until the definitive version with the electric fuel transfer system is available.

- Maximum flying time is currently restricted to 2.5 hours (with a 1.5 t payload) on account of heavy oil foam formation.

- The air-drop opening desired by the KG is not possible at present. A hatch in the floor is not possible without major design changes, while drops from the door pose a threat to the undercarriage. A bailout hatch in the aft fuselage that can be used for air drops is in the works, however. Bulky loads cannot be dropped under any circumstances. Rechlin will investigate flight with the fuselage tail cone removed.

- The definitive strengthened nosewheel will appear on the 26th aircraft.

The Me 323 V14 had four Ju 88 power units. (Peter)

29/6/1942 Meeting of Department Heads at the Headquarters of the Air Armaments Minister [7]

Startup date for the Me 323 cannot yet be estimated. Performance measurements not yet available.

1/7/1942 Delivery Program 222 [8]

963 examples of the DFS 230 B-2 have been delivered, but there is no production at present. 770 Go 242s have been delivered up to now, with 641 still on order. 99 examples of the Go 244 have been delivered and another 351 have been ordered for the period to May 1943. Deliveries of the Me 321 total 200, and no more are to follow. Deliveries of the Me 323 with GR 14 M have not begun, and the total on order is 143, which are to be delivered by September 1943.

The numbers contained in this plan—1,411 Go 242s and 450 Go 244s—were not definitive at this time; instead they were used in the procurement of materials for a certain period. The RLM could, if the need arose, amend the contracts.

3/7/1942 Messerschmitt

Messerschmitt test pilot Baur reports on two flights at Ainring in a DFS 230 equipped with two Argus pulse jets. Two Argus pulse jets, each producing 150 kg of thrust, were mounted beneath the wings with light metal shields between the wings and tubes. A He 45 towed the DFS 230 to a height of 600 m where, at a speed of 180 kph, the pulse jets were ignited. The noise was equivalent to the Bf 110, however, the airframe was shaken badly. After five minutes of operation the tubes glowed red hot. Instead of the claimed thrust of 150 kg the pulse jets produced just 90 kg, which enabled the machine to fly straight and level at 110 kph.

7/7/1942 Meeting of Department Heads at the Headquarters of the Air Armaments Minister [7]

The commander of proving centers suggests that the Me 321 be approved for operational use with a maximum payload restriction of 11 tons. The General Staff will advise.

11/7/1942 Messerschmitt AG Augsburg [4]

A meeting is held between Herr Friebel and others of the RLM and Professor Messerschmitt, Herr Croneiß, Fröhlich, and others of the Messerschmitt AG. Topic of discussion is the RLM's desire that the Me 323 D-1 and D-2 should, if at all possible, be able to fly with a single load of 20 tons. This could also be achieved with the help of a He 111 H-6 tow plane. Messerschmitt promises to install a forward tow coupling in the Me 323 V12 by 25/7/1942. The He 111 will be procured for testing by the *E-Stelle* Rechlin. As the V12 is presently damaged, the experiment is pushed back to the end of August. H. Friebel will test-fly the Me 323 V14 with Jumo 211 J power plants to assess visibility from the cockpit.

Beginning with the D-3 with Jumo 211 J power plants, Messerschmitt will install adjustable rudder pedals. *E-Stelle* Rechlin has tested the Me 323's range and the results surpass the figures provided by the Messerschmitt AG. The Me 323 has a range of 755 km at ground level, approx. 850 km at an altitude of 2,000 m, and approx. 950 km at 4,000 m. Under these circumstances the installation of additional fuel tanks (2 x 500 liter) in the D-1 and D-2 is no longer being considered.

11/7/1942 *E-Stelle* Rechlin [9]

As the characteristics of the undercarriage taken from the Go 242, with its rigid axle, were extraordinarily bad, GWF

Rigid tow coupling of a He 111 and Go 242. (DFS)

The new swing arm with friction damper, here attached to a He 111 by means of an experimental steel tube structure. Above the friction sphere is the cable for opening the coupling. (DFS)

This photo has not been identified, but it is probably associated with the report of 18/7/1942. (E-Stelle Rechlin)

designed a new outrigger undercarriage which was tested by the *E-Stelle* Rechlin. The test-bed, aircraft BD+XM, was equipped with two 1100 x 375 wheels on the main undercarriage and a 685 x 250 tailwheel on the nosewheel unit. The results of previous trials with the Go 244's outrigger undercarriage were less than satisfactory. The overall impression of the main undercarriage was of improved, but not yet satisfactory shock absorbing characteristics. Braking power was criticized as inadequate.

The nosewheel suffered blown tires and failures of the wheel fork and shock strut. Better results have been achieved with a larger wheel (950 x 350).

18/7/1942 *E-Stelle* Rechlin

Department E4-I issues a report entitled "Transient Magnetism in Aircraft Induced by Vertical Intensity of the Magnetic Field." A Go 242 (Werk.Nr. 0024, TD+IN) is mentioned in the report.

21/7/1942 Meeting of Department Heads at the Headquarters of the Air Armaments Minister [7]

The development and construction of 200 Me 321 airframes has required an expenditure of 44.5 million RM (*Reichsmark*). The sum of 827,000 RM has been spent on development of the Me 323 and the conversion to four or six engines per aircraft. Junkers' big glider required the expenditure of 32.5 million RM. This tremendous expenditure has produced results that are far from satisfactory and shows that extreme care must be exercised when pursuing new ideas, if large-scale misdirection of materials and labor is to be avoided.

CB+ZB, often used for experimental purposes by DFS, behind the He 111 with the lightened towing gear. (DFS)

The He 111 / Go 242 combination takes off. (DFS)

1942/43 DFS Ainring [9]

The original rigid-tow mount was too heavy, which ultimately led to its failure to enter service with the air force. Since then DFS has developed a new outrigger mount, which in addition to pivoting vertically also has a limited lateral range of motion.

24/7/1942 Institute for Flight Testing of the German Research Institute for Gliding Flight. Ernst Udet; Ainring

In Studies and Reports No. 680, Stamer describes trials involving a He 111 with DFS 230 and He 111 with Go 242 using a ball-and-socket rigid-tow system. Numerous test flights have demonstrated that the combination of a He 111 H-5 and DFS 230 with 1,200 kg payload is fully ready for service use.

The flight trials with the He 111 H-5 and the Go 242 had to be suspended, as the mass of the empty Go 242 proved too great in relation to the He 111 and the swing arm was deflected to the stop limit. It does not appear that approval for service use will be possible, especially with a loaded Go 242.

24/7/1942 Chief of the General Staff [2]

The General Staff makes demands of the aircraft procurement program. Replacement of the Go 244 by a new interim transport superior in payload (1 truck) and range is considered necessary. The Go 242 cannot be abandoned because of supply reasons.

This demand probably led to the Gotha projects P-35 and P-39 (see 12/8/1942).

28/7/1942 Meeting of Department Heads at the Headquarters of the Air Armaments Minister [7]

Very negative reports are received concerning the Go 242, even though the air force commented favorably on the aircraft just a short time ago. Concerning this, *Oberstleutnant* Petersen reports that the air force has installed considerable extra weight and that operations are being flown without taking the aircraft's restricted performance into consideration. GL/C-TT is tasked with issuing a T-GL to explain the type's operational capabilities to the units. Oberstabsing. Alpers tables a catch-up program for the Go 244. The *Generalfeldmarschall* is of the view that the Go 244 should be removed from the program and replaced by something better by 1944 at the latest.

29/7/1942 Air Armaments Minister Development Conference [7]

Petersen reports that the Me 323 has completed a 100-hour test (*see Me 323 V12*). The aircraft's [handling] characteristics are now in order, but it is not approved for instrument flight. The aircraft may also be flown by average pilots without special training. The problem is with which motors to continue the program. A requirement was issued for carriage of the 20-ton assault gun. This is not possible with the Gnôme et Rhône power plants.

Petersen proposes leaving the aircraft as it is (with Gnôme et Rhône power plants), to approve it with an 11-ton payload excluding the assault gun, and to add no more work capacities. Milch rejects this and asks about the planned numbers. Alpers gives them as 300, of which none have yet been delivered. The 300 can be built by the summer of 1943, however, engines are only available for 180 aircraft. The Jumo 211 was envisaged for the rest and that is causing problems.

Friebel advises that Messerschmitt recently reported that the Me 323's framework is 2 tons heavier than planned and thus has a tare weight of 26 tons. As the gross weight cannot be increased for performance reasons payload is thus 11 tons. The Me 323 has a range of 700 km with an 11-ton payload, and for the Africa case 1,500 km with a 7-ton payload. As we will definitely not have any transports before 1944 and only a very few after that, the Me 323 will be needed everywhere. Friebel, as well as the proving center, has suggested the Ju 88 power plant and six motors. This would result in a service ceiling of 4,000 m. The present cockpit will have to be extended outwards, however, which will result in extensive structural and static changes in the forward part of the aircraft.

Milch wants to know if it is possible to fly the aircraft with fewer engines. According to Friebel, once in the air the Me 323 flies very well on four engines.

Milch asks when the 180 aircraft can really be completed. The answer: by about February 1943. In the opinion of Vogt of Blohm & Voss, the aircraft's stability characteristics are not yet in order, but the aircraft is an obvious choice because of its ability to carry 10 tons. Milch says of the Me 323 that it cannot achieve the main purpose for which it was designed and built in the first place. He would rather have five Ju 52s than one Me 323, because it is good for nothing. He believes that the Me 323 would be finished after five weeks in Russia. Instead of being a durable machine it is a highly sophisticated, heavy bird that is incapable of instrument flight. And, as it cannot be flown on instruments, he considers its use in Russia in winter completely out of the question.

11 tons over 700 km is certainly not the performance that was desired, but it is outstanding for certain purposes. Therefore, he wants to propose to the *Reichsmarschall* that the 180 machines for which there are engines be built as quickly as possible, and to wait a while before making further decisions. Later in the meeting consideration is

The failure of the nosewheel leg was one of the less serious incidents associated with early Go 244 operations. (Kössler)

given to using 140 Alfa-Romeo twin-row radial engines on hand in Italy to equip another 20 Me 323s. It is thus possible to build 200 aircraft, and they are to be built at the maximum sustainable rate. Any further design work on the aircraft is out of the question.

July 1942 K.G.z.b.V. 106 [27]

In July 1942 the unit loses five of 37 Go 244s for reasons other than enemy action.

4/8/1942 Meeting of Department Heads at the Headquarters of the Air Armaments Minister [7]

Stabsing. Grube gives a report on Air Fleet 4's operational experience with the Go 244. A complete transport unit was formed on the Go 244. Operations were similar to those with the Ju 52. The unit fitted the aircraft with radios, armament, and extra fuel tanks. As a result gross weight probably reached 8 tons, even though the aircraft is only authorized for 6.8 tons. The unit also made modifications to the tail section to improve takeoff. As a result of overloading of the aircraft and improper use there were 75 forced landings and several serious accidents in the period from 21/6 to 10/7/1942. The commander of Air Fleet 4 therefore grounded the aircraft.

The OBS also made complaints about the Go 242. Ribs were found to have delaminated through exposure to sunlight. Because of turbulence in the operational area towing can no longer be justified without modified dual controls.

Air Fleet 4 has been advised of technical issues concerning the Go 244 in a telex from the Technical Office. The *Generalfeldmarschall* requests that Operations Staff 1 T issue clear orders to the units for use of the aircraft.

Genst.Gen.Qu.6 expresses a desire that the strengthened Go 244, 15 of which have been completed, be sent to Air Fleet 4 as quickly as possible.

The *Generalfeldmarschall* considers the Go 244 a bad design on account of its limited range and limited operational potential. The aircraft can only be used as a transport with restrictions. He criticizes all of the responsible offices, because until now all reports about the aircraft have been positive. No mention was made about the aircraft's weaknesses. GL/C-B is ordered to ascertain for how many aircraft material has already been cut and to advise LF ST 1 of the number. The point of the proposal is to continue building only with the materials already cut, to immediately ban the cutting of additional material, and make up the shortfall by increasing production of the Ju 52. The goal is to increase production of the Ju 52 from its current rate of about 40 aircraft to 70. LF ST 1 T is asked to comment on this. GL/C-B is to report on the possibility of increased production on 11/8/1942.

4/8/1942 Air Armaments Minister Development Conference [7]

The start of development of the Ju 252/Wood (Ju 352) is discussed at the meeting. Gotha is to assist. Concerning the Go 244, Milch says, "In any case, further cutting of materials for the Go 244 is being stopped. The aircraft that have been started will be completed, but anything else would be a waste."

Polte: "I believe I heard that parachute training with the Go 244 is to begin. Our people are supposed to become familiar with the aircraft. But if the aircraft will no longer be available, the training would be nonsense."

Milch: "Do they have enough Jus?"

Polte: "They intend to employ the 244 in the air fleet somehow, and expect that this machine will be there later. They are therefore switching training to the 244. The people must therefore be told that they won't be getting any. As said, there is something going on there, and as I said, I only heard about it in passing."

Milch: "That makes no difference to me; we must stop it [production] no matter what. Continuing to build this machine is something that can't be justified." (A new report about operational experience with the Go 244 after the grounding was lifted is then read out.)

Vorwald: "It was reported to me yesterday that the aircraft has been loaded with 8.3 tons instead of 6.3."

Milch: "In any case it is again obvious from the report that nothing encouraging can have been produced when the machine was in production. If the aircraft is flown as it should be flown, adhering to the load factors, it has neither a decent range nor a decent payload, and as well it must do without radio equipment, armament, etc. It also has no protected fuel tanks (Shout: only jettisonable). Therefore we will be done with it and concentrate on the Ju 252/Wood."

With this the Air Armaments Minister essentially sealed the fate of the Gotha P-39 project. The Ju 352 was envisaged as the only transport to be built in the future.

It had been planned to also use the Go 244 for the dropping of parachute troops. As this marked the beginning of the end of the Go 244, the question arose as to how the parachute troops should proceed. It would be shown that the dropping of parachute troops from gliders—for whatever reason—was thought to be practical. Therefore, the Go 244 B-3 was later converted back into the Go 242 B-3 transport glider and fitted with specialized equipment.

11/8/1942 *E-Stelle* Rechlin [15], [9]

The *E-Stelle* has tested a Go 244 (VC+OJ, Werk.Nr. 00010) with wooden propellers (alternative solution to save aluminum) and both axle- and outrigger-type undercarriages. The combination of wooden propellers and outrigger undercarriage results in a reduced low-level cruising speed of 170 kph at maximum gross

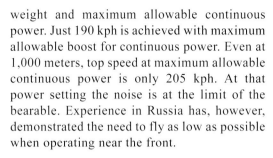

weight and maximum allowable continuous power. Just 190 kph is achieved with maximum allowable boost for continuous power. Even at 1,000 meters, top speed at maximum allowable continuous power is only 205 kph. At that power setting the noise is at the limit of the bearable. Experience in Russia has, however, demonstrated the need to fly as low as possible when operating near the front.

12/8/1942 Gotha [2]
On this date the Gothaer Waggonfabrik produces a design description for a three-engine successor to the Go 244, the P-39 project.

17/8/1942 *E-Stelle* Rechlin [15], [9]
The strengthened nosewheel and outrigger main undercarriage improve taxiing characteristics and stability, but they weigh 140 kg more and, because of the increased drag, maximum speed at low level drops by 23 kph at empty weight and combat power, and at empty weight and economical cruise by 8 kph to 175 kph, or almost to the prescribed climbing speed. The drop in rate of climb with full payload (7.8 tons) and combat power from 2.3 m/sec to 1.25 m/sec is assessed as unacceptable. Handling

The wide-track main undercarriage (here of the Go 244 C-2) produced far too much drag. The bulky nosewheel also reduced the aircraft's performance. (German Museum)

Comparison of the Go 244 B-2 (here still with the wide-track outrigger undercarriage) with the P-39 project. (Gothaer Waggonfabrik)

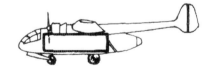

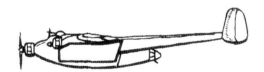

Go 244

P-39

characteristics about the lateral and normal axes also deteriorate.

In its present form the new undercarriage is not usable for performance reasons. The company has already been asked to create an improvement by fairing [the undercarriage].

17/8/1942 Meeting of Department Heads at the Headquarters of the Air Armaments Minister [7]

Production of the motorized transport glider is running down. The emphasis is shifted to the Ju 352. Capacities and materials made available through the cancellation of the Go 244 are to be made available for the start-up of the Ju 352.

20/8/1942 Meeting of Department Heads at the Headquarters of the Air Armaments Minister [7]

Production of the Go 244 comes to an end. Orders have already been issued that workers assigned to the Go 244 be assigned to the Bf 110 increased production program.

26/8/1942 Meeting of Department Heads at the Headquarters of the Air Armaments Minister [7]

The *Reichsmarschall* (Göring) agrees that production of the Go 244 will end at 450 machines. The *Generalfeldmarschall* (Milch) gives his approval to assigning priority to the Bf 110 at the cost of the Go 244. The supply of motors for the Hs 129 is to be taken into consideration when designing the Go 244 program. The Go 244 production run-down program is to be delivered to the *Generalfeldmarschall*.

27/8/1942 *E-Stelle* Rechlin [9]

Taxi and landing shock measurements are carried out on the Go 244's nosewheel shock strut. The measurements reveal that the failure load of the shock strut is reached and exceeded during taxiing. This explains the numerous failures of the nosewheel strut. Following the failure of the nosewheel strut during the 31st takeoff during ongoing trials, the *E-Stelle* restricts the early version to a gross weight of 6.8 tons. Measurements with the modified undercarriage with larger nosewheel will also be carried out after its arrival in Rechlin.

Thermal measurements of the power plants of the Go 244 equipped with Gnôme et Rhône 14 M engines were carried out using Go 244 Werk.Nr. 0000047 (TE+UK)—with Gnôme et Rhône 14 M 7 and 14 M 6 with three-blade Ratier propellers—and Go 244 Werk.Nr. 000010 (VC+OJ) with Gnôme et Rhône 14 M and four-blade Heine propellers. In the climb at 170 kph cylinder head temperatures were within allowable limits, but too high in level flight. The oil coolers (from the Potez 63) are found to be satisfactory in central European areas but too small for tropical use.

1/9/1942 Meeting of Department Heads at the Headquarters of the Air Armaments Minister [7]

Run-down of Go 244 production is to take place as soon as possible, so that the industry is relieved of this aircraft.

14/9/1942 Meeting of Department Heads at the Headquarters of the Air Armaments Minister [7]

As a batch of 25 Me 323s with Alfa-Romeo [engines] is very unfavorable from the point of view of cost and supply, the General Staff is asked to decide if it can be dispensed with.

15/9/1942 Meeting of Department Heads at the Headquarters of the Air Armaments Minister [7]

Obstlt. Pasewald speaks about the transfer of Me 323 production from Messerschmitt to Zeppelin: Zeppelin has declared its willingness to take over production and further development of the Me 323. Messerschmitt must assist the Zeppelin Company by releasing designers. To be decided is whether the Me 323 should be developed for other power plants. Those in question are the Jumo 211 and Alfa Romeo. Approximately 25 aircraft can be equipped with the Alfa Romeo. In view of the small number of aircraft and relatively minor performance increase (1 to 2 ton increase in payload) development costs are not considered justified. The Air Armaments Minister's Liaison Office in Paris can make another 200 Gnôme et Rhône power plants available to Messerschmitt.

A proposal is made to develop a six-engined Me 323 using the DB 603 standard power plant. A useful payload of 30 tons is to be expected with this [engine]. The *Generalfeldmarschall* is in agreement with the transfer of the Me 323 to Zeppelin. Messerschmitt must release as many designers as are required for the continuation of the work.

All of the Me 323s contained in the program are to be equipped with Gnôme et Rhône motors. The Me 323's potential payload is to be thoroughly checked and determined based on a calculated range of 800 km. Payload is to be limited so as to guarantee good takeoff and flight characteristics. Development toward a 30-ton payload with DB 603 engines is to be contracted to the Zeppelin Company and carried out with the utmost speed.

20/9/1942 *E-Stelle* Rechlin [15], [9]

In the judgment of the *E-Stelle*, converting the Go 244 with Gnôme et Rhône power plants to the improved undercarriage is impossible on performance grounds. An increase in gross weight from 6.8 to 7.8 tons (maximum gross weight) can therefore also not be authorized. In addition to the drop in performance, the undercarriage also causes a considerable deterioration in handling. The aircraft is weakly stable to instable about the lateral and normal axes. GWF was immediately given the task of achieving a significant reduction in drag. Joints and struts are to be carefully faired, the old nosewheel strut replaced by a new steel tube strut which is stronger and has significantly better aerodynamics than the old one, and tests are to be carried out with smaller wheels (935 x 345 in place of 1100 x 390 mainwheels and 840 x 300 nosewheel instead of 950 x 350). Even after these improvements, however, conversion of the Go 244 with Gnôme et Rhône engines to the new undercarriage is not possible for performance reasons.

As the performance of the Go 244 with variable-pitch propellers is already poor, it is incomprehensible that the Gnôme et Rhône variable-pitch propellers are to be replaced with fixed-pitch wooden propellers to the benefit of the Hs 129. First of all, the Go 244s delivered can definitely not be converted to the new outrigger undercarriage. Further, as altitude increases, the wooden propellers produce a physically unbearable noise level on account of the increase in rpm.

The *E-Stelle* advises against the use of the Russian M 25 and M 62 motors. These power plants are designed for significantly faster aircraft; consequently, similarly poor results can be expected with respect to cooling and propeller effectiveness as with the Gnôme et Rhône 14 M. Apart from supply difficulties arising from the plethora of different types, Rechlin's experience with Russian power plants has been very bad with respect to reliability.

In order to make the aircraft into a suitable interim transport with the ultimate undercarriage, the *E-Stelle* requests the installation of the BMW 132 L or M, which produce approximately 170 HP. (*With the envisaged BMW 132 Z, climb performance is no better than with the Gnôme et Rhône.*) With their greater operating maturity and reliability and the experience the transport units already have with this power plant, the large number of engine failures, some with fatal consequences, would fall to a minimum, just as the spark plug and filter problems and cooling difficulties would no longer be present. As a power plant, the BMW 132 is scarcely heavier than the Gnôme et Rhône. With its higher cruise power of about 170 HP and its aerodynamically-superior installation, despite its greater diameter (the fixed split collar is deleted) cruise and climb speeds will be so improved that the BMW 132 model will be able to be retrofitted with the ultimate undercarriage and thus finally be flown at full gross weight. As the BMW 132 is a low-level engine, there is no performance loss even with fixed-pitch propellers, as with the Gnôme et Rhône with its maximum boost altitude of 4,000 m. The somewhat higher fuel consumption will cause range to drop, but this can be compensated for by installing the larger fuel tank.

For the above reasons the planned conversion of an aircraft with outrigger undercarriage to skis for winter use has not taken place.

30/9/1942 Aircraft Program No. 22 E [7]

Messerschmitt Leipheim has so far delivered 15 Me 323 with six Gnôme et Rhône 14 N power plants. Obertraubling has only delivered one, but it has not been collected. The planned maximum production of the aircraft is 23 per month, and the plan runs until February 1943. The 25 Me 323s with six Alfa Romeo power plants are to be built in the period from April to September 1943.

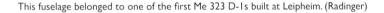

This fuselage belonged to one of the first Me 323 D-1s built at Leipheim. (Radinger)

The Go 242 A-1 was produced in greater numbers than any other variant of the Gotha transport glider. (Obermaier / Petrick)

308 Go 244s have been built, and 142 are to follow by August 1943. 931 examples of the Go 242 have been built to date, and production is to continue at 20 per month until 1945.

1/10/1942 C-Amts Program [8]

308 Go 244s have been built by 30/9/1942. The delivery of 31 Go 244s is planned in October and 25 in November. 15 Go 244s are to be produced each month from December 1942 to April 1943, and the last 11 of the 450 Go 244s authorized by Göring are to be delivered in May 1943. The Ju 252 (Wood) (*later to become the Ju 352*) is the envisaged replacement for the Go 244. Production is to begin in autumn 1943 and run up to 200 per month by March 1945.

931 examples of the Go 242 have been built by 30/9/1942, and the monthly delivery of 20 examples is planned into 1945.

3/10/1942 Messerschmitt AG [9]

The project office writes a report on wind tunnel measurements using a model of the Me 323 with Ju 88 power plants and gun turrets in DVL's medium tunnel. The installation of the power plants results in worsened visibility from the cockpit, making it necessary to modify the cockpit arrangement. The tests, using a 1:26.2 scale model, are intended to determine the most favorable type of cockpit, as well as the best arrangement of gun turrets.

12/10/1942 *E-Stelle* Rechlin [15], [9]

Trials with the Go 244 with 950 x 350 nosewheel and 1100 x 375 mainwheels resulted in no complaints, even at a gross weight of 7.8 tons. In order to keep drag and weight increases within limits, the final wheel sizes are selected as 840 x 300 for the nosewheel and 935 x 345 for the mainwheels. A test bed with these wheel sizes is presently being prepared by the company. An ultimate decision can be expected by mid-October. Adequate braking power is assured by the use of the 935 x 345 double-brake wheels from the Bf 110.

28/10/1942 Peenemünde-West Experimental Station [9]

Report 2334/42 by the *Luftwaffe* experimental station deals with rocket-assisted takeoff experiments using a DFS 230 glider with two Rheinmetall R I 502 powder rockets (1,000 kg thrust for 6 sec.). The experiments were supposed to determine:

1. the operating safety of the Rheinmetall rockets

2. the practicability of rocket-assisted takeoffs by the DFS 230

3. the necessary modifications to the takeoff aids already installed in the aircraft on the production line

In some cases the rockets burned unevenly, turning the aircraft as much as 60° off heading, and the pilot was unable to correct even using all of his strength. On one of the four takeoffs a rocket burned through and scorched the wing, consequently, the *E-Stelle* is withholding approval of the rockets due to unreliability.

30/10/1942 Meeting of Department Heads at the Headquarters of the Air Armaments Minister [7]

Concerning the development of the Me 323, the following matters must be addressed:

1. The installation of other motors (4 x DB 603 or 6 x Jumo 211)

2. Strengthening of airframe to 60-tons (for larger loads, like a 22-ton tank)

3. Forward relocation of the cockpit (necessary with fatter engine nacelles)

Carriage of the 22-ton tank appears impossible, but a takeoff roll of not more than 800 m is demanded, as well as a climb rate of at least 3.5 m/sec and instrument flight capability. The 25 aircraft with Alfa Romeo motors are to be built, possibly with Gnôme et Rhône 14 R motors as replacements. The Gnôme et Rhône 14 R is roughly comparable to the BMW 801 A, and its development was completed near the end of the war with France.

31/10/1942 Gothaer Waggonfabrik [8, RL 3/1122]

GWF writes to the RLM (Vorwald) that there is a shortage of workers. As production of the Bf 110 G-3 and G-4 series was supposed to begin in November 1942, and as the four-blade propeller for the Go 244 has been blocked, it is proposed that people be shifted from production of the Go 244 to Bf 110 production. This will result in a drop in Go 244 production.

1/11/1942 C-Amts Program [8]

The Go 244 E-1 (Werk.Nr. 830), with an experimental installation of two BMW 132 Z power plants, is tested in Gotha.

This is the first mention of the existence of a Go 244 with BMW 132s. The BMW 132 was thus not installed in the Go 244 V1, as claimed by some writers, but not until much later as a replacement for the Gnôme et Rhône. Amazingly, the BMW 132 Z from the Ju 52 was chosen. Like the Gnôme et Rhône 14 M, it was not powerful enough and therefore offered little prospect of satisfactory flight performance.

In the aircraft program, 14 Me 323 prototypes appear under Messerschmitt, including one with four Bloch power plants, two with four LeO, one with four Alfa Romeo, and one with four Jumo 211 J. Also present are three prototypes with six Bloch power plants and six with Gnôme et Rhône motors.

More detailed information in the chapter Me 323 Prototypes.

1/11/1942 GL/C No. 25 574/42 secret command matter [8, RL 3/2685]

A list of aircraft types taken into service by the air force also includes the Go 244 B and Go 244 C. The Go 244 B has Gnôme et Rhône 14 M06/14 M07 power plants with Gnôme et Rhône variable-pitch propellers, and the Go 244 C Gnôme et Rhône 14 M04/14 M05 power plants with four-blade fixed-pitch propellers.

2/11/1942 Conference Air Armaments Minister/ General Staff [7]

The Go 244 can be halted immediately. The aircraft already completed can be converted into gliders if possible.

2/11/1942 K.G.z.b.V. 106 [27]

K.G.z.b.V. 106 moved back to the Reich and turned in its 32 remaining Go 244s. During five months of operations it has lost one Go 244 to enemy action and ten to other causes.

2/11/1942 DVL Berlin Adlershof [1]

The Aerodynamics Institute of the German Aviation Research Institute publishes a report on the development of a propeller-driven siren (like that of the Ju 87) for the DFS 230.

3/11/1942 Meeting of Department Heads at the Headquarters of the Air Armaments Minister [7]

A program proposal is submitted for the termination of the Go 244 and continued production of the Go 242.

The DVL positioned the siren above the fuselage. The photo depicts an operational machine. (Bundesarchiv Koblenz 10 II-565-1407-04)

17/11/1942 Meeting of Department Heads at the Headquarters of the Air Armaments Minister [7]

The *Generalfeldmarschall* authorizes the conversion of Go 244s into gliders, and at Dir. Frydag's suggestion the Menibum Company is selected for the task. All other work on the Go 244 is to be halted immediately.

23/11/1942 Meeting of Department Heads at the Headquarters of the Air Armaments Minister [7]

A priority system with four levels is implemented to deal with labor or materials shortages. Level I includes fighters, night-fighters, and dive-bombers. The Ju 52 is in Level II and the Me 323 is in Level III.

23/11/1942 Conference Air Armaments Minister/ General Staff [7]

The Genst.6.Abt. requests 20 Go 242s (per month). The Go 244 is halted immediately. Those aircraft already completed and those in the hands of the units will be converted into gliders as soon as possible. Genst.2.Abt. and GL/C-B agree that the aircraft are to be stripped and converted at Olmütz or Eger.

1/12/1942 Meeting of Department Heads at the Headquarters of the Air Armaments Minister [7]

Production of the Me 323 with six Gnôme et Rhône engines is under way at 140 machines, to be followed by 25 aircraft with Alfa Romeo motors. *Oberst* Vorwald points out that the Alfa Romeo will not be available in the future, as *Reichminister* Speer has rejected as excessive Italian demands for compensation. Director Verdier is

to be contacted to determine whether the old Gnôme et Rhône 14 N, which is built in Limoges, can be delivered in sufficient numbers (6 x 20 + 60 spares = about 200 motors per month). If sufficient workers are made available, from January 1943 production of the Me 323 can be increased from 12 to 20 aircraft. *Generaloberst* Fromm promises 1,000 armed services convicts. GL/A W-Wi will attempt to procure concentration camp inmates.

While Mannesmann is fabricating components for the Me 323, it also starts producing components for the Ju 352. Mannesmann must switch production to the Ju 352 at the end of 1943. Continuation of the 323 at the expense of a delay in production start-up of the Ju 352 is unacceptable. The 323 will continue at 20 aircraft per month.

The question of the DB 603 is set back until the industry advisor concludes his discussions concerning continuation of the Gnôme et Rhône 14 N. Stabsing. Friebel points out that as of 1/12/1942 development of the Me 323 has passed from Messerschmitt to Zeppelin.

1/12/1942 Zeppelin Company [4]

On the transfer of Me 323 development to the Zeppelin Company, it issues a memorandum describing the direction of development pursued to date. Production of the previous series with Gnôme et Rhône engines, whose payload is 14 tons according to the latest flight results (at a maximum allowable gross weight of 50 tons for performance reasons), will end. It was intended that this should be followed by an airframe strengthened to 60 tons, with which 24 tons could be transported in special cases. The Jumo 211 J in Ju 88

The original installation of the Argus pulse-jet used for static tests on the ground. (Aders)

power units promised by the RLM appeared particularly suited to this. In addition to a strengthened airframe and wing, the new variant would require a new undercarriage and especially a revised cockpit positioned further forward and also higher. The view from the old cockpit with the Ju 88 power units was rejected by the RLM and the *E-Stelle* as unacceptable. In order for this version to follow on a timely basis the design office had to have additional personnel. The RLM did not release the Ju 88 power units, however, and development of the new cockpit was delayed in part by a shortage of designers and in part by a lack of interest on the part of the [technical] office. At the present time, therefore, a timely continuation cannot be anticipated under any circumstances. To prevent a production gap, Messerschmitt has suggested that production of the previous airframe continue with other power plants (e.g. 4 x BMW 801 or 4 x Alfa Romeo). The 60-ton airframe is being developed as a further stage with the forward cockpit and 6 x Jumo 211 J or 6 x Alfa Romeo, or 6 x DB 603 or 6 x BMW 801. A projected third stage is a 75-ton airframe with installation of 6 x DB 603 or BMW 801 or similar power plants. Despite numerous

visits to the RLM by Messerschmitt and Zeppelin, it has not been possible to force a clear decision or to incorporate a specific engine into the plans. Consequently. the entire Me 323 affair is so delayed that continued production is only possible if the airframe is built with the minimum possible changes.

This is essentially the starting shot for the Me 323 E variant.

3/12/1942 Commander of Proving Centers [7]

Hauptmann Späte reports on a trip to Messerschmitt Augsburg and to Hörsching, near Linz. Purpose of the trip was to gather information on the Me 328. He speaks of the recent test flights by the Me 328 and a DFS 230 test bed with 150-kg (thrust) Argus pulse jets at Hörsching.

5/12/1942 Special Commission F 2 Obertraubling [20]

The head of the Special Commission F 2 informs the GL/C (*Oberst* Vorwald) that the requested 32 Me 323 D-1 aircraft with Bloch power units and Ratier propellers cannot be built in a single batch, as there are only enough serviceable engines for 26 aircraft. The available power plants are sufficient only until the beginning of January 1943, and the last six aircraft cannot be expected until the end of the program in July 1943. Only flexible mounts are approved for the Me 323 D-2 with LeO power units and Heine wooden propellers, and these are not available at the moment. For planning purposes, production of the Me 323 D-2 cannot be expected until February 1943. For the 29 Me 323 D-3 aircraft ordered with LeO power units and Ratier variable-pitch propellers, the propeller spare parts situation with regard to propellers is not assured. Therefore, production of the Me 323 D-6 is to begin first and the LeO power units with normal rigid mounts used up, but then it will be replaced by the Me 323 D-2. Consequently, the Me 323 D-6 also cannot be built in one batch.

18/12/1942 Operational Experience Report [4]

Flg. Hauptingenieur Müller of K.G.z.b.V. 1/323 reports that the Me 323 has proved very successful. Only the propellers give cause for frequent complaints. He criticizes the aircraft's poor range on internal fuel, but this is soon to be addressed. The armament is practically unusable, and as an interim step the unit has installed the dorsal gun position from the He 111.

21/12/1942 Conference GL1/Genst. 6. Abt. [7]

As it is to be expected that the Me 323 with Gnôme et Rhône power units will sooner or later be used as a transport in the east, the General Staff requests that materiel be procured for winter operations (heated oil return line on the Gnôme et Rhône motor).

December 1942 Procurement CE 2 [4]

The RLM believes that it may eventually be possible to make He 111 H-6 power units with Jumo 211 engines available for the Me 323.

December 1942 Messerschmitt [4]

A preliminary investigation by Messerschmitt/Zeppelin reveals that a version of the Me 323 with He 111 power units would have superior visibility from the cockpit compared to the Gnôme et Rhône 14 N. Zeppelin proposes abandoning the planned 60-ton variant and strengthening the existing airframe to 55-56 tons by replacing a few elements of the lattice framework. The envisaged variant would also have lighter control forces through the use of internally-balanced elevators and rudder and ailerons with larger Flettner tabs. The fuselage is to be lightened through a thorough overhaul. Redesign of the cockpit will not be possible, but the armored glass is to be replaced with Plexiglas. The two flight engineers are to be replaced by one in the leading edge of the starboard wing, and the radio operator placed on the opposite side, so that the crew can see and speak to each other. Armament is to be strengthened and the fuel capacity doubled.

8/1/1943 Air Armaments Minister Development Conference [7]

Friebel speaks about the Me 323 engine question: the required number of Gnôme et Rhône 14 N engines is assured for 140 aircraft. Things look bad for the follow-on orders, as only a currently unknown number of captured engines can be used for these. They, and the procurement office, have therefore looked around at German power plants and placed their hopes on the Jumo 211. The initial plan to use the Ju 88 power unit would have required extensive modification of the airframe (raising of the cockpit), as the long power units with forward radiators causes an unacceptable deterioration in view from the cockpit. Use of the much slimmer He 111 power units, on the other hand, would result in a view from the cockpit that is superior even to the existing model. Friebel proposes that planning for the Me 323 with He 111 power units begin, and that a contract be issued for construction of a prototype by Zeppelin. While the use of a liquid-cooled engine is a disadvantage because of its greater vulnerability, it must be considered because of the potential gap in production, while use of the more powerful Jumo 211 will deliver twice the payload (19 tons compared to the present 9 at a rate of climb of 4 m/sec).

Thus began development of the Me 323 F with He 111 power units. The Me 323 F was based on preliminary work by Messerschmitt on the Me 323 D-3, but the first development contract went to Zeppelin.

Petersen adds: The Me 323 has proved itself, and it makes sense to push it forward in view of the transport situation. In my opinion the unreliability of the liquid-cooled engine weighs against it. With six engines there will always be something wrong with one of them, and the aircraft will be grounded. In Italy it will be impossible to leave the aircraft sitting around for even half an hour, otherwise they will be attacked with fragmentation bombs and machine-guns. He sees six propellers all turning in the same direction as another disadvantage, fearing it will lead to stability problems. He would therefore prefer to have production of the Me 323 continue with Gnôme et Rhône 14 N power plants.

Mahnke speaks about the 14 N procurement situation: The 14 N is currently not in production, and only spare parts are being built in the unoccupied area. A total of 2,000 to 2,500 14 N motors have been built. Some of these are still in France; 350 have already been located. It is planned, however, to construct the Gnôme et Rhône 14 R in Paris as successor to the 14 N. The 14 R uses fewer strategic materials than the 14 N, which would be an advantage, and in Paris there would be better control.

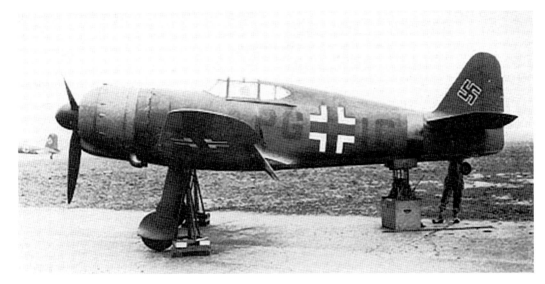

The Gnôme et Rhône 14 R was envisaged for the Me 323 for a long time, but during the war it only flew in prototypes of the Bloch 157. (Mankau)

The first engine has been on the test bench and flown in a fighter in Bordeaux. The assessment was good. If the production tools are taken to Paris, production can start in ten to twelve months. Expected monthly output is 80 to 100 examples.

Milch, Vorwald, and Mahnke reach the conclusion that there are still about 500 Gnôme et Rhône 14 N power plants on hand, but that 1,200 are needed until production of the 14 R begins. The question of the Jumo 211 is urgent because of the 700 missing engines. Vorwald observes that the Jumo 211 can only be a stopgap, as production is to end in summer or autumn 1944, and afterwards the Gnôme et Rhône 14 R is to take its place. Milch agrees, and if they order the prototype immediately, then that would mean they would need a single batch of 700 engines in Heinkel power units. Then the 14 R should take its place.

Friebel does not think it will be difficult to fly the aircraft with six propellers turning in the same direction, but he will confirm this by having six same-handed engines installed in an aircraft. *The six same-handed propellers were tested on the Me 323 V8.* When questioned by Milch, he surmises that a prototype with Jumo 211s could be complete in three months, but the matter has not yet been checked.

21/1/1943 Air Armaments Minister Development Conference [7]

The question of engines for the Me 323 is also raised at this meeting. Pasewald asks whether it is worthwhile starting production of the Gnôme et Rhône 14 N in the Lyon factory if they later switch to the Jumo 211 and possibly the Jumo 213. The Jumo 211 will bestow a considerable increase in payload, and it will be possible to install really effective defensive armament. Vorwald and Mahnke respond that production must start in order to

maintain numbers of the Me 323. Also they do not intend to resume production, but rather to produce 1,000 motors from the 40,000 parts that have been found. They would be used until production of the Me 323 with the Jumo 211 starts. More cannot be delivered, but the question arises whether they really need the Gnôme et Rhône 14 R. Messerschmitt has offered to build 30 Me 323s per month, and Pasewald would like to take advantage of that, especially as the machines require no strategic materials. They must economize with the Gnôme et Rhône 14 N in such a way as to continue without a serious drop in numbers until conversion to the Jumo 211, which is to take place in 1944. There is further discussion of the use of the Jumo 211 in the He 111 and the Me 323, and a decision on starting production of the Gnôme et Rhône 14 R is reserved.

21/1/1943 Gothaer Waggonfabrik [8, RL 3/1122]

At the instigation of the RLM (Herr Alpers) a meeting is held in Gotha concerning the conversion of the Go 244 into the Go 242. 227 aircraft are ready for conversion, which is to be carried out from May to June 1942 by Letov, Basser (Zwickau), Menibum (Hamburg), and Klemm (Böblingen). GWF is to produce the modification directive and provide parts. The rest of the Go 244s are currently not available. Conversion at the Hagenow and Breslau-Gandau bases is not possible.

26/1/1943 Meeting of Department Heads at the Headquarters of the Air Armaments Minister [7]

Concerning the Me 323 engine question, *Oberst* Vorwald of the General Staff states that a proposal has been made not to start production of the Gnôme et Rhône 14 N and to make the Me 323 more economical by installing the Jumo 211/43, and later the Jumo 213. In the interim,

The Me 323 D-6 profited from the decision to continue building the Gnôme et Rhône 14 N (German Museum)

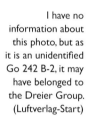

I have no information about this photo, but as it is an unidentified Go 242 B-2, it may have belonged to the Dreier Group. (Luftverlag-Start)

however, it has turned out that the Gnôme et Rhône 14 R has a good performance; consequently, production should begin. Generaling. Mahnke states that the stock of captured Gnôme et Rhône 14 N engines is only sufficient for five or six months of aircraft production. They have 380 complete motors from unoccupied France. Gnôme et Rhône and its subcontractors have parts in storage for 1,400 motors, of which 1,000 are to be assembled. The rest are envisaged as spares. The question remains to be answered whether the difference in performance between the Jumo 211 (1,230 hp) and the Gnôme et Rhône 14 R (1,670 hp, production start early 1944) is sufficient compared to the Jumo 213 (1,800 hp). The Gnôme et Rhône 14 R has so far proved reliable in testing, and production will begin if the Air Armaments Minister so decides. In Mahnke's opinion, they can use

the remaining Gnôme et Rhône 14 N until production of the Gnôme et Rhône 14 R begins and cover the rest with Jumo 211s. Conversion to the Jumo 213 should be abandoned. Stabsing. Friebel subsequently points out that while the Gnôme et Rhône 14 R has greater takeoff power (1,600 hp) than the Jumo 211 (1,425 hp), no use can be made of it because combat power is the same. Payload and armament are the same. On the development side, it appears justifiable to initially fill the gaps with the Jumo 211 and later switch to the air-cooled Gnôme et Rhône 14 R, but not with an increase in performance in the future. With a requirement for heavier armament and greater range performance would drop. Vorwald stresses the special importance of the air-cooled engine, the basic demand of the transport pilots, which is answered by the Gnôme et Rhône 14 R.

This Go 242 was towed aloft by a He 111. The photo shows Gefreiter Zwick testing the partially-deployed braking parachute in level flight. (Krieg)

The Ju 290 and Me 323 served side by side as transport aircraft for a brief time. (Bundesarchiv Koblenz 10 11-561-1130-33)

1/1943 Gotha [1]

The Gothaer Waggonfabrik delivers three DFS 230 B-2 (Werk.Nr. 522, 523 and 526) to Japan.

9/2/1943 Memorandum Headquarters Air Armaments Minister [2]

Three of the latest Go 244s are assigned to Proving Center Command. The aircraft are assigned to a transport unit under Hptm. Braun based at Tempelhof, and there are tested in action. *E-Stelle* Rechlin E2 becomes involved and submits an assessment of the performance and handling characteristics of that version of the Go 244.

The purpose of the testing is not clear to me, as by then it had been decided to convert the Go 244s into Go 242s. There may have been an association with the plan to deliver the Go 244 to Japan at a later date.

17/2/1943 Berlin [2]

The representative of the German Export Office, Ernst Priger, writes a memorandum stating that the Go 244 can be delivered to Japan, that the engine question is resolved, and the BMW 132 engine would now be installed.

2/3/1943 Stuttgart

At Stuttgart-Ruit, *Gefreiter* Zwick tests a Go 242 with ribbon braking parachute.

5/3/1943 Air Armaments Minister Development Conference [7]

As the Ju 290, which was originally thought of as a transport aircraft, is being used for the much more important role of strategic reconnaissance, the Me 323 is to bolster the transport sector. Plans are made to increase monthly production from 20 to 30, and it is believed that, if requested, this number can be increased further in 1945. Licensed production in Italy is also discussed.

9/3/1943 Meeting of Department Heads at the Headquarters of the Air Armaments Minister [7]

At the request of the Air Armaments Minister, production of the Me 323 must be increased considerably.

3/1943 Gothaer Waggonfabrik [8, RL 3/1122]

Special Commission F 12 produces a summary of Go 242 and Go 244 production numbers to March 1943 and planning until year's end 1943. (The table is found in the appendix.)

1/4/1943 RLM (GL/C E2) [3], [30]

The RLM development office issues Technical Guideline No. 63/43 for the design of an assault glider and universal transport glider. Demanded are:

Purpose:

Main Role:

Combat action by assault groups against key points in the enemy's defenses.

Secondary Roles:

a) Dropping of parachute troops in towed flight

b) Dropping of supply containers in towed flight

c) Airborne landing operations with airborne troops and heavy weapons in lightly defended or enemy territory

d) Transport of weapons and equipment of all types

Mode of Operation:

Rigid- or cable-tow behind all modern bomber and twin-engine fighter aircraft. Creation of glider trains must be possible. Takeoff without tow plane using powder takeoff aids (rockets). Targeted approach in a glide or in a braked dive after release with subsequent short landing.

Performance:

Maximum allowable airspeed while towed 330 kph. Glide ratio 1:14. Landing speed as low as possible, roll-out or slide-out distance as short as possible.

Handling Characteristics:

Adequate stability about all axes (instrument flight in rigid-tow, certain instrument capability in free gliding flight).

Payload:

Twelve men, one VW Kübel or one gun.

As the old tow planes were about to disappear at this time, and production of the He 111 was also scheduled to end in summer 1944, in the long run the transport gliders would have to rely on the Ju 188 and Ju 388. These new tow planes could not reasonably operate at speeds of approximately 250 kph, however, which meant that they could not tow the DFS 230 and Go 242. Consequently, towing speed was to be increased to 330 kph and the gliders made similar in size to the Ju 388.

There was renewed development activity. The DFS, together with the Gothaer Waggonfabrik, resumed development of the DFS 230. This led to the DFS 230 V7. The new variant was initially assigned the designation DFS 230 D-1, but this was later changed to DFS 230 E-1. GWF also worked on other projects. Dipl.Ing. Kalkert, director of the Erla Repair Works (REWE) and designer of the Go 242, was tasked with the development of a new transport glider [26]. [30]. The higher towing speed resulted in a reduced wing span on the DFS 230 V7, the other Gotha projects, and the Ka 430.

The Go 244 B-2 RJ+II was flown by the E-Stelle Rechlin until April 1944. (Regel)

In the south of France DFS 230s were assembled in the open air. (Krieg)

The desire for rigid-tow is understandable, as this was the only method that allowed trouble-free instrument flight. Based on the experience with the He 111/Go 242 combination, however, it appears doubtful to me whether the Ju 188 could really have used the rigid-tow method with the new transport gliders because of their relative sizes.

In the literature it has sometimes been stated that Gotha built the DFS 230 V7 as a modern successor to the DFS 230 B on its own initiative and without informing the RLM. The authors then express amazement at the "incompetent" RLM, which did not allow the new DFS 230 to be built. Apparently they failed to notice that a contract was issued at the same time for the Ka 430, which was of similar size. I find it astonishing that one could seriously believe that an aircraft developed by

the Gothaer Waggonfabrik without an RLM contract, and thus contrary to standard RLM procedure, would subsequently be selected for production by the same RLM. The Gothaer Waggonfabrik or the DFS would have received a development contract from the RLM like the Erfurt Repair Works.

7/4/1943 Gothaer Waggonfabrik [2]

The GWF writes to the representative of the German Export Office, Herr Prieger, informing him that it has delivered three DFS 230s to Japan and has now heard that the Japanese are also interested in the Go 242 and Go 244. The company therefore requests approval to export two Go 242s and two Go 244s. The Go 244 is equipped with Gnôme et Rhône 06/07 engines, but also with the Gnôme et Rhône 04/05. As well, a prototype aircraft has

The success of the Go 242 on all fronts caused the General Staff to increase the required number of gliders. (Nidree)

been fitted with BMW 132 Z motors and sent to Rechlin, where it is under test. The testing appears to be proceeding satisfactorily. After various improvements the machines with the other engines are also back under test, likewise with satisfactory results.

And so—provided the testing yields positive results—there are no more reservations about delivering the Go 244 to Japan. It is, however, suggested that the aircraft be delivered with BMW 132 Z motors as, apart from the issue of spare parts, the Japanese are already familiar with this engine. This suggestion is, of course, made pending a decision by the technical office.

It would subsequently be determined that the delivery of complete aircraft was impossible for transport reasons. The plan was abandoned on 7/2/1944, after which discussions turned to licensed production. Drawings were submitted to the Japanese trading partner in summer 1944. It cannot be determined whether license production took place.

Spring 1943 Southern France [13]

Two parachute divisions, 250 transport aircraft, 570 transport gliders, and 200 tow planes are assembled in Southern France undter the command of XI Air Corps to counter the anticipated invasion by the Allies in southern Europe.

12/4/1943 Messerschmitt AG Licensed Production Division

The Messerschmitt Company makes a proposal for continuation of the Me 323. It envisages the construction of 54 Me 323 D-1, 50 Me 323 D-2, and 39 Me 323 D-6 with Gnôme et Rhône 14 N power plants at Leipheim and Obertraubling by 31/7/1943. 110 Me 323 E-1s—also with Gnôme et Rhône 14 N power plants—are to be built from August 1943 to April 1944. In the period February to September 1944 100 Me 323 F-1 with Jumo 211 F engines are to be constructed, and from June to December 1944 another 100 Me 323 F-2 with the same power plant. Production of the Me 323 G-1 with Gnôme et Rhône 14 R power plants is supposed to begin in September 1944. Monthly production of the Me 323 is to be 10 in October 1943, rising to 30 in July 1944 and continuing at that rate until September 1945. By then a total of 775 aircraft will have been produced, including 15 prototypes.

20/4/1943 Gothaer Waggonfabrik [8, RL 3/1121]

At Gothaer Waggonfabrik headquarters the company Metallwerk Niedersachsen informs Dr. Berthold, head of Special Commission F 12, that it will not be able to meet the deadlines foreseen in the delivery plan for the conversion of 21 Go 244s into Go 242s in the months April to August, first because hangar space at Stendal was taken from it, and second because it has not received

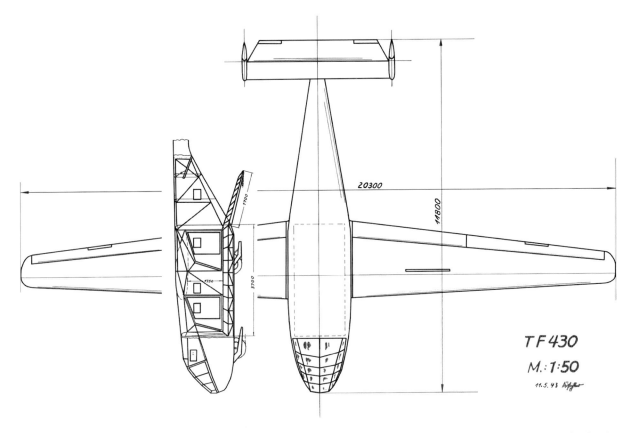

20300
11800

TF 430
M.: 1:50
11.5.43

In its initial configuration, the TF 430 (later Ka 430) resembled the Go 242. Only in terms of size, stress limits, and the new rear loading hatch did it correspond to the RLM guidelines. (Mankau)

any conversion kits from Gotha. Furthermore, the aircraft to be converted have suffered weather damage, requiring the delivery of replacement parts, such as tail booms and wings.

20/4/1943 Erfurt Repair Works [30]

Fliegerhaupting. Kensche of the RLM and Ing. Köhler of the REWE discuss the construction of the new combat glider (as per the guidelines of 1/4). The meeting report reveals that the new type is essentially a strengthened, modernized DFS 230 with a cantilever wing and widened fuselage. It is envisaged that the aircraft will carry armament. The undercarriage is to be designed as a skid combined with raisable wheels. A jettisonable undercarriage, like that of the DFS 230, is out of the question. Dual controls are demanded for the cockpit. The first pilot is to have armor protection. A good downward view is a requirement for precision approaches, as is general view for bad weather flight.

An initial series of 30 aircraft is anticipated, and Köhler is to determine if the REWE can construct the nine planned prototypes with its own personnel.

30 aircraft surely would not justify the development of a new aircraft. These must have constituted a pre-production

series which, if successful, would be followed by additional aircraft. These requirements surely also applied to the GWF with respect to the DFS 230 V7.

11/5/1943 Meeting of Department Heads at the Headquarters of the Air Armaments Minister [7]

Obersting. Alpers hands out several documents concerning the changes to the program:

1. Increase in output of Go 242 to 40 aircraft as per a request by Genst.6.Abt.

2. Resumption of DFS 230 in January 1944. Increase to 40 aircraft.

It can be concluded from this activity that the DFS 230 and Go 242 transport gliders had proved extraordinarily successful and were desired in the greatest possible numbers by the General Staff. Logically, the Air Armaments Minister wanted to improve the DFS 230 if it was to reenter production. This resulted in a new type with a widened fuselage to accommodate an increased payload. With the steel-tube framework of the DFS 230's fuselage the associated costs were relatively minor. Finding a suitable company to build the aircraft would

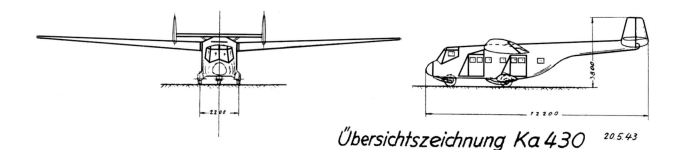

Übersichtszeichnung Ka 430   20.5.43

television, two DFS 230s were fitted with automatic Patin and Askania three-axis autopilots and test-flown with and without crews.

20/5/1943 Erfurt-North Repair Works
A drawing bearing this date reveals that the REWE has modified the cockpit of the new transport glider, which has by then been assigned the type designation Ka 430.

18/6/1943 Meeting of Air Armaments Minister Department Heads Concerning Procurement [7]
Production of the Me 323 is lagging behind the plan. Reason is the transport of power plants, which is taking too long.

21/6/1943 DFS Ainring [9]
The DFS begins testing the DFS 230/Bf 109 Mistel combination.

25/6/1943 Gothaer Waggonfabrik [10]
The GWF makes a proposal for an amphibian (Gotha Project P-52) based on the guidelines issued by the development office for the "Design of an Assault Glider and Universal Transport Glider."

The Erfurt Repair Works submitted a similar proposal based on the Ka 430 on 20/7/1943, and on 20/10/1943 the DFS reported on tests carried out with a DFS 230 equipped with floats. It would therefore appear that the RLM and the General Staff had an interest in commando operations against reservoirs and hydro-electric plants at that time. Supply missions in support of submarines were also included in the envisaged range of roles. While these projects and

prove much more difficult. The type would later be given the designation DFS 230 C-1. As guidelines for the development of a new transport glider were issued on 1/4/1943, resumption of DFS 230 production must be seen as an interim measure.

11/5/1943 Erfurt-North Repair Works
On this date Ing. Köhler of the REWE signs off on an early design of the TF 430 transport aircraft.

14/5/1943 DFS Ainring [9]
The DFS reports on experiments with Patin and Askania three-axis autopilots in the DFS 230 transport glider. As part of the program to develop a system to remotely pilot aircraft from the ground or another aircraft by means of

The DFS 230 + Bf 109 Mistel in its initial configuration. The trestle placed the load directly onto the undercarriage. To make it easier for the pilot of the Bf 109 to see the DFS 230's wingtips, bright yellow markings were applied and red and white striped rods mounted beneath them. (DFS)

Unlike the Go 242 A-1, the Go 242 B-2 had a fixed outrigger undercarriage. (Mathiesen)

experiments produced no tangible results and were soon halted, the plans did lead to an order for 66 float-capable Go 242 C-1s (see 11/4/1944), which was not filled, however.

28/6/1943 Gothaer Waggonfabrik [8, RL 3/556]

Bertold, head of Special Commission F 12, writes to the RLM GL/C-B 2/1 that, according to Program 223 Issue 1, the Robert Hartwig Company of Sonneberg was originally supposed to build the A-1 variant of the Go 242. When the program was finalized it had already become clear that the company was to build aircraft for use as transports. Construction was to be as before, with a fixed undercarriage and no skids.

After confirmation with GL/D-E I T NC these aircraft were given the new type designation "8-242 B-2." Hartwig will build 405 examples of the A-1 and 961 of the B-2.

When one considers that the Hartwig Company was building on average 20 Go 242s per month, and was the only manufacturer of the type at that time, then this contract would have extended for four years, or into the summer of 1947.

9/7/1943 Erfurt-North Repair Works [26], [30]

Inspection of the Ka 430 mockup. In the minutes of the mockup inspection it is stated that the cockpit canopy can be made smaller and that the windscreen panels should be moved back as far as possible and sloped 30°. The pilot's seat is to remain on the right and the left seat is to be fitted with a folding back to provide access to the cargo area. The planned armament is unsatisfactory, especially as the MG 81 Z positioned in the left windscreen panel impairs vision and interferes with the controls.

10/7/1943 Erfurt-North Repair Works [30]

As a result of demands from II Corps for the ability to shoot forward and possibly to the rear, it is ordered that an equipment set be provided for the Ka 430 for the installation of a revolving mount with DL 131/1 turret. The rearward-firing armament is eliminated.

20/7/1943 Erfurt-North Repair Works [30]

The Erfurt Repair Works creates a project based on the Ka 430 which envisages emergency landings on inland seas and even on the high sea. Three variants are examined: A with two main floats, B with a central float beneath the fuselage and two auxiliary floats, C with an inflatable float, and D an amphibian. Only the first two appear practicable, and both must take off from prepared fields. Water takeoff is impossible.

21/7/1943 Erfurt-North Repair Works [30]

A meeting is held in which details of the Ka 430 undercarriage are finalized. As a rule the Ka 430 will land on wheels. Landing on skids is only envisaged 5% of the time, when the aircraft is employed as an assault glider, because of the shorter stopping distance. The air force demands that after such a landing it must be possible to place the aircraft back on its wheels without specialized equipment. Therefore, the undercarriage must be designed so that the skid can be lowered in flight into a position lower than the wheels by means of a folding strut. On the ground the latter will be released by means of a cable and subsequently raised by hand.

1/8/1943 Erfurt-North Repair Works [30]

Construction of the Ka 430 V1 begins.

3/8/1943 Meeting of Department Heads Air Armaments Minister [7]

Consideration is given to transferring Bf 109 production in part from Regensburg to Obertraubling to disperse fighter production. The Me 323 would continue with eight aircraft initially as a suggestion.

By the time this drawing was made the Ka 430 had a conventional vertical tail. The drawing also depicts the jettisonable skids. (Mankau)

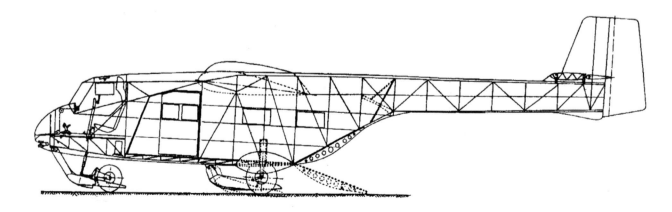

This aircraft on the Gran Sasso has a door in front of the wing and a braking parachute, but no braking rockets. The often made claim that DFS 230 C-1s with braking rockets were used on the Gran Sasso is false. (Bundesarchiv Koblenz 10 11-567-1503A-02)

A propaganda photo taken after the rescue operation on the Gran Sasso. Exiting the aircraft through the side hatch was a laborious exercise. (Press Photo)

12/8/1943 Erfurt-North Repair Works [30]
Inspection of the Ka 430 cockpit mockup.

14/8/1943 Erfurt-North Repair Works [30]
Second inspection of the Ka 430 mockup.

14/8/1943 *E-Stelle* Rechlin Report E2-WB
High-altitude flights with a B-17 and instrument flights with a He 111 using the rigid-tow method are carried out on behalf of the Gräfeling Aviation Radio Research Institute. Until repairs on the B-17 are completed the glider and DFS crew are in Kolberg. The experiments are subsequently concluded at Rechlin. Further rigid-tow testing after equipment is installed in DFS 230 NC+SW. Date 17/8/1943. (Experiments on behalf of the Gräfeling Aviation Radio Research Institute conclude on 4/9/43.)

16/8/1943 Zeppelin Company [7]
K. Eckener, head of the Special Commission F 34, submits to the GL/C a program proposal for continued

production of the Me 323, which also includes the termination of the Me 323 F.

17/8/1943 Meeting of Department Heads at the Headquarters of the Air Armaments Minister [7]

In the office consideration is being given to no longer building the Me 323 at Leipheim and Obertraubling in order to create additional capacity for the Me 262. Responding to an objection that the *Führer* places great importance on the Me 323, Milch declares that "one can't have everything. The *Führer* will have to decide what is important. The war will not be won or lost with the 323, but with fighters. That would settle the matter for him. If they don't have the fighter, then the ability to produce anything would be destroyed."

24/8/1943 Gothaer Waggonfabrik [8, RL 3/556]

With reference to a meeting on 16/8/1943, the head of Special Commission F 12 in the Gothaer Waggonfabrik Company is informed that delivery of materials for production of the DFS 230 cannot be expected before February-March 1944. This means a delay of about six months in the delivery plan requested by the RLM GL/C B-2. Construction of wings and final assembly are to be handled by the Mráz Company. Fuselages will come from the Stratilek Company of Hohenmauth and tail sections from Novotny, Tinischt.

Here there are already indications that the production life of the new series of DFS 230 gliders will be brief on account of development already underway toward higher airspeeds.

12/9/1943 Gran Sasso

Soldiers of the 12th Company, LLG 1 land on the Gran Sasso in DFS 230 gliders and free Mussolini.

9/1943 Erfurt-North Repair Works [30]

Final Ka 430 mockup inspection without serious complaints.

4/9/1943 *E-Stelle* Rechlin

The *E-Stelle* reports on towing trials with a Ju 88 A-4 and an empty Go 242. Results better than expected. Tests with a loaded aircraft continuing.

18/9/1943 *E-Stelle* Rechlin

After loading the Go 242 with 1.2 tons and the Ju 88 with full armament, 2,000 liters of fuel, and a crew of two, takeoff roll was found to be at least 1,400 m with a wind of 6 m/sec. Rate of climb approximately 1.8 m/sec. Testing was suspended, as operational use in this form and with further necessary increases in weight is out of the question. The Ju 88 is rejected as a tow plane because of unsatisfactory performance.

22/9/1943 Gotha [2]

On this date drawings are completed of a Go 242 with a conventional central fuselage.

29/9/1943 RLM [7]

GL/C – BCI approves Eckener's program proposal of 16/8 and thus abandons the Me 323 F with He 111 power units. The two prototypes with this power plant, the V16 and V17, will still be built.

The date of the experiments with floats is not contained in the report. (DFS)

The Me 321 units were disbanded and the big gliders scrapped. As this photo shows, the ballast boxes remained in the Me 321s until they were scrapped. (Petrick)

5/10/1943 Meeting of Department Heads Air Armaments Minister [7]

II./Transportgeschwader 5 has suffered the total loss of some of its Me 323 G aircraft, and all aircraft have subsequently been grounded. *Me 323 G appears in the document, but this is a typographical error, as the units only flew the Me 323 D and E.* Milch asks for the cause. Petersen: debonding of the Kaurit [urea formaldehyde resin glue], which cannot stand up under the sun. The wings must be recovered and then inspected regularly. Hübner: That is being discussed with Messerschmitt. A strip of wood is being placed over it. It may also have been caused by bad glue. Milch: The M 20 had the same problem before. Perhaps it is a fundamental error. Hübner: That always happens where linen lies on metal.

10/1943 *E-Stelle* Rechlin [9]

Trials are carried out with an Ar 232 towing a Go 242 to 6.8 t and 5.7 t. No problems.

In his account of the Ar 232 (JET & PROP 2/96) Kössler mentions that the Ar 232 A-08 and B-02 were tested at Rechlin with DFS 230 and Go 242 gliders in October 1943. After installation of the necessary equipment the Ar 232 performed flawlessly as a tow plane, however, its use in this role made no sense, as the Ar 232/DFS 230 combination had a payload of just 4.5 tons, while the Ar 232 A-0 alone was capable of carrying 4.1 tons.

20/10/1943 Institute for Flight Testing of the German Research Institute for Gliding Flight. Enst Udet; Ainring [9]

Institute Director Stamer publishes Studies and Reports No. 740 "Towing Procedures." It contains a brief description of the development of the towing procedure. Particular attention is given to the systematic experiments carried out in the years 1938 to 1943. These were:

1. Short tow
2. Old-style rigid tow
2a. Long and rigid tow
2b. Rigid tow with ball-and-socket coupling
3. Multiple tow
4. Towing of motorized aircraft
5. Lifting rotor tow
6. Pickup tow
7. Mistel tow
8. Carried takeoff
9. Volga takeoff procedure

The report also contains photos of a DFS 230 on floats, as well as dive brakes and rocket brakes for the DFS 230.

Autumn 1943

30/11/1943 Meeting of Department Heads Air Armaments Minister [7]

Topic of discussion is Delivery Plan 225, which, because of materiel issues, contains a significant reduction compared to Delivery Plan 224. The Me 323 initially continues with eight aircraft per month.

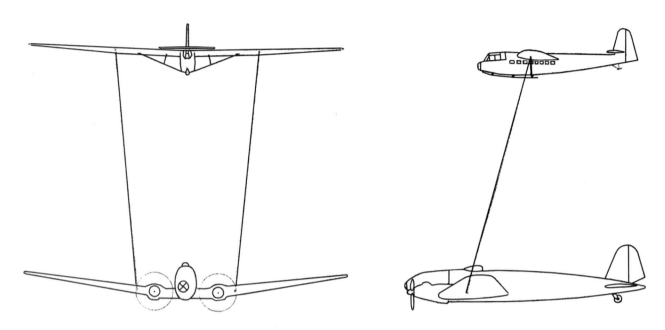

Prinzipskizze „Auftriebsschlepp"

Development sketch of the "Lift Tow" procedure (retouched). (Mankau)

8/11/1943 Memorandum GL/C-B 2/II [8, RL 3/556]

The Hartwig Company cannot carry out the Go 242 program expansion in its present state because of space limitations. It is therefore necessary to move assembly from Sonneberg to Gotha. Furthermore, there are neither sufficient labor forces nor materials to cover the sharp increase in production. Special Commission F 12 was provided with a list of the main shortage materials for the 10-ton coupling. Special Commission S 12 will check to see to what extent assistance with materials can be provided. Until production startup of the 10-ton coupling, which was ordered late by Special Commission F 12, C-B2/1 will help out with couplings (about 240 examples). Couplings for the production series were never procured domestically. Special Commission F 12 will therefore submit a new delivery plan for the production series and retro-conversion to C-B 2/I as quickly as possible. From the retro-conversion of Go 244s to Go 242s, the Letov Company delivered the last 35 aircraft as Go 242 B-3s in November.

Beginning with the first Go 242 B-2, installation of a smoke discharger system as an equipment set was requested for the first 150 aircraft. Installation has so far not taken place.

Installation of the 10-ton coupling on production aircraft thus did not begin before November 1943. At that time only the Go 242 B-2 was in production. The Go 242 B-3 was also being produced by conversion.

In order to exploit capacity, the Mráz initially constructed wings for the DFS 230, specifically a strengthened version. A prototype of the strengthened version was supposed to be completed in Gotha in December 1943. As per a request from the GL/C-Fert., this version would receive the designation DFS 230 C-1 instead of DFS 230 A-3. The delay in commencement of DFS 230 production was due exclusively to shortages of materials (steel tube) and work on the production jigs.

After discussion with the C-E 3, it was determined that the sheet steel casings for the rockets are not being delivered domestically, but are within the delivery scope of the airframe.

The prototype was the DFS 230 V6, and here the designation DFS 230 C-1 was assigned for the first time. The developed version was probably given the designation DFS 230 D-1 at the same time.

15/11/1943 Conference Air Armaments Minister/General Staff [7]

Construction of the Go 242 must continue.

1/12/1943 RLM [2]

The Reich Minister of Aviation issues conversion plan 225/1 GL/C-B No. 18289/43. It states that 334 Go 244

At this time the DFS was engaged in trials with a Mistel consisting of a DFS 230 B-2 and a Bf 109 E. (DFS)

B-1/C-1 production aircraft were converted back into Go 242s, specifically:

- 184 aircraft rebuilt as Go 242 A-1 (64 by GWF, twelve by Menibum Hamburg, 36 by Letov, 50 by RWE, 22 by Klemm).

- 140 aircraft rebuilt as Go 242 B-3 with installation of parachutist and double-tow equipment (20 by Gotha, 95 by Letov, 35 by RWE).

I only know of this conversion plan as a copy from the Pawlas sources (and it does not agree with the information in the book [2]). Therefore, I cannot say whether it contains transcription errors, or the anomalies were already present in the original. First one must ask why they would convert the Go 244 B-1 into the Go 242 A-1. It is much more likely that they retained the axle undercarriage, and thus converted back to the Go 242 B-1. But 334 Go 244s is also higher than the number given in March 1943. Then it was stated that 301 Go 244s were used to produce Go 242s. The C-Amts program of 1/10/1942 spoke of 308 Go 244s.

1/1944 C-Amts Monthly Report [1]
The Mráz Company is supposed to deliver the first DFS 230 C-1. Three are planned for February, eight for March, 15 for April, and 22 for May.

8/1/1944 Ainring [9]
In Studies and Reports No. 754 the DFS reports on research into the "Mistel towing method" using a DFS 230 and Bf 109 combination. Flight testing of the combination began on 21/6/1943. After several flights the support braces were modified, and the second series of tests began on 16/7/1943. Flight trials revealed problem-free flight, takeoff, and landing characteristics. Combined landing and separation in the air are possible. Flights with transfer of control movements from the upper aircraft to the control surfaces of the lower are in preparation (see DFS 230: Research Aircraft).

10/1/1944 Gotha
The Gothaer Waggonfabrik submits to the RLM a proposal for a new towing method: the lift-tow. In this method the towed aircraft, attached by two cables, flies about 9 meters above the tow plane and takes over part of its weight. The two aircraft are joined near the center of gravity. GWF promises better performance with the new towing method (rate of climb of the combination is improved by 50 to 100%) and improved stability of the towed machine, so that instrument flights and even pilotless gliders appear possible. A more significant advantage, however, is that with this method aircraft can be coupled whose flight speeds actually do not match. GWF considers it possible that even the Bf 110 and Fw 190 could tow the DFS 230 or Go 242, which using the normal towing method would not be fully flyable at an allowable towing speed of 200 to 240 kph on account of their high wing loadings.

This towing method also solved the problem that was going to arise when production of He 111 ended, as the Ju 388 was unable to tow the Go 242. Lift-tow would allow use of the Go 242 to continue.

The Ka 430 V1 at Erfurt. (Mathiesen)

These dive brakes were tested by the DFS. (DFS)

1/2/1944 Meeting of Department Heads at the Headquarters of the Air Armaments Minister [7]

Mahnke proposes that the Gnôme et Rhône 14 R be cancelled and the BMW 801 be used for the Me 323 instead. Milch asks if there are enough motors and if it will fit. Mahnke observes that they could allow it, and that, according to communications from Messerschmitt and BMW, it will fit. Milch: "Verify that! Messerschmitt has never told me a single thing that proved to be sound after it was checked. I am very mistrustful that it will work."

7/2/1944 GL/-B2 [8]

In the Aircraft Delivery Preview it is planned to increase production of the Go 242 from the current 25 per month to 35 per month beginning in May 1944. Production of the DFS 230 is to start in March with three aircraft and be increased to 35 per month by the end of the year, after which production will continue at that rate. Eight Me 323s are to be delivered in February, after which production will continue at six per month.

7/2/1944 Zeppelin Company [7]

The head of Special Commission F 34, K. Eckener, writes to Obersting. Alpers of the RLM (GL/C-B2) that he has learned that the office intends to equip the Me 323 F and G with the BMW 801 instead of the Gnôme et Rhône 14 R. According to Eckener, the low monthly requirement and the uncertain situation in France weigh against the Gnôme et Rhône 14 R. However, given the advanced state of preparations for series production, the sudden stopping of all production is not advisable. BMW-Paris (the parent company of Gnôme et Rhône) is proposing the production of 500 Gnôme et Rhône 14 R power plants, given that design of the Me 323 F power plant system with 14 R engines is complete and material orders are under way. According to Delivery Plan 225/1 of 1/12/1943, 64 examples of the Me 323 F are supposed to be built. As Zeppelin had to release 24 designers to Dornier by order of the Air Armaments Minister, elimination of the Me 323 G and thus extension of the Me 323 F to about 110 aircraft cannot be avoided. If the 14 R runs out, the relatively small F series will have to be split into the F-1 with Gnôme et Rhône 14 R and the F-2 with BMW 801 engines. It would make sense to do without the Gnôme et Rhône 14 R completely and equip all Me 323 Fs with the BMW 801. A higher priority level is needed, however, to ensure a follow-on to the Me 323 E.

29/2/1944 Air Armaments Minister Conference [7]

Mistel tow is cancelled.

I suspect that this meant that the Mistel tow using the Bf 109 and DFS 230 was cancelled.

4/3/1944 C-Amts Program [20]

The Aircraft Construction and Development Program is shortened and the Me 323 dropped.

15/3/1944 Gl/C [8, RL 3/1121]

The GWF receives a telex (RLM GL/C No. 14830/44) informing it that the Go 242 and DFS 230 are being dropped from the program immediately.

This advisory did not mean that production was to cease immediately, rather that no further contracts would be issued.

27/3/1944 Erfurt-North Airfield [26]

The Ka 430 V1 (DV+MA) makes its maiden flight. At the controls is Fl.Obering. Herbert Pankratz of the *Luftwaffe* Proving center.

29/3/1944 Ainring/Erfurt [26]

A DFS 230 is ferried from Ainring to Erfurt for testing of new dive brakes intended for the Ka 430.

30-31/3/1944 Erfurt [26]

The new dive brakes are tested on DFS 230 D-IDCP. The purpose of the tests is to determine whether the Ka 430 should be fitted with dive brakes or a ribbon parachute like the DFS 230.

The short period of time between the Ka 430 V1's maiden flight, the delivery of the DFS 230, and the subsequent testing of the dive brakes makes it appear unlikely that the Ka 430's dive brakes were being tested on a DFS 230 here. The DFS had already shown dive brakes on the DFS 230 in Report No. 740 of 20/10/1943. This was probably just a system comparison.

11/4/1944 Gothaer Waggonfabrik [8, RL 3/1121]

GWF writes to the RLM (GL/C Ba 2) to advise that 66 Go 242 C-1 aircraft are still required.

11/4/1944 Gothaer Waggonfabrik [9]

GWF assigns the Hermann Göring Aviation Research Institute in Brunswick-Völkenrode to carry out wind tunnel measurements on a model of the Go 345. The tests are carried out in July 1944.

28/4/1944 GL/C-B 2/1 [8, RL 3/1121]

In Telex No. 15134/44, the RLM advises GWF (H. Berthold) that 43 of the 231 Go 242 B-2 aircraft still to be completed by the Hartwig Company (Sonneberg, Thuringia) as part of the program run-down are to be delivered as Go 242 C-1s.

None of the documents I am familiar with offer any clue as to the subsequent fate of the Go 242 C-1; however, the records of the Quartermaster-General show that the Hartwig Company built only the B-2 during the run-down of the Go 242. On display in the German Technical Museum

Company drawing of the Go 345 as a pinpoint-landing aircraft with Argus pulse-jets and braking rockets in the nose. (Gothaer Waggonfabrik)

in Berlin is the fuselage framework of a Go 242 A, which was allegedly supposed to have been converted into a Go 242 C. I have not been able to confirm this information, however.

15/5/1944 Aircraft Program
According to the program, the following have been delivered to the air force:

Me 323	Leiph.	Obertr.	Quantity
D-1	21	32	53
D-2			34
D-6			55
E-1	46	10	56
Total	93	105	198

18/5/1944 Luftschiffbau Zeppelin [4], [20]
The company submits a project proposal for the Z Me 323 H. The introduction states that development and production of the Me 323 is completely interrupted and that the project was conceived for a possible resumption. In order to keep design costs down, the Z Me 323 H will incorporate design features of the Z Me 323 G, which is 2/3 complete, and the Me 323 F, which is complete.

23/5/1944 (*Reichsmarschall*) [8]
In meetings with the *Reichsmarschall* concerning air armaments, it is decided that a number of aircraft types should be cancelled or production thereof halted as soon as possible. Among these types are the Ju 88/Ju 188 and the Ju 52, Ju 352, and Me 323 transport aircraft. Production of the He 111 is to continue at 80 per month, exclusively for the transport role, and it is to be replaced by the Ar 432. The DFS 230 and Go 242 transport gliders are not mentioned, however, the decision to end production of these types had already been made on 15/3/1944.

27/6/1944 Erfurt [26]
Maiden flight of the Ka 430 V2 (DV+MB).

1/7/1944 (*Reichsmarschall*) [8]
The *Reichsmarschall* holds a meeting at which conclusions are drawn from a *Führer* Order of 30/6/1944. Hitler had ordered the total cancellation of the heavy bomber (He 177) and given fighters absolute priority. Monthly production of fighters was to be increased to

The drawing on the right originates from 1944, but the English subtitle was added at Brunswick-Völkenrode on 30/10/1945. The heading was inserted using the computer. (Gothaer Waggonfabrik)

Windkanalmodell Go 345
Wind tunnel model of the Go 345

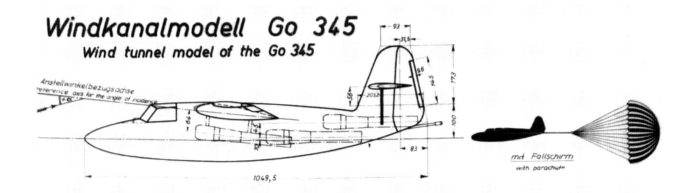

Anstellwinkelbezugsachse
reference axis for the angle of incidence

mit Fallschirm
with parachute

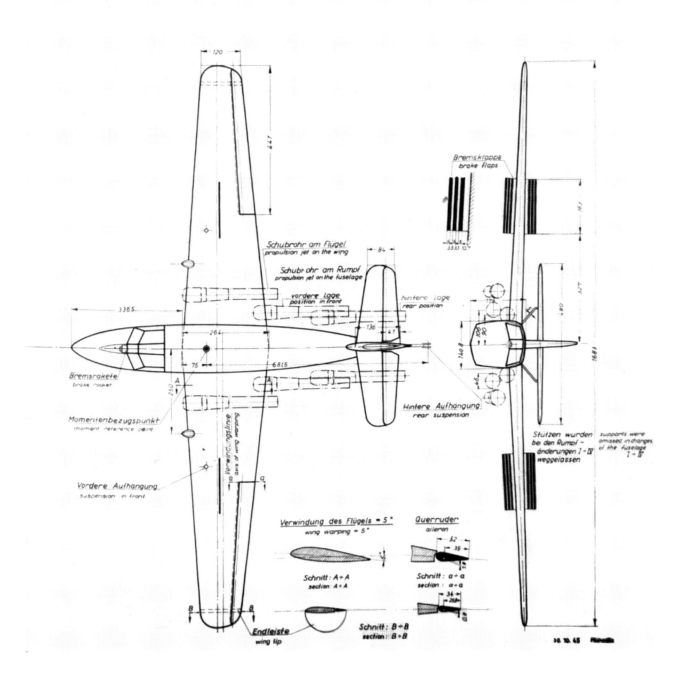

Bremsklappe
brake flaps

Schubrohr am Flügel
propulsion jet on the wing

Schubrohr am Rumpf
propulsion jet on the fuselage

vordere Lage
position in front

hintere Lage
rear position

Bremsrakete
brake rocket

Momentenbezugspunkt
moment reference point

Vordere Aufhängung
suspension in front

Verwindungslinie
axis of wing warping

Hintere Aufhängung
rear suspension

Stützen wurden
bei den Rumpf-
änderungen I – IV
weggelassen

supports were
omitted in changes
of the fuselage
I – IV

Verwindung des Flügels = 5°
wing warping = 5°

Querruder
aileron

Schnitt: A + A
section: A + A

Schnitt: a + a
section: a + a

Schnitt: B + B
section: B + B

Endleiste
wing tip

3,800, plus 400 heavy fighters (*Zerstörer*) and 500 night-fighters. These demands also had effects on other aircraft types. 20 types will be dropped, including the Ju 352 and Go 242. The DFS 230 will continue, however, with 10 aircraft per month. Production of the He 111 is to end in January 1945, and the Ju 52 shall be produced in France as long as possible. The wooden construction Ar 432 is envisaged as the principle transport, and as a tow plane for gliders the Ju 188. The Me 323 is not mentioned.

Ju 188 is probably a typo, for the Ju 188 had already been cancelled on 23/5/44 in favor of the Ju 388.

3/7/1944 Gotha [2]

The Gothaer Waggonfabrik produces a project description of the Go 345. The date of publication and presentation to the RLM is not known. Several drawings in the description were made on this date.

18/7/1944 *Luftwaffe* Proving center Command Type Report No. 1470/44 [1]

Technical notes concerning Study 1036 on the basis of the current testing situation.

Transport Glider: Re DFS 230: Resumption of production does not appear warranted, as with the cancellation of the He 111 a suitable tow plane no longer exists. As well cargo capacity, load-carrying ability, and allowable tow speed are obsolete. As the Ju 388 is the only potential tow plane, it is suggested that the Ka 430 be built in quantity instead of the DFS 230.

The counterpart of the Ka 430 was the DFS 230 D-1 (later E-1), which had a comparable wingspan and load capacity. But the DFS 230 D-1 (E-1) was also largely a new design and shared few components with the A and B variants. As before with the comparison between the DFS 331 and the Kalkert-designed Go 242, the Ka 430 was more practical, as it was much easier to load. As the Ka 430 was also more modern and safer on account of its tricycle undercarriage, Kalkert also won this competition. The DFS 230 V7 was the sole prototype of the DFS 230 D-1 (E-1). For the difference between the D-1 and E-1 see the type summary.

19/7/1944 Gothaer Waggonfabrik [8, RL 3/1121]

The head of Special Commission 12, Berthold, writes to the RLM that a contract for five Go 345 prototypes and ten Me 328 prototypes has arrived, but the documents are not yet clear.

Wind tunnel experiments with a model of the Go 345 took place at the aviation research institute in Brunswick in July 1944. The tests included investigations into power plant position and the braking parachute.

Special Commission F 12 makes a counter proposal to Delivery Plan 226 of 10/7/1944, according to which only 20 DFS 230 C-1 are to be built during the period from April to October 1944. A series of 170 DFS 230 D-1s is to follow

beginning in October, with deliveries of 10 aircraft per month from December 1944 on.

By this time a change in designation had taken place. The production version of the DFS 230 V7 with large fuselage and 300 kph towing speed, thus the counterpart of the Ka 430, was now called the DFS 230 E-1. The DFS 230 D-1 referred to here was a new development, essentially a DFS 230 C-1 with shortened wingspan to enable it to achieve the higher towing speed. As the decision in favor of the Ka 430 and thus against the DFS 230 E-1 had probably already been made, the new DFS 230 D-1 served to bridge the gap until production of the Ka 430 began.

21/7/1944 Gothaer Waggonfabrik Memorandum

On 20/7/1944 two representatives of the DVL demonstrated the Kl 25/Mü 17 lifting rotor-tow combination at the airfield of the Gotha base. As with GWF's lift tow, the towed aircraft flies above the tow plane, but it is connected by just one cable and is therefore not suited to pilotless towing. The FFG will also test the double cable tow in the future. The demonstration had to be halted because of an air raid. The *Habicht* (Goshawk) glider used by GWF in testing its lift tow method was destroyed in the raid and the Ju 87 tow plane damaged.

As the operational use of the Go 242 (Water) ordered by the *Reichsmarschall* is only possible using lift-tow, and it is also envisaged for the P-56, P-57, and P-58 projects, it is proposed that a new DFS Habicht/Ju 87 combination be procured, and further that the DFS 230 V7 be equipped with tow couplings for the lift tow method.

The Go 242 (Water) was assigned the designation Go 242 C-1. As this memo reveals, the Go 242 C-1 was supposed to be towed by a He 111 H using the lift tow method. The P-56 project was a pilotless, winged fuel tank which was to be towed by a Fw 190 for increased range. The P-57 project was a flying bomb towed in the same manner, and the P-58 project was probably a combat glider in the style of the BV 40.

24/7/1944 Gothaer Waggonfabrik [8, RL 3/1121]

In a telex the RLM (GL/C-B 2) asks the Gotha Company to change the DFS 230 series built by Mráz to the D-1. Skids and fixed undercarriage are envisaged.

25/7/1944 Gothaer Waggonfabrik [8, RL 3/1121]

At a meeting, it is agreed that the Mráz Company is operating at full capacity as a result of producing wings for the Ar 396. Should wing production lead to free wood [working] capacity, there would be nothing standing in the way of filling the DFS 230 contract.

7/1944 GL/C2 C-Amts Monthly Reports [1]

The Mráz Company delivered the first DFS 230 C-1 in April. One more followed in May, 9 in June, and in July deliveries end with three more aircraft. Thus, a total of 14 DFS 230 C-1s have been delivered.

7/1944 Gothaer Waggonfabrik [8, RL 3/1121]

Special Commission 12's monthly report contains the following regarding transport gliders:

Series Production

Hartwig built 17 Go 242 B-2

Mráz built 3 DFS 230 C-1

Development

Go 242 A-1 Werk.Nr. 0113 928

Prototype installation of 2 tow couplings in the wing leading edge

Go 345

Fuselage construction complete, other work in progress

DFS 230 A-1 Werk.Nr. 0125144

Prototype installation SF radiosonde

DFS 230 C-1 Werk.Nr. 170008

Conversion to D-1 variant (300 kph) and installation of 2 tow couplings in leading edge of wing

8/1944 Gothaer Waggonfabrik [8, RL 3/1121]

Special Commission 12's monthly report contains the following regarding transport gliders:

Series production cancelled
Development

Go 242 Werk.Nr. 0113 928

Installation of wing tow

Go 345

90% (without power plant) complete

DFS 230 A-1 Werk.Nr. 0125144

Installation and testing Kröte Land

DFS 230 C-1 Werk.Nr. 170008

Conversion to D-1 is complete

DFS 230 C-1 Werk.Nr. 170010

Conversion to D-1 under way, completion date 5/9

DFS 230 C-1 Werk.Nr. 170011

Conversion to D-1 under way, completion date 25/9

DFS 230 V7

Conversion for lift tow

Habicht

Conversion for lift tow

Summer 1944 Gotha [1]

The Gothaer Waggonfabrik creates a data summary for the DFS 230. The construction year 1939 is given for the DFS 230 A/B. For the DFS 230 C-1 (V6) it is 1943, and 1944 for the DFS 230 D-1 and DFS 230 V7. Also mentioned is the E-1 variant, without a construction year, however. The Gothaer Waggonfabrik is listed as builder for all DFS 230s.

Pawlas [1] does not indicate when the summary was compiled. I have seen copies of the documents on which it was based in the German Technical Museum in Berlin. They also offer no date. Several authors associate the DFS 230 D-1 to F-1 with Gotha's chief designer Hünerjäger. I have found no confirmation of this.

Second Half of 1944 Gothaer Waggonfabrik [14]

The DFS 230 V7 (pilot Roehlike) and a Ju 87 B-1 (pilot Rentrop) are used to test the lift-tow method. The tests are continued with a Ju 87 D-2 and a DFS 230 E.

Unfortunately I do not have the original records, so I must rely on the source [14], which is apparently based on Gothaer Waggonfabrik test reports. These tests are confirmed by Bruno Lange (Das Buch der deutschen Luftfahrttechnik) and Nowarra (Die Deutsche Luftrüstung 1933 – 1945). No dates of the test reports are offered in the sources. One can narrow down the time frame, however, from the conversion of the prototypes in July 1944 after the decision in favor of the Ka 430 and the absence of fuel for such experiments (see 31/1/1945). While the Ju 87 B and DFS 230 V7 combination is clear, the DFS 230 E could in fact have only been the V7. The dimensions in [14] support this conclusion.

9/1944 Rechlin [26]

The Ka 430 V3 crashes at the *Luftwaffe* proving center in Rechlin.

22/9/1944 Rechlin (Report No. 369/44) [9]

The proving center reports on damage to wood components of various aircraft types. Concerning the Ka 430 the specialist writes: "After arrival of the aircraft from the manufacturer the aileron and landing flap jacks resembled raw box boards. Approximately 30% of the protecting outer surface was not preserved at all, and in the remaining places so poorly preserved that every single wood fiber acted like a dagger (photos [slides] could not be taken on account of the total loss [of the aircraft])...."

17/10/1944 Erfurt [26]
Maiden flight of the Ka 430 V5 (DV+MC)

18/10/1944 Erfurt [26]
First towed flight of a Ka 430 behind a He 111 H-6 (DJ+SI).

25/11-23/12/1944 Rechlin [26]
The Ka 430 V4 is tested at Rechlin. Flights also made using rigid tow.

4/12/1944 *Luftwaffe* High Command, Gen.Qu. Az 11 No. 24 290/44 (Chief Supply Dept. II) [7]
The Quartermaster-General creates a summary of the DFS 230, Go 242, and Me 323 transport gliders delivered to the air force.

Total Deliveries DFS 230 Transport Glider							
Company	1939	1940	1941	1942	1943	1944	Total
Hartwig			308				
Bücker			180				
Gotha			32				
Erla			178				
BMM			322	74		Mráz 14	
Total	28	455	1020	74		14	1591
Total Deliveries Go 242 Transport Glider							
Gotha			253	469	178		
Hartwig			213	264	151		
Total			253	682	442	151	1528
Total Deliveries Me 323 Transport Glider							
Leiph.				12	55	26	93
Obertr.				16	86	3	105
Total				28	141	29	198

This table includes the aircraft delivered to the air force. Not included are prototypes, which remained with the companies and at research and test establishments.

6/12/1944 Stress Testing Center GL/C-E 2
The testing center lays down the allowable weights for the Go 242 under the file reference number Az.89/C-E 2/FP I M No. 5337/12.43. The data are included in tables in the appendix.

January 1945 Gothaer Waggonfabrik [14]
The Go 242 A-1 Werk.Nr. 0113 928 is successfully tested in lift-tow. The military situation prevents the operational use of the procedure, however.

25/1/1945 *Luftwaffe* High Command, Quartermaster-General No. 981/45 [7]
Summary of the state of deliveries of the DFS 230 transport glider to allied and friendly nations as of 31/12/1944.

	1942	1943	
Italy	10	50	Delivered in February
Rumania	15	23	Delivered in October and November

31/1/1945 Erfurt-North [26]
Testing of the Ka 430 behind a Ju 88 C-6.

31/1/1945 Erfurt-North [26]
Final test flight of a Ka 430 behind a Ju 88 C-6 (PB+VW). Testing is subsequently halted because of lack of fuel.

30/4/1945 Breslau/Berlin
On this day the last sorties by DFS 230 and Go 242 gliders towed by He 111 H and Do 17 E are flown to supply Berlin and Breslau.

GLIDERS AND AIRCRAFT IN ACTION

Neetzow and Schlaug [13] have described operations by transport gliders and their crews extensively and in detail. Griehl [16] also includes a description of the relevant units. For this reason, coverage of glider operations here is limited to a brief illustrated section.

Loads Carried by Transport Gliders and Transport Aircraft

The DFS 230 delivered troops straight to the battlefield. (Bundesarchiv Koblenz 10 1L-569-1579-14)

The Go 242, on the other hand, was used to transport troops from place to place. (Bundesarchiv Koblenz 10 11-641-4546-17)

Among the preferred cargos were drums of fuel. (Mathiesen / Pawlas)

The Me 323 was capable of transporting about 20 drums of gasoline to Africa. (Bundesarchiv Koblenz 10 11-552-0822-22)

The Go 242 and Me 323 brought many wounded home. (Bundesarchiv Koblenz 10 11-641-4550-29 and 10 11-561-1142-21).

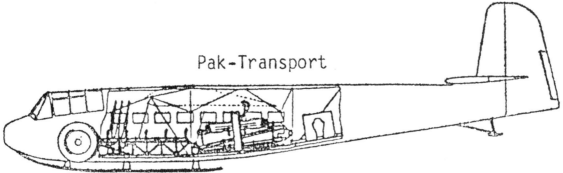

Pak-Transport

The DFS 230 was only capable of carrying small or disassembled loads. (Bundesarchiv Koblenz 10 11-561-1142-21 /Schlaug)

The Go 242 was capable of transporting food and fodder. (Bundesarchiv Koblenz 10 II-561-1138-13)

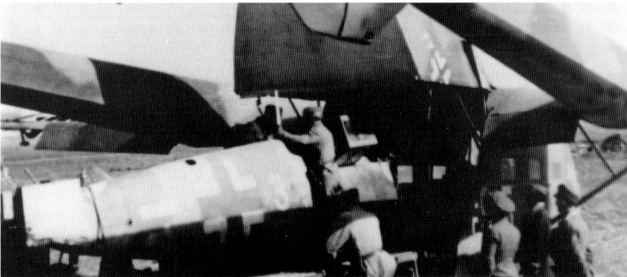

The Go 242 was even capable of transporting
whole vehicles. (Bundesarchiv Koblenz 10
11-434-0949-09)

The Go 242 was often used to transport aircraft motors and components,
such as the BMW 801 of a Fw 190 and the fuselage of a Bf 109 seen here.
(Bundesarchiv Koblenz 10 11-332-3096-12 and Petrick)

Me 321 loading experiments during the development phase. (Radinger)

Sample Me 321 payloads from a Messerschmitt film. The aircraft was initially used to transport drums of fuel. (Pawlas)

The Me 323 transported everything within its weight and size restrictions: here new engines and scrapped power plants. (Petrick)

German Gliders in World War II

In addition to other vehicles, the Me 323 also transported engines and crane trucks for its own use. (Bundesarchiv Koblenz 10 1L-667-7148-04).

The more capable Me 323 D-1 disgorges an Opel Blitz Maultier. (Bundesarchiv Koblenz 10 11-559-1085-07)

The Me 323 also transported artillery pieces to Africa. (Bundesarchiv Koblenz 10 11-559-1085-08)

Transport and Assembly of Gliders

As a rule, DFS 230s were transported to the area of operations by rail. (Mathiesen)

This also applied to the Go 242. (MM Photo Archive)

At the destination rail station soldiers unload the DFS 230 wings and transport wagon. (Krieg))

The components of a Go 242 are reloaded onto a trailer and taken to the airfield. (Nidree)

Right: at the airfield the ground crew unload the fuselage, wings, and other components. (Nidree)

No special aids were needed to assemble the DFS 230. (Griehl)

A field crane and four personnel were needed to assemble a Go 242. (Nidree)

Assembly in a hangar followed a similar pattern. (Nidree)

The Me 321 could only be assembled at the production site. It was then towed to its operating airfield. (Radinger)

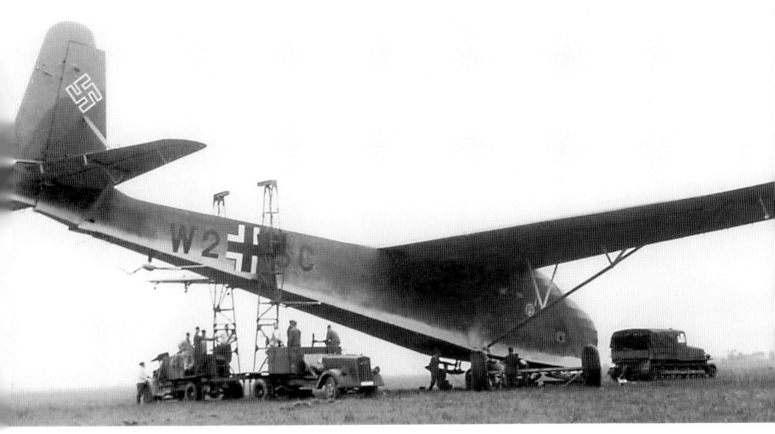

Takeoff preparations for the Me 321 were always lengthy. Special trucks first had to lift the glider onto the undercarriage which, fitted with Ju 90 and Bf 109 wheels, weighed approx. 1.7 tons. Then takeoff rockets were mounted on the loaded glider. Men and vehicles had to be transported to the operational site before the glider landed. (Petrick)

Towing the Glider
on the Ground and
Airfield Tow Vehicles

Relatively small vehicles, like the Opel Blitz or this 55-hp Hanomag SS 55, were sufficient to tow the DFS 230. (Bundesarchiv Koblenz 10 11-566-1491-37)

A 55-hp Lanz Bulldog in Luftwaffe service. (Bundesarchiv Koblenz 10 IL-567-1523-03)

A 100-hp Hanomag SS 100 Gigant towing a Go 242 B-2. (Pawlas)

185-hp Daimler Benz 12-ton prime mover towing a Go 242 A-1. (Bundesarchiv Koblenz 10 11-561-1130-24)

A 150-hp Faun could also be used to tow the Go 242. (Nidree)

The Me 323 E-1 required powerful vehicles such as the Faun ZR 567. (Bundesarchiv Koblenz 10 II-668-7197-03)

Two prime movers (Zgkw. 12 t and Praga T6-SS) struggle to tow a Me 323 D-1 on soft ground. (Bundesarchiv Koblenz 10 11-552-0822-36)

ACCIDENTS

Pilots of DFS 230s used as combat gliders often had to land in difficult terrain. Many gliders were wrecked in such landings and many soldiers lost their lives. (Mathiesen)

This Go 242 came to grief atop a railway car. (Mathiesen)

Removal of a damaged transport glider.

German Gliders in World War II

The fuselage of this Go 242 survived a forced landing relatively intact. Not so the wooden tail booms, however. (Nidree)

It was a relatively common occurrence for one of the outer tow planes to exceed a certain angle, which caused the machine to veer. If this happened during takeoff, the pilot could not turn back to the center without braking. The pilot's only option was to release the tow cable, resulting in a forced landing by the glider. In this case the Bf 110 that swung even crashed. (Petrick)

This Me 321 A-1 lost its ballast box in a hard landing. (Petrick)

TYPE OVERVIEW

DFS 230

In the German Technical Museum in Berlin (Historical Archive) there are Gothaer Waggonfabrik documents (data sheets and a technical description) concerning the DFS 230. I have summarized the information they contain in tables (see appendix). The DFS 230 table resembles one by Pawlas [1], which is based on the same source; however, Pawlas mixed up the internal and external fuselage widths. I measured the width of the fuselage of the DFS 230 in Wunstorf. This is 0.8 meters between the wings. The following description of variants is based primarily on the variant summary in the appendix. The aircraft handbook [33], which describes the DFS 230 A-1, was also used. Another original source I used was the "Replacement Parts List Transport Glider DFS 230" published by Gothaer Waggonfabrik in September 1941. Based on the components it contains, it probably applies only to the DFS 230 A-2. Some of the statements are based on my own observations and conclusions.

DFS 230 V1 to V3

(there is no information concerning the V4)
Of this group, the DFS 230 V1 can be described, as it is illustrated in a report on mountain testing. It was silver overall and differed in the following respects from the DFS 230 A-1 (see DFS 230 B):

- · The nose was more rounded

- ··The fuselage spine was straight from the cockpit to the fin.

- · The cockpit glazing consisted in part of bulged Plexiglas panels.

- · There were seven windows instead of eight on the left side of the fuselage.

- On the right side of the fuselage there were seven windows and no hatch.

These illustrations from the handbook probably depict the three prototypes. (Handbook)

The three DFS 230 A-0 gliders in the foreground have the simple cockpit glazing. The aircraft in the background has additional windows and probably dual controls. (German Museum)

In 1940 the camouflage scheme was changed, as may be seen on this DFS 230 A-0. (Selinger)

- ·· The rudder was smooth and had no trim tab.
- ·· The horizontal tail was of a different shape.

The DFS 230 V2 and V3 were probably similar in appearance. In the draft handbook of 3/9/1939 two other DFS 230s are illustrated in addition to the V1. Their registrations are: D-5-241, D-5-271, and D-5-289 (DFS 230 V1). These might be the three prototypes.

DFS 230 A (A-0)

Built in 1937/38, the DFS 230 pre-production machines can be divided into two groups. The first had one pilot seat and was definitely designated DFS 230 A in the beginning. Later it was renamed DFS 230 A-0 to differentiate it from the standard production aircraft. The aircraft basically resembled the V1, but were painted overall gray (probably RLM 63 or RLM 02). It is known that Hartwig built 18 DFS 230 A-0 (see 17/2/1941). According to the aircraft development program of 1/10/1937, 30 were under construction, thus Gerner must have built the remaining twelve.

DFS 230 B (Pre-Production)

The pre-production series also included machines with additional windows or openings behind the cockpit, dual instrumentation, a second control stick, and a second pilot's seat. Some of these aircraft were also painted gray. It is not known if these training aircraft, which were used to train pilots in 1938/39, had their own designation. It cannot be ruled out, however, that they were later designated DFS 230 B or B-1.

DFS 230 B (Calibration)

I have two copied pages of a DFS report from the German Aviation Research 1941 yearbook, on which a DFS-230-B is depicted. This is no training aircraft, however. Instead, it is a calibration aircraft with modified wing. The fuselage has different windows and door compared to the normal DFS 230 A-0. The drawing reveals the shape of the early DFS 230's horizontal tail (see DFS 230: Research Aircraft).

DFS 230 V5

The DFS 230 V5 was built by Gothaer Waggonfabrik and represents the first prototype of the DFS 230 A-1 series. It probably looked identical to the production aircraft. It was completed in March 1939 and subsequently tested.

This pre-production machine has dual controls and extended glazing to improve the instructor pilot's view. (Petrick)

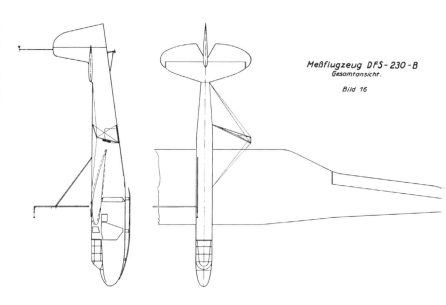

Meßflugzeug DFS-230-B
Gesamtansicht.
Bild 16

The early DFS 230s had a rounded nose, bulged cockpit glazing, a straight fuselage spine from rear to front, and tail surface contours that differed from those of later variants. The fuselages of these experimental machines had the door in a different location and minimal glazing. (DFS)

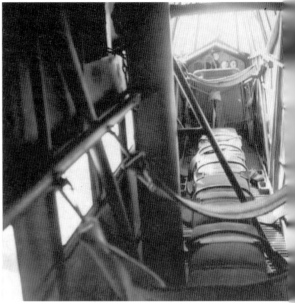

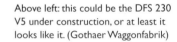

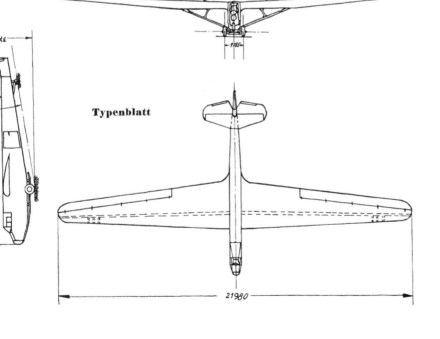

Längsschnitt

Typenblatt

Above left: this could be the DFS 230 V5 under construction, or at least it looks like it. (Gothaer Waggonfabrik)

Above right: the diagonal strut beneath the wing inside the fuselage and the channel for the aileron control cables (left next to the bench seat) made it almost impossible to climb from the rear to the front. The DFS 230 A-1 was therefore loaded from the front and the back. The soldiers seated in front of the strut faced forward and had lap belts. The four soldiers seated behind them faced the rear and had additional shoulder belts. (Mankau)

Drawings from the DFS 230 A-1 handbook.

Close-up photos of the DFS 230. (Gothaer Waggonfabrik)

DFS 230 A-1

Purpose: Assault glider for nine soldiers

Identifying Features: Jettisonable undercarriage for takeoff, single-piece canopy, one entrance door on left side

The DFS 230 A-1 was the first variant of the transport glider to be built in quantity. Hartwig is known to have built 30 DFS 230 A-1 machines, the last of which was completed on 24/1/1940. There is no evidence that additional aircraft were built and it is also improbable. The type was used mainly to transport combat teams (ten men). Six sat facing forward; they entered and exited the aircraft through the cockpit canopy. Four faced rearward and left the aircraft by way of the door on the left side of the fuselage, which was also used to load and unload radio equipment or heavy machine-guns. A characteristic of the early DFS 230 A-1 was the absence of a loading hatch on the right side of the aircraft. Instead there were eight windows.

DFS 230 A-2

Purpose: transport aircraft for troops and equipment (gun aircraft)

Identifying Features: similar to the A-1, additional loading hatch on right side of fuselage, rear bench seat removable for use as cargo transport, folding canopy hood, and fittings for equipment racks.

Six members of the DFS 230 A-1's crew had to enter the aircraft through the cockpit. (Modell Magazin)

In this photo one can see both early DFS 230 A-1s (without side hatch) and DFS 230 A-2s (with side hatch). Both variants wear the same finish. (Schlaug)

Right: there were variations in the camouflage scheme. The DFS 230 received new camouflage in about summer 1940. The overall gray scheme (RLM 02) was replaced by RLM 71 upper surfaces and RLM 65 undersides. The dappled camouflage scheme followed later. (Petrick)

The tubular framework had to be modified to allow introduction of the side hatch. The rear bench seat was removable. (Gothaer Waggonfabrik)

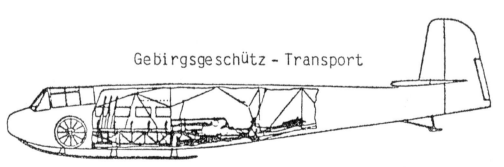

Gebirgsgeschütz - Transport

Typical load for the DFS 230 A-2. (Schlaug)

German Gliders in World War II

DFS 230s after landing with the rear cockpit fairing closed and open.
(Mathiesen / Barbas)

This DFS 230 A-2 displays the opaque folding cockpit fairing over the second pilot's seat and the loading hatch, both typical of this variant. (German Museum)

According to the DFS 230 pilot's notes of June 1942, compared to the A-1 the DFS 230 A-2 had an additional loading hatch, a folding canopy hood, and fittings for equipment racks.

A Gotha type summary indicates that, unlike the A-1, the DFS 230 A-2 had auxiliary controls (See Page 30). This enabled the man behind the pilot to control the aircraft if the pilot was disabled. This eventuality was quite possible,

when one considers that the unarmored glider came within range of even small arms while landing. The pilot's notes attribute the dual controls to both the DFS 230 A-1 and A-2, which contradicts the DFS 230 A Handbook of 4/11/1939 and the Gotha Replacement Parts List of September 1941. I cannot explain this contradiction, however, I tend to believe the type summary, which would mean that only the DFS 230 A-2 had auxiliary controls.

The DFS 230 A-1 had a complement of ten, and was designed to transport a lightly armed combat team. In the Air Armaments Minister's aircraft summary of 1/6/1942 the DFS 230 A-2 was designated a gun aircraft with a complement of six. That means that in this form the rear bench seat was absent or could be removed for transporting a gun.

On the DFS 230 A-1 the fixed fuselage began right behind the cockpit glazing. Behind the glazed hood of the A-2, with its sloped side panels, there was a rearwards-folding hood which was triangular in shape when viewed from the side. When raised, it made it easier for the forward-facing soldiers to enter or exit the aircraft. As the DFS 230 A-2 was also designed as a cargo transport, the larger opening also made it easier to load the forward fuselage. On the A-2 series the folding hood was not transparent, while on the later DFS 230 B-2 it had glazed windows.

DFS 230 A-3

Purpose: transport aircraft for troops and equipment

Identifying Features: like the A-2, probably with tropical equipment

GWF, Erla, and BMM built 114 DFS 230 A-3 in the second half of 1940. The distinguishing features of this variant are not known. It is possible, however, that it was a tropical variant, as a number of aircraft types were being prepared for use in Africa at that time. It is therefore likely that, as with other types, the equipment included sun blinds and rifles.

DFS 230 B-1

Purpose: not mentioned in handbook

Identifying Features: not known

In the handbook draft L.Dv.559 of 4/9/1939 [33] it states that the dual-control training version was supposed to be called the DFS 230 B-2, and no B-1 is mentioned. Neither is there any reference to a B-1 in the pilot's notes [34], [35], in which the DFS 230 A-1, A-2, and B-2 variants are mentioned. The documents I discovered concerning delivery numbers not only offer some clue as to the possibility that DFS 230 B-1s were delivered, but they also leave a very small number of aircraft which cannot be assigned with certainty to other variants. Overall, however, I cannot find any definitive proof that a DFS 230 B-1 variant existed. The DFS 230 B-1 is only mentioned in the Gotha summary, without, however, offering a key difference from the B-2.

Photos and films do, however, confirm that there were pre-production aircraft with dual controls. It is possible that these training aircraft from the pre-production series were at some point designated DFS 230 B-2, but at present that cannot be proved.

DFS 230 B-2

Purpose: transport aircraft for troops and equipment, training aircraft

Identifying Features: like the A-2 without auxiliary controls, but with dual controls, second pilot's seat, greatly-increased cockpit glazing

The DFS 230 B-2 was originally conceived as a training aircraft to supplement the DFS 230 A-1. The flight instructor sat behind the student, not beside him, as claimed in many publications.

Later, however, it was decided that all production of the DFS 230 should switch to the B-2 variant. This change essentially took place in February 1941. The reason for the

A pre-production machine with dual controls, second pilot's seat, and extended glazing for the instructor pilot (possibly designated DFS 230 B-1). (Petrick)

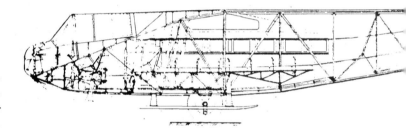

The DFS 230 B-2 had a glazed cockpit fairing and two pilot's seats. (Mankau / Ries)

decision was that the air force could no longer afford to use transport aircraft exclusively for training. The DFS 230 B-2 could be used as a training aircraft with dual controls, but after removal of the second pilot's seat also as a transport glider.

Through the door one can see the second pilot's seat of the DFS 230 B-2 and the bench seat also present in other variants. (Modell Magazin)

Factory-fresh DFS 230 B-2 still without braking parachute and associated equipment. (Mathiesen)

DFS 230 B-2 with extended cockpit glazing. (Mathiesen)

The normal pilot's seat and the dual instrumentation required more space, consequently, the DFS 230 B-2 could accommodate just nine men. The folding hood behind the cockpit glazing was needed to allow the troops in the rear to get out over the second pilot's seat. Externally, this variant was identifiable by its glazed folding hood. The extra glazing improved the view of the flight instructor. Initially triangular in shape, the side panels were later made even larger.

DFS 230: Second Door on Left Side of Fuselage

Note: There follows an explanation of the difference between a door and a hatch. A door is attached to the fuselage by a hinge, while a hatch is not. Some doors could be easily removed and thus functioned like a hatch.

The DFS 230 was originally conceived solely for the purpose of transporting ten soldiers. The first six sat in front of the wing spar and had to enter and exit the aircraft through the cockpit. Their bench seat was welded in place. The four in the rear sat on the left side of the aircraft behind the wing and had a door. From the beginning, the rear seat could be removed to increase cargo space. As the door offered poor access to the cargo area, beginning with the A-2 variant the DFS 230 was provided with a hatch on the right side of the fuselage behind the wing strut. While this allowed the rear part of the cargo hold to be loaded reasonably well, the area in front of the strut was still poorly accessible. To provide access to this area, another door was installed in front of the wing strut on the left side of the fuselage. Pawlas [1] maintains that this door was an exclusive feature of the C-1 and identifies all DFS 230s with this door as C-1s, but he is wrong. His own sources reveal that the 14 DFS 230 C-1 aircraft were not built until 1944, however, the door was present long before that. I have been unable to prove whether this door was retrofitted or was installed on the production line from the start.

DFS 230: Armament

No defensive armament was envisaged for the DFS 230 and none was retrofitted. An offensive capability was, however, felt to be necessary. At first, therefore, a MG 34 was mounted rigidly on the right side of the fuselage beside the cockpit. After the glider cast off the man

The door on this DFS 230 A-2 is still on its hinges. The aircraft has been modified for rigid tow and braking parachute. (Schmalwasser)

MG 34 with pull cord for cocking and firing. A blast shield is mounted alongside the muzzle to protect the fabric skin. (Bundesarchiv Koblenz 10 II-565-1425-20)

The second man
operated the
side-mounted
MG 34 and the
fourth man the
MG 15 atop
the fuselage.
(Bundesarchiv
Koblenz 10
11-568-1529-27f)

German Gliders in World War II

The rigidly-mounted MG 34 had a very restricted field of fire. Consequently, a second gun position with an MG 15 was placed atop the fuselage behind the cockpit. The fourth member of the crew manned the MG 15, which was able to provide covering fire after landing. The gunner stood during the landing approach and wore a special harness. (Aders / Petrick)

An armament of two MG 15s and one MG 34 must probably have been extremely rare. The arc-shaped mounting rail was probably installed to enable the gunner to fire past the man in front. (Mathiesen)

The wide snow skid could be fitted on the standard attachment points without modification. (Griehl)

Above: DFS 230 A-2 CB+MW was at Ainring in February 1941 and at Leipheim in March. (Mathiesen)

Below: the pilot climbs into the cockpit. (Mathiesen)

The ladder is removed as the DFS 230 is made ready for takeoff. (Mathiesen)

The three He 72 tow planes as seen by the ground crew and the pilot. (Mathiesen / Krieg)

CB+MW during takeoff. (Mathiesen)

behind the pilot could open a small hatch, reach out, and cock the weapon. The pilot aimed with a fixed sight, and on his command the second man operated the MG 34. The weapon could then be removed after landing.

DFS 230: Skis

As part of mountain trials, the DFS put the DFS 230 on skis, mounting a broader skid on the standard skid's three attachment points. The trials were so successful that in mid-August 1941 the RLM asked the General Staff if it wished to have some DFS 230s equipped with skis. The answer was yes, and at the end of September 1941 it was confirmed that 200 sets of DFS 230 skis were to be delivered in the months December 1941 to February 1942. Then, in mid-October 1941 it was determined that most of the skis were to be delivered in February 1942. According to the pilot's notes, the undercarriage was removed when skis were installed.

DFS 230: Trainer for Me 321 Pilots

The future pilots of the Me 321 faced two special challenges. First they would be sitting high above the ground, and second, their glider had to be towed into the air by several tow planes simultaneously. At least one DFS 230 was placed on a raised undercarriage in order to simulate these conditions. The aircraft is known to have flown in February 1941. The main undercarriage was essentially that of the Fi 156, while the original nosewheel was probably a tailwheel from a machine like the Me 210. One Ju 52 or three He 72s served as tow planes. Some students made just a few flights in the tall DFS 230 towed by a Ju 52, before practicing the triple tow in a Ju 52 towed by three Bf 110s, the tow cables attached to the shut-down central engine of the Ju 52.

DFS 230: Conversion to Fa 225

Purpose: transport aircraft for troops and equipment

Identifying Features: lifting rotor, fixed undercarriage

The DFS 230's slide after landing was uncomfortably long for use as a combat glider. One of the attempts to shorten this involved combining the fuselage of a DFS 230 B-2 with the rotor of the Fa 223. At the beginning of 1942 the Focke-Achgelis Company was instructed to begin design work on a variant of the DFS 230 modified in this way. For a time, consideration was also given to providing the aircraft with a motor, but for space reasons this was not possible and Focke-Achgelis limited itself to the unpowered Fa 225. A standard rotor and rotor head from the Fa 331 were mounted on a tower above the DFS 230 fuselage. A shaft ran from the rotor head down through the fuselage,

German Gliders in World War II

The Fa 225 lifting rotor vehicle and a mockup of the Fa 225's instrument panel. (Nowarra)

ending in a cable drum directly beneath the fuselage. Before takeoff a cable was wound onto the drum and its free end attached to the ground. During takeoff, the unwinding cable caused the rotor to turn. In 1943 the DFS 225 was tested with He 46 and Ju 52 tow planes, and the hopes of a significantly reduced landing run were fulfilled. It was also found, however, that the towing speed of 180 kph was significantly lower than that of the normal DFS 230 (210 kph), which was not especially high anyway. Glide ratio was reduced from 1:11 to 1:5. The project was therefore abandoned in favor of the braking parachute and rocket braking.

DFS 230: Rocket-Assisted Takeoff

Following the successful experiments by the DFS on the Seethaleralpe (see DFS 230: Research Aircraft), on 15/5/1941 the RLM decided to procure an initial batch of 50 powder takeoff-assist rockets for broader-based tests with the DFS 230. Rheinmetall had continued development of powder rockets, and from the St-H8 evolved the R I 502, which was similar in thrust and appearance. The RLM also issued a modification directive (No. 16) for the installation of the rocket system in the DFS 230. The ability to install takeoff assist rockets was mentioned and illustrated in the edition of pilot's notes [34] issued in June 1942, indicating that there was at least an interest in takeoff aids. In its report No. 2334/42, however, the Peenemünde-West Experimental Station stated that testing of the rockets and the takeoff procedure had to be abandoned because of inadequate safety in operation, and that the rockets could not be approved for use because of their reliability. I have no further information as to the use of rockets in connection with the DFS 230, however, guideline No. 63/43 issued by the RLM for the design of an assault glider and universal transport glider on 1/4/1943 envisaged the use of powder rockets for uncoupled takeoffs. The Rheinmetall R I 502 was also investigated as a takeoff aid for the Go 242 and Me 262.

The Fa 225 being towed by a He 46. (Mankau)

These movie stills show that the powder takeoff-assist rockets were also tested on the Ju 52. I have no further details. (Mankau)

Dive brakes deployed: these were designed to reduce glide angle and facilitate pinpoint landings. (Mathiesen)

Below: because of the DFS 230's limited maximum speed (250 kph), it was not permitted to dive steeper than 60° even with the braking parachute. The parachute is collared. During a precision approach to the target, meaning below 250 m, maximum allowable dive angle was 30°. (Mankau)

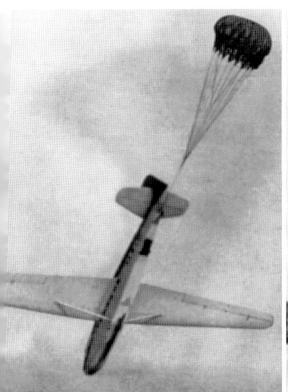

Not until 2 meters above the ground, after flaring for
landing, was the parachute to be un-collared (fully deployed).
(Bundesarchiv Koblenz 10 11-568-1531-32)

The parachute collapsed after a landing run
of about 30 meters. (Petrick)

German Gliders in World War II

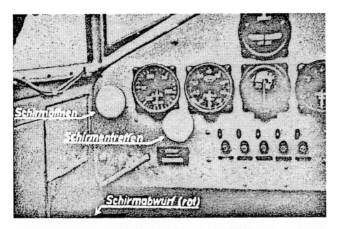

Instrumentenbrett DFS 230 mit Bedienungsgriffen

The pilot had to pull the handles marked "Schirmentreffen" (un-collar parachute) and "Schirmöffnen" (open parachute) carefully and in the correct sequence in order to avoid an accident. (Handbook)

DFS 230: Short Landing

The unarmored DFS 230 was extremely vulnerable during the approach to land. Initially, the only possibility for shortening the landing procedure was the use of air brakes.

The air force pushed for a further shortening of the landing procedure. A braking parachute had already been used in the high mountain experiments. The braking parachute was further developed for use as a dive and landing brake, enabling the glider to dive and shortening the approach and landing distance. The ability to dive was desirable to enable the glider to descend quickly from altitude. In order to ensure controllability in the dive, in the beginning the parachute was used only partially deployed.

Use of speed brakes was strictly forbidden when flying with the braking chute. The load had to be securely tied down to avoid shifting. The braking parachute was attached beneath the rear fuselage. The tail skid was modified to avoid fouling the parachute. Mounted behind the tail skid was a spur-like extension with slide and parachute coupling. The cable ran from the parachute along the right edge of the fuselage to the coupling. The parachute could be retrofitted to any DFS 230 A-1, A-2, or B-2.

The DFS 230 could also be landed on its undercarriage. As this had no brakes however, the landing run was relatively long. If a shorter landing run was required, the undercarriage was jettisoned shortly after takeoff or immediately before landing. Some aircraft were fitted with a braking spur to reduce the length of the slide after landing.

As this was seldom available, however, the units sometimes helped themselves by winding steel wire

Some parachute-equipped DFS 230s were also fitted with a rearview mirror to enable the pilot to check the parachute's deployment state. (Bundesarchiv Koblenz 10 11-569-1579—28))

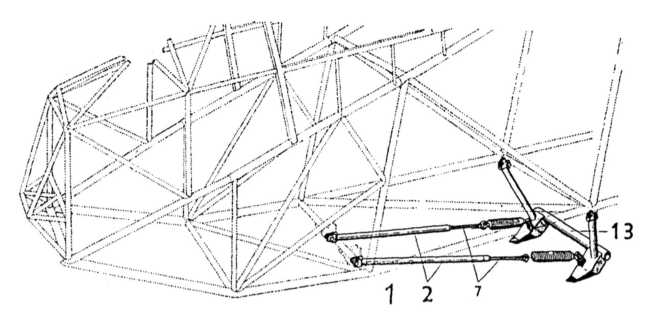

Drawing of the braking spur system taken from the replacement parts list.

In the beginning the braking rocket system consisted of 48 Leinen-Sander rockets. In addition to the braking rockets, the test machine also had the Mistel mounting shoe for use with the Fw 56. (DFS)

Windows were retrofitted in the fuselage sides in front of the pilot to improve his view when initiating the dive and in the dive itself. (Griehl)

around the landing skid. This was not what the air force wanted, however. The DFS therefore experimented with braking rockets mounted in the nose, which were ignited after touchdown.

Used by the DFS in many research projects, DFS 230 B-2 CB+ZB is seen here during trials with braking rockets and braking parachute. The smoke produced by the rockets also helped conceal the aircraft. (DFS)

The ultimate braking rocket configuration: three Nebelwerfer rocket motors. The rockets could be retrofitted onto any DFS 230. The rockets were kept covered to keep them clean. (Petrick)

Photos from the German
Aviation Research
Yearbook 1941. (DFS)

DFS 230: Research Aircraft
The DFS 230 was used extensively by the DFS for research purposes. The known activities are described here.

DFS-230-B
For its initial experiments the DFS used the DFS-230-B, a modified DFS 230 A-0. The drawing on Page 127 and the photos above are from a DFS report in the 1941 German Aviation Research Yearbook. At present I have no more information, but the aircraft was undoubtedly used to test wing profiles.

Technical Reports Vol. 8 (1941) contains a report on profile drag measurements on rough wings, which were also carried out using the DFS 230 B. It is extremely likely that this aircraft was a one-off. To my knowledge the designation DFS 230 B was not used again.

Photos from Technical Reports Volumes 8 and 11. (DFS)

From Long to Rigid-Tow

In the period 1939 to 1941 time was also given to the development of various towing methods. The objective was to make the glider-tug combination instrument-flight capable. This led from the use of long towlines to short ones and finally to rigid-tow. On 9/5/1940 the DFS issued a comprehensive report on its experiments. This stated that the most practical towline lengths were 1.5 to 10 meters, and with 6- to 8-m towlines it was possible to fly through clouds and over long ranges in almost any weather. Turbulence and unskilled flying would lead to yawing and pitching, however, requiring heightened attention on the part of the pilot.

Rigid-tow eliminated or significantly reduced the pitching and yawing; consequently, the pilot's workload was greatly reduced. The space requirements, course stability, and maneuverability of the glider-tug combination were better than with the long tow method, which seemed important for operational use. Instrument flight was possible and did not impose an increased workload on the pilot of the tow plane. The original towing apparatus was heavy and required reinforcements in the fuselage to absorb the undamped lateral forces of the glider.

Because of the high weight of the experimental model, a 140-kg production version of the rigid-tow apparatus was developed at Lemwerder, but this was still too heavy and was rejected by the *Luftwaffe*.

By mid-1942 the DFS developed a lighter tow arm, which weighed 70 kg and required no counterweight. The pivoting arm's spherical receptacle made possible friction-damped movement vertically and laterally. The coupling on the glider had to be placed lower and was protected by a cone-shaped shield on the pivoting arm.

Type Overview

Test flights with 10- and 2-meter towlines. (DFS)

First rigid-tow tests. (DFS)

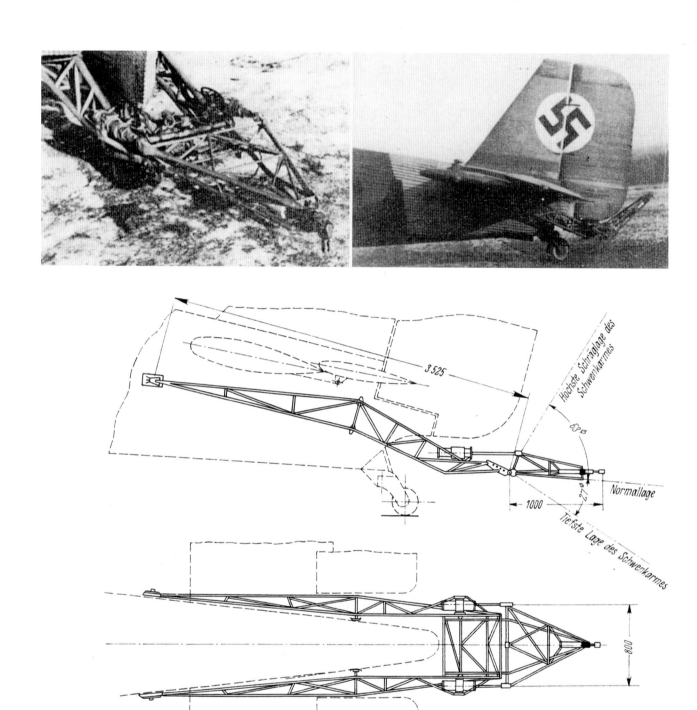

The first rigid-tow apparatus developed by the DFS. It weighed 200 kg
and its use required a counterweight of equal weight in the nose of
the Ju 52. (DFS)

An electric winch was installed in a Ju 52 so that the tow length could be varied smoothly down to rigid-tow length. (DFS)

Lemwerder style rigid-tow apparatus. (Nowarra)

The Ju 52 / DFS 230 combination takes to the air
with the improved rigid-tow coupling. (Nowarra)

In flight photo of a Ju 52 / DFS 230 combination using
the Lemwerder type rigid-tow coupling. (Nowarra)

The rigid-tow method was initially tested using a Ju 52 glider tug. Subsequent trials were carried out with He 46, Hs 126, and He 111 tow planes. Satisfactory results were only obtained when the weight of the glider was not more than 1/3 that of the tow plane. The He 111 / DFS 230 combination yielded the best results and was adopted for service use. (DFS)

XI Air Corps subsequently conducted trials with the Do 17 E, however, it is not known to have been used operationally. (DFS)

The DFS 230 V1 prior to the catapult takeoff. (DFS)

DFS 230 A-2 with two takeoff-assist rockets and broad
skid for use on snow. (DFS)

German Gliders in World War II

Use of the DFS 230 in the High Mountains

In October 1940 the DFS began studying the use of the DFS 230 in the high mountains. There followed the previously described landing and subsequent catapult takeoff on the Grand Venice Glacier on 19/10.

The procedure was still too time consuming, and the DFS fitted a DFS 230 A-2 with a braking parachute and powder rockets to enable the aircraft to land on small surfaces and, after being turned around, takeoff again. The experiments were conducted successfully on the Seethaleralpe on 27 and 28/2/1941.

Rheinmetall St-H8 powder takeoff-assist rockets, which produced 500 kg of thrust for six seconds. The wing's fabric skin had to be covered with metal to protect it against the hot gas jet. (DFS)

DFS 230 A-2 (NC+SA) with the ribbon braking parachute developed by the Stuttgart Aviation Technical Institute. The snow skid had an additional brake. (DFS)

In October 1942 this DFS 230 B-2 was used to determine the aerodynamic effects of high- and low-mounted wings on the horizontal tail. (Kössler)

Aerodynamic Experiments

Like the DFS 230 B, the DFS used other DFS 230s for basic aerodynamic research.

Sirens

After the Ju 87 achieved great effect using sirens, in 1942 the German Aviation Research Institute E.V. (Registered Association) and the DFS investigated similar installations on the DFS 230. The DVL system was used operationally.

A pressure-sensing device like this was used to measure the pressure distribution behind the wing. (Kössler)

The DFS selected the nose as the location for the noise generator, while the DVL placed it on the fuselage. (Bundesarchiv Koblenz 10 11-565-1407-15)

The wheels of the Klemm sat in guide shoes on the DFS 230's wing. The tail was supported by a four-legged tail brace. Forces were transferred by a pyramid of cables beneath the Klemm 35's center of gravity. (DFS)

Mistel Tow

Another goal was to combine aircraft from different speed classes. The DFS 230's normal towing speed of 200 kph was scarcely higher than the landing speeds of the Bf 109, Bf 110, and Ju 88. To fly at such speeds those aircraft had to adopt a nose-up attitude. This placed the wing at a greater angle of attack and increased lift, but drag also rose sharply. The DFS therefore developed procedures in which the glider took over part of the lift of the tow plane. The best known example of this was the so-called "Mistel" tow. With it the DFS hoped to create combinations which, for example, would enable fighter groups to transport their own baggage in self-towed gliders. Also considered was the idea of carrying fuel in the glider to increase the fighter's range.

The first experiments with a DFS 230 B-2 and a Kl 35 began in September 1942. The combination had to

be towed into the air by a Ju 52. The Klemm's 105 hp motor did not even provide enough power to maintain level flight. The combination performed flawlessly in the air and separation in flight caused no problems. The combination could be controlled from either aircraft and could be landed together. This first Mistel was used only for testing.

The experiments continued in October 1942 with a Fw 56 *Stösser* (Sparrow Hawk). This combination was also initially towed aloft by a Ju 52. To pilot Stammer of the DFS the combination appeared suitable for use, but problems arose when an attempt was made to tow the combination behind a He 111 (RN+EE) using rigid-tow. The combination swung vertically during takeoff. On 19/10/1942 there was a near catastrophe when the Mistel began bouncing so forcefully during the takeoff run that the towing apparatus broke, the Mistel struck

The switch to the Fw 56 resulted in a Mistel with improved characteristics. A braking parachute may be seen under the fuselage of the DFS 230. (DFS)

This photo shows the wheel shoes for the Kl 35 and Fw 56. During the Mistel trials DFS 230 CB+ZB had the previously-described braking rocket installation in the nose in addition to the braking parachute. (DFS)

The Bf 109's propeller was located directly above the DFS 230's first pilot's seat. Understandably, it was soon decided to fly the DFS 230 from the second pilot's seat. (DFS)

An additional glazed door was installed in the left side of the fuselage to improve the pilot's view from the second seat and to facilitate his exit from the aircraft if forced to bale out. During the initial flight trials the DFS 230 still wore a typical glider code with two groups of numbers. (DFS)

the ground and slid into a field, damaging the starboard wing.

The first Mistel combination capable of taking off under its own power, a Messerschmitt 109 E atop a DFS 230 B-2, became available in June 1943. Because of the increased weight, the undercarriage of the DFS 230 was replaced by a new one using the mainwheels of a W 34 and a tailwheel from a Hs 126. The struts joining the aircraft maintained the interval between them, while the tension forces were absorbed by a cable running from the Bf 109's center of gravity to the fuselage midpoint of the DFS 230. Flight testing began on 21/6/1943. No problems were encountered during takeoff, combined flight, and combined landing. Airspeed with the Bf 109's engine at cruise setting was 200 kph. As the combination's thrust line was clearly above the DFS 230, it had to be trimmed tail-heavy in order to fly straight and level. On separation, however, this trim setting caused the DFS 230 to pitch up. The slipstream of the Bf 109's wing, which passed over the DFS 230's tail, further increased this tendency. During the first flight the DFS 230's canopy struck the coupling beneath the Bf 109. For safety reasons, therefore, in subsequent trials the DFS 230 B-2 was flown from the rear seat.

The initial testing of this combination was carried out at Hörsching, which had a runway long enough for the untried Mistel. After the combination demonstrated good takeoff characteristics, the trials were moved to Ainring, the DFS' home airfield. Poor separation characteristics led the DFS to modify the cradle, and the cable was eliminated. During this modification the DFS 230 was also given a different code. Flight trials resumed on 16/7/1943. As behavior during separation was still not satisfactory, an air brake was installed ahead of the forward struts. The Mistel was subsequently tested extensively at Ainring. On 8/1/1944 the DFS certified the combination's flight, takeoff, and landing characteristics as entirely satisfactory, and expressed a desire to continue development to link the controls of the two machines so that the glider's control surfaces would react to control inputs from the powered machine. The RLM initially showed little enthusiasm for the idea, for this type of Mistel tow was set aside at a meeting held by the Air Armaments Minister on 29/2/1944.

The forward mount with the subsequently-added dive brake. (DFS)

The Mistel was tested in this configuration at Ainring. (DFS)

These water trials with the DFS 230 took place in the Main River in summer 1943. It would have been extremely difficult to unload the aircraft, and even commandos would have had difficulty exiting the aircraft; consequently, the idea was abandoned. (Schlaug)

This only looks like a water landing. In fact, the aircraft "got wet" during flooding in southern France in 1943. It has a noise generator. (Krieg)

Water Landing

In the summer of 1943 the RLM saw a probable need for gliders to be able to land on the water. According to witnesses, the intention was to deposit commando teams on Russian reservoirs near dispersed tank production sites. The commandos would blow up the hydro-electric plants and then make their way back to their own lines.

The Gothaer Waggonfabrik therefore initiated development of the P-52 amphibian project, while the Erfurt Repair Works offered a suitably-modified Ka 430. The DFS also investigated other ways of using the DFS 230 on water, but the experiments did not produce any tangible results.

The DFS 230 on Floats

The DFS also worked on a DFS 230 on floats. It would have been able to take off on an undercarriage and land on the water.

A DFS 230 was placed on floats in 1943. The space between the floats was greater than normal, and the jettisonable undercarriage was located there. The aircraft was at Ainring in September 1943 and was then moved to the Chiemsee, a lake in Bavaria.

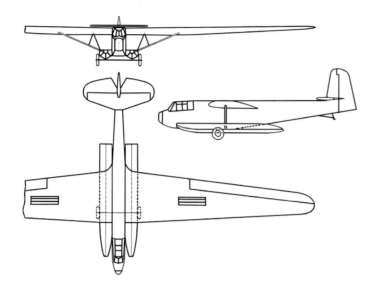

Left: concept drawing of a DFS 230 on floats mounted close to the fuselage. The date on the drawing is illegible. (Mankau)

Center: DFS 230 A-2 on floats.

Bottom: DFS 230 on the Chiemsee. According to witnesses, attempts by the tow plane to pull the cable from the water and take off with the glider were unsuccessful. Takeoff was only possible on wheels. (Petrick)

The He 111 flew low over the stationary DFS 230 and tried to snag the tow cable from the two poles, but the elastic cable broke. (Modell Magazin)

The pickup box was housed in the fuselage of the tow plane. (DFS)

Pickup-Tow

The idea of gliders towed behind passenger aircraft, to be released over small airfields which did not justify a landing by the airliner, was conceived early on. It was proposed that a cable pickup system be used to enable the airliner to subsequently fly over the airfield and take the glider back into the air. The concept was patented by the Hungarian Banhidi.

In 1943 the RLM tasked three research facilities in Rechlin, Ainring, and Trebin/Schönberg with the development of a pickup method. One pickup method used a cable polygon. The DFS looked into the use of an elastic cable, using the He 111 and DFS 230 among other types. At the free end of the cable there was a lug which was held up by posts. According to a report dated 20/10/1943 the method proved unusable in this form, as it was not possible to get the glider to the speed of the pickup aircraft in the time available.

The pickup tow first appeared possible when the idea was conceived of placing the tow cable in a pickup box made of plywood slats. When the cable was snagged, it was pulled out of the box for a time and energy destroyed by breaking the slats. As a result, resistance rose gradually and the tow cable was not overstressed. So much for the theory. In practice the steel cable frequently snapped. No use with aircraft is known.

Lift-Tow

The DFS developed a lift-tow procedure, in which the towed aircraft flew above the powered aircraft and the tow cables bore a portion of its weight. One possible use was for bombers to tow rocket fighters into the area of operations, where they would separate and ignite their rocket motors. As the rocket fighter had a relatively small wing area it could not provide sufficient lift at the speed of the towing aircraft to fly independently, as in rigid-tow.

Dive Brakes

The DFS converted one aircraft with larger dive brakes for comparative trials with the braking parachute.

Three-Axis Autopilot

DFS in-house report No. 73 of 14/5/1943 described how two DFS 230s were fitted with three-axis autopilots as test-beds for television devices. One was fitted with a Patin autopilot, which was in production and installed in a variety of aircraft, and the other an Askania pneumatic autopilot. Demanded of the systems were:

1) Stabilization of the three axes

2) Turn rates of 1° to 10° per second

3) The ability to engage a remote control system

4) Ability to conduct rigid-tow flights in which the aircraft was automatically controlled

5) The ability to carry out unmanned, remotely-controlled flights and remotely-controlled landings

The Robbe was an attempt to create a transport device for an unmanned weather station. It would have been transported to its destination using the lift-tow method and gently deposited there. Development of the Robbe was abandoned because of the danger of collision in turbulent conditions. (Griehl)

These dive brakes are clearly larger than the production version. (DFS)

One of the two DFS 230s with reinforced skid, air brakes, and antenna array on the fuselage. (Kössler)

DFS 230 V 6 Rumpfbreite 1000 mm Systemmaß

Fahrwerk 8-230.280   (Start- und Landefahrwerk)

Reifen 650x180 p₀=2,8 atü oder 660x160 p₀=3,5 atü, bremsbare Räder
Federstreben 8-2649, Spurweite 1400 mm.
Federstrebe in Rumpfseitenwand geführt, Abstützstrebe nach vorn,
Rad an Kragachse gelagert.

Keilkufe 8-230.   (Bremslandung)

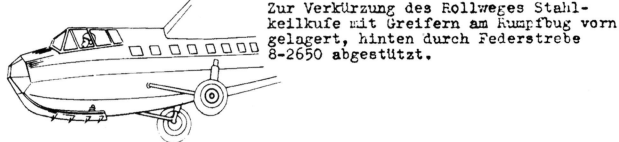

Zur Verkürzung des Rollweges Stahl-
keilkufe mit Greifern am Rumpfbug vorn
gelagert, hinten durch Federstrebe
8-2650 abgestützt.

Company drawing and specification for the DFS 230 V6. (Gothaer Waggonfabrik)

The long-range goal was to control aircraft from the ground by means of television cameras, in particular automatic landings and navigation. Because of the higher risks associated with automatic landings, in addition to the autopilots both aircraft were fitted with stronger skis combined with the shock struts from the Fieseler Storch with 30 cm of travel. The undercarriage was strengthened and, in order to allow the DFS 230 to be towed aloft by a Ju 52, Cardan shaft couplings were installed. To control the glide angle, four fan-shaped retractable spoilers were installed above and below each wing. Fully-extended, they increased the rate of descent by 4 to 6 m/sec. During trials, the aircraft fitted with the Patin autopilot made ten to twelve automatic landings and the Askania-equipped machine 30 to 40.

The topic of Report 73 was the equipping of the two aircraft with three-axis autopilots. Whether, and in what form, the aircraft were equipped and tested with television cameras I cannot say.

DFS 230 V6

On 11/5/1943 a decision was made to resume production of the DFS 230 in January 1944. The new aircraft was to be an improved version, the DFS 230 C-1. Built in December 1943, the DFS 230 V6 was the prototype of this new variant. It had a broader fuselage, with an internal width of 1 meter. Like the DFS 330, the prototype was built by Gothaer Waggonfabrik. The number and arrangement of seats was the same as that of the DFS 230 A and B. A special feature of this prototype was a fixed undercarriage for landing and takeoff. I am not aware of a picture or a definitive drawing

of the DFS 230 V6, but the drawing from a Gothaer Waggonfabrik undercarriage summary probably depicts the undercarriage arrangement.

DFS 230 C-1

Purpose: transport aircraft for troops and equipment

Identifying Features: like the B-2, fuselage width 1 meter

According to the Gothaer Waggonfabrik information, the internal width of the DFS 230 C-1's fuselage was one meter, with a jettisonable undercarriage comparable to that of the A-2 and B-2. The wing and tail section must have been adopted unchanged from the DFS 230 B-2. I know of no photos or original drawings of such a machine. Pawlas [1] adds that the C-1 variant had an additional door in front of the wing strut. He identifies the aircraft in a series of photos as C-1s because of the extra door in front of the wing strut, but he is wrong. I know of no photos of the DFS 230 C-1. The door was probably there, but I have found no proof to confirm this.

The Mráz Company built 14 examples of the DFS 230 C-1 from April to July 1944. They cannot, therefore, have taken part in the rescue of Mussolini on the Gran Sasso on 12/9/1943 as claimed by a number of authors. Production of the DFS 230 C-1 by Mráz also did not begin as quickly as the RLM desired. Thus, possible quantity production moved into a period in which the envisaged tow plane (He 111) disappeared from production. As the DFS 230 C-1 was obsolescent, even with the modifications, and was unsuitable for towing behind the Ju 388, it was decided that production would end in July 1944.

Two photos of an unidentified DFS 230 with wide fuselage and machine-gun position in the nose. (JET & PROP)

(Nowarra)

DFS 230 D-1

Purpose: transport aircraft for troops and equipment

Identifying Features: like the C-1, shortened wingspan, stressed for 300 kph

Original documents contain differing information about the DFS 230 D-1. In one it is designated the production version of the DFS 230 V7, while a Gothaer Waggonfabrik type summary states that the DFS 230 D-1 was essentially a C-1 with shortened wings. Both are correct, but one after the other. The first variant was created in the time period mid-1943 to mid-1944 and is described in the chapters DFS 230 V7 and E-1.

In mid-1944 a situation arose in which the *Luftwaffe* preferred the Ka 430 over the DFS 230 V7, but production of the Ka 430 could not begin until 1945. It was therefore decided to modify the DFS 230 C-1—production of which had just begun—so that it could be towed by the Ju 388 at 300 kph. The new variant with shortened wings was given the designation DFS 230 D-1, and work began on the conversion of three DFS 230 C-1s. One DFS 230 D-1 was

completed in August 1944. Whether the other two, which were supposed to be delivered in September 1944, were also completed cannot be confirmed. Nothing more came of plans to produce the DFS 230 D-1 in quantity.

I know of no photos with captions confirming a DFS 230 D-1, consequently, it is impossible to describe the machine's appearance.

DFS 230 ?

There are several photos of a broader (fuselage) DFS 230 that has retained significant components of the [original] fuselage framework. Some of the photos were taken at Zellhausen [23]. The conversion is so extensive and so professional that I do not believe that it was carried out by any unit. The new cockpit with the machine-gun position moved to the nose suggests a prototype with a higher planned towing speed. As I have no information about any additional variants, I assume that the photos depict a prototype of the DFS 230 D-1. If this is so, then one can ask if the DFS 230 C-1 had a similar cockpit canopy. As it is impossible to estimate the wingspan from the photos, the subject may also have been a DFS 230 C-1.

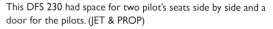
This DFS 230 had space for two pilot's seats side by side and a door for the pilots. (JET & PROP)

The DFS 230 V7 offered much more room than the DFS 230 B-2, but like the earlier variants it was still difficult to load. The Ka 430's tricycle undercarriage was safer but also heavier than the tailwheel undercarriage illustrated here. (German Museum)

DFS 230 V7

When, in mid-1943, it became obvious that few He 111 glider tugs would be available in 1945 and that the only possible replacement was the Ju 388, development began of a successor to the DFS 230 and Go 242 which would be suitable for operation with the Junkers machine. The Ka 430 was designed by a team led by Kalkert, director of the Erfurt Repair Works (REWE), essentially as a smaller development of the Go 242, and the DFS 230 V7 by the Gothaer Waggonfabrik under Hünerjäger as an improved and enlarged DFS 230. As both were designed to the same specification, the two gliders were similar in size and performance. The Ka 430 was selected as the more modern and practical design. The DFS 230 V7 remained a one-off and was—based on place of origin

and timing—the prototype for the planned DFS 230 D-1, later E-1, series. As far as is known, there were no other prototypes or production aircraft, and thus no other changes; the aircraft depicted in the drawing of the DFS 230 E-1 is identical to the V7. In [14] there is information concerning the use of the DFS 230 V7 to test the lift-tow method in combination with a Ju 87 B-1. In preparation for these tests, windows were installed in part of the cockpit floor to provide the pilot with a better view of the tow plane flying beneath him. The two tow cables were usually attached at the center of gravity points in the wings. Bomb racks were placed on the upper surfaces of the Ju 87's wings, spaced 4.7 meters apart. The attachment points on the undersurfaces of the glider's wings were 9 meters apart.

Without a loading platform the hatch in the fuselage was not very helpful. With its ventral hatch, the contemporary Ka 430 was much simpler to load. (Petrick)

The wings and tail section of the DFS 230 V7. One can see from its wing and tail section that it was obviously derived from the DFS 230 B-2. (Petrick)

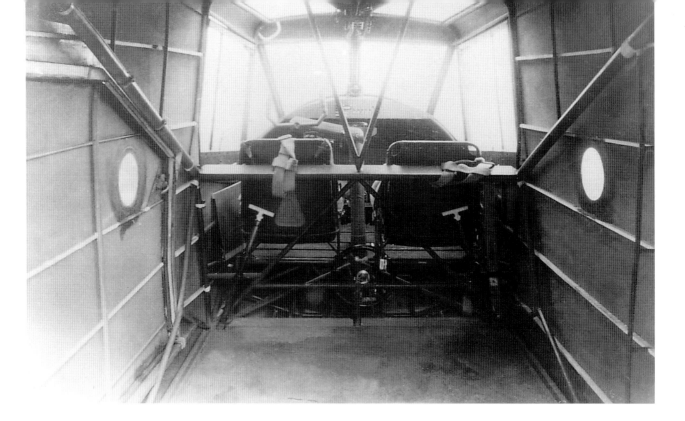

DFS 230 E-1

Purpose: transport aircraft for troops and equipment

Identifying Features: fixed undercarriage for takeoff, larger fuselage, reduced wingspan, stressed for 300 kph

In the documents with which I am familiar, the Gothaer Waggonfabrik initially designated the production version of the V7 the DFS 230 D-1, and then, after another D-1 was inserted into the series, this was changed to the DFS 230 E-1. With the RLM's decision in favor of the Ka 430, however, the DFS 230 E-1 was not required and therefore never materialized. A Ju 87 D-2/DFS 230 E combination is mentioned in a lift-tow [14] test report, but this is only an indication that in the second half of 1944 Gothaer Waggonfabrik still viewed the DFS 230 V7 as the basis for the E series. The drawing above, which is also printed in [1], depicts the V7 as the prototype of the planned D-1 series.

DFS 230 F-1

Nowarra (*Die Deutsche Luftrüstung 1933 bis 1945*), Green (*Warplanes of the Third Reich*), and Redemann (*FLUG REVUE 5/1980*) claimed that the DFS 230 V7 was the prototype of the F-1 variant. Nowarra and Green do not mention the E-1 at all and Redemann only as a listing. The DFS 230 F-1 is also mentioned in [1] in a type summary. No clear difference between it and the E-1 is discernible. An undercarriage summary by the Gothaer Waggonfabrik dated 31/8/1944 also appears in [1]. In it are described the undercarriages of the A-2, B-2, V6, C-1, and F-1 variants and two special undercarriages. The D-1 and E-1 variants and the V7 are not mentioned, but the undercarriage

Like that of all German transport gliders, the fuselage of the DFS 230 V7 consisted of a fabric-covered steel tube framework. The floor was made of wood. The control yoke could be swung to the right, like that of the Ka 430. (Petrick)

According to this drawing, the DFS 230 V7 was originally envisaged as the prototype for the D-1 series. (Mankau)

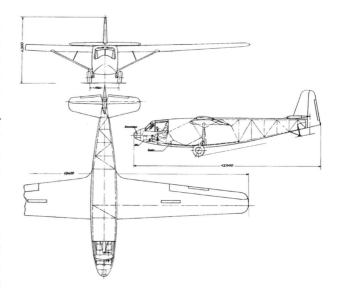

described for the F-1 is similar to that of the V7 and the E-1, and the Systemmass 1500 identified with the F-1 confirms the link to the V7. I believe the designation F-1 to be a typographical error which the authors have promulgated. In any case, I have found no credible evidence of any difference between the E-1 and F-1, and from this I conclude that there were plans for an E-1 variant, but not for an F-1.

Tow Planes for the DFS 230

Ju 52

In the beginning the DFS 230 was only towed by the Ju 52.
(Mathiesen)

Ju 52s and DFS 230s ready for takeoff. (Nowarra)

The rigid-tow method was developed using the Ju 52 and DFS 230. (Petrick)

The tow coupling on the Ju 52. (Mankau)

He 45

This He 45 lacks a tow coupling, but otherwise it is similar to the glider tug version. (JET & PROP)

He 46

As the number of DFS 230 gliders grew, obsolete reconnaissance aircraft like the He 46 were pressed into service as glider tugs. The performance and speed of the He 46 matched those of the DFS 230, but their numbers in the tow units were rather low. (Mathiesen)

As most He 46s came to the transport glider units from training schools, most also retained their old paint schemes. Camouflage was not applied until later. (Mathiesen)

Four-letter codes were typical for the He 46 glider tug. (Schlaug)

Hs 126

Beginning in the summer of 1940, the newly-formed Luftlandegeschwader 1 (LLG 1) flew the Hs 126 alongside the Ju 52. The unit consisted of three Gruppen, each with three Staffel. In autumn 1942, III./LLG 1 operated the Hs 126/DFS 230. (Bundesarchiv Koblenz 10 11-566-1492-17)

Attaching the tow cable to a Hs 126. (Bundesarchiv Koblenz 10 11-565-1425-37)

German Gliders in World War II

Do 17 E

In autumn 1942 I./LLG 1 was equipped with
Do 17s and DFS 230s. (Schlaug)

Do 17s stand ready to tow DFS 230s. The gliders are equipped
with noise generators. (Bundesarchiv Koblenz 10 11-565-1407-35)

Avia B 534

In autumn 1942 II./LLG I was equipped with Avia B 534s and DFS 230s. (Kössler)

The combination was not a success, because of the different cruising speeds of the Avia 534 and the DFS 230. (Mathiesen)

Ar 65

In the winter of 1942, IV./ LLG 1 was temporarily established with the Ar 65 and DFS 230. (Mankau)

Ar 65 with auxiliary tanks, tow coupling, and winter camouflage. (Klassiker der Luftfahrt)

Ju 87 R

Propaganda photo taken by a war correspondent showing the Ju 87 R serving as tow plane for the DFS 230. (Bundesarchiv Koblenz 10 11-567-1523-35)

From 1943 the Ju 87 R was frequently used as a glider tug, initially replacing the Avia B 534 in II./LLG 1. (Bundesarchiv Koblenz 10 11-565-1407-31)

Tow coupling on the Ju 87 R. (Griehl)

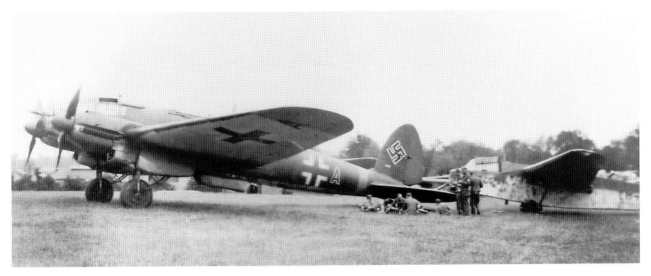

A rigid-tow Staffel (17./LLG 1) equipped with the He 111 and DFS 230 was formed in winter 1942. (Petrick)

The He 111 was used to tow both the Go 242 and the DFS 230. (Schlaug)

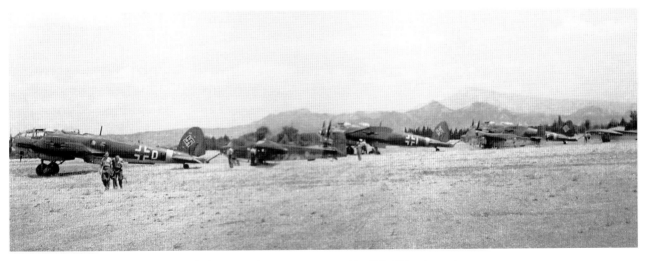

Glider-tug combinations are prepared for flight. (Schmalwasser)

The He 111 was capable of towing two DFS 230s simultaneously. The first was attached to the Ju 52 using the rigid coupling. The second DFS 230 was connected to the first by means of a medium-length towline. The cable was attached to the braking parachute coupling in the tail of the first glider. (Griehl)

DFS 203

In 1940 there were plans to create a research aircraft from two DFS 230s, with the two fuselages joined by an instrumented wing, which was to be variable in shape and angle of incidence. According to a DFS report entitled "Wind Tunnel Tests on the Model of the Twin-Fuselage DFS 203," a 1/20 scale model was tested in the DFS 2-meter free stream wind tunnel from 3/10/1942, with interruptions during the period 27/8 to 16/12/1940. The purpose of the tests was to determine to what degree the instrumented wing was affected by the fuselages and outer wings and to determine the longitudinal and lateral stability of the aircraft created by combining two normal transport glider (DFS 230) fuselages. In addition to the model illustrated here, there was also one with a length of 605 mm. Both could be fitted with the two types of horizontal tails illustrated here.

This twin predated the He 111 Z and may have influenced the design of the latter. It is not known if the DFS 203 was built, but the DFS later worked on a similar project for higher airspeed, the DFS 332.

Drawing of the wind tunnel model. The measurements apply to the model, which was 1/20 the size of the planned full-size aircraft. (Mankau)

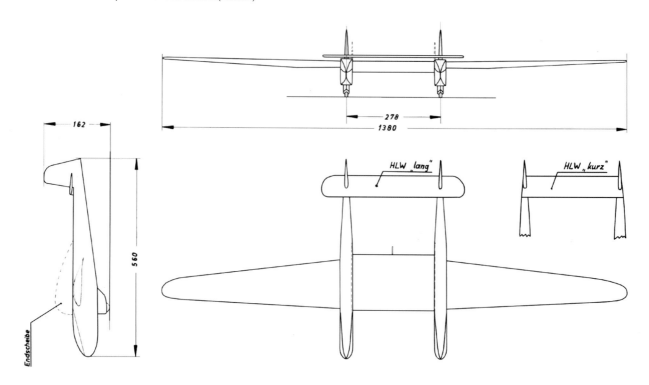

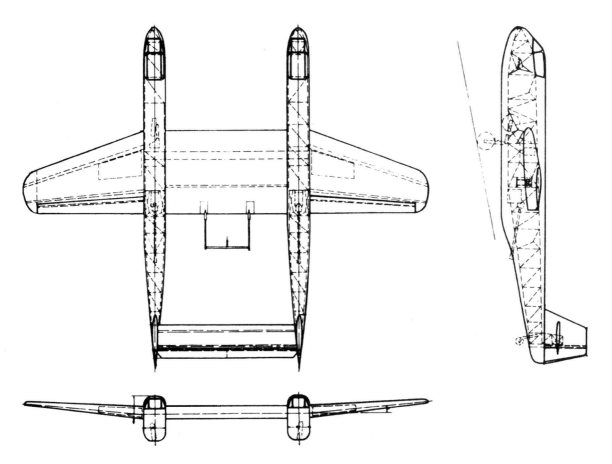

The DFS 332, a high-speed research aircraft. (Mankau)

Wind tunnel model of the DFS 203

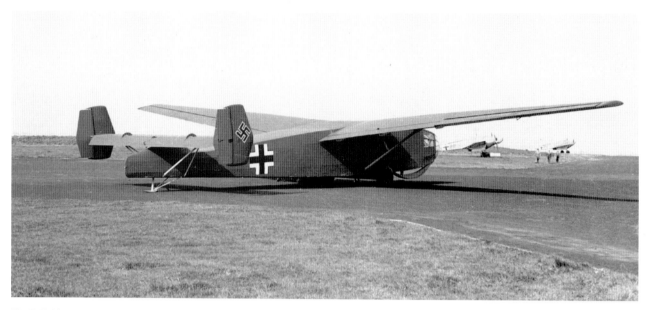

The DFS 331 V1 with no code and two bracing struts beneath each side of the horizontal tail. (German Museum)

The DFS 331 V1 with code and three struts under each side of the tailplane. The forward skids were faired (presumably for tests to determine a possible increase in speed). The mainplane was braced by struts which were usually faired. (Krieg)

DFS 331 V1 to V3

Purpose: transport aircraft for troops and equipment

Identifying Features: jettisonable undercarriage

The General Staff ordered the development of a larger transport glider even before the successful capture of Fort Eben Emael in Belgium on 10/5/1940, for it was mentioned at meetings at the RLM in May 1940 and five prototypes were under construction by the Gothaer Waggonfabrik in June. These were the parallel designs DFS 331 and Go 242. As the DFS was not set up for the construction of such a glider, the RLM had contracted Gothaer Waggonfabrik to build groups of prototypes. The DFS sent designer Jakobs and six colleagues to Gotha to develop the DFS 331. According

to their own statements, the DFS people were already upset when they left Gotha after discovering that their Gotha colleagues were carrying out industrial espionage by night. It was said that differences arose between Jakobs, designer of the DFS 331, and Laiber, who was responsible for the Go 242.

The size of the gliders was chosen so that they could be towed by the Ju 52 or a He 111 powered by the Jumo 211 or DB 601. According to plans in September 1940, three prototypes of the DFS 331 and two of the Go 242 were to be completed in the months September to November. The DFS 331 V1 flew for the first time on 30/9/1940 at the *Luftwaffe* airfield in Gotha. According to the C-Amts Program, the V2 and V3 were still under construction at the beginning of November. As testing was successful,

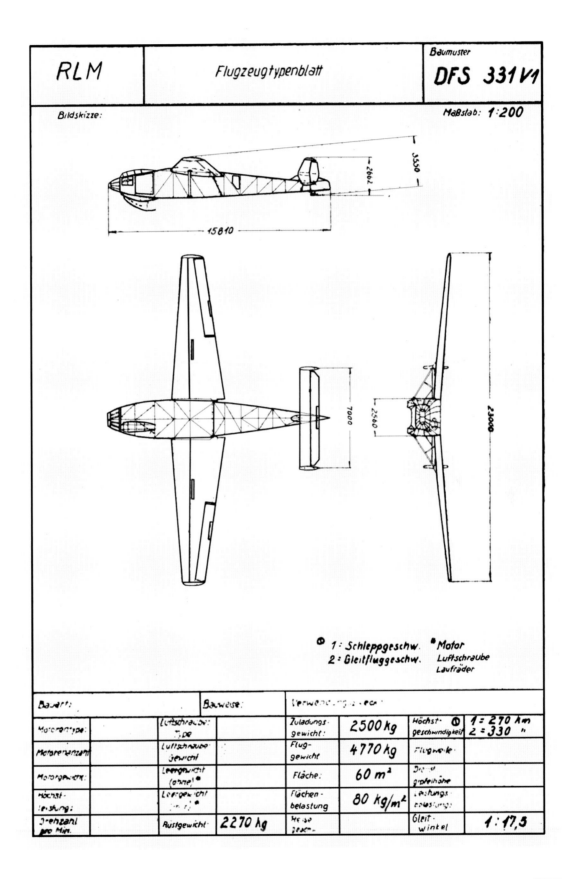

RLM	Flugzeugtypenblatt	Baumuster DFS 331 V1

Bildskizze: Maßstab: 1:200

① 1 : Schleppgeschw.   **"** Motor
      2 : Gleitfluggeschw.   Luftschraube
                     Laufräder

Bauart:		Bauweise:	Verwendungszweck:			
Motorentype:		Luftschraube Type		Zuladungs-gewicht:	2500 kg	Höchst-geschwindigkeit ①	1 = 270 km 2 = 330 "
Motorenanzahl		Luftschraube gewicht		Flug-gewicht	4770 kg	Flugwerk:	
Motorgewicht:		Leergewicht (ohne) "		Fläche:	60 m²	Dienst-gipfelhöhe	
Höchst-leistung:		Leergewicht (mit) "		Flächen-belastung	80 kg/m²	Leistungs-belastung:	
Drehzahl pro Min.		Rüstgewicht	2270 kg	Reise-gesch.		Gleit-winkel	1 : 17,5

Here the DFS 331 V1 has an incomplete code and—as in the previous photo—three bracing struts under each side of the tailplane and unfaired struts between the wing and fuselage. For reasons unknown, the rear part of the letter K in the code is missing. (Krieg)

DFS 331 V1 with incomplete code and three bracing struts. The front part of the K is missing because of the addition of an extra door. The wing struts are faired. (German Museum)

the RLM issued a contract to the Erfurt Repair Works (REWE) for the construction of 20 Zero-Series (pre-production) aircraft in the period January to May 1941. On 19/1/1941 *Flugkapitän* Franke from Rechlin test-flew the DFS 331 V1 at Gotha and was enthusiastic about its handling characteristics. The REWE was, however, not in a position, or was unwilling to complete the contract. It only wanted to assemble the pre-production aircraft and gave the job of building components to subcontractors. These had no experience in building aircraft, however, and moreover, the REWE did not pass on the design drawings produced by the DFS. As a result of this, and changes made by the contracting agency (for example, dual controls and armor), the DFS 331 pre-production series fell so far behind that the RLM chose the Go 242, by then completed, and on 24/3/1941 ordered the REWE to cease all work on the DFS 331. The DFS 331 V1 had been ferried to the DFS in Darmstadt and there underwent extensive and successful testing. The DFS 331 V2 was sent to the DFS— also in February—after construction by GWF had reached the 80% complete point. Assembly of the aircraft was completed there, but I do not know what happened to it after cancellation of the program. On 1/2/1941 the V3 was not yet complete and its subsequent fate is uncertain. All of its components were, however, complete when the type was cancelled.

The DFS 331 did not fail because of technical or design flaws, but rather because of the REWE's incompetence or unwillingness.

The DFS 331 V1 can be recognized by its overall dark (RLM 70?) finish, while the V2, of which only a single photo taken from the front is known, had pale blue undersides. In the course of development the DFS 331 V1 underwent several modifications. The first photos show it in camouflage and with *Balkenkreuze* (wing and fuselage crosses) but with no code letters. At that stage it had two bracing struts on each side from the fuselage to the horizontal tail. The modifications saw the number of struts increased to three on each side.

The nose of the DFS 331 was extensively glazed. (Petrick)

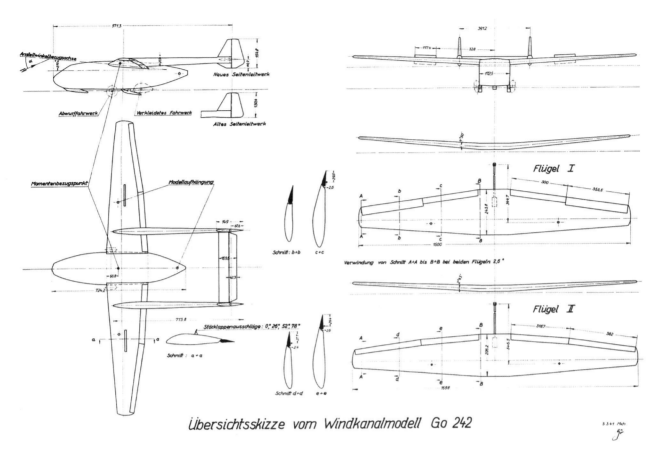

Drawing of the Go 242 wind tunnel model. (Aviation Research Institute)

Go 242

Go 242 Wind Tunnel Models

On 10/8/1940 the Gothaer Waggonfabrik assigned the Hermann Göring Aviation Research Institute to carry out wind tunnel measurements on a model of the Go 242. The tests were conducted in the period from October 1940 to February 1941 and documented in a report dated 30/4/1941.

Go 242 V1 to V3

Development of the Go 242 began in parallel with that of the DFS 331. In the beginning it looked as though, after its experience with the DFS 230, the RLM favored the larger glider from DFS. Gotha was supposed to build three prototypes of the DFS 331 and only two of the Go 242, and they were even ordered later. The first prototype, the Go 242 V1, flew on 9/11/1941, or more than one month after the DFS 331 V1. After company trials at Gotha, in January 1942 the V1 was tested by

the *E-Stelle* at Rechlin. The decisive test flights took place on 21/1/1942. These tests were so successful that, at the beginning of February 1942, the RLM decided to order production of the Go 242 beyond the pre-production series. The Go 242 V1 returned to Gotha in February. There it was supposed to be fitted with a motor (probably an As 10 in the nose). The Go 242 V2 was completed in January 1942 and sent to Rechlin for further testing. During trials at Rechlin the weak design of the tail booms and empennage became apparent when the tail booms broke off during a landing and the empennage failed during high-speed trials. The latter incident resulted in the death of a crewman and the loss of the aircraft. Meanwhile, the RLM had ordered the Go 242 V3, which was ready to fly in February 1942. In March 1942 the Go 242 V1 and V3 underwent service trials with the air landing wing (*Luftlandegeschwader*) in Hildesheim. I have found no information as to the fate of the prototypes after March 1941.

Go 242 A-0 after landing with extended nose skid. (Nowarra)

Slide from the data sheet for the aircraft type Go 242 A-0. VS+OQ was probably the last of the 17 Go 242 A-0 pre-production machines. (Type Sheet)

Go 242 A-0

Purpose: transport aircraft for troops and equipment

Identifying Features: jettisonable undercarriage for takeoff, three skids (forward one retractable), small tail booms

According to the *C-Amts* Program of 1/11/1940, 20 Go 242 pre-production aircraft were to be built in Gotha. At that time the V1 and V2 were not yet completed. On 2/11 GWF offered to build an initial series of 10 pre-production machines using primitive means. Jigs were planned for the next ten pre-production machines, and these would be used for subsequent production aircraft. Testing of the DFS 331 and Go 242 in January 1941 obviously proceeded to the general satisfaction of all parties, but the GWF had made ground against the DFS, as its industrial capacity put it in a position to complete the 20 pre-production aircraft on time. The exact fate of the 20 machines is not known. They were most probably used for trials. Referring to original sources, Pawlas [2] writes only 17 Go 242 A-0 were built. That fits, for the two aircraft with the *Werknummer* 00018 and 00019 are known to have been the Go 244 V1 and V2, and 00020 probably the Go 244 V3. Werk.Nr. 00010 was also later converted into a Go 244 and tested at Rechlin. 00010 had the aircraft code VC+OQ and 00018 VC+OR. It is therefore reasonable to assume that the 20 Go 242 A-0s and the Go 244s converted from them bore the codes VC+OA to VC+OT.

Go 242 A-0 after landing with extended nose skid. (Nowarra)

In the cockpits of the prototypes the control cables were uncovered. (Luftwissen)

In the prototypes the control rods were also exposed on the left side behind the pilot. Under the right pilot's seat is the prone position for the gunner manning the C-1 gun position. At the front of the cargo compartment are weight sacks used to trim the empty aircraft. (Luftwissen)

Go 242 A-1

Purpose: combat glider

Identifying Features: jettisonable undercarriage for takeoff, 875 x 320 mm or 950 x 350 mm balloon tires, three skids, 6-ton coupling in nose

After the successful trials on 21/1/1942 a contract was issued for the Go 242 A-1 production version, which was to be built by Gothaer Waggonfabrik, AGO, and especially Hartmann until about mid-1943. Reference was made to the in-flight failure of the tail booms on one of the prototypes. GWF strengthened the tail booms of the Go 242 A-1 by increasing their depth. I am unaware of any other significant differences between the Go 242 A-1 and the A-0.

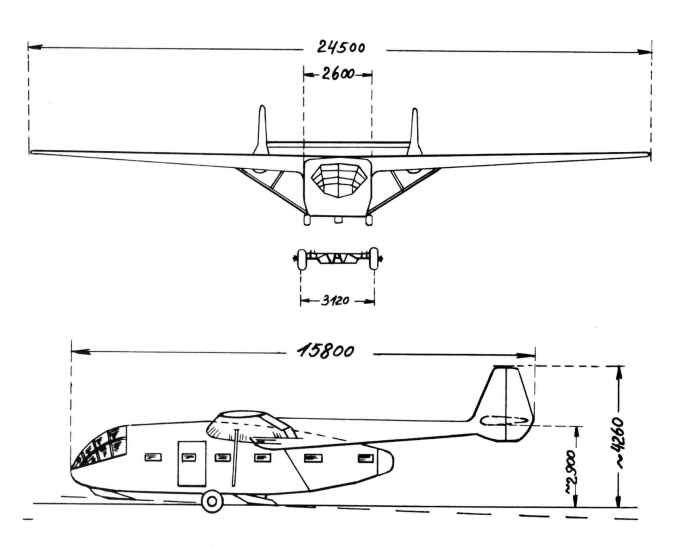

General arrangement drawing of the Go 242 A-1. (Gothaer Waggonfabrik)

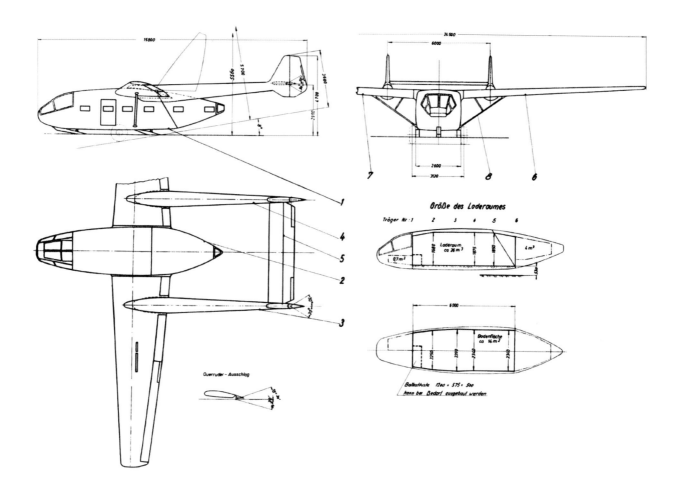

This Gothaer Waggonfabrik drawing depicts the Go 242 A-1. The most important dimensions and details also apply to all other variants, however. The differences are shown in the applicable drawings. (Gothaer Waggonfabrik)

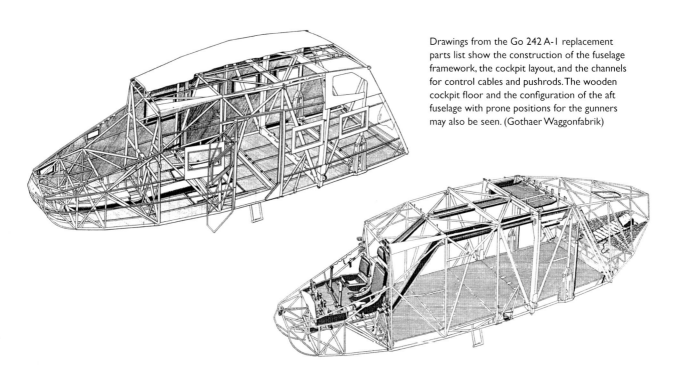

Drawings from the Go 242 A-1 replacement parts list show the construction of the fuselage framework, the cockpit layout, and the channels for control cables and pushrods. The wooden cockpit floor and the configuration of the aft fuselage with prone positions for the gunners may also be seen. (Gothaer Waggonfabrik)

The instrument panel could be swung to the right when the second pilot took control of the aircraft. He did so by placing the tip of his foot in the hemisphere-shaped receptacle beneath the instrument cluster. (Mankau)

There was often an armor plate in front of the first pilot. He had a normal control column and yoke with which to fly the aircraft. The second pilot, on the other hand, had only a telescoping control stick, in order to provide him with the necessary freedom of movement when firing from the hatch in the roof of the canopy. (JET & PROP)

The drawings in the replacement parts list show the mat on which the nose gunner lay and the jettisonable undercarriage. The latter was used on the prototypes and the A-series. 875 x 320 mm balloon tires were initially used. 950 x 320 tires were adopted later, increasing payload by 300 kg. (Gothaer Waggonfabrik)

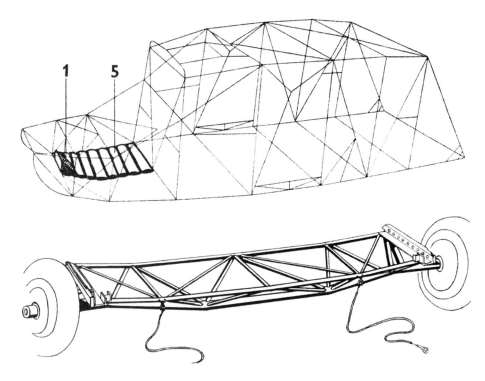

The interior of an empty Go 242 A 1. The sand box, for ballast when the aircraft was flown empty, and the channels for the control cables and pushrods may be seen. (Nidree)

German Gliders in World War II

Photographs of the Go 242 A-1 show a wide variety of camouflage schemes and code styles. (Bundesarchiv Koblenz 10 II-641-4549-15)

(Bundesarchiv Koblenz 10 II-641-4547-36)

Go 242 A-2

Purpose: combat glider

Identifying Features: jettisonable undercarriage, 875 x 320 mm or 950 x 350 balloon tires, double tow coupling = 10 ton forward and 6 ton behind (+50 kg), use of braking parachute possible

In May 1942 the Go 242 A-2 was planned as a variant of the Go 242 employing mixed construction. I do not know exactly what was meant by this, as the Go 242 was a mixed construction design anyway. In any event the plan was abandoned, making the designation available for other use.

The Me 321 large transport glider was originally supposed to be towed by three twin-engined aircraft—preferably the He 111. This so-called *Troikaschlepp* proved extremely dangerous, however, and the RLM had Heinkel develop the He 111 Z, essentially two He 111 H-6 bombers joined by a new wing center-section, which was capable of towing the Me 321 by itself. The He 111 Z V1 was tested successfully in Bavaria in the second half of May 1942, and Heinkel was issued a contract to build a total of ten as quickly as possible. At that time there were still about 110 Me 321s. Most were delivered in the second half of 1942. The cost of using the Me 321 was so great, however, that it was proposed that the He 111 Z also be used to tow the Go 242. The He 111 Z had more than enough power to tow the Go 242, and so it was proposed that it tow two at a time. For safety reasons it was undesirable to tow the two gliders side by side, but to place them one behind the other the Go 242 A-1 had to be modified. In order to attach the gliders one behind the other, it first needed a coupling in the nose that was strong enough to tow both gliders, specifically a ten-ton coupling. Then a second coupling (six-ton coupling) had to be installed beneath the tail hatch. The second coupling could also be used to attach the braking parachute that had since been developed. The designation Go 242 A-2 was assigned to differentiate the modified Go 242 from the original version. Available documents show that the existing Go 242 A-1s were retrofitted with the braking parachute. It is likely that those machines were also modified for double towing. In any case, there is no evidence that A-2 series aircraft were new-build machines. The first operational use of the He 111 Z with two Go 242s took place on 11/2/1943 by *I./Luftlandegeschwader 2*. The last probably took place in July 1944.

I have only found the designation He 111 Z in the documents in the Heinkel Archive. For a short time in May 1942, consideration was given to a He 111 Z-2 long-range bomber. If this had been realized, the glider tug would surely have been renamed He 111 Z-1, but as the long-range bomber never got off the drawing board, the designation remained He 111 Z.

Left: until mid-1943 it was standard practice for the RLM to issue serial numbers (Werknummern) and manufacturer's codes (Stammkennzeichen) sequentially and in blocks. It is therefore not unusual that the three aircraft depicted here have manufacturer's codes from the block DL+DA to DL+DZ. (Kössler / Petrick / Bundesarchiv Koblenz 10 II-561-1138-21)

Here a Go 242 with an aft fuselage towline coupling is transported by road. (Schlaug)

A Go 242 A-2 and an A-1 under tow, as seen from the left fuselage of a He 111 Z. (ECPA)

A Go 242 A-2, and behind it a Go 242 A-1, ready for takeoff. (Schlaug)

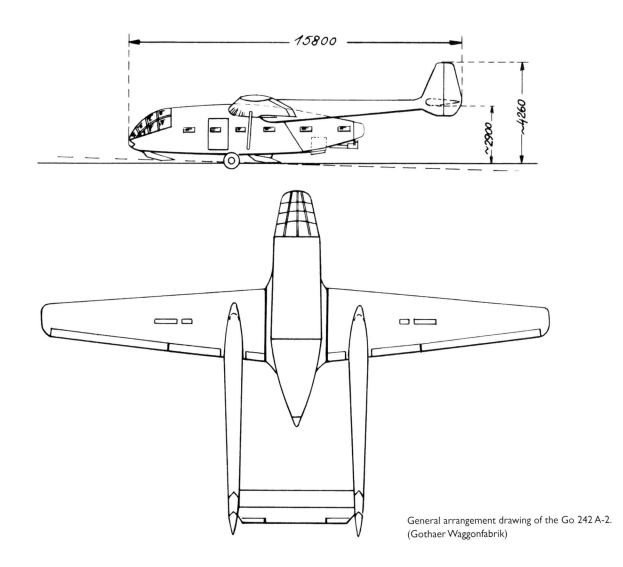

General arrangement drawing of the Go 242 A-2.
(Gothaer Waggonfabrik)

Visible beneath the rear fuselage of this Go 242 A-2 is the second towline coupling and the attached braking parachute cable. The nose skid is equipped with a retractable braking spur. (Petrick)

Go 242 B-1

Purpose: transport glider

Identifying Features: nosewheel, fixed undercarriage with one-piece axle, tire size 950 x 350 mm, single brake, 6-ton coupling in the nose

It was important for a combat glider to able to stop as quickly as possible after landing. For this reason the glider was designed to take off from a jettisonable undercarriage and land on skids. For pure transport duties, however, it made more sense to land on a wheeled undercarriage, for then it could take off again as soon as it was unloaded. If the undercarriage was not jettisoned the Go 242 A-1 could land on wheels, but without brakes the landing roll was long. As the requirement for pure transport gliders was relatively great, Gothaer Waggonfabrik developed a tricycle undercarriage with the braked mainwheels on a single axle. If necessary, the axle undercarriage could also be jettisoned.

Production of the Go 242 B-1 variant with its axle undercarriage began at about the same time as the Go 244 B-1 interim transport, which required such an undercarriage anyway. With production increasingly shifting to the Go 244 by mid-1942, the number of Go 242 B-1s produced was initially small. Not until the Go 244 B-1 was halted and even converted back into a transport glider were further Go 242 B-1s built. According to the conversion delivery plan of 21/12/1943, 184 Go 244 B-1s were converted back into Go 242 A-1s.

It seems more probable to me that the aircraft were converted into Go 242 B-1s, but that is unproven.

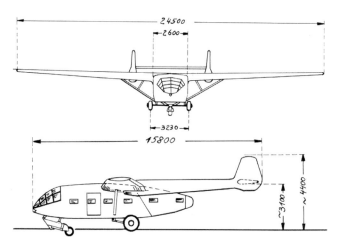

General arrangement drawing of the Go 242 B-1 (Gothaer Waggonfabrik)

This may have been an early, jettisonable version of the Go 242's tricycle undercarriage. (Luftwissen)

The camouflage schemes worn by the Go 242 B-1 were just as varied as those of the A series. (Griehl / Nidree / German Museum)

The Go 242 B-1 had two machine-gun mounts above the second pilot's seat. (IWM)

The undercarriage of the Go 242 B-1 was similar to that of the Go 244 B-1. (German Museum)

Go 242 B-2

Purpose: transport glider

Identifying Features: like the B-1, but with: outrigger undercarriage with larger shock struts recessed in the fuselage sides, wheel size 935 x 345 with dual brakes (+100 kg), double tow coupling = 10 t forward and 6 t aft

To allow a 250 kg increase in payload at the same maximum allowable weight, part of the Go 242 B-2 series was built with a weaker and thus lighter floor.

As the undercarriage of the Go 242 B-1 was unsatisfactory, its inadequate load-bearing capacity first becoming apparent in the Go 244 B-1, GWF saw itself forced to develop an outrigger undercarriage for the Go 244. At first the shock struts were completely outside

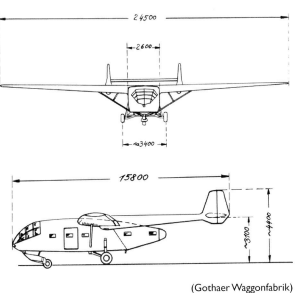

(Gothaer Waggonfabrik)

the fuselage and the bracing struts were attached to the lower corners of the fuselage. This resulted in an unacceptable increase in drag, leading GWF to modify the outrigger undercarriage, fitting smaller wheels and recessing the shock struts in the fuselage sides. This resulted in acceptable drag and improved taxiing characteristics compared to the axle undercarriage. The outrigger undercarriage was prepared for production of the Go 244 B-2, but when this failed to materialize the outrigger undercarriage flowed into production of the Go 242 B-2. With 256 examples built, it was the second most numerous variant after the Go 242 A-1. According to available records, the Go 242 B-2 was built from the late summer of 1943 until production of the Go 242 ended in the summer of 1944, and all were new-build aircraft.

Few photos of the Go 242 B-2 are known. The main undercarriage shock struts were recessed in the fuselage sides. (Propaganda Service Photo)

The absence of forward windows in the tail hatch of this captured machine is suggestive of the B-3 series. The aircraft also has a 6-ton towline coupling for attaching a second glider. (Mankau)

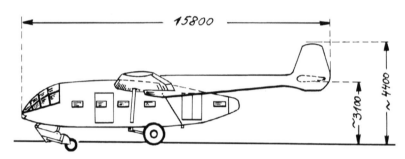

(Gothaer Waggonfabrik)

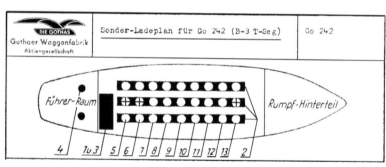

Section of the Go 242 B-3 loading plan. The numbers "1" and "3" stand for the ballast box (36 kg) and ballast (420 kg). The weight of the bench seat "2" was 244 kg. The two pilots "4" and the paratrooper positions "5" to "13" were each allocated 100 kg. Positions 5, 6, and 13 on the center bench seat were not used during exercises, and operationally they were only occupied when the aircraft took off from a concrete runway. (Gothaer Waggonfabrik)

Go 242 B-3

Purpose: transport glider

Identifying Features: like the B-1, but with: rear fuselage modified for dropping of parachute troops (+ 50 kg), three rows of seats (+ 244 kg), double tow installation with 10 t coupling forward (+ 50 kg)

The *Luftwaffe* employed two types of airborne troops at the beginning of the war: the paratroopers and soldiers brought to the ground by gliders. Later it was decided to also drop parachute troops from gliders. This was perhaps not the original intention, for the paratrooper equipment was initially installed in the motorized Go 244 B-3, a few examples of which were delivered to the *Luftwaffe*. There were also a number of Go 244 B-3s at various stages of construction. When the Go 244 was converted back into the Go 242, all Go 244 B-3s were fitted with paratrooper equipment and thus became Go 242 B-3s. The conversion delivery plan of 21/12/1943 offered by Pawlas indicates that 95 aircraft were only fitted with paratrooper equipment during conversion. Whether this is true and what they intended to do with the paratrooper gliders, I cannot say. It is possible that the doors in the aft fuselage were not used for dropping parachute troops at all, but for the dropping of cargo. This often happened in areas where landing and takeoff were not possible. It seems certain, however, that the Go 242 B-3 variant was solely the product of conversion from the Go 244, and according to the quoted conversion delivery plan 20 aircraft were converted by Gotha and 95 by Letov.

Three bench seats of this type were installed in the Go 242 B-3. (Nidree)

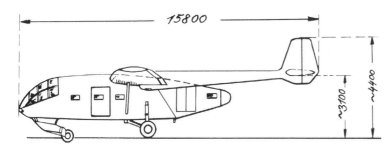

Go 242 B-4 (Gothaer Waggonfabrik)

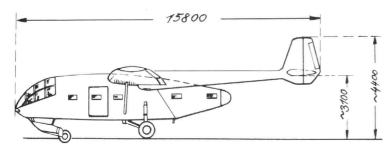

Go 242 B-5 (Gothaer Waggonfabrik)

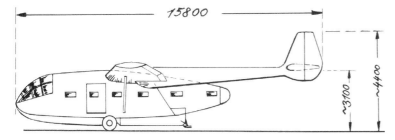

Go 242 C-1 (Gothaer Waggonfabrik)

Go 242 B-4

Purpose: transport glider

Identifying Features: like the B-2 with lighter floor, but also: paratrooper equipment in aft fuselage (+ 50 kg), three rows of seats (+ 244 kg)

The Go 242 B-4 variant appears in several GWF documents, but there is no indication that the type was actually built. As the Go 244 B-2—and thus the Go 244 B-4 paratrooper version as well—was dropped, there was no corresponding retro-conversion, and according to the records the B-2 was the only other variant of the Go 242 to be built.

Go 242 B-5

Purpose: transport glider

Identifying Features: like the B-2, dual control columns with internally-balanced rudders, wooden floor light version

The dual control columns and internally-balanced rudders were measures intended to improve the Go 244's single-engine handling (see Go 244 B-5 and C-2). It is probable that a few Go 244 B-5s (11) were so equipped, and when these were retro-converted the result was the Go 242 B-5. This is not confirmed. The glider did not need these modifications, and the only new gliders being built were B-2s.

Go 242 C-1

Purpose: transport glider (marine) for special operations

Identifying Features: fuselage floor designed as a float, takeoff from jettisonable undercarriage, light aft fuselage, two auxiliary floats on the wings, empty weight 3,500 kg. Payload 3,020 to 3,300 kg.

Several authors have linked the Go 242 C-1 with the attack on the British fleet in Scapa Flow that was allegedly planned in 1944. The gliders were supposed to have delivered Italian assault boats to the target area. After landing on the water the light aft section of the fuselage was to be jettisoned, allowing the assault boats to leave the gliders and carry out the attack. It is confirmed that Göring ordered an operation involving the Go 242 (Water) (see 21/7/1944). The operation would only require the float fuselage to support the Go 242 for a short time, and no consideration was given to taking off again. On 11/4/1944 GWF still believed that 66 Go 242 C-1s were required. On 28/4 the number was just 43, to be built by Hartwig and diverted from B-2 production. On 1/7/1944, however, the order was issued for production of the Go 242 to run down, and as revealed by the *C-Amts* monthly reports from 1944 and the Quartermaster-General's records of 4/12/1944, just 151 Go 242 B-2s were built and delivered in 1944. The Go 242 C-1 was therefore built as a prototype or was created by conversion. The Gothaer Waggonfabrik believed that use of the Go 242 C-1 was only possible using the lift-tow method.

With two MG 34s firing forward, two to the rear, and two from each side, the Go 242 was capable of all-round defense. The machine-guns were not normally carried, however. (Gothaer Waggonfabrik)

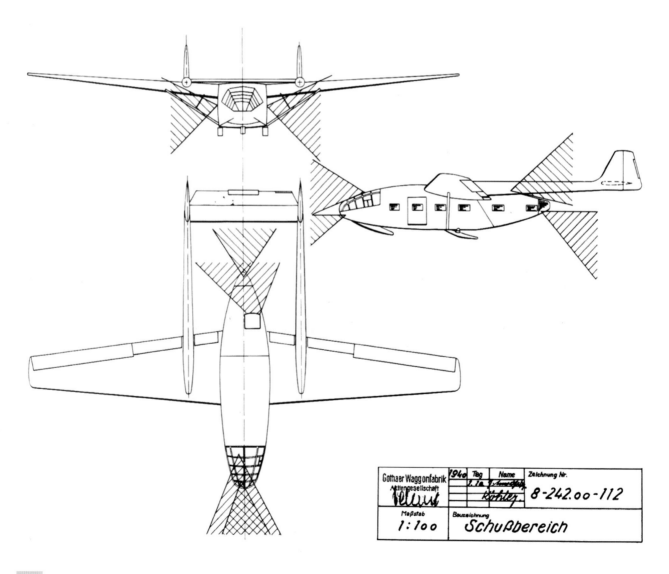

The two aft machine-guns and one side-mounted weapon are visible on this Go 242. (Bundesarchiv Koblenz 10 11-641-4546-22)

While provision was made for the gun position under the cockpit floor, as a rule it was not used. The position was too dangerous, especially in an assault landing. (Petrick)

Go 242: Armament

From the start of development, it was anticipated that eight mounts for MG 34 machine-guns should be installed in the Go 242. Only the forward upper machine-gun would be operated by a member of the crew, the rest being served by soldiers being transported in the aircraft. As plenty of MG 15s were available, these were often used instead of the MG 34.

Go 242: Skis

In order to maintain operational readiness, even in heavy snow, in 1941 the General Staff decided that it made sense to equip a small number of aircraft with skis. On 17/7/1941 30 sets of skis were ordered for each of the Go 242 and Go 244, for use in the winter of 1941/42. The skis were subsequently developed, and in the winter of 1941/42 were tested at the Dorpat testing establishment behind a He 111 H-6 (also on skis). The maximum payload of the ski-equipped Go 242 was 2,500 kg. There were no restrictions on the use of the ski-equipped Go 242. As the Go 244 was underpowered as it was, the use of skis was out of the question. There are a few photos taken during development and testing, but I have never seen any operational photos.

Go 242: Short Takeoff Rockets

On 12/6/1942 the *Luftwaffe* experimental station at Peenemünde-West reported on function testing of Go 242 Werk.Nr. 24 (TD+IN) with takeoff-assist rockets (2 x Walter RI 202 b each producing 500 kg of thrust for 30 sec = 1,000 kg for 30 sec; and 4 x Rheinmetall

The side-mounted machine-guns were operated by the soldiers. (Bundesarchiv Koblenz 10 11-641-4546-15)

R I 502 each producing 500 kg of thrust for 24 sec = 2,000 kg for 24 sec). Both types were initially used in static tests and then in flight. The Walter devices were found to be acceptable in terms of flight characteristics, the only complaint being the poor positioning of the ignition handle. Nevertheless, the experimental station rejected their use with the Go 242, for while takeoff distance was reduced, rate of climb to parachute release

A number of Go 242s featured two mounts for MG 15 machine-guns above the cockpit. As there was just one opening in the roof, however, the second pilot could only operate one machine-gun. An MG 15 could also be mounted above the pilot's seat. (Mathiesen)

The Go 242 TD+IN was tested with various add-ons, here with the undercarriage of the Go 242 B-1 with skis. (E-Stelle Rechlin)

The E-Stelle Rechlin tested the skis at Dorpat using TE+DU. (E-Stelle Rechlin)

The skis were installed in place of the wheels. (E-Stelle Rechlin)

altitude—which was already marginal—was further reduced. The poor climbing performance also made it impossible to increase the glider's payload.

The Rheinmetall powder takeoff-assist rockets were jettisoned by parachute as soon as they had burnt out. There was some blistering of the aft fuselage, but this was repairable. Most of the rockets were also reusable. They also delivered an acceptable reduction in takeoff roll and did not impair climbing performance, therefore, the experimental station found them sensible. At the time of the trials, however, the Rheinmetall rockets were still unreliable and were out of the question for operational use. Sometimes the rockets failed to ignite, and sometimes the heads blew off, allowing burning gases to escape the front of the rocket.

Pending availability of the more reliable Rheinmetall R I 502 powder rockets, the experimental station recommended the use of Walter devices on the He 111 H-6 glider tug. Simultaneous use of the Walter units on the He 111 and the Go 242 did not appear justified.

Arrangement of the takeoff-assist rocket control panel: at the front is the safety switch; AKS-M for Walter rockets; and four AKS-M 7 for igniting the Walter rockets individually. (E-Stelle Rechlin)

To date I have not discovered any photos or reports to confirm the use of takeoff aids with the Go 242 apart from these trials.

Go 242 with Walter R I 202 b takeoff-assist rockets. Each produced 500 kg of thrust for 30 seconds. (E-Stelle Rechlin)

Go 242 with Rheinmetall R I 502 rockets (anchored for static tests). (E-Stelle Rechlin)

The two photos below depict Go 242s taking off with the aid of R I 202 b rockets and R I 502 units. E-Stelle Rechlin)

Me 321 Braking Parachute

Powilleit [31] reported that the Me 321 had a braking parachute in the tail box which he employed when landing on the undercarriage to avoid overrunning the airfield. I have not seen any photos of a Me 321 with a deployed parachute.

Installing the box housing the braking parachute. (Zeppelin Company)

During precision landings, the parachute was not fully opened until the glider touched down, in order to shorten the stopping distance. The same applied to normal landings when the parachute was used to shorten the stopping distance. (Krieg)

The Go 242's maximum allowable speed was 290 kph. The maximum speed for opening the parachute was 230 kph, but the preferred speed was 140 to 180 kph. The dive angle could vary between 20° and 45°. Dive speed was 190 to 280 kph. At about 300 meters above the ground the dive angle was reduced to 20° to 25°. The pilot began flaring for landing at about 20 meters above the ground. (Krieg)

Tow Planes for the Go 242

Ju 52

The Ju 52 was the first tow plane employed for the Go 242 A-1 and was soon replaced by the He 111. (Bundesarchiv Koblenz 10 11-622-3340-07)

Ju 52 with Go 242 over the Mediterranean. (Bundesarchiv Koblenz 10 11-434-0949-25)

Lacking a wheeled undercarriage, early versions of the Go 242 could not be flown home immediately after unloading. (Nowarra)

View of the Ju 52 tow plane from the cockpit of a Go 242. ((JET & PROP)

The Go 242 A-1 flew above the He 111. (Bundesarchiv Koblenz 10 11-641-4547-25)

The He 111 was the most frequently used tow plane for the Go 242. These three He 111s are the tugs for the Go 242s on Page 197. (Bundesarchiv Koblenz 10 11-641-4548-24)

A He III glider tug does an engine run-up in preparation for takeoff from a Russian airfield. (Bundesarchiv Koblenz 10 II-331-3026-01A)

The same He III from the rear. (Bundesarchiv Koblenz 10 II-331-3026-06A)

German Gliders in World War II

(Radinger)

(ECPA)

The He 111 Z was originally developed to tow the Me 321, but it was also capable of towing the Go 242. As one glider barely taxed the five-engined machine, the Go 242 A-2 was developed so that another Go 242 could be attached. (Mankau)

The He 177 / Go 242 combination was tested by the DFS, but only for the purpose of a special operation. (Schmitt)

Go 244

GWF began development of a powered version of the Go 242 in September 1940, even before the glider had made its first flight. At first the idea was to install a relatively small motor (Argus As 10 C) in the fuselage nose to significantly extend gliding distance and to enable the glider to fly home with a crew of two and 170 kg of fuel. In February 1941 it was decided to convert the Go 242 V1 into an engine test-bed; however, this never came to pass. Performance calculations had shown that the desired improvements could not be achieved with the central motor. The return flight, in particular, was impossible with the small engine. This variant thus disappeared from planning.

GWF subsequently turned to another solution. It was a relatively simple matter to install engines in front of the tail booms, which promised to turn the glider into a cheap and simple interim transport. The Ju 52 was certainly a successful transport aircraft, but it used a great deal of aluminum, which was more urgently needed for fighters and bombers. A powered version of the Go 242, which was made of steel tube, linen, and plywood, appeared to make possible an additional transport aircraft without placing any great strain on the aviation industry. The RLM promised further relief by using French-built motors (Gnôme et Rhône 14 M), propellers (Gnôme et Rhône and Ratier), and instruments. Russian power plants were also considered as an alternative. The first two prototypes of the powered Go 242, later renamed Go 244, flew in the spring of 1941. Testing at the *E-Stelle* Rechlin began in January 1942, and production by Gotha began at the same time. The results of the 100-hour trials, concluded at the beginning of February 1942, were encouraging, although some improvements were demanded. Weak points were poor single-engine handling and inadequate range and payload, all caused by insufficiently powerful engines, and the poor taxiing characteristics of the axle undercarriage adopted from the Go 242 B-1. It was originally hoped that these shortcomings could be addressed, and an initial batch of 450 machines was ordered with the option for further production. The first series was called the Go 244 B-1 and was characterized by its axle undercarriage. The *E-Stelle* Rechlin only approved the Go 244 B-1 for a payload of 1.2 tons and limited equipment. Gotha was already working on a stronger outrigger undercarriage in April 1942, which was to lead to the Go 244 B-2 variant. Also in development were the Go 244 C-1 and C-2, equivalent to the B-1 and B-2 but with four-blade fixed-pitch wooden propellers instead of three-blade variable-pitch metal propellers. The Go 244 was also intended for use as a transport for parachute troops. To this end doors and jump equipment were installed in the aft fuselage. These modifications resulted in the Go 244 B-3 (based on the Go 244 B-1) and were planned for the Go 244 B-4 (based on the B-2). The pilots of *Kampfgruppe* z.b.V. 106 began retraining on the Go 244 B-1 at Hagenow in April 1942, and on 19 June the Go 244 was released for frontline use. At that time Messerschmitt was having serious problems with the Me 210, which Gotha was supposed to build under license. The RLM ordered GWF to shift production capacity from the Me 210 to the Go 244, and for a time hoped that the Go 244 could replace the Go 242 entirely. In mid-1944 production concentrated almost exclusively on the Go 244. By 1/7/1942, 99 Go 244s had been delivered to the *Luftwaffe* with another 351 on order and in production.

At the end of June 1942, K.G.z.b.V. 106 moved to Kirovograd and operated from there with an average strength of 34 Go 244 B-1s. The unit equipped the Go 244 with radios and armament, causing gross weight to rise. It also flew with higher than authorized payloads. Instead of a gross weight of 6.8 tons, the aircraft were generally flown at a gross weight in excess of 8 tons. This overstressed both the undercarriage and engines, and the result was a series of accidents—some serious—and forced landings. The Air Armaments Minister became aware of the poor results at the front. As a result, at the beginning of August 1942 he ordered production of the Go 244 limited to the initial batch of 450, which was to be completed by May 1943. 308 of the planned 450 Go 244s had been completed by 1/10/1942. Production of the type was halted, and GWF instructed to allocate all resources to production of the Bf 110.

The sturdier outrigger undercarriage of the Go 244 B-2 increased drag, resulting in a deterioration in performance; consequently, it was not possible to increase the payload as had been hoped. The performance of the two variants with wooden propellers was even poorer because of their reduced effectiveness. These variants were not delivered to the *Luftwaffe*, and on 2/11/1942 the Air Armaments Minister halted all production of the Go 244. The Ju 352 had been chosen to replace the Go 244 as an interim transport, and the Go 244 was to be retro-converted into the Go 242, which in fact took place from November 1942 into 1943. Although production was halted, GWF continued development of the Go 244 into February 1943. That month three improved Go 244s were handed over to the testing establishments. That spring a Go 244 E-1 with BMW 132 Z motors was also tested at Gotha and Rechlin. Nothing is known of the results of these tests, but it is certain that production was not resumed, nor were existing Go 244s modified to the new standard.

Type Sheets Go 244/917, 918, and 919 TB-Fl were produced for the Go 244, and authors Pawlas [2] and Engel [29] used these to compile their variant summaries. I have not seen these type sheets, therefore, I can only cite and make reference to them.

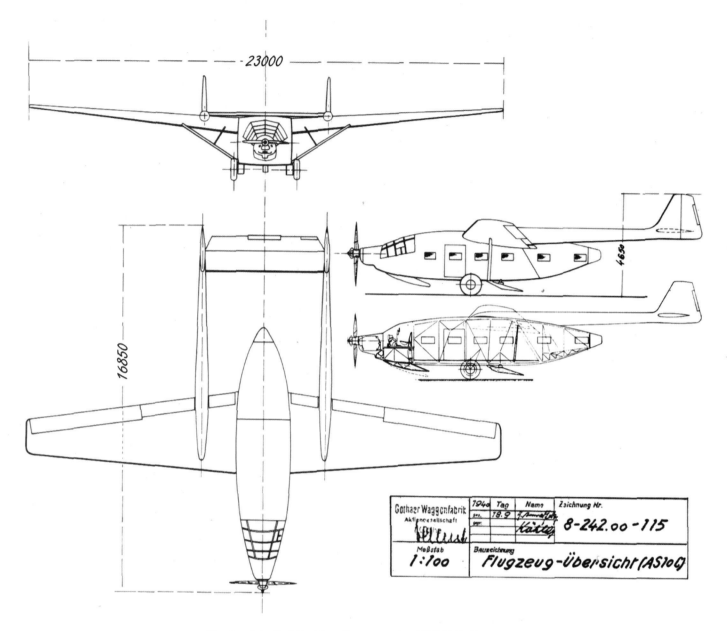

Drawing of the Go 242 with auxiliary motor dated 18/9/1940. (Gothaer Waggonfabrik)

Go 244 V1 and V2

Purpose: transport aircraft for troops and equipment

Identifying Features: converted from the Go 242 A-0 with axle undercarriage, early style engine nacelles, and nosewheel

The Go 244 V1 (WN 2420000018 (VC+OR)), powered by two Gnôme et Rhône 14 M engines, was tested at Gotha in April 1941. In June 1941 it was joined by the Go 244 V2 (2420000019, VC+OS). As the serial numbers show, these machines were taken from the Go 242 pre-production series. At the beginning of January 1942 the V2 went for type testing to Rechlin, where it received a generally favorable evaluation. It was, however, only authorized up to a gross weight of 6.8 tons (instead of 7.8 t), which had the effect of lowering maximum payload from the desired 2.5 tons to just 1.2 tons. The reasons were poor engine-out characteristics (inadequate trimming capacity, insufficient power from the Gnôme et Rhône 14 M 04/05 engines) and a weak undercarriage.

Go 244 V3 to V6

Purpose: transport aircraft for troops and equipment

In the period that followed, Gothaer Waggonfabrik and the *E-Stelle* Rechlin tested several more Go 244s with different power plants and undercarriage configurations. The V3 to V5 may have been test-beds for undercarriages, paratrooper equipment, etc. I have not, however, discovered any records containing prototype (V) designations for these aircraft. Pawlas [2] offers a data sheet for the Go 244 V1 to V6 and claims that they were powered by BMW 132 Z engines (660 hp) with Escher-Wyss variable-pitch propellers. As it has been proven that the V1 and V2 were powered by Gnôme et Rhône engines, this data sheet probably applies only to the versions equipped with the BMW 132 Z. Given what we now know there was only one such machine, and it was designated the Go 244 E-1. The Go 244 V6 could have been a prototype of the Go 244 E-1. According to the type sheet the V6 had a maximum speed of 230 kph at a height of 1,000 m, a cruising speed of 210 kph, and a range of 360 km on 690 liters of fuel. Tire sizes were 950 x 350 and 685 x 250.

Go 244 A-1 and A-2 (status February 1942)

On 10/2/1942 the RLM envisaged the production of two variants of the Go 244. First the Go 244 A-1 powered by two French Gnôme et Rhône 14 M engines was to be built at the rate of about 15 per month until May 1943. Also planned were 20 Go 244 A-2s with Russian M 25 engines. Production of the Go 244 A-1 was to run down

As the Go 244 V1 was based on the Go 242 A-0, it also had the old style tail booms. (Mankau)

from June 1944, and only about 20 Go 244 A-2s were to be built per month, although the power plant question had still not been cleared up by December 1943. As the Go 244 A-1 used the undercarriage of the Go 242 B-1 it was probably renamed the Go 244 B-1; in any case the designation Go 244 A-1 was not used for production aircraft. The use of Russian power plants never got beyond the planning stage, resulting in the cancellation of the Go 244 A-2 (and possibly also the Go 244 D-1). While the Russian power plants nominally provided sufficient power, they had been designed for medium altitudes and were thus found to be unsuitable. As well, the captured engines were of many different types and quality was poor. It has yet to be proven that a Russian power plant was ever installed in a Go 244.

The Go 244 V1 (VC+OR) before, during, and after takeoff. (Mankau)

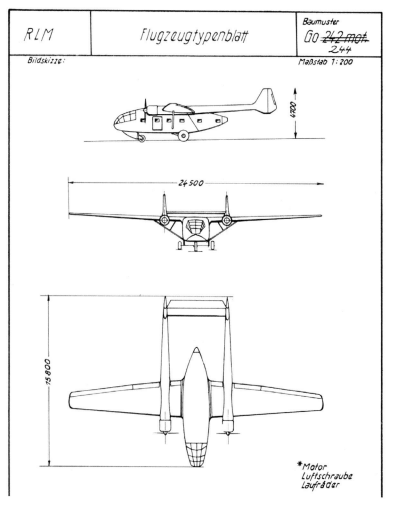

RLM	Flugzeugtypenblatt	Baumuster Go ~~242 mot.~~ 244
Bildskizze:		Maßstab 1:200

24 500

15 800

*Motor
Luftschraube
Laufräder

Aircraft type sheet depicting the Go 242 mot. or Go 244. The wing struts are the same as those of the Go 244 V1.

Go 242 B/244 and C/244 (status May 1942)

On 19/5/1942 the RLM issued the pilot's notes for the Go 242 B and C/244. According to this publication the Go 242 B-1/244 was a motorized version of the Go 242 A-1 with variable-pitch propellers and Gnôme et Rhône 14 M 06/07 power plants. The Go 242 B-2/244 was similar to the Go 242 B-1/244 and was supposed to be derived from the Go 242 A-2 (mixed construction). Planned as parallel variants were the Go 242 C-1/244 and C-2/244 with Gnôme et Rhône 14 M engines and wooden fixed-pitch propellers. The pilot's notes were unquestionably based on an out-of-date draft, for at the time of publication the Go 242 B-1/244 had already become the Go 244 B-1. As well, the Go 242 A-2 was not built in the form described, and the Go 244 B-2 differed significantly, having a different undercarriage in particular.

German Gliders in World War II

Following evaluation by the E-Stelle, the RLM increased production of the Go 244 B-1 to 60 per month (at that time the Go 242 production rate was about 20 per month). (Modell Magazin)

Two views of a Go 244 B-1 of Kampfgruppe 106 in Russia. (Petrick)

(Petrick)

Go 244 B-1

Purpose: transport aircraft for troops and equipment

Identifying Features: powered aircraft derived from the Go 242 B-1 with fixed undercarriage.

The first Go 244 B-1 production aircraft was delivered in September 1941, followed by eight in October and 21 in November. Production then stopped for a few months, as testing had revealed a number of shortcomings that required design changes, particularly with respect to the undercarriage. Only after subsequent testing, modifications, and receipt of approval from the *E-Stelle* Rechlin on 10/2/1942 did production resume in March 1942. At the same time the first operational unit (K.G.z.b.V. 106) was familiarized with the type at Hagenow.

On account of the axle undercarriage taken from the Go 242 B-1, the maximum allowable gross weight of the Go 244 B-1 was restricted to 6.8 tons. K.G.z.b.V. 106 equipped its Go 244 B-1s with radios, defensive armament, and auxiliary fuel tanks. In order to permit a reasonable payload, the aircraft were flown at a maximum allowable gross weight of 8.3 tons.

As a result of overloading the aircraft and its incorrect use, the unit experienced 75 emergency landings and several serious accidents in the period from 21/6 to 7/10/1942. The commander of Air Fleet 4 therefore grounded the aircraft. After the transport unit had been expressly forbidden to overload the aircraft operations resumed, although it was clear to the Air Armaments Minister that if the Go 244 was flown with the prescribed loadings it would have neither a reasonable range nor payload and would have to do without radio equipment, armament, etc. The aircraft also did not have protected fuel tanks. He therefore decided to limit production to the batch already under construction (450 aircraft). He probably did so in the hope that with an improved undercarriage as an interim solution, the Go 244 would still be usable for some time. When continued development failed to produce the desired results (see Go 244 B-2 to Go 244 C-2) production of the Go 244 was halted on 2/11/1942. The Air Armaments Minister also decreed that as many Go 244s as possible were to be converted back into gliders. At the beginning of November K.G.z.b.V. 106 returned to Germany and handed in its remaining Go 244 B-1s. Thus ended the story of the Go 244 B-1. Beginning in autumn 1942 and into 1943 most aircraft were converted back into Go 242 B-1s.

Pawlas [2] states that, according to the conversion plan of 21/12/1942, 184 Go 244 B-1/C-1 were converted into Go 242 A-1s. I cannot state for certain that this is false, but I find it rather implausible. After removal of the fuel tanks and power plants the Go 244 B-1 was no longer overloaded and could retain its axle undercarriage. The records also show that the Go 242 B-1 retained the undercarriage of the Go 244 B-1. The Go 242 B-1 therefore already existed, and the Luftwaffe also wanted to have the Go 242 as a pure transport aircraft with a fixed undercarriage (see Go 242 B-2). It therefore seems more likely to me that the Go 244 B-1s retained their undercarriage when converted and thus became Go 242 B-1s.

Go 244 B-2

Purpose: transport aircraft for troops and equipment

Identifying Features: 840 x 300 nosewheel, fixed outrigger undercarriage with large shock struts in fuselage, wheel size 935 x 345 with dual brakes

Apart from the outrigger undercarriage, the Go 244 B-2 was similar to the Go 244 B-1. As the characteristics of the fixed axle undercarriage taken from the Go 242 B-1 were extremely poor, and it was too weak for the desired payload, a new outrigger undercarriage was designed by GWF and tested by the *E-Stelle* Rechlin. The test-bed (BD+XM) was initially fitted with 1100 x 375 mainwheels and a 685 x 250 nosewheel; however, the nosewheel suffered burst tires and failures of the nosewheel fork and shock strut. A makeshift solution, a larger balloon tire (950 x 350), was then successfully tested on the nose gear. In order to keep weight and drag increases within reason, the *E-Stelle* Rechlin finally selected wheel sizes of 840 x 300 for the nosewheel and 935 x 345 for the mainwheels. On the first test-beds the outrigger undercarriage was completely outside the fuselage (see Go 242 C-2). Also, a change had been made to an unfaired steel nosewheel leg. The increased drag caused by the exposed undercarriage and larger wheels reduced airspeed by up to 23 kph at combat power at low altitude, and rate of climb to an unacceptable 1.25 m/sec. The *E-Stelle* therefore categorized the outrigger undercarriage as "not usable for performance reasons" and directed the company to bring about an improvement by fairing. GWF therefore returned to the old-style faired nosewheel and partly recessed the main undercarriage struts in the fuselage.

Production of the Go 244 B-2 with the original outrigger undercarriage was limited to a few prototypes, of which I have never seen a photograph. The improved, partially recessed undercarriage was not available when production of the Go 244 began, but it was used on the Go 244 B-2.

This photo shows the Go 244 B-2 with narrow-track main undercarriage and 840 x 300 tire on the nosewheel and 935 x 345 tires on the mainwheels. (German Museum)

Go 244 B-3

Purpose: transport aircraft for troops

Identifying Features: like the B-1, but with jump equipment in the rear fuselage (doors for paratroopers) and consequently 100 kg heavier

Pawlas [2] offers a type sheet for the Go 244 B-3. It states that it was a transport aircraft derived from the Go 244 B-1 in 1941 with four-blade fixed-pitch wooden propellers. 13 prototypes were supposedly built and tested at the front. According to Engel [29], the Go 244 B-3 was a conversion from the Go 242 B-1 (in contrast to the Go 244 B-1, which was converted from the Go 242 A-1).

The wooden propellers were used by the C-series, however. Thus, this data sheet is only partially correct, or it was correct at a certain point in time. We know that Go 244s with jump equipment in the aft fuselage were delivered to the *Luftwaffe* and used at paratrooper schools. We also know that Go 242s retrofitted with the axle undercarriage were designated Go 242 B-3s. I therefore conclude that the Go 244 B-3 was similar to the B-1 but with jump equipment in the aft fuselage. If

one believes the conversion delivery plan of 12/12/1943, then 130 Go 242 B-3s were created by retro-conversion. Consequently, I conclude that these 130 aircraft were originally built as Go 244 B-3s, although only a small percentage were actually delivered to the *Luftwaffe* before production was halted. These could have been the 13 prototypes mentioned by Pawlas.

Go 244 B-4

Purpose: transport aircraft for troops

Identifying Features: like the B-2, but with jump equipment in the rear fuselage (doors for paratroopers) and consequently 100 kg heavier

Pawlas' information offers no clue as to the identifying characteristics of the Go 244 B-4, and Engel calls it a conversion of the Go 242 B-2. That is also of no help, as the Go 242 B-2 appeared after the Go 244 B-2. As the Go 244 B-1 was supposed to be switched to the outrigger undercarriage, it was surely also planned to create a version equipped for dropping parachute troops. This would have been the Go 244 B-4, but like the B-2 it did not enter production.

This photo of a Go 244 C-2 provides an excellent view of the wide-track main undercarriage which produced so much drag. (German Museum)

Go 244 B-5

Purpose: transport aircraft for troops and equipment

Identifying Features: like the B-2, with dual control yokes and internally-balanced ailerons

According to Pawlas [2], the Go 244 B-5 was a transport aircraft from the year 1942. Named as a characteristic is its use of VDM variable-pitch propellers. Engel [29] writes that it was a new-build aircraft. Eleven aircraft were built with the B-1's axle undercarriage, the rest with the outrigger undercarriage of the B-2.

To improve single-engine handling, Gotha developed the double control yoke and ailerons with internal balancing and larger trim tabs. They appear to have been installed in some of the last Go 244 B-1s (11 aircraft). These were probably designated Go 244 B-5 to differentiate them [from the B-1], but were never delivered. In the retro-conversion program they produced the Go 242 B-5.

Go 244 C-1

Purpose: transport aircraft for troops and equipment

Identifying Features: like the B-1, but with Gnôme et Rhône 14 M 04/14 M 05 power plants with four-blade fixed-pitch wooden propellers.

The Go 244 C-1 was similar to the Go 244 B-1, but had four-blade fixed-pitch wooden propellers (each assembled from two two-blade propellers) with a diameter of 2.7 m. The Go 244 was born in a time of shortages. A shortage of Gnôme et Rhône and Ratier variable-pitch propellers, which were also required for the Hs 129, led to the decision to equip some Go 244s with fixed-pitch wooden propellers. The Go 244 V1 (VC+OR, Werk.Nr. 00018) was tested with wooden propellers by Gotha in February 1942, or at the same time that the Go 244 V2 was undergoing type testing at Rechlin. The type of propeller used is not known. In summer 1942 the *E-Stelle* Rechlin tested wooden propellers with diameters of 2.7 and 2.8 meters on VC+OJ, a Go 244 with the Werk.Nr. 00010, formerly a Go 242 A-0. The aircraft was flown with both the old axle and new outrigger undercarriage. Performance was poor, and cockpit noise levels were unbearable at altitudes between 1,000 and 1,500 meters; consequently, on 11/8/1942 the *E-Stelle* approved the Go 244 C-1 with 2.7-meter propellers, axle undercarriage, and restricted payload (6.8 ton gross weight) as an emergency solution only. As the propellers tested had proved unsatisfactory on account of their high rpm and associated noise levels they were banned by the RLM, which ordered the development of new, slower-turning propellers. These were still not ready in October 1942, and as the RLM ordered an immediate halt to Go 244 production on 2/11/1942, production of the Go 244 C-1 never began. There was just one known prototype, aircraft VC+OJ.

The E-Stelle Rechlin tested the Go 244 C-2 and, after finding its performance unsatisfactory, refused to authorize its use. Note the fairings on the main undercarriage struts (see also 17/8/1942). (German Museum)

Inside the cockpit of the Go 244 C-2. (German Museum)

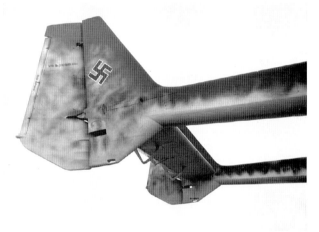

The Werknummer is Go 242 000 884, which indicates that this Go 244 C-2 was a converted Go 242 with the modified rudders. (German Museum)

Go 244 C-2

Purpose: transport aircraft for troops and equipment

Identifying Features: like the B-2, but with Gnôme et Rhône 14 M 04/14 M 05 power plants with four-blade fixed-pitch wooden propellers.

The Go 244 C-2 had the outrigger undercarriage of the Go 242 B-2 and the four-blade wooden propellers and Gnôme et Rhône 14 M 04 / 14 M 05 power plants of the Go 244 C-1. The high drag of the outrigger undercarriage and the poor effectiveness of the wooden propellers caused performance figures to drop, however, and on 20/9/1942 the

E-Stelle Rechlin denied approval. No examples of the Go 244 C-2 variant are known apart from the prototype VC+OJ and the aircraft illustrated below.

Go 244 D-1

I have no information concerning the Go 244 D-1, however, as a Go 244 E-1 appears in the records it is probable that the Go 244 D-1 was also planned. It is reasonable to assume that it was a variant with Russian M 25 or M 62 engines. This variant was cancelled because of poor quality (of Russian aero engines) and the problems with the multitude of variants, supply difficulties, and cooling issues.

Go 244 E-1

The idea of equipping the Go 244 with BMW 132 Z motors was conceived in the summer of 1942. This engine powered the Ju 52 and had proved extremely successful. On 20/9/1942 the *E-Stelle* Rechlin suggested equipping the Go 244 with either the BMW 132 L or M (instead of the less powerful BMW 132 Z), arguing that only thus could a usable interim transport be created. The BMW 132 L promised greater reliability, and for the first time opened the possibility of enabling the Go 244 to achieve its envisaged gross weight of 7.8 tons with the new outrigger undercarriage.

Just one prototype was converted, however: the Go 244 E-1, Werk.Nr. 830, with BMW 132 Z engines. It was tested at Gotha in November 1942 with successful results. The aircraft was then tested at Rechlin in March-April 1943. In spring 1943 GWF attempted to obtain a license to export the Go 244 E-1 to Japan, but the type was neither built for the *Luftwaffe* nor exported to Japan. If we accept that the Go 244 V6 was identical to the single Go 244 E-1, and that the information in the type sheet is correct, then the performance of this variant was very modest and surely would not have received the *E-Stelle* Rechlin's approval. Quantity production was thus senseless.

There is no information as to the Go 244 E-1's appearance. The records do reveal, however, that the Go 244 E-1 was not intended to fly with uncowled BMW engines, as some authors have interpreted the Go 244 V1 with uncowled engines. It is more likely that the Go 244's BMW 132 Z power plants would have had NACA cowlings with cooling gills similar to the outer engines of the Ju 52. The aircraft probably had three-blade Escher-Wyss variable-pitch propellers.

Go 244 Engine Questions

In the prewar period, the National-Socialist government forced the German aircraft and aero-engine industry to construct aircraft for the planned war to come. It was not, however, conceived to immediately make good the losses that would occur in war. As Hitler drove Germany from one theater of war to another, supplying the army and air force became ever more difficult, and the authorities began concentrating on what was most important. As they were of particular importance, high value aero-engines and aircraft were built in Germany, while production of less important types, trainers, and transports, for example, was halted or moved to occupied territories. As early as September 1940 the RLM began considering relocating Ju 52 production to France and equipping it with Gnôme et Rhône power plants. The envisaged designation was Ju 52 F, but the plan never came to fruition.

In 1941-42 BMW was more than overtaxed with production of the BMW 801. The BMW 132, whose most powerful variants (D, K, etc) powered a variety of prewar types like the Do 17, Ju 86, Fw 200, and He 115, was no longer powerful enough for frontline bombers. It was only still needed for the Ar 196, spares, and in its less powerful form (BMW 132 Z) for the Ju 52, and it hindered production of the BMW 801. In September 1942, therefore, the RLM decided to transfer production of the engine to Gnôme et Rhône.

In the beginning, aircraft and aero-engine plants in occupied France simply kept operating under the direction of German companies. Gnôme et Rhône came under BMW's direction, as both produced air-cooled radial engines. In 1941-42 the *Luftwaffe* used the French-built Caudron C 445 trainer and the Gnôme et Rhône

The K-version of the Gnôme et Rhône 14 had been in production since 1932. Production of the Gnôme et Rhône 14 M began in 1936. The engine illustrated here is the 1942 model. (Handbook)

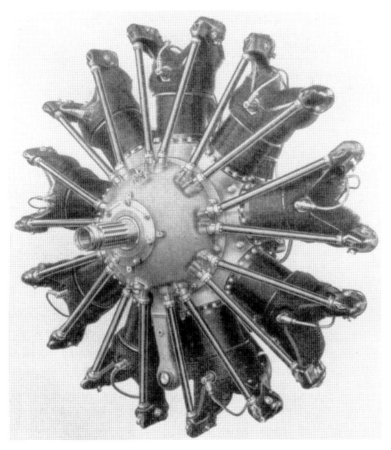

14 M engine. In 1939 Gnôme et Rhône had a capacity of 250 engines per month, which was probably still the case in 1941-42.

Like others, the engineers of the Gothaer Waggonfabrik were certain that they had calculated the Go 244's performance in advance. As maximum speed and altitude were not important design objectives, they had endeavored to create an interim transport capable of carrying a roughly 2-ton payload approximately 400 km using the lightest possible power plants with correspondingly low fuel consumption. This was equivalent to the range of a Ju 52 towing a Go 242 glider. Power plants in the 700 hp class seemed sufficient to meet this requirement.

The proven BMW 132, thousands of which were in service with the *Luftwaffe*, seemed the obvious choice. The BMW 132 Z was particularly interesting, as it powered the Ju 52, and its use would have given the transport units a standard power plant. As mentioned before, however, BMW lacked the required production capacity.

The Gnôme et Rhône 14 M was in the same power class and there was capacity for it,

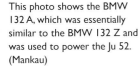

This photo shows the BMW 132 A, which was essentially similar to the BMW 132 Z and was used to power the Ju 52. (Mankau)

Gnôme et Rhône 14 M with variable-pitch propeller (2.55 m diameter) on a Go 244. The oil cooler was inadequate for tropical use. (German Museum)

The BMW 132 L was a more powerful version of the BMW 132 introduced in 1939. It had no gearbox (in contrast to the otherwise identical BMW 132 M). It powered the Fw 200 Condor which made the record-breaking flights to New York and Tokyo in 1939. (Mankau)

at least temporarily. It is therefore not surprising that GWF turned to this power plant. The Gnôme et Rhône 14 M was more powerful (742 hp at 2,000 m) than the BMW 132 Z (660 hp at 1,000 m), but it was designed for a different purpose. The engine was originally installed in the Potez 63, a three-seat fighter and light bomber (similar to the Bf 110 B). It flew almost twice as fast as the Go 244 (450 kph instead of 220 kph) and four times as high (rated altitude of 4,000 m instead of 1,000 m). As the power plants were ill-suited to the Go 244, its low airspeed resulted in cooling problems when fully loaded. Another problem was that the oil coolers, which were taken from the Potez 63, were inadequate for tropical operations.

The Gnôme et Rhône 14 M's superchargers were set to provide maximum continuous power at a height of 4,000 meters, where the Go 244 did not fly. In Russia the aircraft as a rule flew as close to the ground as possible. To avoid engine damage, the motors could only be flown for long periods at authorized continuous power. For the Gnôme et Rhône 14 M that was 570 hp at the maximum boost altitude of 4,000 m. At low level, the typical operating height, maximum continuous power was just 490 hp. Experience in Russia showed that the Gnôme et Rhône 14 M's performance was too modest for the Go 244. Poor quality, incorrect use, and overloading resulted in numerous engine failures, some with fatal consequences. The low power output became

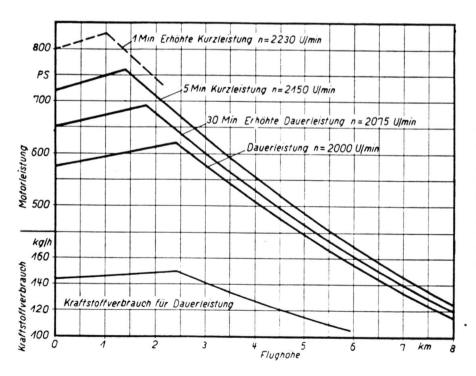

In 1939 engines were not yet capable of sustained periods of high output. Authorized continuous power at low level was about 72% of maximum output. Altitude also affected engine performance. Because of decreasing air density, output fell as height increased. This could be offset through the use of superchargers. These were designed to provide maximum continuous power at the preferred altitude.

especially critical when the sturdier outrigger undercarriage was installed, and it became totally unacceptable when it was decided to replace the metal variable-pitch propellers with fixed-pitch wooden units.

Faced with the Go 244's engine problems, in 1942 GWF again turned to the BMW 132 Z. This was a low-altitude power plant designed with a maximum boost altitude of 900 meters. Its maximum output was 660 hp, and maximum continuous power was about 445 hp at low level. Use of the BMW 132 Z in the Go 244 E-1 therefore came at no cost to low altitude performance and promised greater reliability. But production was barely adequate for the Ju 52. As well, the BMW 132 Z would do nothing to address the Go 244's performance deficit.

The Russian M 25 and M 62 engines were even more powerful than the Gnôme et Rhône 14 M, but they were also high-altitude engines designed for higher speeds. They thus appeared ill-suited to the Go 244, apart from the problem of poor quality.

The *E-Stelle* Rechlin proposed the use of the BMW 132 L or M, and only this would have cleared up the situation and turned the interim transport into a usable aircraft. In 1942, however, these engines were only being built in small numbers and were about to go out of production. The lack of a suitable power plant ultimately sealed the fate of the Go 244.

The next-largest motor was the Bramo 323 P, which produced 1,000 hp for takeoff. It was not considered for the Go 244 as it was probably too large. GWF did envisage this engine for the P-35 and P-39 projects. Two Bramo 323s were to have powered the P-35 transport, giving it a range of 1,300 km with a 2.5-ton payload.

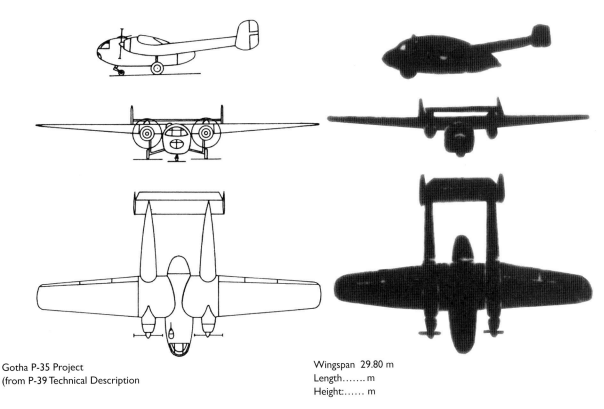

Gotha P-35 Project
(from P-39 Technical Description

Wingspan 29.80 m
Length.......m
Height:...... m

Gotha Projects for a Successor to the Go 244

Note: I was not able to see any original documents related to the Gotha projects described here. All information and drawings are based on the Pawlas [2], [3] and Nowarra [12] publications. Pawlas does, however, provide facsimiles of documents or reproduces their wording.

Go P-35

Gothacr Waggonfabrik began work on an improved interim transport even while the Go 244 was still under development. In July 1942 the General Staff also requested the development of a new interim transport to replace the Go 244. We know of the P-35 and P-39 projects, and related documents may be found in Pawlas [2]. It was envisaged that the P-35 would be powered by two Bramo 323 engines. The records reveal two versions, one with a fixed, wide-track undercarriage and one with retractable landing gear. Gothaer Waggonfabrik was apparently unable to interest the RLM in the project, and it was abandoned.

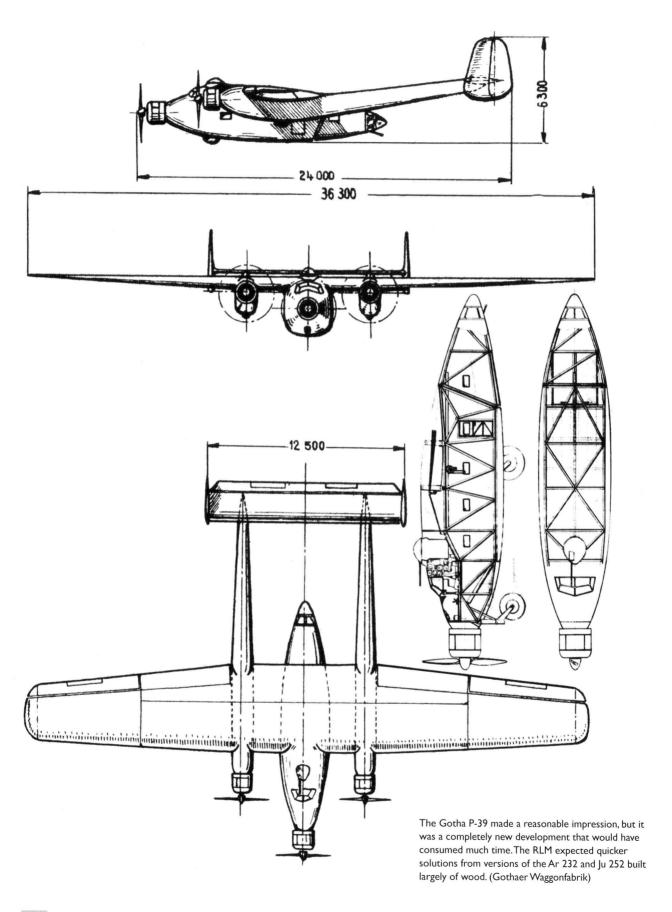

6 300

24 000

36 300

12 500

The Gotha P-39 made a reasonable impression, but it was a completely new development that would have consumed much time. The RLM expected quicker solutions from versions of the Ar 232 and Ju 252 built largely of wood. (Gothaer Waggonfabrik)

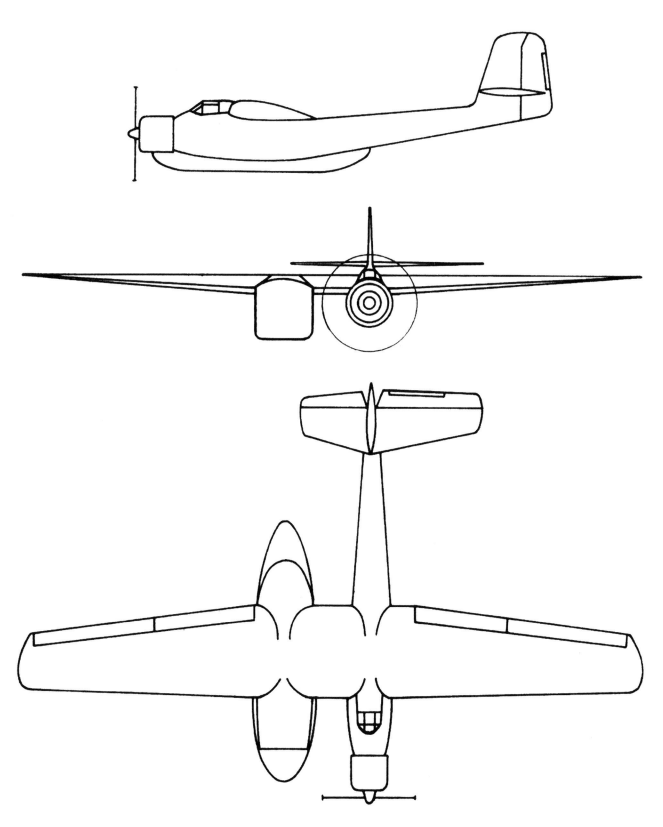

Gotha Project P-40 B (from Nowarra)
Wingspan: 24.99 m
Length: 16.37 m
Height: 5.13 m

Go P-39

Like the Go 244, the P-35 would have had poor single-engine characteristics; therefore, the GWF designed another transport, the P-39, with three Bramo 323 engines. The design description is dated 12/8/1942 and is reproduced by Pawlas [2]. The RLM was also unable to warm up to this design and decided in favor of the Ju 352, also powered by the Bramo 323. This decision was probably influenced by the fact that the aluminum Ju 252 had flown well, and the RLM proceeded with a redesigned version built of wood. In retrospect this decision was ill-advised, for the Ju 352 was underpowered with the Bramo. Thus, it was a repeat of the bad experience with the Go 244.

Nowarra deserves credit for collecting many documents about German aircraft in the period from 1933 to 1945 and having made them accessible to a wide audience. He did not restrain himself, however, from filling gaps in knowledge with fantasy, and he also often made mistakes in interpreting the information before him. His statements are therefore to be treated with caution. On the other hand, I have also found many of the drawings published by him in original documents, such as the Gotha P-3001 and P-3002 projects, for example. I therefore conclude that the drawings published by Nowarra really did come from GWF, and that the project numbers given are correct. Furthermore, in this examination I presume that higher project numbers were assigned at a later date. As the P-39 project followed the Go 244, it follows that the P-40 to P-46 projects were developed afterwards.

In comparing the drawings with the dimensions it becomes apparent that they must contain errors. If one accepts the wingspans of several projects as accurate, then for the length there must be a difference of up to 1 meter between the drawing and the dimensions offered. I have no explanation for this.

Go P-40 B

In addition to larger transports, work was also done on smaller machines similar to the Go 244, but with different power plants. The P-40 B project was an asymmetrical aircraft with a radial engine, which Nowarra identifies as the BMW 801. Given the shortage of BMW 801s and the unusual design, which was a completely new development, the RLM's interest was surely minimal.

Go P-45 and P-46

Projects 45 and 46 were essentially a Go 244 with the Gnôme et Rhône 14 M engines replaced by a central Jumo 211. This solution was unsatisfactory, however, as the Jumo produced less power than the two GN 14 M. The P-45 project had a central fuselage with a loading hatch in the rear. The P-46 had twin tail booms like the Go 244.

Gotha Projects for a Successor to the Go 242

After it became clear that the RLM wanted no more small interim transports from GWF and desired only transport gliders, work began on projects aimed at producing an improved Go 242 or a replacement. Reference has already been made to the critical situation that was anticipated when production of the He 111 ended. GWF began working on an improved version of the Go 242, but then switched to smaller and faster transport gliders suitable for operation with the Ju 388, the envisaged future glider tug.

Go P-47

Compared to the DFS 230, the Go 242 was already easier to load and unload. Two shortcomings remained, however: additional ramps had to be carried for the loading of motor vehicles, engines, and other bulky items. As well, as the rear of the fuselage could not be raised in flight it was not possible to air-drop loads. As well, the twin tail boom arrangement produced more drag than a conventional fuselage. A new design was therefore created to address these shortcomings. Project P-47 was designed near the turn of the year 1942/43 and had a conventional central fuselage with a cargo hatch in the rear. This hatch made it possible to load the aircraft on the ground without specialized equipment, and also enabled the dropping of cargo and paratroopers in flight. But the advantages of this project were probably not great enough, and the RLM decided to continue production of the improved Go 242 B.

The drawing and dimensions are from Nowarra. I have found no other sources concerning the project. But the drawing and dimensions do not seem to belong together, for according to the drawing, a wingspan of 26.82 meters results in a fuselage width of about 3.5 m. In contrast, the Go 242 had a fuselage width of just 2.6 m.

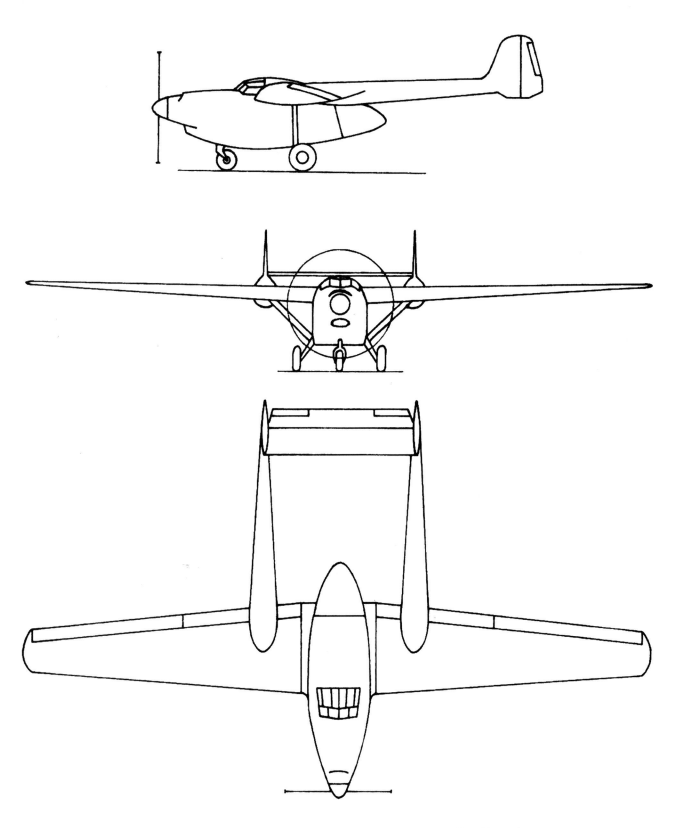

Gotha Project P-46 (from Nowarra)
Wingspan: 24.50 m
Length: 15.04 m
Height: 5.31 m

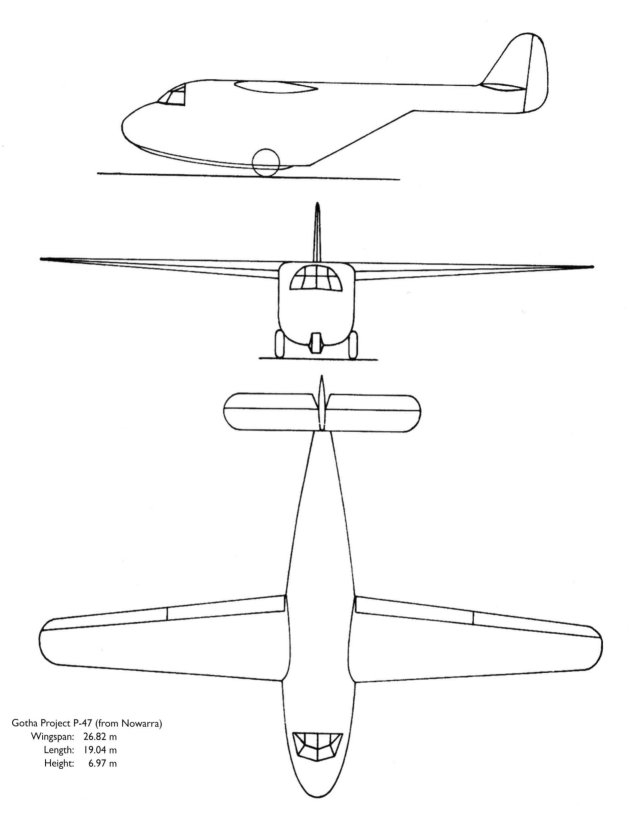

Gotha Project P-47 (from Nowarra)
Wingspan: 26.82 m
Length: 19.04 m
Height: 6.97 m

Go 242 with Conventional Fuselage

There is a drawing dated 22/9/1943 of a wind tunnel model of a Go 242 with a conventional central fuselage. A test-bed with this feature was also converted from a standard Go 242. In the literature this Go 242 with central fuselage is usually associated with Herr Kalkert and his Ka 430. Kalkert stopped working for GWF in 1940, however, and moved to the REWE, where he designed the Ka 430.

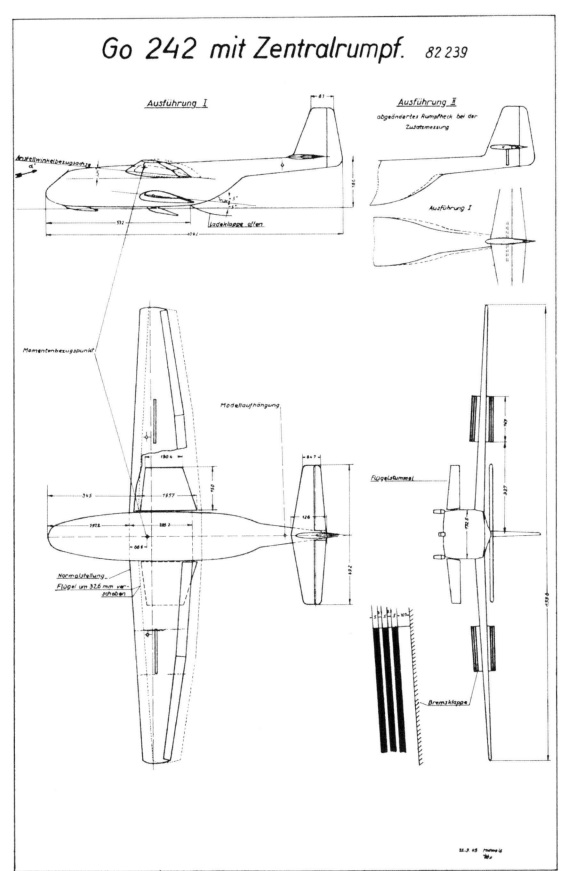

Go 242 mit Zentralrumpf. 82 239

Drawing of a wind tunnel model of the Go 242 with single tail from 22/9/1943. (Gothaer Waggonfabrik)

This experimental machine was made of components from a variety of aircraft. The wing appears to have come from a Go 244. The aircraft has no control surfaces and was thus not flyable. In this form the aircraft was used solely for loading exercises. (Petrick)

The drawing offers no clue as to whether it was produced by GWF or REWE, and it is also not known with certainty where and when the test-bed was created. It is therefore impossible to say whether the Go 242 with central fuselage was part of GWF's development process, or was built by REWE as a test-bed for the Ka 430. I tend to attribute it to GWF, for the final Ka 430 mockup inspection took place at the end of September 1943, and wind tunnel tests with a model of the Ka 430 would have made more sense.

Go P-50

With production of the He 111 scheduled to end, the RLM's development office issued guidelines for the design of an assault glider and universal transport glider which was to accommodate twelve men, a VW Kübel, or an artillery piece. In the competition for this transport glider GWF worked on the DFS 230 V7 and also looked into other solutions. Among these were the projects P-50/1 and P-50/2. The P-50/2, in particular, appears too large to meet the fundamental requirement of operation with the Ju 388 glider tug.

The following data and drawings are from Nowarra. The dimensions
and canard or shoulder wing layout are confirmed by Bruno Lange.

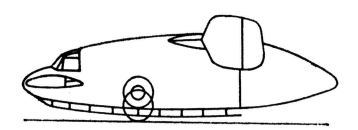

Gotha Project 50/I (Nowarra)
Wingspan: 19.98 m
Length: 10.08 m
Height: 3.38 m

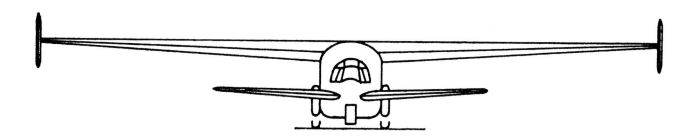

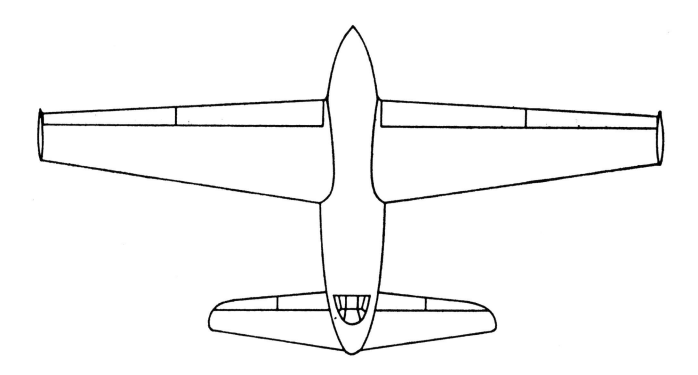

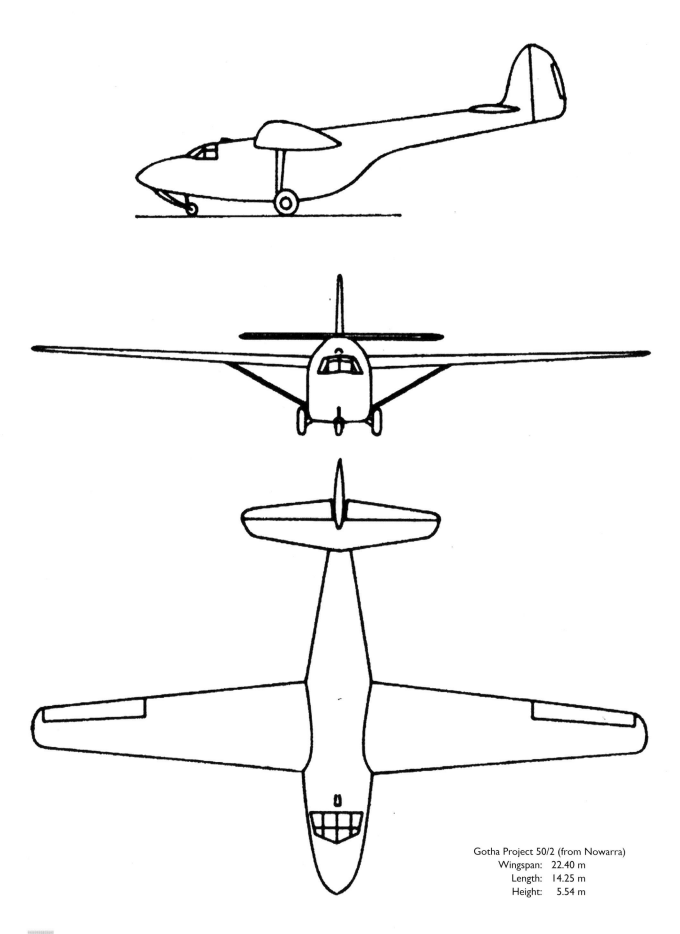

Gotha Project 50/2 (from Nowarra)
Wingspan: 22.40 m
Length: 14.25 m
Height: 5.54 m

Go P-52001

Gotha created the P-52 [3] project on 25/6/1943, following the guidelines set out by the RLM. It was an amphibian with a hinged nose and integrated loading ramp. The amphibian was supposed to land just off the coast and then taxi to shore using an integrated motor. The project was not pursued by the RLM.

The drawing of the Go P-52 was restored from a copy. The positioning of the engines for water travel is recognizable, but unfortunately cannot be reproduced in better quality.

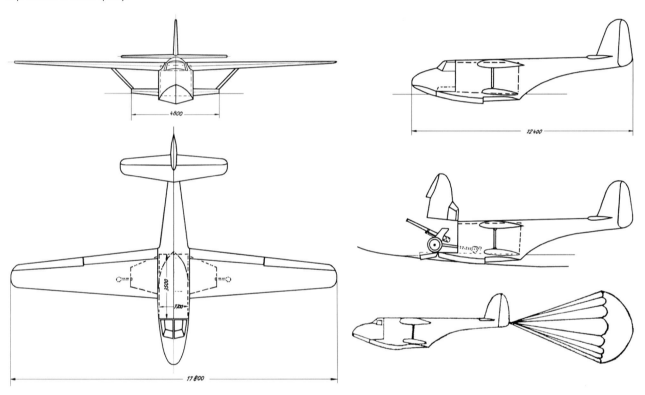

Gotha Project P-52 (Gothaer Waggonfabrik)
Wingspan: 17.80 m
Length: 12.40 m
Height: ...... m

Go P-53 ?

A P-53 project by Gotha appears in the literature. It also had a folding nose, but this aircraft was designed to operate from land. A noticeable feature is the wide axle, which was already outmoded in 1943. That is all I know about this project. In particular, I cannot even state whether this drawing even depicts the P-53 project, for as will be seen, the designation P-53 was assigned to another project that bore no similarity to this one and became the Go 345.

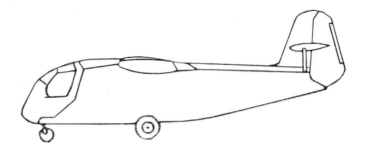

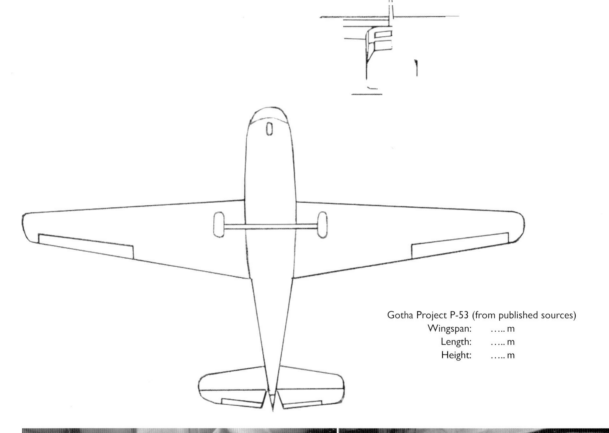

Gotha Project P-53 (from published sources)
Wingspan: ….. m
Length: ….. m
Height: ….. m

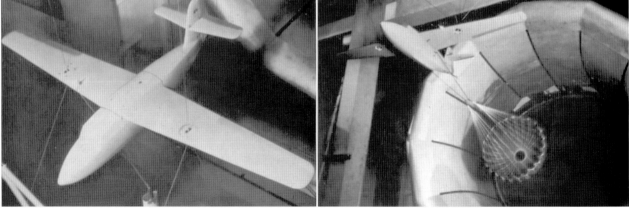

Model of the Go 345 in the wind tunnel of the Hermann Göring Research Institute at Brunswick-Völkenrode. (Gothaer Waggonfabrik)

German Gliders in World War II

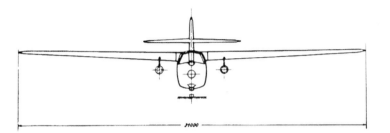

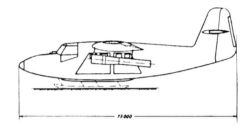

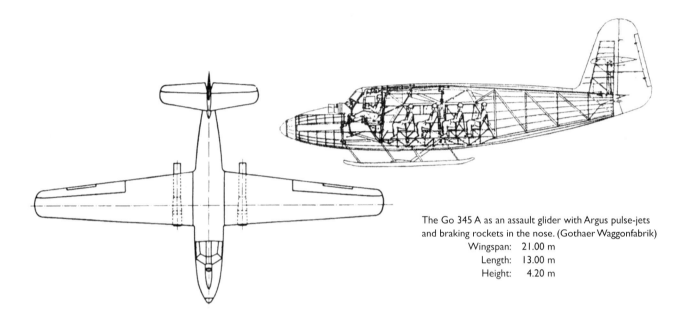

The Go 345 A as an assault glider with Argus pulse-jets and braking rockets in the nose. (Gothaer Waggonfabrik)

Wingspan: 21.00 m
Length: 13.00 m
Height: 4.20 m

Go 345

Go P-53

Initial development work on the P-53 project was carried out in the second half of 1943. At the end of 1943 Gothaer Waggonfabrik presented an aircraft design whose distinguishing characteristic was that it could, unlike a normal aircraft, make its approach to land in a dive. The design bore the designation P-53 Z. On 5/4/1944 GWF made an application to the German Aviation Research Institute for wind tunnel measurements, some of which were for the P-53 project. The request was approved, and on 11/4/1944 GWF sent the necessary instructions to the LFA Brunswick. The P-53 Z aroused sufficient interest in the RLM for it to approve further development as the Go 345, and on 3/7/1944 GWF produced a technical description of the Go 345. The wing tunnel measurements took place in Brunswick in July 1944, and a report was written the same month.

Go 345 A

Purpose: assault transport glider

Identifying Features: jettisonable undercarriage and landing skid (nosewheel and fixed outrigger undercarriage also possible), Argus pulse-jets. Braking parachute, braking rockets in nose

While the Gothaer Waggonfabrik's P-35 to 52 projects found little favor with the RLM, the P-53 Z project, which became the Go 345, was approved for development. The project had to adapted to meet the guidelines for the design of an assault transport glider and universal transport glider, and consequently there were two variants.

The first variant, a combat glider with a crew of ten, was to have been capable of employment as a pure glider with braking rockets. It was also envisaged that two Argus pulse-jets could be installed beneath the wings. The idea was for the aircraft to be towed to altitude and then continue under its own power, provided by the pulse-jets. It was also envisaged, however, that it might take

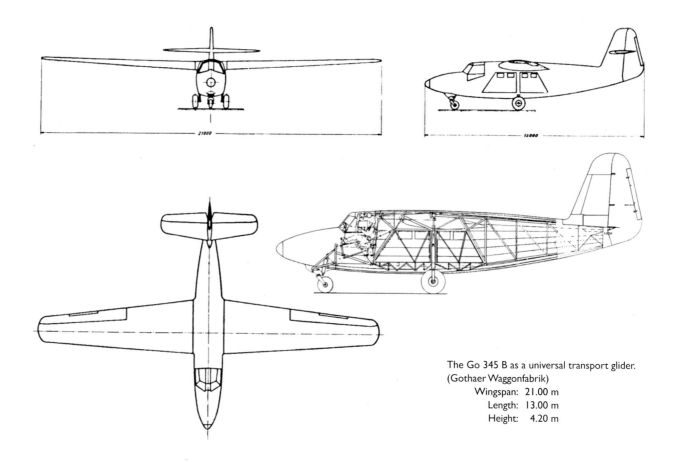

The Go 345 B as a universal transport glider.
(Gothaer Waggonfabrik)
Wingspan: 21.00 m
Length: 13.00 m
Height: 4.20 m

off from concrete runways under its own power, possibly with the assistance of takeoff rockets. The machine's defining characteristic, however, was its ability to make pinpoint landings. The Go 345 would dive almost vertically onto the target, initially slowed by a large dive brake. Maximum diving speed during this phase was 300 kph. A braking parachute would be deployed at about 600 meters above the ground, reducing descent speed to 90 kph. Then, at 10 meters above the ground braking rockets would be ignited, killing the aircraft's remaining speed. The aircraft would touch down on its nose and then slide over the ground on the fuselage keel, which was in the shape of an arc. A weight suspended from the nose on a 10-meter cable ensured that the braking rockets were ignited at the correct height. If the braking rockets failed, the impact energy would be absorbed by the 1.8-meter nose cone, which was designed as an energy-absorbing body. The wings and tail section were supposed to separate from the aircraft, with the fuselage sustaining no serious damage. This goal was an ambitious one, especially if one considers that, in modern automobiles, the safety of the passenger compartment is only assured to a speed of about 50 kph. The Go 345 was, however, also designed for normal short landings on its skid using the braking rockets.

Go 345 B

Purpose: universal transport glider

Identifying Features: nosewheel, fixed outrigger undercarriage

The second version was a conventional glider suitable for towing behind a Ju 388. The Go 345 was larger than the Ka 430 and, like the DFS 230, had to be loaded through side doors.

On 19/7/1944 Berthold, director of Special Commission 12, wrote to the RLM that a contract had been issued for five Go 345 prototypes, but that the documents were not yet clear. In July 1944, however, the Go 345 V1 was already being built, for the fuselage had already been reported complete. In August 1944 the Go 345 V1 was 90% complete, but without engines. And the Go 345 V1 and V4 were mentioned in a GWF memorandum dated 17/9/1944. According to it, the V1 was faster and heavier than the V4. One may conclude from this that the V1 was the prototype of the assault glider, and the V4 the prototype of the universal transport glider. The memo does not, however, indicate whether both prototypes really existed or the status of the remaining prototypes.

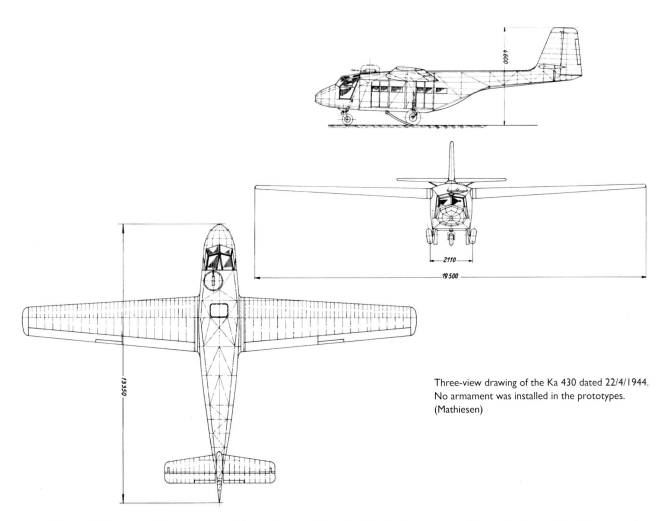

Three-view drawing of the Ka 430 dated 22/4/1944.
No armament was installed in the prototypes.
(Mathiesen)

This is the last record known to me. I do not know if the Go 345 V1 was ever completed, whether it was fitted with power plants and braking rockets, and whether work was begun on the remaining prototypes.

Ka 430

Purpose: transport aircraft for troops and equipment

Identifying Features: fixed outrigger undercarriage

Krieg [26] and Lommel [30] have provided detailed accounts of the Ka 430's development history.

Albert Kalkert was responsible for the design of the Ka 430. He is attributed with heading the development of the Go 242 and the Ka 430, and this is surely correct. However, much of what has been written about what he did in the interval between these two developments is open to question. On 1/10/1940 Kalkert moved from the Gothaer Waggonfabrik to the Erfurt Repair Works (Mitteldeutsche Metallwerke as of 15/5/1944). That was before the maiden flight of the Go 242 on 9/11/1940. In addition to his post as director of the REWE, for a time he was the Air Armaments Minister's deputy for the DFS 230 industry program. Krieg [26] also attributes the Gotha

P-47 to P-50 projects to him, and almost all authors associate him with the Go 242 with conventional single fuselage. Gotha project P-39 is known to have originated in the summer of 1942, and in my opinion the P-47 to P-50 projects came later, or at a time when Kalkert had already been with the REWE for two years. GWF was working on the Go 242 with single fuselage in autumn 1943, which was already too late to serve as a research aircraft for the Ka 430.

The Ka 430's origins can be traced back to the RLM guidelines of 1/4/1943 for the design of an assault glider and universal transport glider. At a meeting of the RLM and the REWE on 28/4/1943, it was decided that the new machine should have dual controls, a dorsal turret as an equipment set (*Rüstsatz*), and a combined skid with retractable wheels. The REWE initially received a contract for nine prototypes and a batch of 30 production aircraft. A preliminary design was to be ready by 4/5/43 (see TF 430 drawing of 11/5/1943). There is a drawing of the Ka 430 dated 20/5/1943 which still has the twin tails of the old design but is otherwise identical to the later production models.

The first inspection of the Ka 430 mockup probably took place at the REWE in Erfurt-North on 9/7/1943, and the final inspection in September 1943.

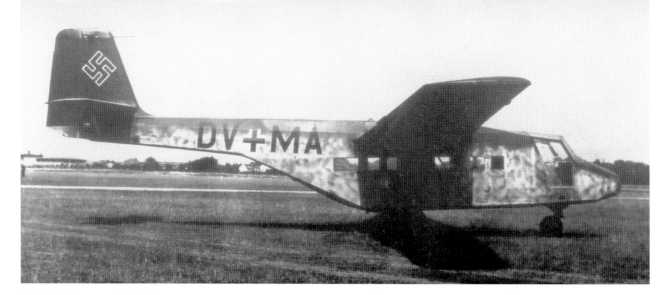

Ka 430 VI during testing. (Griehl)

The Ka 430 VI lacked armament, dive brakes, and skids. (Mathiesen)

Ka 430 V1 to V7

Construction of the Ka 430 V1 (DV+MA) began on 1/8/1943, and its maiden flight took place on 27/3/1944 with Rechlin pilot Pankratz at the controls. All of the control actuators proved much too weak and had to be immediately stiffened. In March 1944 the dive brakes from the DFS 230 D-IDCP were tested for comparative purposes. The Ka 430 V1 was towed to Rechlin and back during the period from 9 to 13 June 1944 and was tested at Rechlin from 15 to 26 June. The Ka 430 V1 proved to have heavy controls, and above 300 kph control forces were impossible. The V1 was therefore sent back to the builder for improvement. It underwent further testing at Erfurt-North from 5 to 9 August 1944. The nature of the subsequent testing of the Ka 430 V1 is not known. The V1 was used purely for flight trials and was neither equipped with armament nor dive brakes. The landing skids were also not fitted.

The Ka 430 V2 (DV+MB) flew for the first time on 27/6/1944. As it also displayed control problems, it was modified and did not resume testing until 6/7/1944. Its subsequent fate is not known. A reconnaissance aircraft photographed a Ka 430 at Rechlin on 15/10/1944, and as only the V1 and V2 were flyable at that time, it is possible that the V2 was sent to Rechlin.

The problems with the first two prototypes resulted in the V3 undergoing a prolonged modification process even before its maiden flight. On 27/6/1944 it was recorded as not yet having flown. On 20/7/1944 the Mitteldeutsche Metallwerke was bombed and the He 111 H-5 glider tug (VE+CT) was destroyed. Two of the three prototypes (V1 to V3) were damaged. The damage was obviously minor, however, for they were available again a short time later. The Ka 430 V3 appears in a report which states that it crashed at Rechlin prior to 22/9/1944.

The absence of wing struts and the use of recessed shock struts made the Ka 430 capable of 300 kph. (Mathiesen)

The single-tail fuselage with special loading ramp made it possible to drop loads in flight. (Mathiesen)

The Ka 430 V1's cargo compartment, which could be loaded without extra ramps. (Mathiesen)

The report describes the extremely sloppy preservation of the wooden components.

It was envisaged that the Ka 430 V4 would go to Rechlin for weapons trials. Testing was supposed to begin in November 1944. On 12/11 and 18/11/1944 the armament was still not ready for testing because of missing parts. On 18/11 the *E-Stelle* also complained about extraordinary wood damage caused by inadequate preservation, demanding that it be repaired by specialist personnel at the Mitteldeutsche Metallwerke. The repairs were subsequently carried out in the period from 15 to 23/12/1944. There is no information concerning the outcome of the weapons installation tests.

The Ka 430 V5 (DV+MC) flew for the first time on 17/10/1944. Rigid-tow behind a He 111 (DJ+SI) was first tested on 18/10/1944. The Ka 430 V5 was tested at Erfurt in January 1945, with rigid-tow behind a He 111 and cable-tow behind a Ju 88 C-6 (PB+VW). Testing was subsequently halted due to lack of fuel. The Ka 430 V6 and V7 were completed but were not tested.

Cockpit of the Ka 430. (Mathiesen)

Type Overview

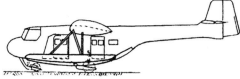

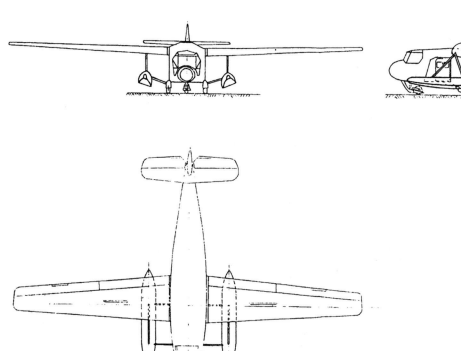

Ka. 430
Entwurf A
Abb. 1
M. 1:100

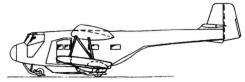

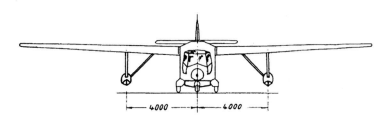

— 4000 — 4000 —

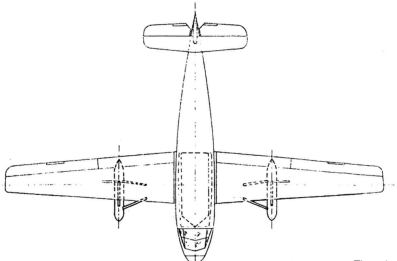

Ka. 430
Entwurf B
Abb. 3.
M. 1:100

These drawings are dated 20/7/1943. Both versions were
designed to take off from prepared airfields. (Krieg)

Ka 430 Pre-Production Series

A few Ka 430s were ferried to Halle and Esperstedt just before the Americans arrived in Erfurt. They were probably prototypes. Twenty fuselages belonging to the pre-production series were found in the factory.

Ka 430 Seaplanes

As described in the descriptions of the DFS 230 and Go P-52, in 1943 efforts were made to enable transport gliders to land on the water. The Ka 430 was also involved in these investigations.

The objective of simplified construction resulted in the Ju 322 using components which were largely straight-lined. The rear fuselage was relatively flat (and probably also narrow) and served as a tail boom. The fin was small, which had an adverse effect on longitudinal stability. The rudder had a large trim tab, surely in an attempt to achieve manageable rudder control forces. (Schlaug)

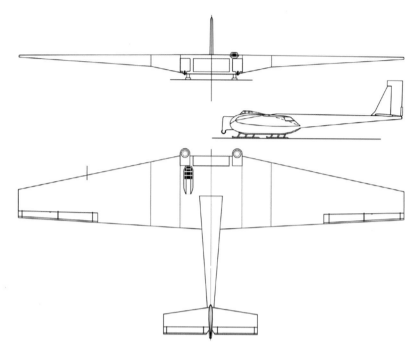

Attempted reconstruction of the Ju 322 V1 based on the photos. In conceiving the Ju 322, the designers appear to have directed the wing forces into spars above and below the cargo compartment. Thus, the wing was very deep near the fuselage, and the Ju 322's layout resembled that of the Junkers G 38. The wingspan is believed to have been 62 m. With no fuselage forward of the wing the Ju 322 was tail-heavy, and therefore the tail surfaces could not be enlarged. (Mankau)

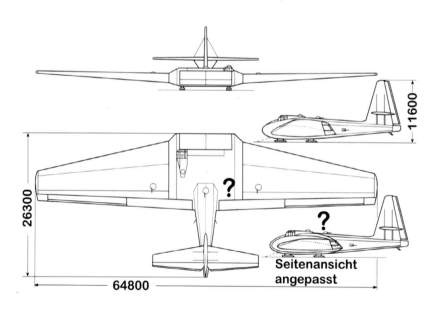

An aircraft could not be built from this drawing, for the views do not fit together. Even if one matches the wing in the side view with the other drawings, it is still unclear how the fat fuselage was to join the wing at its rear edge, and how the landing flaps might look. (Mankau)

Ju 322 (Warsaw-North)

Since the FlugRevue article by Heumann, the codename Warsaw-East has been attributed to the Ju 322. I have only seen the name Warsaw-North in the few surviving records, therefore that it is what I call it.

The paucity of records makes a description of the aircraft difficult. It is known that the combination of a short fuselage and small tail surfaces made it laterally unstable and impossible to fly under tow. As well, design errors reduced the aircraft's payload to 12 tons instead of the design target of 20 tons. As the tail could not be made larger due to weight considerations, and thus the flight characteristics could not be improved, the project was abandoned. The literature states that materials for 100 aircraft had been procured. According to an Air Armaments Minister's conference on 12/6/1941, it is possible that 315 machines may even have been ordered.

A drawing of the Junkers EF 94 project allegedly dating from 3/12/1940 was shown in FLUGREVUE, and it later appeared in other publications. This project only resembled the Ju 322 in principle. The huge tail surfaces, the armament in turrets, and the forward overhang of the fuselage in front of the wing suggest that the EF 94 was an improved successor to the Ju 322 rather than an original preliminary design. Some of the dimensions can be attributed to the Ju 322.

Me 321 (Warsaw-South)

The Me 321 was conceived for one-time use and was therefore cheaply designed. It was equipped with landing skids to achieve a short landing distance. The wing spar was a lattice structure of steel tube construction, rectangular in cross-section. Wing ribs, nose fairing, and tail section were all of wooden construction and the rest, including the lattice fuselage framework, were fabric-covered. The wing was mounted atop the fuselage to provide room for the transport of tanks. For reasons of controllability the outer wings had

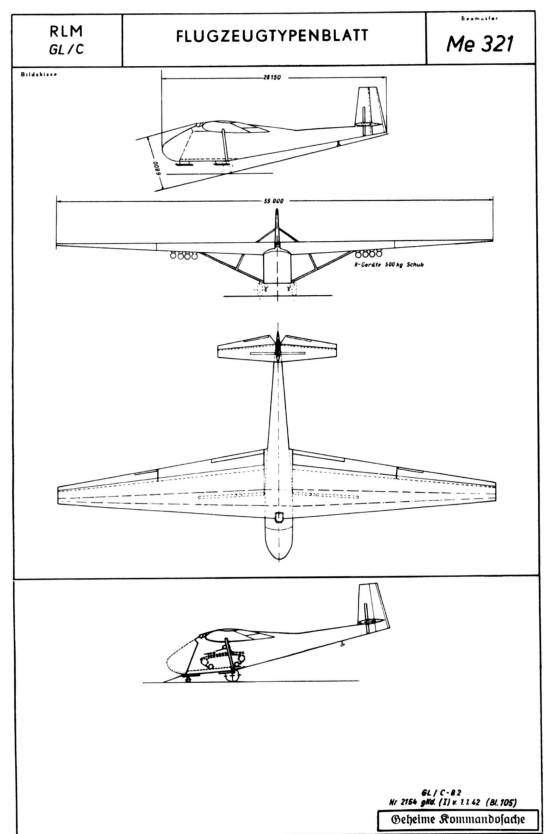

Bildskizze

28150

6800

55 000

R-Geräte 500 kg Schub

GL/C-82
Nr 2154 gKd. (I) v. 1.1.42 (Bl. 105)

Geheime Kommandosache

Me 321 aircraft type sheet dated 1/1/1942. The sketch depicts the machine with no dihedral on the outer wings. Poor controllability demonstrated by the Me 321 V1 resulted in the introduction of 6° of dihedral. (Type Sheet)

The Me 321 could not be flown empty. Without a payload, the aircraft's ballast box had to be filled with approximately 4 tons of sand or bricks. If an empty return flight was planned, the ballast box first had to be loaded into the fuselage nose, as seen here. (Mathiesen)

6° of dihedral, however, this came at the cost of reduced directional stability. Initially it was thought that a single pilot was sufficient for a typical 400-km mission, however, poorly designed control surfaces resulted in excessive control forces, making a co-pilot appear necessary to assist the pilot. As an initial measure a second elevator control was installed, this being operated by a second pilot sitting on a beam behind the pilot. Messerschmitt began designing a two-man armored cockpit at an early stage, but because of the tight production schedule the first half of the Me 321s produced had to be built with the one-seat cockpit. The co-pilot was also responsible for trimming the aircraft. The crew also included a flight mechanic, whose main task was to jettison the undercarriage after takeoff.

While the Ju 322 did not even get out of the starting gate, the Me 321 (in keeping with its name) proved to be a gigantic planning error. It was never used in the role for which it was conceived—transporting men and equipment behind enemy lines. Operating it as a transport glider behind the *Troika* (three tow planes) was a pointless exercise. It was capable of transporting 80 full 200-liter drums of fuel

(16,000 liters), something it accomplished several times, but to do so three Bf 110s had to be fueled (3,600 liters of fuel for an 800 km return trip). For the *Troika* to take off a sufficiently large airfield was needed, along with a transport glider and glider pilots, tow aircraft and pilots, ground personnel for the Me 321 and the tow planes, a number of vehicles, including the two vehicles with hydraulic lifts and the truck for attaching the takeoff rockets, a loading team with loading engineer for the Me 321, and a special unit for the takeoff rockets, plus a doctor and medics. As the Me 321 at first jettisoned its undercarriage after takeoff, the vehicles with hydraulic lifts at least had to be available at the landing site (thus driving there and using fuel). The same task could have been accomplished with seven Opel Blitz trucks and approximately 2,500 liters of fuel for the trip there and back. Another consideration was the need to fly the three tow planes to the departure airfield at great cost, while trucks could be transported by rail. Not until the advent of the He 111 Z glider tug, the two-seat cockpit of the Me 321 B, and undercarriage landings did the Me 321 become halfway practical.

The prototype had no defensive positions, few windows, no code, and small crosses. This is probably the Me 321 V1. (Pawlas)

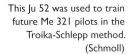

This Ju 52 was used to train future Me 321 pilots in the Troika-Schlepp method. (Schmoll)

Me 321 V1 to V5

The Me 321 V1 made its first flight at Leipheim on 25/2/1941 with *Flugkapitän* Bauer at the controls, and it was towed by a Ju 90. Not until the 6th flight on 8/3/1941 was the glider towed into the air by three Bf 110s.

On 14/3/1941 the *Luftwaffe* pilot Powilleit, who had previously been trained only on the DFS 230, took the Me 321 aloft (the seventh flight ever by a Me 321). Because of a misbalanced aileron the aircraft swung so sharply to the left that Powilleit had to release the tow cable to the Ju 90. In the ensuing landing the narrow nose skid caught in the soft ground and the Me 321 V1 overturned. The aircraft was almost totally destroyed, but the three *Luftwaffe* crewmen escaped injury. As a result of this incident, subsequent Me 321 pilots received preliminary training in a Ju 52 whose central propeller had been removed and replaced by a tow coupling.

The Me 321 V2 with the code W1+SB flew for the first time on 24/3/1941 and made four more flights by 10/5, all with three Bf 110 tugs. The last two flights were made with 22 tons of ballast and the use of eight takeoff rockets. According to a test report dated 10/5/1941,

after these flights Messerschmitt considered testing of the Me 321 concluded to the degree that it could be flown by any pilot with transport glider experience.

Bauer flew the V3 (W1+SC) for the first time on 4/4/1941. The V4's maiden flight took place on 9/4/1941 and that of the V5 on 10/4/1941. In both cases Ing. Bernhard Finsch of the *Erprobungsstelle* was at the controls. What test purposes the Me 321 V1 to V5 served is not known. Their codes identify them as the first machines in the first Leipheim production batch. As testing was largely concluded, the prototypes were probably used for training in the ensuing period. The V2 and V3 also flew at Obertraubling at the beginning of 1941.

Me 321 A

Purpose: transport glider

Identifying Features: jettisonable undercarriage for takeoff, four skids, single-seat cockpit, no armament in nose doors

The Me 321 A was built with the single-seat cockpit, although it was possible to replace this with the two-seat

With its few side windows, W1+SF was intended to transport materiel. (Petrick)

As the nose skids were at first too narrow, they could become hung up in soft ground, resulting in damage to the airframe or even overturned aircraft. (Petrick)

version. Messerschmitt ordered replacement two-seat armored cockpits for all Me 321s. Whether they were actually delivered and installed is not known. 100 Me 321 A gliders were originally supposed to be built in the period from April to June 1941. In fact, deliveries began in May 1941. There were Me 321 A troop transports with numerous windows and a possible second floor, and cargo or tank transports with few windows.

Me 321 B

Purpose: transport glider

Identifying Features: jettisonable undercarriage for takeoff, four skids, two-seat cockpit, gun positions often present in upper part of nose doors, twin wheels often present in nose

The Me 321 with two-seat armored cockpit was called the Me 321 B. 100 examples of this version were also supposed to be built, half in Leipheim and

half in Obertraubling. Apart from the two-seat armored cockpit, no differences from the A are known. Some Me 321 Bs had gun positions in the upper part of the nose doors.

The *Luftwaffe* took delivery of 166 Me 321s by December 1941. As Messerschmitt found itself still six aircraft in arrears on 16/3/42, more were delivered. Messerschmitt probably built the 200 gliders that had been ordered, however, some were converted into test-beds and prototypes for the Me 323, while others succumbed to accidents before they were delivered to the *Luftwaffe*.

Me 321 Braking Parachute

Powilleit [31] reported that the Me 321 had a braking parachute in the tail box which he employed when landing on the undercarriage to avoid overrunning the airfield. I have not seen any photos of a Me 321 with a deployed parachute.

W5+SA must have been one of the first Me 321 B production aircraft with the two-seat cockpit. Note the modified camouflage on the aircraft in and in front of the hangar, and the gun position installed in the nose door. (Petrick)

The nose skids were widened as an initial step toward improved landing safety. When the Me 321 B / He 111 Z combination began regular transport flights, the big gliders were fitted with twin nosewheels for conventional wheeled landings. (Petrick)

The braking chute cable can be seen under the tail surfaces. (Petrick)

Tow Planes for the Me 321

Ju 90

The Ju 90 (Werk.Nr. 0002, KB+LA) was used on the very first towed flight by a Me 321 and made many other towed flights, especially ferrying empty gliders and retrieving them after landings away from base. The aircraft was originally envisaged for supply flights to Africa and was fitted with Pratt & Whitney Twin Wasp motors, which were much more powerful than the BMW 132 H engines that powered Lufthansa Ju 90s. (Kössler)

The BMW 801-powered Ju 90 V7 (GF+GH) takes to the air from Obertraubling on 27/10/1941. (Nowarra)

To enable the pilots of the Ju 90 V7 (and Ju 90 B KB+LA) to see the glider, rearview mirrors were mounted well out from the fuselage. (Bundesarchiv Koblenz 10 II-561-1130-39)

The additional thrust of eight takeoff-assist rockets was required to get a fully-loaded Me 321 airborne. (Petrick)

After the Ju 90, three Bf 110 E were used in the so-called Troikaschlepp tow method. The Bf 110s were fitted with larger radiators, rearview mirrors above the cockpit, and on both sides of the fuselage steel cables which transferred the towing forces from the tow coupling in the tail to the wing spar. The Bf 110 flying on the left outside position was later fitted with a tow coupling relocated to the right side, in order to reduce the tendency to swing (see 16/5/1941). (MM Photo Archive)

He 111

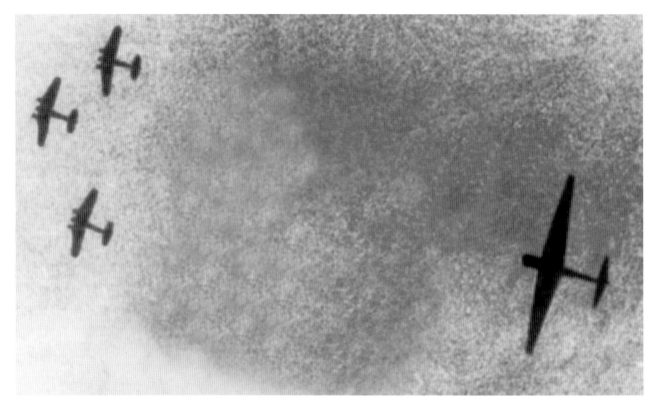

The He 111 H was a superior tug for the Me 321. It had better climbing performance, and two aircraft were sufficient to tow an empty glider. The left outside aircraft in this towing formation also tended to swing, however, and an outrigger coupling was designed for it as well. This glider-tug combination required a wide runway. (Schlaug)

He 111 Z

(Mankau)

The pairing of the Me 321 B with dual controls and the He 111 Z resulted in the first truly practical glider-tug combination. The Me 321 usually retained its undercarriage to facilitate takeoff from the destination airfield. (Schlaug)

Preparing the Me 323 A VI for takeoff. The aircraft still has no code and is fitted with eight takeoff-assist rockets. (Messerschmitt)

WI+SZ in flight. The engine cowlings have been removed because of overheating problems. Compared to its original state, the machine now has a code and a modified paint finish on the lower fuselage. (Petrick)

Me 323

On 21/5/1943 the chief designer of the Me 321/323, Obering. Frölich, wrote that, even as the glider was being built, Prof. Messerschmitt suggested motorizing it to free it of the troublesome towing process during supply missions. He obviously obtained the RLM's approval, for on 13/3/1941 he received a preliminary contract for development of the Me 323.

Me 323 A V1 (Me 323 V1 a)

Work must have begun before this, however, for the first flight of a four-engine Me 323 is

This photo depicts the Me 323 A VI after 20/5/1941, wearing the code WI+SZ. Though an initial production variant, the aircraft has the two-seat cockpit. The closely-cowled engines led to overheating problems. The left nose door appears to have been repaired. (Peter)

The first six-engined Me 323, the Me 323 B VI or Me 323 VI. As the only six-engined Me 323 at that time, it still has a Me 321 style code. (Radinger)

An Me 323 with four Bloch power units (Me 323 V2?) on final approach. Behind it, above the Me 321, is a six-engined prototype. Like the other 14 prototypes, the four-engined variants also had a faired undercarriage. (Lange)

mentioned in Karl Baur's logbook on 21/4/1941, less than two months after the maiden flight of the Me 321 V1. The Me 321 V2 had only completed two flights, and the V3 to V5 one each. The aircraft was possibly seen as a prototype for the four-engine Me 323 A variant, but because of the great haste the power plants and undercarriage were not yet ready, and the Me 323 A V1 had more the character of a test-bed converted from a Me 321.

Photos show that the machine had four Gnôme et Rhône 48/49 motors in LeO 451 nacelles. The poor climbing performance of the four-engine Me 323 A V1 was revealed on its very first flight, which almost ended in the church tower of Günzberg. The first flights also revealed that the cooling characteristics of the Mercier engine cowlings taken from the Lioré et Olivier LeO 451 bomber were inadequate for the slow-flying Me 323.

Me 323 B V1 (Me 323 b V1)

On 2/8/1941 the Air Armaments Minister decided that five six-engine Me 323s and ten four-engine Me 323s should be built from the first batch of 200 Me 321s. Thus 15 prototypes were probably envisaged at that time.

The first test flight of the first six-engine Me 323 (W9+SA) took place at Leipheim on 6/8/1941 with Baur at the controls. On 28/11 pilot Fries conducted taxiing trials over obstacles with the Me 323 B V1 to test its undercarriage, and on 27/2/1941 it was noted that only the V1 and V11 were completed in 1941. Thus W9+SA was the Me 323 B V1 or Me 323 V1.

Me 323 Prototypes on 1/11/1942 according to C-Amts program [8]					
	W.Nr.		Engine	Location	Remarks
V2	801	4	Bloch	Dornst.	loading tests
V3	802	6	Bloch	Truppe	delivered on 1/10
V4	803	6	Bloch	Leiph.	installation of Blohm & Voss controls
V5	804	4	Leo	Obertr.	mothballed after handling trials
V6	805	4	Leo	Obertr.	mothballed after vibration tests
V7	806	6	GnR	Obertr.	under assembly with production engines
V8	807	6	GnR	Leiph.	mothballed after testing with non-handed propellers
V9	808	6	GnR	Obertr.	under assembly with production engines
V10	809	6	GnR	Obertr.	flight testing with production engines and new tail
V11	810	6	Bloch	Leiph.	flight trials with internally-balanced control surfaces
V12	811	6	GnR	Leiph.	cannibalization envisaged, 100-hour and factory trials completed
V13	812	4	Alfa	Leiph.	trials with Alfa-Romeo engines'
V14	813	4	Jumo 211 J	Leiph.	trials with Jumo engines completed. Cockpit conversion under way
V15	814	6	GnR	Obertr.	final assembly with production wing and new tail
Additions from other sources					
V16	1160001	6	Jumo 211 F	Leiph.	1st prototype for Me 323 F
V17		6	Jumo 211 F	Obertr.	2nd prototype for Me 323 F (completion uncertain)
V18 - V19		6	Jumo 211 F		V18-V19 April 1943 envisaged as prototypes for Me 323 F-1, not realized
V20 - V24		6	Jumo 211 F		April 1943 envisaged as prototypes for Me 323 F-2, not realized
V25 - V30		6	GnR 14 R		April 1943 envisaged as prototypes for Me 323 G-1, not realized
V18	130027	6	GnR 14 N		Me 323 E, testbed with Dornier

Like the other 15 prototypes, the Me 323 V8 (DT+DQ) was unarmed. (German Museum)

Me 323 V2 to V21

Fifteen Me 323 prototypes were initially planned, ten of them four-engined. This breakdown was subsequently changed. On 27/2/1942 five four-engine and five six-engine Me 323s were complete, and three six-engine machines were nearing completion. Two more aircraft were being prepared to receive Alfa Romeo and Jumo 211 J power plants.

The above table provides information on the power plants, test purposes, etc. of the 15 prototypes on 1/11/1942. It is notable that only three more four-engine machines are listed in addition to the V13 and V14, although five were complete on 27/2. Two had obviously been modified in the meantime (possibly the V7 and V9).

Me 323 A/B

In a logbook entry dated 14/10/1941, *Flugkapitän* Karl Baur identified the four-engine W1+SZ as a Me 323 A and the six-engine W9+SA as a Me 323 B. The Me 323 A and B variants are also mentioned in a January 1942 Messerschmitt memo concerning the hydraulic system, but in a similar memo written just a few days later the only variants mentioned are the C and D. The A and B variants do not appear in later documents.

They were probably not built for the following reasons. Aircraft type designations were issued by the RLM. "Me" stood for the Messerschmitt development company and its designer. Equipping the aircraft with engines was identified by the number 323 (as opposed to the 321 glider), while the letters stood for different airframes. "A" was the airframe with a single-seat cockpit and "B" with the two-seat one. Both variants had skids and a jettisonable undercarriage. As the Me 323 was to be equipped exclusively with the fixed, rough field undercarriage (and thus represented a new airframe), it is logical that the airframe designation moved to the next letter, like the Go 242 A/Go 244 B.

Me 323 C

Purpose: transport aircraft for troops and equipment

Identifying Features: four engines, fixed ten-wheel undercarriage

The four-engined variant of the Me 323 was given the most space in the Me 323 offer description of May 1941. The aircraft was supposed to be capable of carrying one 22-ton tank, or two 9-ton tanks, or vehicles of all kinds up to 3 meters in height, or an 88-mm anti-aircraft gun with crew, or military units up to 175 men with equipment, or up to 22 tons of goods. The RLM viewed this version as the main production variant until at least August 1941. It was most likely thought that the type's poor takeoff performance could be addressed by the use of takeoff-assist rockets or a He 111 tow plane, but this was surely only justifiable in isolated cases, such as the execution of an airborne landing operation. The ability to take off unassisted was an absolute necessity for normal transport operations. The five four-engine prototypes, which began flying in January 1942, must have confirmed the type's inadequate takeoff performance; therefore, as airborne landings were no longer a priority, the four-engine Me 323 C was not approved for production.

Me 323 D

Purpose: transport aircraft for troops and equipment

Identifying Features: six engines, fixed ten-wheel undercarriage, armament in fuselage only

Six-engine production version by the Messerschmitt AG in 1942/43. The aircraft were built by Messerschmitt AG in Leipheim and Obertraubling, with deliveries beginning in July 1942.

The aircraft construction division of the Zeppelin Airship Works was established in 1942. On 1 December of that year, with the same personnel, the aircraft division took over the further development, modification, and testing, and probably also production of this type. Production suffered because the necessary power plants could not be procured fast enough and in sufficient numbers. Initially Gnôme et Rhône 14 N engines from captured Bloch 175 and LeO 451 bombers were envisaged. At the end of July 1942 it was believed that 180 of the 300 aircraft planned by summer 1943 could be so equipped. Another 120 were to be built with Jumo 211 J motors in Ju 88 power units. There was also the possibility that 140 air-cooled Alfa Romeo engines might be procured from Italy to equip 20 to 25 Me 323s. The variants with the Ju 88 power units were halted in September 1942 because of poor visibility from the cockpit. In October 1942 it was decided to build 25 Me 323s with Alfa-Romeo engines. By the end of 1942 planning began to initially equip the Me 323 with He 111 power units after the supply of Gnôme et Rhône 14s ran out. This was an interim solution pending the start of the Gnôme et Rhône 14 R production. Then, beginning in December 1942, it was found that there were still sufficient components in France to continue production of the Gnôme et Rhône 14 N. In January 1943 it was clear that the supply of complete captured engines (380) was sufficient to cover five to six months of production, and that Gnôme et Rhône and its subcontractors still had parts in storage for 1,400 engines, of which 1,000 were to be assembled. Power plants for the Me 323 were thus assured until 1944, and it was decided not to proceed with the variant with Alfa Romeo engines, but to probably build the improved E version.

In July 1942 the RLM placed great emphasis on the Me 323 D-1 and D-2 being able to carry a single load of 20 tons if at all possible, and it considered it not unlikely that this could be achieved with the aid of a He 111 H-6 tow plane. In July 1942 the Me 323 V12 was converted to test this procedure. Trials probably took place in Rechlin at the end of August 1942, but the method is not known to have been used operationally. The D-1 and D-2 variants were initially authorized for an 11-ton payload and, after flight testing, for 14 tons.

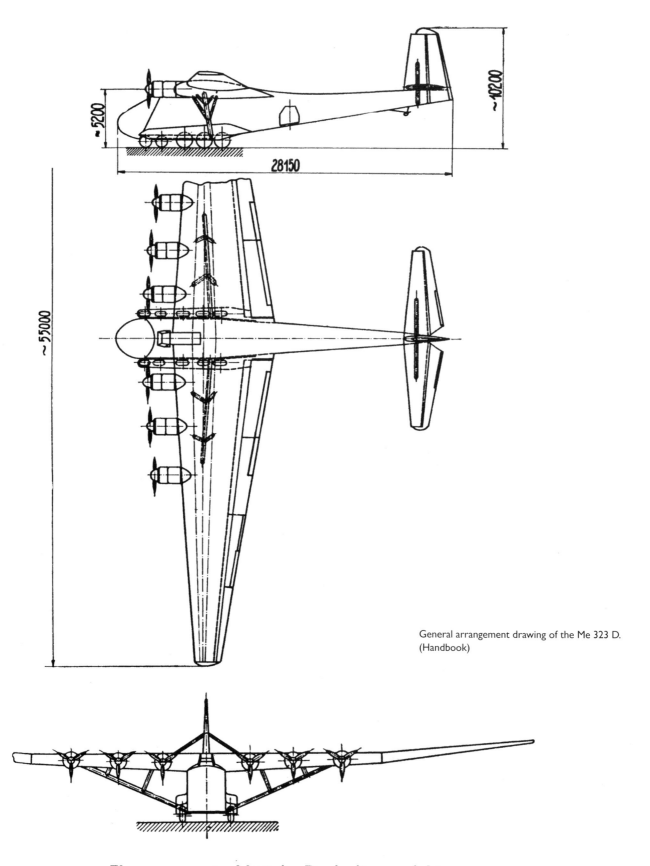

General arrangement drawing of the Me 323 D.
(Handbook)

Flugzeugmusterblatt in Dreiseitenansicht

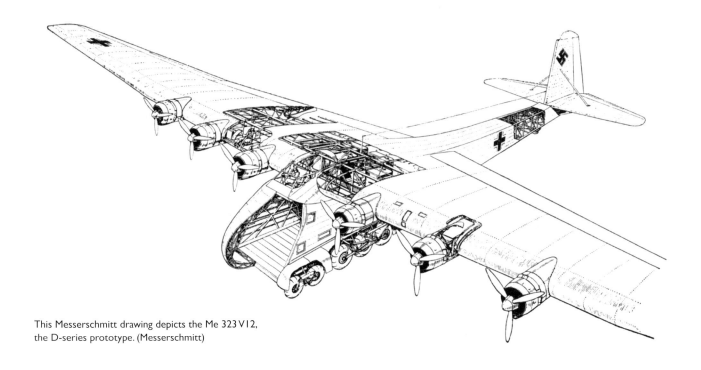

This Messerschmitt drawing depicts the Me 323 V12,
the D-series prototype. (Messerschmitt)

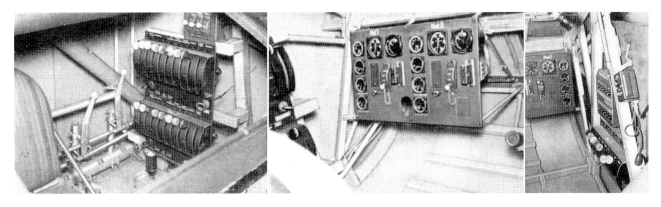

A flight mechanic sat in each wing, monitoring the engines on that side. (Pilot's Notes)

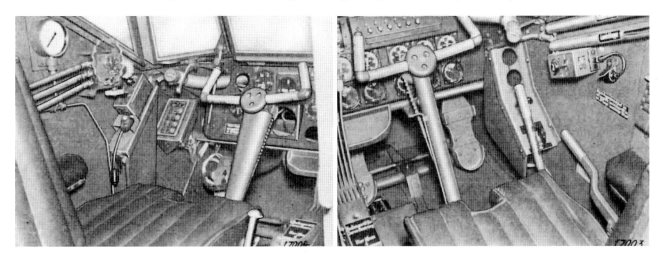

Two pilots flew the Me 323 visually. Seen here is the early Me 323 D cockpit. (Pilot's Notes)

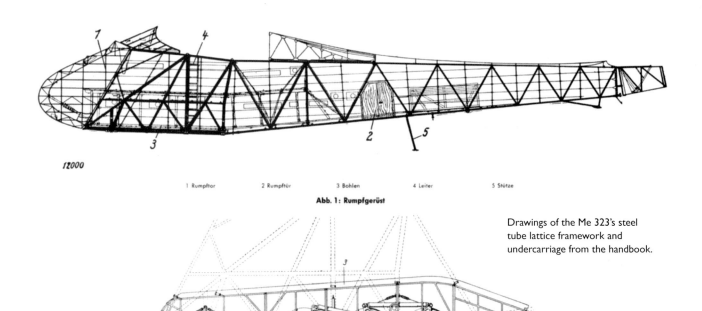

1 Rumpftor   2 Rumpftür   3 Bohlen   4 Leiter   5 Stütze

Abb. 1: Rumpfgerüst

Drawings of the Me 323's steel tube lattice framework and undercarriage from the handbook.

1 Vorderes Fahrgestell   2 Hinteres Fahrgestell   3 Verkleidung

Fahrwerk

Internal view of the fuselage, a fabric-covered steel tube structure with a floor of wooden planks. The ladder to the cockpit may be seen in the center of the photo. (Pawlas)

German Gliders in World War II

In some documents no difference is made between the D-1 and D-2 with respect to payload, while others do. At present I cannot decide which information is correct.

The Me 323 D-1 and D-2 exceeded the ranges originally calculated by Messerschmitt, and the RLM dropped the idea of installing two additional 500-liter fuel tanks.

Me 323 D-1
Purpose: transport aircraft for troops and equipment

Identifying Features: six Bloch 175 power units with Ratier variable-pitch propellers

The Me 323 D-1 was the first production version of the Me 323 and was distinguished by the installation of complete Bloch 175 power units from captured aircraft. The three engines arranged on the left wing rotated counterclockwise (Gnôme et Rhône 14 N-49) and those on the right wing clockwise (Gnôme et Rhône 14 N-48). On the Bloch power units the oil cooler was positioned low on the engine mount. The engine mounts were canted 1° upwards and the center section of the engine cowling was in three sections. The Me 323 D-1 was equipped with Ratier three-blade, electrically-driven variable-pitch propellers. While the engines worked well, there were frequent problems with the propellers and failures were commonplace.

Beginning in mid-1941, power plants for the Me 323 were obtained by removing them from captured Bloch 175s that had been assigned to training schools. According to a Messerschmitt delivery plan dated 12/4/1943, 22 aircraft were to be built at Leipheim and 32 at Obertraubling. Leipheim only delivered 21 (according to the aircraft program of 15/5/44), while Obertraubling achieved its target of 32.

Me 323 D-2
Purpose: transport aircraft for troops and equipment

Identifying Features: six Leo power units with Heine fixed-pitch propellers

Revised cockpit of the Me 323 E. (Bundesarchiv Koblenz 10 11-668-7197-27)

The Me 323 D-2 was similar to the D-1, but was equipped with LeO power units (with the same Gnôme et Rhône 14 N 48/49 engines) and—for availability reasons—wooden twin-blade Heine fixed-pitch propellers. The oil cooler on the LeO "power egg" was located on the side of the engine mount, which was canted 6° upwards. The cowling center-section was in four sections, and the engine attachment points differed slightly from those of the Bloch power unit. The power plants were thus not interchangeable. The fixed-pitch

Heine propellers were only suitable for flight at low altitude.

The *E-Stelle* Rechlin tested a Me 323 with these propellers in February 1942 in an effort to find a solution to the heavy vibration caused by propeller imbalance. The vibration was so severe that Messerschmitt refused further flights. At the same time the *E-Stelle* rejected Heine propellers as unsuitable for service use. It was hoped that the problem could be cured by changing the engine mounts. The *E-Stelle* suggested the use of

The large oil coolers beneath the engines identify the Me 323 D-1. For tropical missions two additional oil coolers were mounted beneath the engine mounts of each engine. Between the oil coolers are intakes for the carburetors. Here members of the ground crew are seen attaching takeoff-assist rockets. (German Museum)

A Me 323 D-1, still without a manufacturer's code. (Petrick)

German Gliders in World War II

Twin-blade wooden propellers were the unmistakable feature of the Me 323 D-2. On this example there are machine-guns in the forward upper defensive positions. Of note are the ladders and the swing-like seats for the gunners. (Petrick)

Drawing of the wind tunnel model of the Me 323 D-3. The design office recommended the narrow version cockpit and an arrangement of the gun turrets between Positions III and IV. (Mankau)

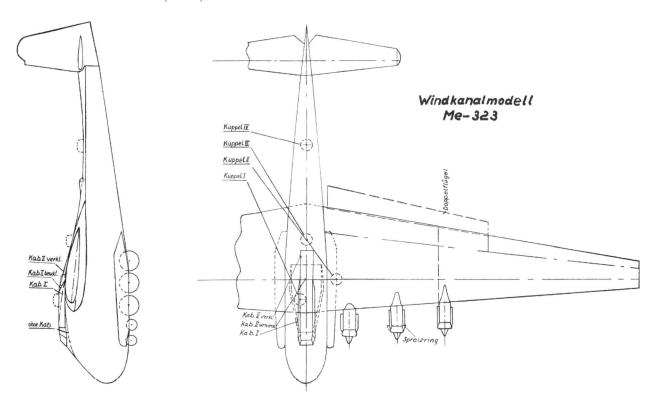

rigid mounts, but the ultimate solution was found to be more flexible mounts. After trials with the four-engine Me 323 V5 and V6, on 21/8/1942 the *E-Stelle* Rechlin recommended using the flexible engine mounts developed by Messerschmitt for the production variant.

Initially the Me 323 D-2 was to have been built alongside the D-1, but the vibration and additional cooling problems delayed production start-up, and in 1942 only the D-1 was produced. As the supply of Bloch power units ran out at the beginning of 1943, and the Me 323 D-2 with flexible engine mounts could not follow until February, at the end of 1942 it was decided to replace it with the Me 323 D-6, which had LeO power units with Ratier three-blade variable-pitch propellers and normal mounts. According to the delivery plan of 12/4/1943, 16 Me 323 D-2s were supposed to be built at Leipheim by June 1943 and 34 at Obertraubling. The two sites produced a total of 34 aircraft between them.

Me 323 D-3

Purpose: transport aircraft for troops and equipment

Identifying Features: six Ju 88 power units, revised cockpit

The Messerschmitt delivery program dated 19/1/1942 stated that after two Me 323 variants with GR 14 N engines a third was envisaged with Jumo 211s. 175 examples were to be built between October 1942 and August 1943. The minutes of a Messerschmitt meeting on 11/7/1942 mention that Herr Friebel of the RLM wanted to fly the Me 323 V14 with Jumo 211 J engines to assess the view from the cockpit. He also wanted a rudder bar pedestal developed by Argus to be installed in combination with adjustable rudder pedals, beginning with the D-3 variant with Jumo 211 J engines. Thus, the Me 323 D-3 was the planned variant with Jumo 211 J engines in Ju 88 power units (photo on Page 57).

At the end of July 1942 the Jumo 211 J in Ju 88 power units was envisaged for 120 Me 323s. Testing of the Jumo-powered Me 323 V14 revealed, however, that the annular radiators reduced visibility to the point that formation flying was impossible. Plans were therefore made to alter the cockpit (taller and farther forward) while simultaneously strengthening the fuselage, wings, and undercarriage to take advantage of the greater

power of the Jumo 211 and increase payload. A report on wind tunnel tests was submitted on 3/10/1942. The RLM considered the cost to be excessive, however, and in September 1942 it cancelled this variant of the Me 323.

Me 323 D-4

Purpose: transport aircraft for troops and equipment

Identifying Features: six Alfa Romeo power plants

On 19/1/1942 Messerschmitt planned the construction of a fourth variant of the Me 323 during the period from April to September 1943. It was to be powered by Alfa Romeo engines. It seems likely to me that this was the Me 323 D-4. It would only have been possible to build 25 examples of this subtype (there were only enough engines on hand for this first batch, and Speer was unwilling to meet the Italians' demands for compensation for additional engines); consequently, the Air Armaments Minister rejected this version at an early stage. The General Staff nevertheless wished for it to be produced temporarily. On 1/10/1942 it was envisaged that six aircraft per month would be built for the period May to September 1943. Continued production of the Gnôme et Rhône 14 N in 1943 caused the Me 323 D-4 to become unnecessary. I have not seen any photos of a Me 323 with Alfa Romeo engines.

Me 323 D-5

Purpose: transport aircraft for troops and equipment

Identifying Features: six Ju 88 power units, revised cockpit, towing equipment

The Messerschmitt delivery program of 19/1/1942 envisaged a fifth variant powered by Jumo 211 engines, deliveries of which were to begin in July 1943. This was the Me 323 D-5. In a GL/A-Rü aircraft type summary dated 1/6/1942, it is stated that the Me 321 could be towed by 3 He 111 H-5, H-6, or Me 323 D-5 or 1 He 111 Z. Therefore, for a time at least, the Me 323 D-5 was thought of as a glider tug for the Me 321. In the beginning, it probably differed from the D-3 in having some reinforcement of the fuselage and wing, which enabled a higher payload. The Me 323 D-5 suffered the same fate as the D-3 because of the planned use of Ju 88 power units.

As the Me 323 D-6's original armament proved inadequate, the units installed a He 111 dorsal gun position with hood, in some cases with two machine-guns. (Petrick)

This is what the power units of the Me 323 D-6 (and, apart from the propellers, the Me 323 D-2) looked like. The LeO power units can also be identified by the vertical pipes which fed air to the oil coolers. The rectangular box in front of the pipes is the cooling air outlet. Power units 1 to 3 on the left side, including oil cooler arrangement and air intakes, were mirror images. (Mankau)

Me 323 D-6

Purpose: transport aircraft for troops and equipment

Identifying Features: six Leo power units with Ratier variable-pitch propellers

The Me 323 D-1, D-2, and D-6 variants are described in Aircraft Handbook D (Luft) T 2323, 1943 issue. According to it, the Me 323 D-6 was similar to the D-2, however, the Heine propellers were replaced by the Ratier units used on the Me 323 D-1. As well, it had rigid instead of flexible motor mounts. This variant was created as an alternative

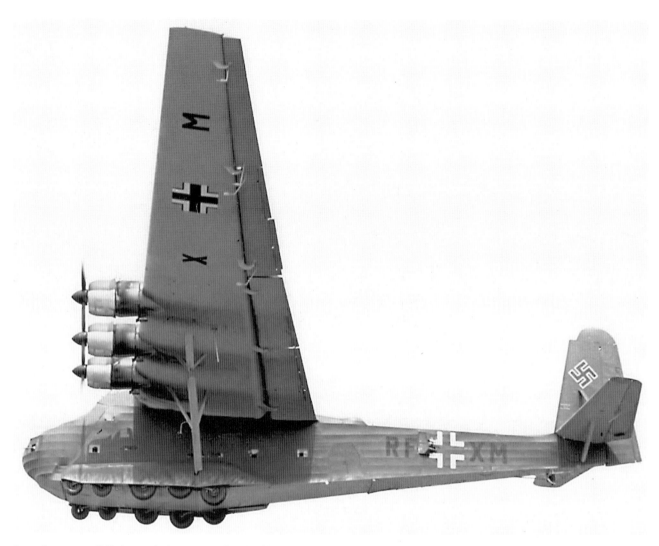

From about spring 1943 the standard armament of the Me 323 D-6 included two MG 131 machine-guns in positions in the center of the nose doors and in the side positions. RF+XM (Werk.Nr. 1139), a Leipheim-built machine, has the strengthened armament. (Petrick)

to the trouble-plagued D-2, and after the D-3 and D-5 had already been cancelled. Solving the propeller vibration problem so delayed production of the Me 323 D-2 that some Me 323 D-6s were built before the D-2 series. The delivery program dated 12/4/1943 envisaged the construction of ten D-6s at Leipheim and 29 at Obertraubling by June 1943. According to the delivery program dated 15/5/1944, 55 Me 323 D-6s had been built.

After the engines removed from French aircraft and the completed engines discovered in France had been used up, 1,000 engines were assembled in France from spare parts. These appear to have made their way into the Me 323 D-6 in the form of LeO power units.

As the original armament installed in the Me 323 D-1 and D-2 proved too weak, it was subsequently bolstered in existing aircraft, while heavier armament was fitted to the Me 323 D-6 on the production line.

Me 323: 1942 Planned Developments

For performance reasons, the Me 323 D-1 and D-2 were restricted to a maximum gross weight of 50 tons with a 14-ton payload; however, loading exercises showed that there was room for a 22-ton tank. In order to exploit this potential Messerschmitt, the *E-Stelle*, and the RLM all wanted to equip the aircraft with more powerful engines.

At the end of July 1942 a proposal was made for a 60-ton aircraft with six Jumo 211 J engines in Ju 88 power units. These would have given the Me 323 a service ceiling of 4,000 meters. However, the cockpit would have to have been raised and extended forward,

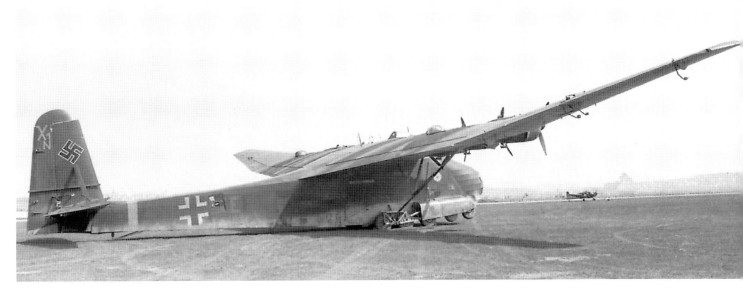

The two EDL 151/20 turrets on the wing were external identifying features of the Me 323 E-1. The photo shows the original short form of turret base. (Bundesarchiv Koblenz 10 11-667-7148-32)

The turret base was later lengthened for aerodynamic reasons. (JET & PROP)

requiring extensive structural changes to the forward section of the aircraft. As a result, in the months that followed versions were also proposed and evaluated with 6 x Alfa Romeo, or 6 x DB 603, or 6 x BMW 801 engines.

In autumn 1942 a third stage was envisaged, a 75-ton airframe with six DB 603 or BMW 801 engines. The *Technische Amt* could not, however, make a timely decision to develop one of the variants. At the beginning of 1943, therefore, they found themselves facing the situation of being able to continue producing the Me 323 only if the airframe remained essentially unchanged.

Me 323 E

According to Luftschiffbau Zeppelin GmbH this was a more highly stressed variant (replacement of some elements of the lattice framework) with increased armament produced since summer 1943. It was designed and built by Zeppelin.

The hesitant behavior of the RLM in 1942 meant that the switch to a Me 323 powered by Jumo 211 engines, originally planned for mid-1943, could not take place. Thus, there was no follow-on to the D-series equipped with captured engines. When, in early 1943, it was decided to resume production of the Gnôme et Rhône 14 N the engine situation became less critical, and it became possible to push back the Me 323 variants with He 111

Me 323 E-1 power units. The bulge beneath the EDL 151/20 turret may be seen. Another feature of the E-1 series is the air intake positioned in front of the machinist's compartment in the wing. (Bundesarchiv Koblenz 10 11-667-7148-35)

power units. Messerschmitt/Zeppelin therefore planned to insert an interim variant, essentially similar to the Me 323 D-6 but with the structural strengthening and heavier armament of the Me 323 F. At Leipheim in the early summer of 1943, the Me 323 V15 was retrofitted with two HDL 151/20 turrets mounted on the wing. Because of the high drag, however, these were soon replaced by EDL 151/20 turrets with shallower cupolas. After testing at Tarnowitz and several modifications by Luftschiffbau Zeppelin, the similarly-equipped Me 323 E-1 entered production in September 1943. Other changes compared to the Me 323 D-6 included improved, integrated gun positions in the fuselage sides.

Me 323 E-1

Purpose: transport aircraft for troops and equipment

Identifying Features: six LeO power units with Ratier variable-pitch propellers, higher stress rating, strengthened fuselage and wing armament

The delivery plan of 12/4/1943 envisaged the construction of 40 Me 323 E-1s at Leipheim and 70 at Obertraubling during the period from October 1943 to April 1944. The plan foresaw a production gap of two months between the end of Me 323 D production and start-up of the Me 323 E-1. According to the *C-Amts* monthly reports, however, just 20 Me 323 E-1s were delivered to the *Luftwaffe* from Leipheim in 1943 and seven from Obertraubling. Another 19 followed from Leipheim and three from Obertraubling by April 1944.

DH 151/1 rotating turret in the nose. (Hellwig)

The 56 Me 323 E-1s are also included in the aircraft program of 15/5/1944.

Me 323 E-2

The E-2 series is frequently mentioned in the literature, however, I have found nothing in the records to confirm its existence. The *C-Amts* monthly reports from the GL/C-2 only record the delivery of Me 323 E-1s until April 1944, when production of the Me 323 ended. The aircraft program of 15/5/1944 likewise makes no mention of the Me 323 E-2. If the Me 323 E-2 did exist, it was only as a conversion of existing aircraft.

Me 323 Waffenträger (Weapons Carrier)

In response to the heavy losses sustained in operations over the Mediterranean, the *Luftwaffe* became interested in improved defensive measures for the Me 323. At first the aircraft were fitted with heavier armament, but then the idea arose of creating a heavily-armed Me 323 *Waffenträger* (literally weapons carrier) to escort

the transports. The idea continued to be pursued even after the surrender of the *Afrikakorps*, and in autumn 1943 a prototype was created. The Me 323 E-1's normal armament was increased to four EDL 151/20 turrets on the wing, one DH 151/1 turret in the nose, two gimbal-mounted MG 131 machine-guns in the locked nose doors, two MG 151 L 151/3 gun mounts immediately behind the nose doors, two MG 151 L 151/3 mounts in the aft side positions, and two gimbal-mounted MG 131s aft in the fuselage floor. All gun positions were armored, and an armored generator was provided to supply power to the weapons. The crew consisted of about 20 men. In addition to the prototype, known *Waffenträger* are SL+HT (Werk.Nr. 1298), C8+GL (Werk.Nr. 330004), and RL+UE (Werk.Nr. probably 330005). Other Me 323s being converted into weapons carriers were destroyed in a bombing raid on Leipheim on 24/4/1944.

This photo shows the inner EDL 151 turrets, the Plexiglas panel over the radio operator's compartment, and the He 111 dorsal gun position on the cockpit roof. On the gunship variant this position was not armed, serving instead as a workplace for the fire control officer. (Hellwig)

Visible in this photo of RL+UE are the DH 151/1 revolving turret, an MG 131 position behind it, and two MG 151/3 positions in the fuselage sides. (Hellwig)

This photo of SL+HT was probably retouched, eliminating the gun position in the aft fuselage. The inner EDL 151 turrets have no weapons, and the outer ones have been overpainted. (Nowarra)

Me 323 F

Purpose: transport aircraft for troops and equipment

Identifying Features: six He 111 power units, revised cockpit, aerodynamic and design improvements, increased payload

The shortage of Gnôme et Rhône 14 N 48/49 engines forced the RLM to look for alternative solutions. The first choice was the Jumo 211 J in the standard Ju 88 power unit (see Me 323 D-3), but this concept was abandoned because of poor view from the cockpit. From a procurement point of view, the use of the Jumo 211 in He 111 power units was first considered possible in December 1942. As this power unit was much more compact, view from the cockpit was even better than that of the original production versions.

Zeppelin subsequently proposed a new variant powered by the Jumo 211 F. While requiring few airframe changes, it promised to have better handling characteristics, increased payload, and improved range. In order to meet the demand for better armament, it was planned to install two MG 81 Z or MG 131 machine-guns in the fuselage nose. Manually-operated MG 151 cannon were to be mounted in bulges on the left and right sides of the fuselage, and a HD 151 position was envisaged on the wing center-section aft of the main spar. Instead of the two machine-gun positions there was to be one in the starboard leading edge of the wing, with the radio operator's compartment in the port leading edge.

At an Air Armaments Minister's development meeting on 8/1/1943, it was proposed that planning for the Me 323 with He 111 power units begin, and that a contract be issued to Zeppelin for construction of a prototype. Zeppelin completed the design drawings by 6/7/1943. In time the weapons system was changed to two EDL 151/20 turrets.

On 8/1/1943 it was the Air Armaments Minister's intention to use the Gnôme et Rhône 14 R as the ultimate power plant for the Me 323, but the production line for this engine was not yet complete. As it was assumed that there were still 500 Gnôme et Rhône 14 N engines on hand, and that 1,200 engines were needed until production of the 14 R began, the missing 700 power plants (about 100 aircraft) were to be Jumo 211s. As of January 1943, however, the engine situation took a

turn for the better because of production of new Gnôme et Rhône 14 N engines, and it was assumed that the changeover would now take place in 1944. On 5/3/1943 it was planned to increase production of the Me 323 from 20 to 30 aircraft per month, and it was believed that this total could be increased further in 1945 if required. Use of the Jumo 211 F was therefore of vital importance and production of the Gnôme et Rhône 14 R reasonable. On 12/4/1943 Messerschmitt planned to build 40 Me 323 F-1 at Leipheim and 60 at Obertraubling in the period from February to September 1944. They were to be followed by 40 Me 323 F-2 at Leipheim and 60 at Obertraubling from June to November 1944.

I am not aware of the differences between the two variants.

In August 1943, however, production of the Me 323 was reduced to eight aircraft per month in favor of fighter aircraft, and as there were sufficient Gnôme et Rhône 14 N power plants, the Jumo-powered version of the Me 323 became superfluous. Consequently, the Me 323 F was no longer present in the aircraft program of 16/8/1943. The Me 323 V16 prototype was completed at the end of 1943 and underwent testing in early 1944.

Concerning the fate of the Me 323 V17, the second Jumo-powered prototype, all I know is that the He 111 power units for it and the V16 were supposed to have been delivered in October 1943.

The Me 323 F was initially supposed to bridge the gap between the Me 323 E and G, but as design work on the G was being held up by a shortage of designers at the end of 1943 it was decided to build the Me 323 F, which was already designed, and which was simpler to handle because of the moderate design changes from the Me 323 E, with Gnôme et Rhône 14 R power plants. The RLM's Delivery Plan 225/1 of 1/12/1943 envisaged the construction of 64 Me 323 Fs with Gnôme et Rhône 14 R engines. The removal of additional designers from Zeppelin further delayed the Me 323 G, so that in February 1944 the construction of 64 Me 323 Fs with Gnôme et Rhône 14 N engines appeared necessary. As production of the Me 323 had fallen to such small numbers in early 1944 that the point of producing the Gnôme et Rhône 14 R in quantity came into question, in January and February 1944 consideration was given to equipping the Me 323 F with BMW 801 engines. All of these plans became moot when the Me 323 was struck from the production lists on 4/3/1944.

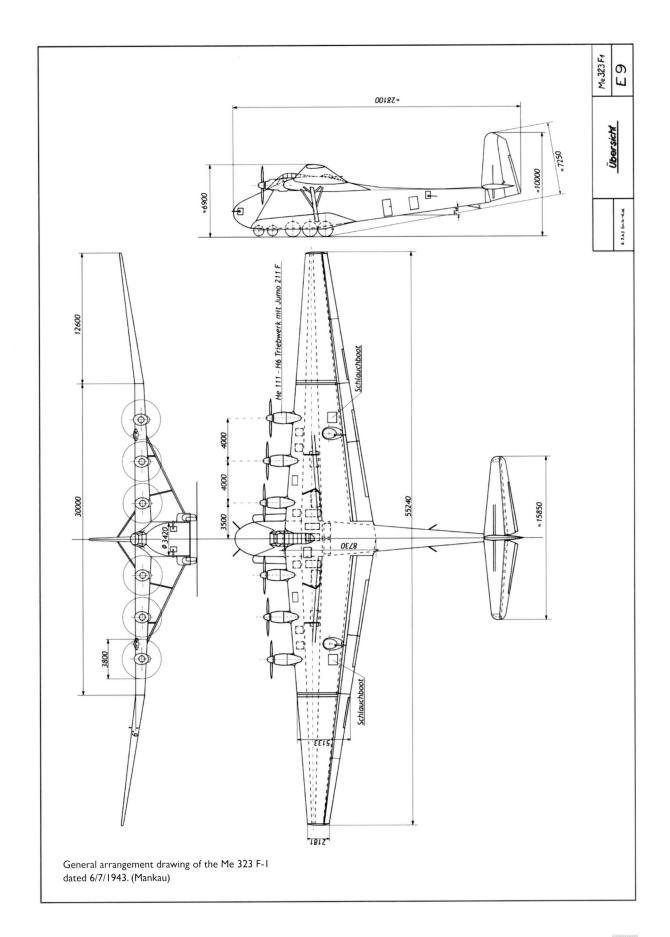

General arrangement drawing of the Me 323 F-I
dated 6/7/1943. (Mankau)

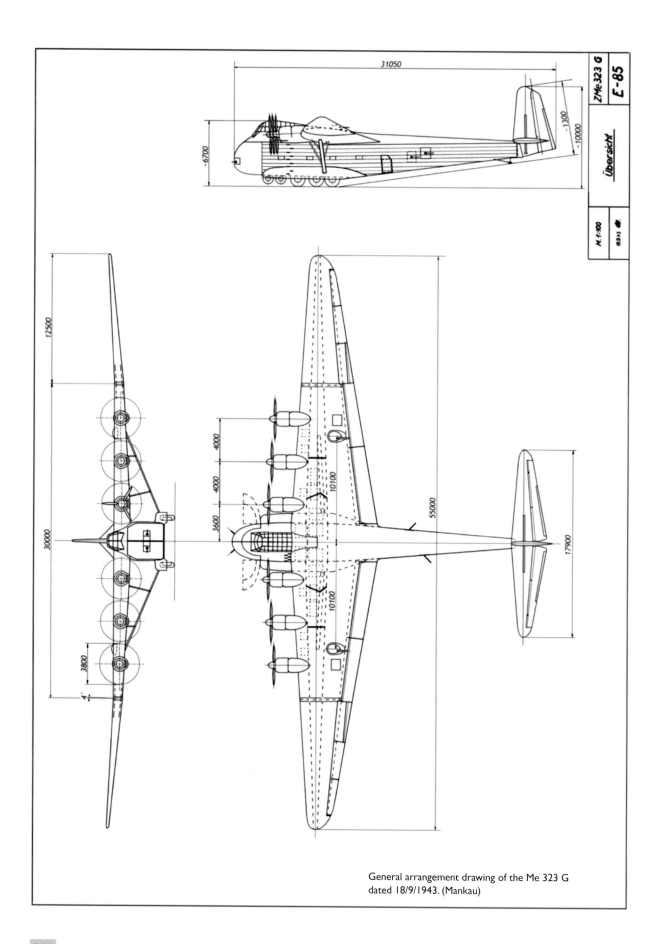

General arrangement drawing of the Me 323 G
dated 18/9/1943. (Mankau)

Z Me 323 G

Purpose: transport aircraft for troops and equipment

Identifying Features: six GR 14 R power plants, largely redesigned

After the end of the French campaign the Germans found complete aircraft, engines, and factories in the defeated nation. They also discovered the completed development project for the Gnôme et Rhône 14 R, an engine roughly comparable to the BMW 801. Prototypes of the engine were built in 1942 and tested on the bench and in fighter aircraft. The power plant was so highly rated that on 8/1/1943 the RLM planned to have it built for use in the Me 323. Production was to begin at the start of 1944 and reach a rate of 80 to 100 engines per month.

Zeppelin developed the G variant with Gnôme et Rhône 14 engines in parallel with the Me 323 F which, apart from its power plants, tail surfaces, and raised cockpit differed only slightly from the E-series. It was envisaged that the Me 323 G would have considerable aerodynamic improvements, structural reinforcements, a cockpit that was higher and farther forward, and a new, stronger undercarriage. On 12/4/1943 Messerschmitt (and Zeppelin) planned to have seven prototypes of the Me 323 G-1 built from January to July 1944. It was expected that production would begin in September 1944. Beginning in January 1945, Leipheim would deliver 12 aircraft per month and Obertraubling 18. Design work was largely complete by the end of 1943. The progress of the war had delayed development and production of the Gnôme et Rhône 14 R, and the plan of September 1943 forecast the start of production by Zeppelin in October 1944 with a monthly rate of 8 aircraft. At a meeting of department heads on 1/2/1944 it was suggested that the Gnôme et Rhône 14 R be dropped and the BMW 801 used to power the Me 323 instead. At that time production of the Me 323 was down to just six aircraft per month; not enough to justify production of an engine, and certainly not the modification of the aircraft. Thus died the G-variant.

Z Me 323 H

Purpose: transport aircraft for troops and equipment

Identifying Features: six BMW 801 engines, airframe similar to Me 323 F, new six-wheel undercarriage

The Z Me 323 H design dates from 18/5/1944. At that point production had been halted and the Me 323 F and Z Me 323 G variants were no longer being worked on. In order to be ready in the event of a resumption of production, chief designer Walter Stender wanted to carry out design work on an H variant. Because of a lack of development capacity, it was based on the Me 323 F rather than the Z Me 323 G, design work on which had not been completed, and minimal design changes were planned. The type was to be powered by BMW 801 engines, which made it possible to increase payload from 11 to 20 tons. The higher payload required structural reinforcements and a suitable undercarriage. All of these changes, plus the heavier power plants, resulted in takeoff weight rising from 45 to 58 tons. To improve the pilot's view, the cockpit was to be raised 25 cm and covered with bulged glazing. The mechanics' spaces were moved to a position close to the fuselage, and it was envisaged that the lighter tail surfaces of the Me 323 F would be used. In order to improve the aircraft's aerodynamic shape the fuselage forward of the cockpit was made more rounded, while aft of the wing it was raised and more sharply rounded. The outer wings were to be plywood-covered. The Z Me 323 H progressed no farther than the project stage because of the course taken by the war.

Me 323 Armament

In the literature the Me 323 is usually described as easy prey for enemy fighters on account of its size, low speed, and inadequate armament. This overlooks the fact that the same applied to almost every known transport aircraft and still does. Such transports were employed in secure areas or flew with fighter protection. The heavy losses suffered by the Me 323s were the result of the *Luftwaffe* sending them deep into enemy territory unescorted. As time went on the Me 323, which was initially lightly armed, was fitted with increasingly heavy defensive armament to make up for the absent fighter escort. This added armament of course came at the cost of reduced payload.

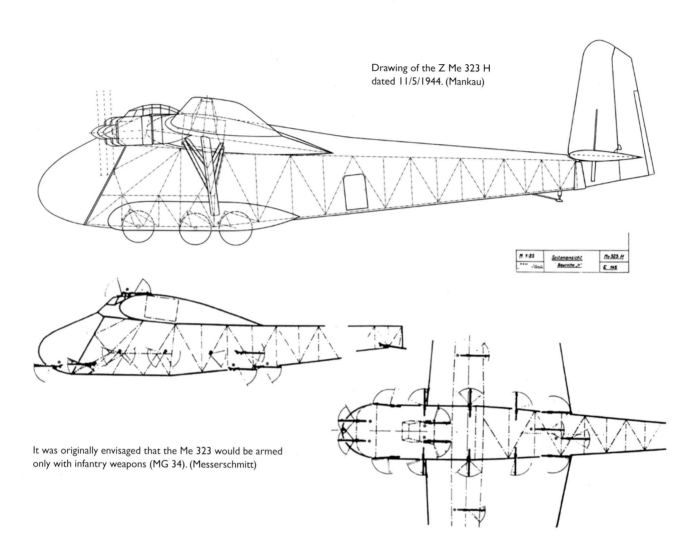

Drawing of the Z Me 323 H
dated 11/5/1944. (Mankau)

It was originally envisaged that the Me 323 would be armed
only with infantry weapons (MG 34). (Messerschmitt)

The prototypes of the Me 323 were unarmed, although the Me 321s being built at the same time had blisters in the nose doors. (German Museum)

Like the Me 321 B, most Me 323s were fitted with Plexiglas blisters in the nose doors, but in many cases no weapons were installed. (Bachmann)

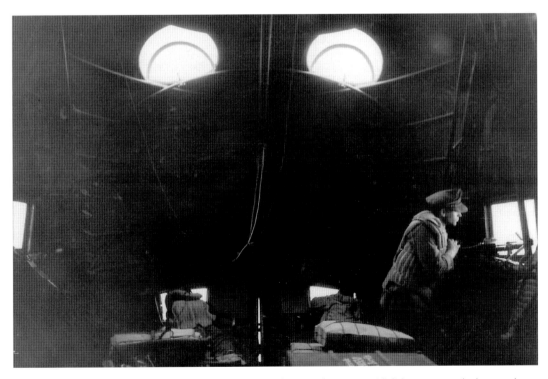

Here the lower gun positions are manned. The upper ones are being used just to provide light, consequently, the area above and in front of the aircraft is unguarded. (Bundesarchiv Koblenz 10 11-552-0822-17)

As a rule, there were no platforms in the nose doors of the Me 323, therefore, the gunners manning the upper machine-guns had to use a makeshift arrangement of ladders and seat harness, as on this Me 323 D-2. (Radinger)

As a result of bitter operational experience, frontline maintenance facilities installed a He 111 dorsal machine-gun position on the canopy roof and MG 131 positions in the bottom part of the nose doors of Me 323 D-1 to D-6. (Bundesarchiv Koblenz 10 11-5587-1051-18)

The interim solution cobbled together by the maintenance facilities was followed by a better-integrated production version, as seen here on a Me 323 D-1. The aircraft has no He 111 dorsal position, however. (Petrick)

Like all Me 323 Ds, this Me 323 D-6 has gun positions on the fuselage aft of the wing, the retrofitted He 111 dorsal gun position on the cockpit roof and, like all late D-6s, armored defensive positions in the fuselage sides. (Hellwig)

A few Me 323 D-1s and most Me 323 D-6s were fitted on the production line with newly-developed nose door defensive positions with MG 131 machine-guns. The weapons in the low positions were much easier to operate than those on the ladder higher up in the door. (Bundesarchiv Koblenz 10 11-628-3486-12)

Unlike the Me 323 D-6, the Me 323 E-1 had EDL 151/20 turrets in
the wing and integrated machine-gun positions in the fuselage sides.
(Bundesarchiv Koblenz 10 11-499-0072-22)

In the ultimate version the turret base projected far to
the rear. For space reasons there was a bulge on the
bottom of the wing beneath the EDL. (Petrick)

Instead of the blisters on the fuselage aft of the wing, the Me 323 E-1 had as standard equipment two EDL turrets with MG 151/20 cannon mounted on the wing. The He 111 dorsal position was also installed on the production line. Here the EDL turrets are seated on the original short bases. (Bundesarchiv Koblenz 10 11-668-7197-16)

The lateral gun positions of Me 323 D-6 RF+XA in comparison with those of Me 323 E-1 RF+XW, one of the first aircraft of this type built at Leipheim. (Radinger)

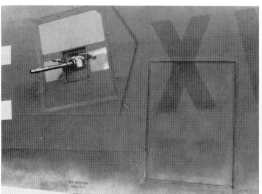
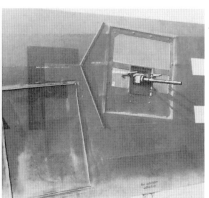

Me 323 Power Plants

Rated at 1,180 hp, the Gnôme et Rhône 14 N in Bloch and LeO power units was the standard power plant of the Me 323 D-1, D-2, and D-6. It was a reliable engine that was initially difficult to procure, but after production was resumed it became available in sufficient numbers to equip all the Me 323 production aircraft built. While it lacked the power to enable the Me 323 to carry its designed payload, it did produce a very useful transport aircraft.

During the period between the end of Gnôme et Rhône 14 N and the start of Gnôme et Rhône 14 R production, the Me 323 D-3 and D-5 were to have been powered by Jumo 211 engines (1,340 hp) in Ju 88 power units, which also gave the aircraft a greater payload. The large diameter of the Junkers engine's radiators seriously hampered the pilot's view from the cockpit, causing it to be rejected and the Jumo variants to be cancelled. In their place it was planned to build the Me 323 F-1 and F-2 variants with Jumo 211 F engines in He 111 power units. These variants were never produced, for with the resumption of Gnôme et Rhône 14 N production in 1943 it initially met the need, and in any case the F-1 and F-2 had only been planned as interim solutions.

Rated at 1,600 hp and roughly comparable to the BMW 801 A, the Gnôme et Rhône 14 R was for a long time seen by the RLM as the ultimate power plant for the Me 323 in the G variant. Because of the worsening military situation, however, development of the engine got no farther than a trial installation in a Bloch 157 fighter and preparations for production in Paris. There is no information as to the power unit configuration planned for the Me 323 G. The Gnôme et Rhône 14 R

Gnôme et Rhône 14 N. (Handbook)

did not enter production before the end of the World War II. A prototype of the Noratlas was equipped with the engine in 1949, but by then its performance was no longer adequate, and the Noratlas was built with Bristol engines.

At the beginning of 1944 the BMW 801, rated at 1,600 hp, also became part of the Me 323 program in the planned Me 323 H variant. This plan was unrealistic, however, as production of the engine was barely adequate for the Fw 190.

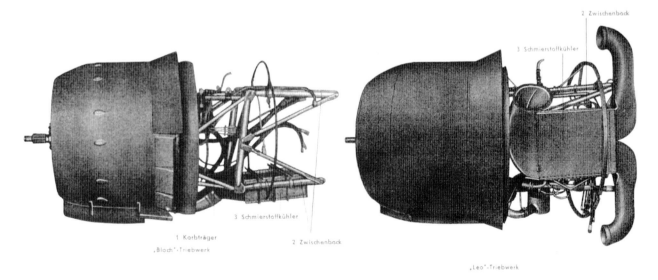

Bloch power unit with the oil cooler beneath the engine mount (left) and the LeO power unit with side-mounted oil cooler (right). (Handbook)

Ju 88 with Jumo 211 J engines and annular radiators. (Nowarra)

He 111 Z with Jumo 211 F engines and retractable radiators. (Lutz)

German Gliders in World War II

Bloch 157 with Gnôme et Rhône 14 R. (Mankau)

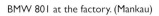

BMW 801 at the factory. (Mankau)

APPENDIX

DFS 230 Specification and Information from Gothaer Waggonfabrik Type Sheets			
Type	A-1, A-2, B-1, B-2	C-1, V 6	D-1
Construction Year	1939	1943	1944
Empty Weight		940 kg	990 kg
Tare Weight	(812) 860 kg	1050 kg	1050 kg
Payload	(1288) 1240 kg	1100 kg	1100 kg
Gross Weight	2100 kg	2150 kg	2150 kg
Wingspan	21,98 m	22,28 m	19,10 m
Fuselage Width	0,80 m		
Length	11,24 m	11,00 m	11,00 m
Load Length	5,40 m	5,40 m	5,40 m
Load Height	1,30 m	1,30 m	1,30 m
Load Width	0,70 m	1,00 m	1,00 m
Allowable Towing Speed	(185) 215 km/h	260 km/h	300 km/h
Gliding Speed	290 km/h	290 km/h	300 km/h
Landing Speed	87 km/h	88 km/h	90 km/h
Fuselage steel tube	steel tube lattice, fabric-covered	steel tube, component construction, fabric covered	
Vertical Tail	Wood, fin covered with plywood, rudder fabric		
Horizontal Tail	Wood, stabilizer covered with plywood, elevator fabric		
Wing	Wood, single spar, plywood leading edge, fabric covered		
Undercarriage	Skid, jettisonable V6 with takeoff undercarriage, tires 650 x 180 mm, track 1.185 m	Skid, jettisonable and landing undercarriage, tires 660 x 180, forward bracing strut, track 1.4 m, 230 C-1 skid,jettisonable undercarriage	undercarriage
Seats	A-1: 1 + 9 A-2: 1 + 9 (1 + 5) B-2: 2 + 7	1 + 9 on bench seat	
Remarks	Narrower fuselage, A-1 to A-3 with single controls, B-1/B-2 with dual controls	Wider fuselage	Wider fuselage, shortened wing, strengthened undercarriage

Go 242/DFS 331 Specifications				
Type	Go 242 A-1/A-2	Go 242 B-1/B-3	Go 242 B-2/ 4/ 5	DFS 331
Construction Year	1941	1942	1943	1941
Tare Weight*	A-1: 3236 kg A-2: 3436 kg	B-1: 3436 kg B-3: 3780 kg	B-2: 3836 kg B-2***: 3586 kg B-4***: 3880 kg B-5***: 3586 kg	2270 kg
Payload* Tare Weight	A-1: 3564 kg** A-2: 3364 kg**	B-1: 3364 kg B-3: 3020 kg	B-2: 2964 kg B-2***: 3214 kg B-4***: 2920 kg B-5***: 3214 kg	2500 kg
Payload, takeoff from paved runway	A-1: 4046 kg** A-2: 3864 kg**	Payload increased by 300 kg		
Normal Gross Weight	6800 kg**	6800 kg	6800 kg	4770 kg
Gross weight, takeoff from paved runway	7300 kg**	7100 kg	7100 kg	
Wingspan			24,5 m	23 m
Fuselage Width			2,6 m	2,56 m
Length			15,8 m	15,81 m
Load Length			6 m	
Load Height			1,9 m	
Load Width			2 m	
Towing Speed			maximum 240 kph	270 km/h
Gliding Speed			maximum 290 km/h	330 km/h
Landing Speed		empty 105 kph, loaded 140 kph		
Fuselage	Steel tube, lattice, fabric covered			
Vertical Tail	Wood, plywood-sheeted fins, fabric-covered rudders			
Horizontal Tail	Wood, two spars, plywood-sheeted stabilizer, fabric-covered elevator			
Wing	Wood, single spar with torsion leading edge, fabric-covered			
Undercarriage	3 skids, jettisonable undercarriage with one-piece axle, tires 875 x 320 mm (also 950 x 350 mm) track 3.12 m	nosewheel, fixed undercarriage with shock struts, tires 950 x 350, single brake, track 3.23 m	nosewheel, fixed undercarriage, tires 935 x 345, dual brakes, track 3.4 m	steel tube, 2 skids, tail skid, jettisonable undercarriage
Seats	2 + maximum of 27 paratroopers			1 + 18
Remarks from specification and type sheets	A-1 with 6-ton nose coupling, A-2 with 10-ton nose fuselage and 6-ton tail coupling and braking chute	B-3 with jump equipment in aft	10-ton nose and 6-ton tail coupling, B-4 with jump equipment in aft fuselage	

* Go 242 weight figures from memo Structural Strength Testing Office Az.89/C-E 2/FP IM No. 5337/12/43.

** Weight figures for Go 242 with jettisonable undercarriage, 950x350 undercarriage and one-time use. For multiple use payload and gross weight reduced by 1100 kg. With 875x320 undercarriage payload and gross weight each reduced by 300.

*** Go 242 with weak floor.

Glider Specification (Successor for Use with Ju 388 Glider Tug)

Type	DFS 230 E-1 DFS 230 V 7	Ka 430	Go 345 Glider (Go 345 V4)	Go 345 Powered Aircraft (Go 345 V1)
Construction Year	1944	1944	1944	1944
Empty Weight	1253 kg	1750 kg	2395 kg	2471 kg
Tare Weight	1300 kg	1810 kg		
Payload	1700 kg	2790 kg	3605 kg	3558 kg
Gross Weight	3000 kg	4600 kg	6000 kg	6029 kg
Wingspan	19,40 m	19,5 m	21,00 m	21,00 m
Fuselage Width	1,72 m	2,06 m	1,8 m	1,8 m
Length	12,50 m	13,35 m	13,00 m	13,00 m
Load Length	4,50 m	3,65 m	4,0 m	4,0 m
Load Height	1,50 m	1,3 m	1,56 m	1,56 m
Load Width	1,50 m	1,45 m	1,4 m	1,4 m
Allowable Towing Speed	300 km/h	320 km/h	310 km/h	350 km/h
Gliding Speed	300 km/h		370 km/h	420 km/h
Landing Speed	96 km/h		120 km/h	120 km/h
Fuselage steel tube	Steel tube, component construction, fabric-covered	Steel tube, lattice, fabric-covered		
Vertical Tail	Wood, fabric-covered fin and rudder	Wood, plywood-sheeted fin, fabric-covered rudder		
Horizontal Tail	Wood, fabric-covered stabilizer and elevator	Wood, plywood-sheeted stabilizer, fabric-covered elevator		
Wing	Pine, steel, main spar, auxiliary spar forward, torsion tubes in front of main spar, behind fabric-covered, bracing struts	Wood, single spar, torsion tubes in front of the main spar with plywood skin, behind fabric-covered	Wood, single spar, plywood sheeting	Wood, single spar with plywood sheeting, 1600 kg tanks in front of main spar, 2 Argus pulse jets under wings
Undercarriage	2 shock struts, tail skid, tires 660 x 160 mm, track 1.96 m	2 shock struts, nosewheel, track 2.11 m	2 shock struts, nosewheel	skid and jettisonable undercarriage
Seats	2 + 15, crew side-by-side, otherwise as desired	2 +	2 + 10, crew side-by-side, otherwise as desired	
Remarks	Wider fuselage, shortened wing new tail section			Payload restricted to 1630 kg for pinpoint landing

Specification, interim transport, projects				
Type	Go 244 B-1	Go 244 C-2	P-35	P-39
Construction Year	1942	1942	1942	1942
Power Plants	G&R 14 M 6/7	G&R 14 M 4/5	Bramo 323 P	Bramo 323 P
Takeoff Power	2 x 700 hp	2 x 700 hp	2 x 1000 hp	3 x 1000 hp
Propellers	variable-pitch, 2,55 m 3-blade	fixed-pitch, 2,7 m Ø, 4-blade	variable pitch, 3,7 m 3-blade	variable pitch, 3,7 m 3-blade
Empty Weight	5100 kg	5380 kg*		
Tare Weight	5224 kg	5500 kg		
Payload	770 kg	560 kg	2500 kg	4000 kg
Total Weight	6800 kg	6800 kg	11500 kg	16000 kg
Wingspan		24,5 m	29,8 m	36,3 m
Fuselage Width		2,6 m		
Length		15,8 m		24,0 m
Payload Length		6 m		6,5 m
Payload Height		1,9 m		2,2 m
Payload Width		2 m		2,5 m
Maximum Speed	290 km/h	255 km/h		350 km/h
Cruising speed	250 km/h	190 km/h	250 km/h	270 km/h
Landing speed	125 km/h	125 km/h	110 km/h	109 km/h
Rate of Climb	2,7 m/sec	1,6 m/sec		4,4 m/sec
Service Ceiling		ca. 8350 m		7900 m
Range		480 km at economical cruise	1300 km	1600 km
Fuselage	steel tube, lattice, fabric-covered			
Vertical Tail	Wood, plywood skin on stabilizer, rudder fabric-covered		Wood, plywood skin on stabilizer, rudder fabric-covered	
Horizontal Tail	Wood, twin spars, plywood skin on stabilizer, elevators fabric-covered		Wood, plywood skin on stabilizer, elevators fabric-covered	
Wing	Single spar with torsion leading edge, fabric-covered		Wood, twin spars, plywood skin	
Undercarriage	Nosewheel 685 x 250 mm, fixed undercarriage with one-piece axle, 950 x 350 mm, single brake, track 3.23 m	Nosewheel 950 x 350 mm, fixed undercarriage with shock struts, tires 1100 x 390 mm, twin brakes, track 3.4 m	Retractable tricycle undercarriage	Retractable tricycle undercarriage
Seats		2	3	3
Remarks	Carriage of 300-l tank in fuselage for increased range possible, but at cost of payload, maximum gross weight 6800 kg	Gross weight could not be increased to 7800 kg because of insufficiently powerful engines	Single-engined flight not possible with full payload	Overloaded range with 3000 kg payload: 4000 km

*The use of four-blade fixed-pitch propellers on the Go 244 C-1/C-2 resulted in a 76 kg decrease in empty weight compared to the corresponding Go 244 B-1/B-2.

Specifications Me 321, Ju 322, Me 323

Type	Ju 322	Me 321 A	Me 321 B	Me 323 D-2
Construction Year	1941	1941	1941/42	1942
Power Plants		-		
Takeoff Power		-		
Propellers		-		fixed pitch, two-blade
Empty Weight			12200 kg	
Tare Weight		12600 kg	13000 kg	28000 kg
Fuel	-	-	-	5340 l
Payload	120000 kg	22000 kg	22000 kg	9500 kg
Payload (without armor)	-	-	-	-
Payload (full extra tanks)	-	-	-	8000 kg
Overload				-
Gross Weight		34600 kg	35000 kg	43000kg
Gross Weight (overload)			39400 kg	-
Wingspan	62,00 m			
Fuselage Width				
Length				
Payload Length				
Payload Height				
Payload Width				
Max. speed empty			250 km/h	232 km/h
Max. speed loaded				219 km/h
Cruising speed			180 km/h	204 km/h
Landing speed			115 km/h	130 km/h
Low level climb rate		8 m/sec with 20-t payload behind He 111 Z		3 m/sec
Service Ceiling				3600 m
Range at Altitude		400 km behind Me 110 E 600 km behind He 111 Z		750 km in 0 km
Fuselage		steel tube, lattice, fabric-covered		
Vertical Tail		wood, plywood skin, partly fabric-covered		
Horizontal Tail		wood, plywood skin, partly fabric-covered		
Wing		steel-tube spar, rectangular in cross-section, wooden ribs,		
Undercarriage				ten-wheel under-rear six
Crew		2	3	5

Me 323 D-1/ 6	Me 323 E	Me 323 F-1	ZMe 323 G	ZMe 323 H
1943	1943/44	V 16 1944	Project 1943	Project 1944
G&R 14 N		Jumo 211-F	G&R 14 R	BMW 801
6 x 1180 PS (PS = h.p.)		6 x 1340 PS	6 x 1600 PS	6 x 1600 Ps
variable-pitch, 3-blade, 3.3 m diameter		variable-pitch, 3-blade, 3.8 m diameter		
	27570 kg	30926 kg	31080 kg	32800 kg
28000 kg	30000 kg	34173 kg	33920 kg	34490 kg
5340 l	5390 kg	5390 kg	5390 kg	5390 kg
11500 kg	9000 kg	11686 kg	12400 kg	
-	9500 kg			
10000 kg	7500 kg			
3000 kg	3000 kg	4000 kg	4000 kg	4000 kg
43000 kg	45000 kg	54000 kg	54000kg	58000 kg
46000 kg	48000 kg	58000 kg	58000kg	62000 kg
				55,00 m
		3,42 m	3,60 m	3,42 m
		28,15 m	31,65 m	28,15 m
		11,00 m		11,00 m
		3,3 – 2,4 m		3,3 – 2,4 m
		3,15 m		3,15 m
260 km/h	253 km/h	305 km/h	310 km/h	
	238 km/h			
250 km/h	225 km/h	260 km/h	290 km/h	
130 km/h	130 km/h		142 km/h	
1,9 m/sec	1,9 m/sec			
4500 m	4500 m	5150 m		
750 km in 0 km 950 km in 4 km	1100 km in 0 m 1300 km in 4 km	optimal 1350 km	optimal 1180 km	
				like the F-1
				like the F-1
				like the F-1
plywood-covered leading edge, rest fabric-covered				like the F-1
carriage, forward four 875x320 wheels, 1200 x 420 with brakes, track 4.1 m		like the Me 323 E, larger wheels	like the Me 323 F, larger wheels	six wheels
7	9	9		9

DFS 230 Production Overview

Note: This is an attempt to combine the various production dates. Used were the Aircraft Development Program of 1/10/1937, the *C-Amts* Monthly Reports from 1941 and 1944, the *C-Amts* Program of 1/10/1940, the Erfurt Repair Works' list of 17/2/1941, and the Chief of Supply Dept. II's total delivery numbers of 4/12/1944. Handwritten sources are not covered. Without taking into account the DFS 230 A-0, which does not appear in the Quartermaster-General's lists, it appears that 50 more aircraft were built than were taken on strength by the *Luftwaffe*. The actual number of aircraft built by BMM in 1942 is not known. It is also not known whether aircraft delivered to allied nations (Italy, Rumania, and Japan) were new-build aircraft or were taken from *Luftwaffe* stocks.

DFS 230	Year		37/38	39	1940		1941					
	Month				1-6	7-12	1	2	3	4	5	6
	Company	Total										
A-0	Harwig			18								
	Gerner			12								
	Total A-0	30		30								
A-1	Harwig	30		28	2							
	Total A-1	30										
A-2	Hartwig	433			109	230	23	42	29			
	Bücker	26				15	11					
	Gotha	9					3	1				5
	Erla	32				4	8	15	5			
	BMM	39				17	9	13				
	Total A-2	539			109	266	54	71	34			5
A-3	Gotha					40						
	Erla					40						
	BMM					34						
	Total A-3	114				114						
B-2	Hartwig	214							8	30	50	40
	Bücker	169					8	18	22	11	7	38
	Gotha	23										23
	Erla	150						15	25	25	23	
	BMM	387						10	17	19	19	31
	Total B-2	943					8	28	62	85	101	155
C-1	Mráz	14										
D-1		3			Not new aircraft, rather conversions of DFS 230 C-1s,							
Total DFS 230		1670	30	28	111	380	62	99	96	85	101	160
Quartermaster-General's Records		1591		28	455							

1941						42	43	44
7	8	9	10	11	12			4-7
25	25	25	11					
19	20	26						
18	23	21						
30	30	39	48	35	35	*74*		
92	**98**	**111**	**59**	**35**	**35**	*74*		
								14
conversions probably carried out by Gotha								
92	**98**	**111**	**59**	**35**	**35**	*74*		**14**
					1020	**74**		**14**

Go 242/244 Production Overview

Note: numbers are incomplete for the period April to December 1943

Go 242 Go 244		Go 242 Production to March 1943 from Tables Produced by Special Commission F 12 Go 244 Total Numbers Based on Plan of March 1943								
Company	Year	1941					1942			
	Month	8	9	10	11	12	1	2	3	4
	Total	Go 242 new construction								
Ago	45	18	4	9	7	1	3	1	1	-
GWF	690	7	25	34	81	90	80	51	85	61
Hartwig	466					8	12	12	20	18
		Taken from Go 242 number								
	301		1	8	21	-	3	-	17	42
		Retro-conversion of Go 244s into Go 242s or								
GWF	194	40 + 44 retro-conversions + 110 new-build								
andere	230									
Total per year		224 Go 242 30 Go 244					432 Go 242 271 Go 244, 22 retro-converted into Go 242s			

		Planning of March 1943 Based on Special Commission F 12 Tables								
Company	Year	1943								
	Month	4	5	6	7	8	9	10	11	12
	Total	Go 242 A-1, A-2 new construction								
Ago	45									
GWF	690									
Hartwig	466	20	20	20	20	20	20	20	20	20
		Taken from Go 242 number for Go 244:								
	301									
		Go 244 Retro-Conversions into Go 242 B-1, B-3								
GWF	194	30	30	20	13					
Other	230	31	46	37	34	34	34	12		
Total per Year										

				1942				1943		
5	6	7	8	9	10	11	12	1	2	3
1										
60	43	54	19							
20	18	20	15	18	20	24	16	20	20	25

for Go 244

| 60 | 46 | 66 | 33 | 4 | | | | | | |

aircraft begun as Go 244s and Completed as Go 242 B-1, B-3

| | | | | | | 5 | 17 | 24 | 25 | 30 |
| | | | | | | | | | | 2 |

**1943/44 Production Based on GL/C-B
Procurement Report 2/8 4401/44**

43	44									
	1	2	3	4	5	6	7	8	9	10

Go 242 B-2 new construction

105	25	18	25	26	20	20	17			

none after September 1942

	151 Go 242 B-2									

Summary of Me 321/323 Serial Numbers and Manufacturer's Codes

Me 321				
	Serial Number	Manufacturer's Code	Production Site	Units
Me 321 A		W1+SA to W1+SZ	Leipheim	26
Me 321 A		W2+SA to W2+SZ	Obertraubling	26
Me 321 A		W3+SA to W3+SZ	Leipheim	26
Me 321 A		W4+SA to W4+SZ	Obertraubling	26
Me 321 B		W5+SA to W5+SZ	Leipheim	26
Me 321 B		W6+SA to W6+SZ	Obertraubling	26
Me 321 B		W7+SA to W7+SZ	Leipheim	26
Me 321 B		W8+SA to W8+SP	Obertraubling	ca. 16
			Summe Me 321	200
Me 323				
Me 323 A V1		W1+SZ		
Me 323 V1		W9+SA	Leipheim	
Me 323 V2	801	DT+DK		
Me 323 V3	802	DT+DL		
Me 323 V4	803	DT+DM		
Me 323 V5	804	DT+DN		
Me 323 V6	805	DT+DO		
Me 323 V7	806	DT+DP		
Me 323 V8	807	DT+DQ		
Me 323 V9	808	DT+DR		
Me 323 V10	809	DT+DS		
Me 323 V11	810	DT+DT		
Me 323 V12	811	DT+DU		
Me 323 V13	812	DT+DV		
Me 323 V14	813	DT+DW		
Me 323 V15	814	DT+DX		
Me 323 V16	160001	DU+QZ		
1942		DT+QB	DT+IB?	
		AT+ID	DT+ID?	
		RD+UE	RD+QE?	
1943		SN+HL	SL+HL?	
Me 321 D-1	1101 to 1122	RD+QA bis RD+QU	Leipheim	21
Me 321 D-2/6	1123 to 1126	RD+QV bis RD+QZ	Leipheim	5
Me 323 D-2/6/E-1	1127 to 1152	RF+XA bis RF+XZ	Leipheim	26
Me 323 D-1	1201 to 1226	DT+IA bis DT+IZ	Obertraubling	26
Me 323 D-1/2/6	1227 to 1252	SG+RA bis SG+RZ	Obertraubling	26
Me 323 D-6	1253 to 1278	VM+IA bis VM+IZ	Obertraubling	26
Me 323 D-6	1279 to 1298	SL+HA bis SL+HT	Obertraubling	19
Me 323 E-1	130015 to 130040	BM+GA bis BM+GZ	Leipheim	26
Me 323 E-1	130041 to 130055	DU+PA bis DU+PO	Leipheim	15
Me 323 E-1	330001 to 330010	RL+UA bis RL+UJ	Obertraubling	10
				200

BIBLIOGRAPHY

1. Karl R. Pawlas: Kampf- und Lastensegler DFS 230 – DFS 331, Luftfahrt Monographie LS1, Eigenverlag Karl R. Pawlas

2. Karl R. Pawlas: Die Sturm- und Lastensegler Go 242 - Go 244 - Go 345 - P39 - Ka 430, Luftfahrt Monographie LS2, Eigenverlag Karl R. Pawlas

3. Karl R. Pawlas: Gotha Go 345, Waffen-Revue 96

4. Karl R. Pawlas: Die Giganten Me 321–Me 323, Luftfahrt Monographie LS 3, Eigenverlag Karl R. Pawlas

5. Karl Kössler: Der Lastensegler DFS 230, FLUGZEUG 3 und 4/1986

6. Deutsche Akademie der Luftfahrtforschung, Beiträge zur Geschichte der Deutschen Luftwissenschaft und -technik

7. Besprechungsprotokolle des Generalluftzeugmeisters aus den Jahren 1941 bis 1944 aus dem Bundesarchiv Freiburg

8. Bundesarchiv Freiburg, Bestand RL 3/

9. Sondersammlung Deutsches Museum

10. Deutsches Technikmuseum Berlin

11. H. J. Nowarra: Deutsche Lastensegler an allen Fronten DFS 230 - DFS 331 - Go 242 - Go 345 - Ka 430 - Me 321 - Ju 322, Das Waffenarsenal, Band 42, Podzun-Pallas-Verlag

12. H. J. Nowarra: Die Deutsche Luftrüstung 1933–1945, Bernard & Graefe Verlag 1993

13. K. Neetzow, G. Schlaug: Deutsche Lastensegler 1938–1945, Eigenverlag

14. Ernst Peter: Der Flugzeugschlepp von den Anfängen bis heute, Motorbuch Verlag, 1981

15. Ch. Regel: Erprobungsstelle Rechlin, in Die Deutsche Luftfahrt, Flugerprobungsstellen bis 1945, Bernard & Graefe Verlag, 1998

16. M. Griehl: Heinkel He 111, Motorbuch Verlag, 1997

17. V. Koos: Ernst Heinkel Flugzeugwerke, Heel Verlag 2003

18. H.J. Ebert und andere: Willy Messerschmitt – Pionier der Luftfahrt und des Leichtbaus, in Die Deutsche Luftfahrt, Bernard & Graefe Verlag 1992

19. H.-P. Dabrowski: Messerschmitt Me 321/323, Schiffer Publishing Ltd. 2002

20. Zeppelin Museum Friedrichshafen: Zeppelins Flieger, Wasmuth Verlag

21. P. Schmoll: Messerschmitt-Giganten, MZ Buchverlag

22. F. A, Vajda, P. Dancey: German Aircraft industry an production 1933–1945, Airlife Publishing Ltd. 1998

23. Heinz Birkholz: Lastensegler DFS 230 als Doppelsitzer, JET & PROP 1/94

24. Georg Schlaug: Der Erstflug des Lastenseglers DFS 331, JET & PROP 1/98

25. Heinz Birkholz: Ein Lastensegler mit Storch-Beinen, JET & PROP 4/98

26. Manfred Krieg: Kalkert Ka 430 – der Lastensegler aus Erfurt, JET & PROP 1/99

27. Karl Kössler: Kampfgruppe z.b.V. 106, Teil 3, JET & PROP 4/02

28. G. Heumann: Unternehmen Warschau: Die Giganten, FLUG-REVUE 12/1964 und folgende

29. B. Engel, Gotha Go 244, Luftfahrt-Geschichte 2/74

30. H. Lommel: DFS 230 "Hochbein, Robbe" , DFS 331 und Ka 430, Luftfahrt History Nr. 11, Selbstverlag 2006

31. H. Powilleit: Vom Segelflieger zum Lastensegler – DFS 230 und Gigant Me 321, Selbstverlag, Kopie im Deutschen Museum München

32. Sammlung Ch. Regel

33. L.Dv.559 DFS 230 A und B Flugzeughandbuch 4.11.1939

34. L.Dv.T.2230 A-1, A-2, B-2 Bedienungsvorschrift Fl Juni 1942

35. L.Dv.T.2330 A-1, A-2, B-2 Bedienungsvorschrift Fl Beiheft 1 Sturzflug- und Landebremsschirm

36. D (Luft) T. 2323 D-1, D-2, D-6, Ausgabe 1943, Flugzeughandbuch

37. Wolf D. Mauder:"Lastensegler im Einsatz" (DFS 230/Go 242/Me 321, Videofilm bibo tv, Bad Homburg

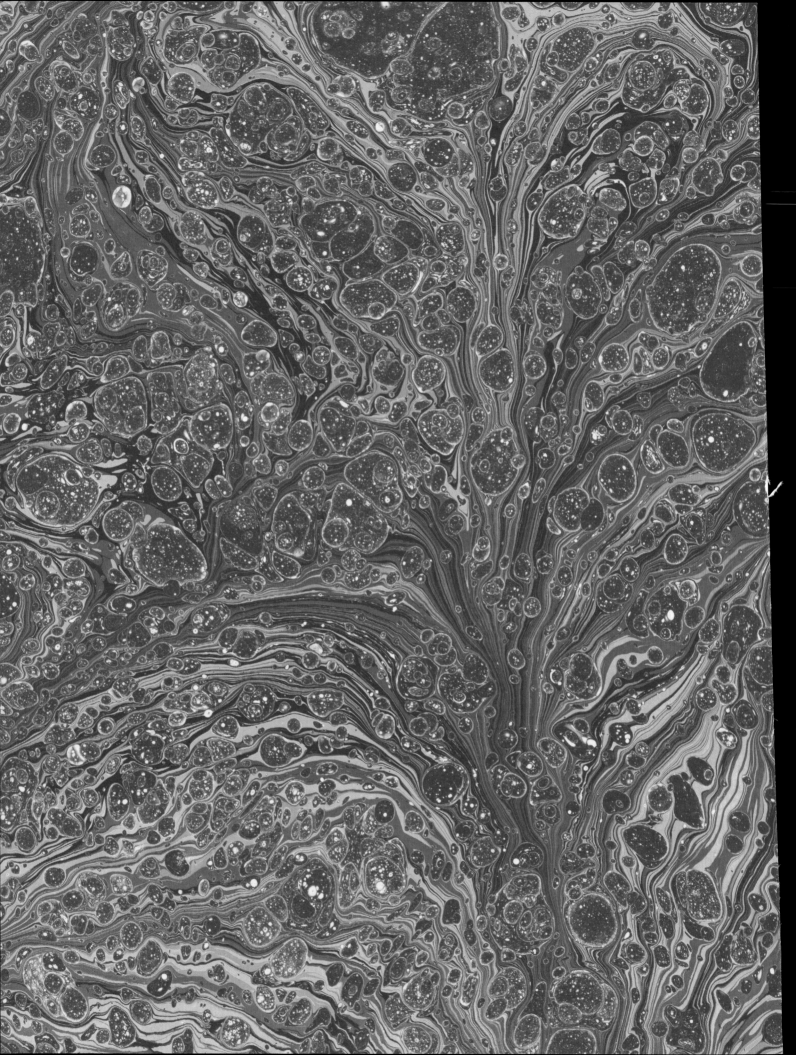